Darwin's Medicine

Darwin's Medicine is the sequel to Brian D. Smith's influential and critically acclaimed *Future of Pharma* (Gower, 2011). Whereas the earlier book predicted the evolution of the pharmaceutical market and the business models of pharmaceutical companies, *Darwin's Medicine* goes much deeper into the drivers of industry change and how leading pharmaceutical and medical technology companies are adapting their strategies, structures and capabilities in practice.

Through the lens of evolutionary science, Professor Smith explores the speciation of new business models in the Life Sciences Industry. This sophisticated and highly original approach offers insights into:

- The mechanisms of evolution in this exceptional industry;
- The six great technological and social shifts that are shaping its landscape;
- The emergence of 26 distinct, new business models; and
- The lessons that enable firms to direct and accelerate their own evolution.

These insights map out the industry's complex, changing landscape and provide an invaluable guide to those firms seeking to survive and thrive in this dynamic market.

The book is essential reading for anyone working in or studying the pharmaceutical, medical technology and related sectors. It provides a unique and novel way of making sense of the transformation we can see going on around us and a practical, focused approach to managing a firm's evolutionary trajectory.

Professor Brian D. Smith began his career as a research chemist in a pharmaceutical R&D lab and then spent twenty years in technical and marketing roles before becoming an academic, author and advisor. Working at The University of Hertfordshire and SDA Bocconi, two of Europe's leading business schools, his research focuses on strategy creation and implementation in pharmaceutical and medical technology markets. Brian also runs a specialist consultancy that advises many of the world's largest companies in this sector. He was the founding editor of the *Journal of Medical Marketing*, has written and co-written four other major books, including *The Future of Pharma* (Gower, 2011), and published over 300 papers and articles – all of which can be seen at www.pragmedic.com.

Darwin's Medicine

How business models in the Life
Sciences industry are evolving

Brian D Smith

Routledge
Taylor & Francis Group

LONDON AND NEW YORK

First published in paperback 2024

First published 2017
by Routledge
4 Park Square, Milton Park, Abingdon, Oxon OX14 4RN

and by Routledge
605 Third Avenue, New York, NY 10158

Routledge is an imprint of the Taylor & Francis Group, an informa business

Copyright © 2017, 2024 Brian D. Smith

Publisher's Note
The publisher has gone to great lengths to ensure the quality of this reprint but points out that some imperfections in the original copies may be apparent.

British Library Cataloguing in Publication Data
A catalogue record for this book is available from the British Library

Library of Congress Cataloging-in-Publication Data
A catalog record for this title has been requested

ISBN: 978-1-4724-2071-8 (hbk)
ISBN: 978-1-03-283707-9 (pbk)
ISBN: 978-1-315-57587-2 (ebk)

DOI: 10.4324/9781315575872

Typeset in Bembo
by Apex CoVangtage, LLC

For Lindsay, Eleanor, Catherine and Rosalind

Contents

Figures

Tables

Foreword and acknowledgements

It has often been said that writing a book is like bringing a child into the world. As I complete this, my fifth book, and consider my three precious daughters, I appreciate the truth in that comparison. In particular, the adage that 'it takes a village to raise a child' springs to mind. In the case of *Darwin's Medicine*, any merit it has is attributable to at least three 'villages' of people who helped me in various ways to create the book.

First, I must thank all those industry life science executives who have contributed their thoughts and ideas so generously. Many are unaware of their contribution, such as the innumerable executives who have invited me to advise them on how to adapt to their changing market and whose real world challenges permeate this book. Others have invited me to speak to them at conferences and meetings, and their questions have provided an important stimulus to my thinking. Most importantly, still others have deliberately and kindly given up their time to be interviewed by me: Jay Galeota, Michael Swinford, Michael Simpson, Hedley Rees, Kevin Lobo, Tom Monroe, Tomasz Sablinki, Bruno Strigini, Marcus Sluijs, David Nexon, Leroy Hood, Elias Zerhouni, Manuel Coelho, Kai Gait, Julian Bradwell, Gary Bell, Daniel Carlin, Andreas Fibig, Cary Pfeffer, Alan Lamont, Angelo de Rosa, Steve Burrill, Richard Klausner, Gordon Howe and Per-Olof Attinger. My profound and personal thanks go to all of them for sharing their time and insight, which went far beyond the limited quotes used in the final version of the book.

Second, I would like to thank all of my colleagues at both of the universities that give me an academic home: Bocconi University in Milan, Italy, and the University of Hertfordshire in the UK. By sharing their varied expertise with me, they have constantly fed and watered my intellectual curiosity and given me new perspectives.

Finally, I must single out the small handful of people who made a very direct and positive contribution to the creation of *Darwin's Medicine*. These include Jonathan Norman, my commissioning editor at Taylor and Francis, whose patience and genuine interest in my ideas encouraged me enormously; Mike Firth, whose illustrations for the book are so much better than the briefs I gave him; and, most of all, Lindsay Bruce Smith, my so-much-more-than-editor for this and all my previous books. Her ability to transmute my poorly punctuated and often incoherent drafts into something readable and presentable was the essential, irreplaceable ingredient in putting this book into your hands.

I hope that *Darwin's Medicine* meets my aims of helping life science companies adapt to the future. Whether you think so or not, I would greatly value your comments and questions about my latest 'child'.

Professor Brian D Smith, Welwyn

Part 1

The future of pharma – reprise

We will now discuss in a little more detail the Struggle for Existence.

Charles Darwin, *The Origin of Species*

1 Introduction and an invitation to skip some pages

As I sketch out the plan of this book, I am sitting on an aeroplane working on my iPad. Like most of us, I multitask, and there are four documents open on my device. The first is a mind-mapping app that I use for planning any important piece of work. It is currently showing an incomplete plan for the book you are now reading. The second is an e-book I am re-reading: *The Origin of Species*, Charles Darwin's most famous book, a work that changed the way scientists look at the natural world and, as I will discuss later in this chapter, the way that management scientists think about organisations and industries. The other open apps are a PowerPoint presentation and a Word document. The PowerPoint is a situation analysis, sent to me by a medium-sized pharmaceutical company, describing how changes in the healthcare funding system, regulatory system and technological environment are combining to make their existing business model obsolete. Their customers won't pay for the drugs they can develop and, to develop the drugs their customers are willing to pay for is too costly and too risky for their shareholders' appetites. Perplexed by what they see as irreconcilable demands of their customers and their owners, they have asked me to review their presentation and to advise them on how to respond to the situation. Their request is typical of the advisory work I do with many pharmaceutical and medical technology companies. The final document open on my iPad is the Word document. It is a report I am about to send to a very large, powerful medical technology company who were faced with a similar situation to the pharmaceutical company. However, they thought about the problem sooner and have tried to adapt to the fundamental, inexorable changes in their market. Their attempts to change have failed, resulting in lots of costs and disruption but no new value for either their shareholders or their customers. Having asked me to assess why their change efforts are not producing the intended results, my report to them describes the deeply embedded behavioural factors that have emasculated their well-intentioned attempts at strategic transformation.

At first glance, the four documents could not be more different. As well as their different electronic formats, they differ in style, content and perspective. The limbs of the mind map are fragments of sentences and probably meaningless to anyone but me. Darwin's beautiful, coherent prose is not as dated as might be expected after 150 or so years but is still recognisably from a different era and much more eloquent than my report. The situational analysis and my report both use a modern business writing style, but they adopt very different perspectives. The first, provided by the CEO of the medium-sized pharma company, concentrates on tangible and mostly quantified factors: failures in the development pipeline, the market access policies of state healthcare systems and the cost differentials between innovative and generic drugs. My report to the medtech company uses tangible observations that I made in the company, such as organisational structures, business processes and intraorganisational conflict, to identify the much less obvious, hidden organisational assumptions, values and behaviours that have defeated them. My report begins provocatively with a famous quote by Peter Drucker: 'Culture eats strategy for breakfast.' It is what the company needs to hear, but not what they want to hear.

Despite all these visible differences, the four documents are underpinned by the common theme of evolution. The PowerPoint presentation describes a pharmaceutical company that senses the pressures on its business model (evolutionary scientists would call them selection pressures) arising from its social and technological environment. The company is casting about for a way to avoid extinction in a market that is very different from the pharmaceutical market of thirty years ago, to which the company was very well adapted. My report for the medtech company describes how even determined leadership and massive resources have not made sufficiently significant difference to avoid failure. It echoes the observation, often falsely attributed to Darwin, that it is not the strongest or fastest that survive, but the ones most capable of change. Darwin's masterpiece explains how biological complexity emerges via natural selection, as species evolve in response to selection pressures arising from the natural environment. As a taster, please read the book's final paragraph, presented in Box 1.1. When I read this passage, I can't help but see the many parallels between the industry in which I have spent my career and Darwin's 'entangled bank'.

Finally, the mind map, fragmented and half-formed as it is, represents my attempt to show how Darwin's beautiful, wonderful, brilliant idea can help pharmaceutical, medical technology and other companies to adapt to the changing market that they occupy. By the time you read these words, that garbled mind map will have grown into the book you are now reading.

Box 1.1   The final paragraph of Darwin's *Origin of Species*

It is interesting to contemplate an entangled bank, clothed with many plants of many kinds, with birds singing on the bushes, with various insects flitting about, and with worms crawling through the damp earth, and to reflect that these elaborately constructed forms, so different from each other, and dependent on each other in so complex a manner, have all been produced by laws acting around us. These laws, taken in the largest sense, being Growth with Reproduction; inheritance which is almost implied by reproduction; Variability from the indirect and direct action of the external conditions of life, and from use and disuse; a Ratio of Increase so high as to lead to a Struggle for Life, and as a consequence to Natural Selection, entailing Divergence of Character and the Extinction of less-improved forms. Thus, from the war of nature, from famine and death, the most exalted object which we are capable of conceiving, namely, the production of the higher animals, directly follows. There is grandeur in this view of life, with its several powers, having been originally breathed into a few forms or into one; and that, whilst this planet has gone cycling on according to the fixed law of gravity, from so simple a beginning endless forms most beautiful and most wonderful have been, and are being, evolved.

This is not my first attempt at applying evolutionary theory to the context of the life sciences industry. This book is a sequel, a follow-on to *The Future of Pharma* (1) that blended ideas from evolutionary economics with the views of industry leaders to anticipate how that industry would change. In that book, I describe how important the industry is to our society, how the industry is threatened by powerful market changes, how evolution works in an economic context and how evolutionary economics applies to the particular context of the pharmaceutical industry. In this next and complementary book, I build on those ideas by expanding the analysis both horizontally and longitudinally. Horizontally, I expand my analysis to consider both pharma and medtech since it seems obvious the sectors have much in common and increasingly are converging. Longitudinally, I move from the prediction of hypothesised evolutionary changes to how these are playing out in reality. Many readers of this book will have read *The Future of Pharma*. However, it is inevitable that some readers of this book will not have read its ancestor and so the remainder of Part 1 is a reprise covering the basic facts of the industry's importance, evolution's mechanism and how evolution helps us make sense of the industry. If you have read *The Future of Pharma* you may wish to skip to the end of Part 1, to Chapter 9 titled 'Watching the Future Unfold'.

2 An important industry at risk

To those of us who work within it, the industry that makes the products used by doctors, nurses, technicians and other healthcare professionals is very fragmented. Not only do we separate pharmaceutical companies from medical technology companies, we see great divisions within each of these sectors. Research-based pharma, generic pharma and biotech are different beasts, although all make what the layman would call drugs. Within any of these sub-divisions, we see further differences. Those who understand the sector differentiate between big pharma and speciality pharma, for example; or, using products as differentiators, between small molecules, biologics and vaccines, to name just a few categories. Similar divisions are generally understood in non-pharma medical technology, which is even more fragmented. In this sector, there are divisions between equipment, such as fMRI scanners or patient monitors, and between disposables, such as dressings and surgical drapes or gloves. And there are further sub-divisions according to technology, such as clinical chemistry, immunoassay or haematology in pathology blood analysers. To the cognoscenti, there isn't really a single industry in the sense of many firms making the same thing, as might be said of the automobile industry. Instead, there are many industries all supplying the products needed to maintain or restore health. But when we consider the impact this sector has had on our world, it is not too simplistic to consider this kaleidoscope of products, applications and technologies as a single industry, as the layman, journalists and others who look at the sector from outside often do.

In *The Future of Pharma*, I write at some length about the impact the pharmaceutical industry has had on the world, both in terms of human health (for example, life expectancy) and its importance to the world economy. We can make the same sort of claims about the wider industry, including medical technology, and there is little point in restating the argument for the importance of the sector. Having a supply of drugs, devices, diagnostics and equipment is systemically important to modern societies and is one of the primary demands of citizens of developing economies. More than that, we constantly raise our expectations and demand solutions to new medical conditions or ones we previously counted as incurable. In particular, as societies age we look to the sector for ways to fight cancers and degenerative diseases such as Alzheimer's disease and to counter the consequences of our modern lifestyles such as obesity related conditions. And, in all countries, health technology is one of the sectors governments see as the 'crown jewels' of a competitive economy, creating wealth, good jobs and foreign earnings. The future of the industry, how it might develop and how it can continue to contribute to our society, is therefore important to all of us, whether we work in the sector, benefit from its inventions or simply want the economic benefits and taxes of a large, successful industry sector.

It seems self-evident that this industry is very important to our society and that we should all be concerned for its future. And yet importance is no defence against change as we can observe in industries as varied as coal mining, shipbuilding and transport. My home village, Welwyn in Hertfordshire in the UK, grew up as a transport hub, a day's coach and horses ride north of London. It is still characterised by buildings that were inns with stables and what we would now call the infrastructure of the horse-dependent world. Of course, that world no longer exists; the inns are good restaurants, their stable yards are car parks and some of the stable blocks are expensive hotel rooms. Welwyn probably smells considerably sweeter than it did in the age of the horse, but it is no longer a transport hub. To my ancestors, the horse-dependent transport industry probably seemed too big to fail and immune to change, but that was naïve.

In current trends, we see the possibility that the now mighty pharma and medtech sectors may similarly fail. In *The Future of Pharma*, I describe how various mega-trends, from globalisation and demographics to economic growth and technological advances, are converging in a way that is, potentially at least, negative for our industry and society. One scenario, described by many industry leaders, is that of commoditisation, in which innovation is no longer profitable and the social and economic contribution of this important industry flattens out. In the closing lines of that book, I described how those of us old enough to appreciate the inevitability of senescence, or whose loved ones suffer from incurable or unmanageable diseases, do not wish for a world where innovation in healthcare slows or flattens out. We want our children to live longer and better than ourselves, just as our lives are better and longer than our parents' and grandparents'. In the world inhabited by my pharma and medtech client companies, there's a real threat of that not happening.

This threat, that an industry we have come to rely on for continuously growing contributions to society would sink into commoditised stagnation, led me to begin my research into this area. At first, I looked at some 'usual suspects' from the management science literature. For example, I spent some time trying to apply Industry Life Cycle Theory (2–4), but this seemed a poor explanation of the past of the sector and an even weaker predictor of its future. That theory relies on certain factors – such as relatively low barriers to entry and exit – that simply don't apply to the sectors I was interested in. As often happens in academic research, I entered a 'slough of despond', to steal a beautiful phrase from Bunyan.

Then, during my happy period at the Open University Business School, I attended an inspiring lunchtime seminar by Professor J. C. Spender. I remember the seminar vividly for two reasons. First, it was at the edge of my knowledge, and I had to work very hard to keep up with his torrent of original thoughts. Second, he made reference to Nelson and Winter in the tone that academics use, when talking to other academics, to imply that 'this is such common knowledge I am not going to elaborate on it'. I blushed inwardly, as I had never heard of Nelson and Winter. I went out, bought and devoured their book, *An Evolutionary Theory of Economic Change* (5), and began the research journey that led to this book being in front of you now.

3   The best idea anyone has ever had

Among practical, hands-on executives, the word 'theory' often has quite negative connotations. It's used as a pejorative and as a synonym for impractical, useless and unsubstantiated. This is unfortunate, ironic, inconsistent and, not to put too fine a point on it, hypocritical. Unfortunate because more accurate synonyms for 'theory' include explanation, rationalisation or elucidation. Ironic because explanation, rationalisation and elucidation are exactly what practical managers strive for. Such negativity is inconsistent because executives only demonstrate it towards theories in social sciences, such as management science, and not to theories in the physical and natural sciences, irrespective of their evidence base. Finally, it is hypocritical because executives, even those who are most sceptical of management theory, use management theory all the time, whether consciously or otherwise. When an R&D Director focuses resources onto a particular avenue of research, the decision is underpinned by an implicit theory about what area of research is most likely to lead to the desired product innovation. The same applies when a Commercial Director instigates a marketing campaign or an Operations Director makes choices about outsourcing. Their decisions are underpinned by an implicit explanation, rationalisation or elucidation of how the world works. John Maynard Keynes's observation in *The General Theory of Employment, Interest and Money* was accurate. He stated, 'Practical men, who believe themselves to be quite exempt from any intellectual influences, are usually the slaves of some defunct economist.'

Arguably, the primary difference between academics and theory-sceptic executives lies in their attitude to theory. Academics acknowledge their reliance on theory and use their scepticism to separate strong theories from the weak. This was summarised beautifully in an insightful editorial in a highly respected academic journal:

> *[Academic] Research in organizations and management places a high premium on theory. The importance of theory is well deserved, given that theories allow us to make sense of the phenomena that surround us in organizations, help us synthesize the insights we gain from our observations and imaginations, and influence the numerous decisions that guide our empirical research, such as the hypotheses we test, the measures we use, and the analytical methods we employ.*
>
> **Edwards**, 2010 (6)

In sharp contrast, many executives deny their reliance on theory. In management science (but interestingly not in the physical or natural sciences), executives are often universally prejudiced against theories. As a result, they often fail to discriminate between the theories that are likely to be useful to them and those that will lead them astray, like a hidden magnet next to their instinctive compass.

Good, strong theories, in management science and elsewhere, have two fundamental properties. They explain a past or current phenomenon and predict its future. Germ theory, atomic theory and the theory of gravity do that for infections, chemical reactions and the motions of the planets respectively. But these are exemplary, exceptionally strong theories that have now been substantiated by massive amounts of evidence. Not all theories are equally strong. As I mentioned, I began my attempt to explain and predict the pharmaceutical and medical technology industries with Industry Life Cycle Theory, but this turned out to be less of a theory and more of a generalisation of industry behaviour, one to which this sector was an interesting exception. J. C. Spender's mention of Nelson and Winter, and the orgy of reading that followed, led me to look at evolutionary theory.

For someone like me, trained as a Chemist then steeped for decades in the life sciences, evolutionary theory seemed an odd place to look for enlightenment in management science. It is, after all, a biological theory, isn't it? Well, no as it turns out. To explain that, allow me to take a step back, with apologies to any evolutionary biologists reading this, to remind readers of the basic concepts of the theory of evolution by natural selection.

Darwin (and indeed Wallace [7]) developed the idea of evolution by natural selection as an explanation of complexity in the natural world. This is clear in the paragraph quoted in Box 1.1 and is the underlying theme of all of Darwin's writing in this area. Why is there so much variety in the natural world? Because naturally-occurring variation in nature is amplified by the differential survival and reproduction of variants. The contribution of Darwin, Wallace and other Victorian scientists (for example, Gregor Mendel, remembered by most of us for his experiments with peas) is all the more remarkable, given that their work was long before the discovery of DNA and genes in the molecular biology sense. Not until the late 1930s and early 1940s did the work of several great thinkers come together into what Julian Huxley called the modern evolutionary synthesis, sometimes called the neo-Darwinian synthesis (8).

Evolution is an incredibly powerful theory. From a few, parsimonious principles it explains life in all its complexity. It also has great predictive power. Karl Popper, regarded by many as the greatest philosopher of twentieth century science, was initially sceptical of evolution as a theory but later reversed his position (9). Philosopher and cognitive scientist, Dan Dennett, famously described evolution as 'the best idea anyone has ever had' (10). It is therefore with some trepidation that I try to summarise the fundamental idea of the neo-Darwinian synthesis in Figure 3.1.

Figure 3.1 introduces some new terms that are important in understanding how evolution works. In *The Selfish Gene* (11), Richard Dawkins coined the term 'replicator', meaning anything which is copied. In a biological system, genes are the replicators, although Dawkins later developed his idea to cover memes, ideas that are copied. Importantly, genes do not interact directly with their environment. Instead, through gene expression, RNA and proteins, they shape the vehicle that is carrying them, and it is that vehicle that interacts with the environment. In biology, the interactors are the organisms carrying the genes, and variation in genes is expressed as variation in the traits of the organism. *Homo sapiens'* large brain is an obvious trait, as is a giraffe's long neck or antibiotic resistance of MRSA bacteria, although these examples arise from the variation of multiple genes rather than a single one. An interactor with a particular trait or set of traits is known as a phenotype.

To the extent that the traits infer greater or lesser ability to survive and propagate (an ability known as fitness by biologists), some phenotypes are selectively favoured over others. To use some jargon, they are 'selected for' by the environment. This selection, when followed by further propagation, leads to an increase in the population of the favoured

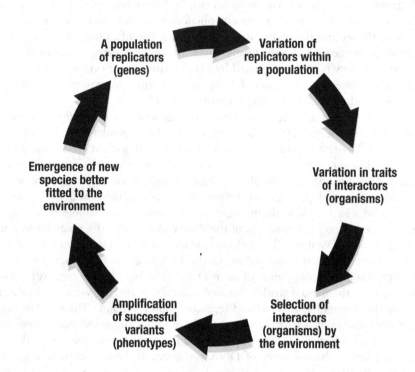

Figure 3.1 The mechanism of biological evolution

phenotype, relative to its less favoured 'rivals'. By this method, the new phenotype is 'amplified'. Eventually, this leads to a new population of interactors, which share the same new replicators (i.e. genes), but which are genetically distinct from their ancestors. Evolutionary biologists call this population of organisms (interactors) sharing the same genes (replicators) a new species. And the process by which it emerges is called speciation.

That, with one more grovelling apology to those evolutionary scientists balking at my gross oversimplification, is how evolution works. One species leads, by variation, selection and amplification, to one or more new species, each shaped by and suited to its environment. I suspect my readers may already be anticipating how evolutionary processes work in an industry but, since the idea is quite central to the rest of the book, I will elaborate on this in the following section.

4   The biologists got there first

Whilst most people think of evolution as a way of understanding the complexity of biological systems, its potential to explain and predict economic systems has been discussed for well over 100 years (12). At first, much of this work saw biological evolution as a metaphor for economic evolution; it's not difficult to see how the 'survival of the fittest' seems to fit with typical free-market thinking. But metaphors have their limitations, and evolutionary theory didn't start to influence academic thinking significantly until the 1980s, when the power of the neo-Darwinian synthesis and the great advances in our understanding of biological evolution gave new impetus to evolutionary economics.

If you are interested in further reading on this new thinking, there are many books on the subject. For a great layman's treatment, I recommend Beinhocker (13), and for a stunning academic tour de force, Hodgson and Knudson (14). However, the seminal work remains the book I mentioned earlier by Nelson and Winter (5).

As I did earlier with biological evolution, I will again risk the wrath of my more specialised colleagues by simplifying economic evolution into a single diagram in Figure 4.1. I am aware of the limitations of this simplification, but I hope it suffices for our purposes.

As you can see, Figure 4.1 illustrates exactly the same mechanism as Figure 3.1 but with different entities involved. In an economic system, the replicators are organisational routines. Nelson and Winter defined these as repeated patterns of activity within the organisation. They might be activities for identifying a market opportunity, for ensuring a production process meets FDA standards or any one of a million other activities. An organisation typically has thousands of them, just as an organism has thousands of genes. Both genes and organisational routines are, if you think about it, information storage and transmission devices. Just as with genes, organisational routines interact with their environment through their interactor vehicle, which is the organisation or firm itself.

Just as genes express themselves and shape the organisation through RNA and proteins, routines express themselves and shape their 'carrying' vehicle through behaviours, processes, strategies, structures and capabilities, and it is that vehicle (the organisation or firm) that interacts with the environment. In economic systems, therefore, the interactors are the organisations (e.g. firms) carrying the organisational routines, and variation in routines is expressed as variation in the behaviours, processes, strategies, structures and capabilities of the firm. Pharmaceutical companies' ability to screen and identify biologically active compounds is an obvious capability, as is a medical technology company's capability to train surgeons to use its devices. In the same way that a phenotypical organism is characterised by its traits, so is a phenotypical firm characterised by its behaviours, processes, strategies, structures and capabilities. As selective pressures act on the firms, selection and

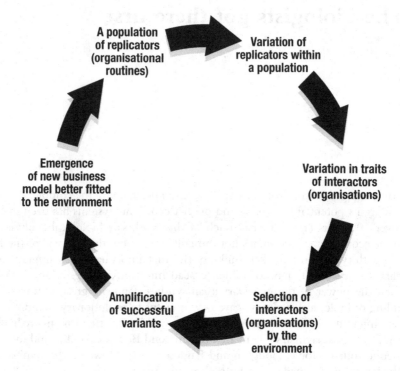

Figure 4.1 The mechanism of economic evolution

amplification lead to the same emergence of a distinct population that is better fitted to the environment. As in biology, this is a process of speciation that leads to one or more new types of firm. The only difference is in the names we use. We call a population of organisms with the same genes (and hence traits) a species. On the other hand, a group of firms sharing the same routines (and hence exhibiting the same behaviours, processes, strategies, structures and capabilities) is called a business model.

With the same apology for simplification to my evolutionary economist colleagues as I gave to my evolutionary biologist friends, that is how evolution works in an economic system such as an industry. One business model leads, by variation, selection and amplification, to multiple new species, each actively shaped by and uniquely suited to its environment. This premise, discussed in detail in *The Future of Pharma*, allows us to explain the past and predict the future of the pharmaceutical and medical technology industries. In the remainder of Part 1 I will summarise my work in that area, so setting the scene for the rest of this book, which examines how those predictions are playing out.

5 Applying evolutionary theory to the pharmaceutical and medical technology sectors

In reprising *The Future of Pharma*, I have so far introduced two premises upon which this book and its predecessor are based. The first is that the pharmaceutical and medical technology sectors are important to our society, both economically and socially. From that it follows that the future development of those sectors is important both to those of us who work in them and also to those of us who benefit from them, which means everyone. The second premise is that all industries, and perhaps especially the pharmaceutical and medical technology sectors, can be usefully thought of as complex adaptive systems. In other words, they are systems made up of entities that interact with one another and subsequently adapt in response to those interactions. From that perspective it follows that we can best understand the past and predict the future development of industries by the use of evolutionary theory. In particular, we can use Nelson and Winter's ideas about evolutionary economics, where organisational routines are the replicators, and firms are the interactors.

So what happens when we apply the concepts of evolutionary economics to our sector? The answer to that question was a large part of *The Future of Pharma* although, as that research developed, it became clear that most of my findings applied equally well to the medical technology sector. In the remainder of this chapter, I will summarise my evolutionary economics–based explanation of the industry's past and its predicted future. Before I do, however, there are a couple more concepts from evolutionary economics that I need to introduce.

The first two concepts concern how evolutionary economists classify the environment in which firms operate. Nelson and Winter saw the environment as consisting of two dimensions: the physical technology environment and the social technology environment, for which I will give a simplified definition and some illustrative examples.

The **physical technology environment** we can define simply as the implications of developments in the physical and natural sciences. For the pharmaceutical and medical technology sectors, the physical technology environment might be thought of in two parts, directly applicable physical technologies and indirectly enabling physical technologies. Obvious examples of the former include pharmacology, nanotechnology, stem cell technology and biomarkers, to name only a few of the vast range of physical technologies that are used and are usable by our sector. Similarly, web-connected devices, big data, social media, real world data and new supply chain technologies such as RFID are just a few examples of the second part of the physical technology environment. These are physical technologies that powerfully but indirectly enable the pharmaceutical and medical technology industry.

The **social technology environment** we can define simply as the implications of developments in the social sciences and societal trends more generally. For the pharmaceutical and medical technology sectors, the social technology environment might also be thought of in two parts, directly relevant social technologies and indirectly influencing social technologies. Regulatory approval systems, health technology assessment (HTA) processes and the structuring and funding of healthcare systems are the most prominent of the very many and different social technologies that are directly relevant in our sector. Similarly, social changes such as demographics, globalisation, disease patterns and cultural changes such as social attitude to risk are just some of the various social technologies that pervasively and inexorably, but indirectly, influence the pharmaceutical and medical technology industry.

At this point, it's worth clarifying an aspect of Nelson and Winter's terminology that has often confused some of the industry executives with whom I have discussed the evolution of the sector. This is the use of the phrase 'social technology' to describe things like regulatory systems or social attitudes. Often and understandably, people unfamiliar with Nelson and Winter are happy to use 'technology' as a term to describe physical technology such as biomarkers, the internet and RFID (although some quibble that they are biological or natural technologies rather than physical). However, to many people the term 'social technology' seems incongruous or inappropriate when applied to social systems, laws, regulations, attitudes and behaviours. I understand the confusion, but I don't want to add to it by using different terminology when writing about Nelson and Winter's work, so I have used the terms physical and social technology in broadly their original sense in my summary explanation in Figure 5.1. That said, the terms chosen by Nelson and Winter in

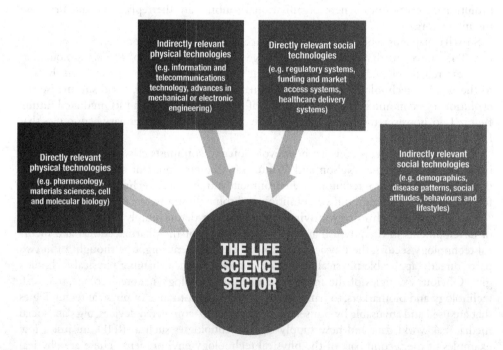

Figure 5.1 The social and physical technology environments of the pharmaceutical and medical technology sectors

the 1980s did not foresee how people's understanding of those words would subtly change over the next decades. For the remainder of this book, therefore, I will talk about the social and technological environments, which will be less confusing for the non-academic, executive reader.

It is the combined social and technological environments to which our industry adapts and it does so by means of variation, selection and amplification of organisational routines. Through adaptation it evolves new capabilities, structures, strategies and business models. And to better describe that adaptation process, I need to introduce another concept from evolutionary theory, that of co-evolution (15).

The idea of the industry adapting to its environment is not an entirely accurate description, because it implies a unidirectional, one-way adaptation that is not a good description of reality. In fact, the industry and the social and technological environments are constantly adapting to each other in a three-way process. For example, a change in the technological environment (e.g. a better scientific understanding of chronic respiratory diseases) might lead to shift in a drug company's strategy (a focus on developing and marketing certain categories of COPD and asthma drugs) that in time leads to a shift in both clinical practice and the design of healthcare services (a shift from institutional to community care).

The important point to extract from this complexity is that pharmaceutical and medical technology companies evolve in response to changes in their social and technological environments. However, they do not do so in a passive, reactive manner. More accurately, the industry co-evolves in continuous, incremental steps with the social and physical technological environments, which are in turn co-evolving with each other and with the industry. This complex, incremental, three-way co-evolutionary process is summarised in Figure 5.2.

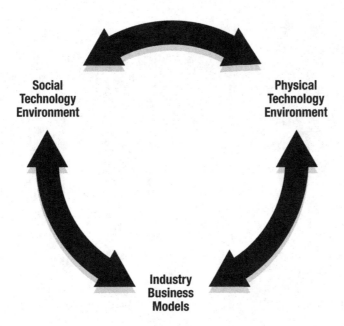

Figure 5.2 The co-evolution of business models with their environment

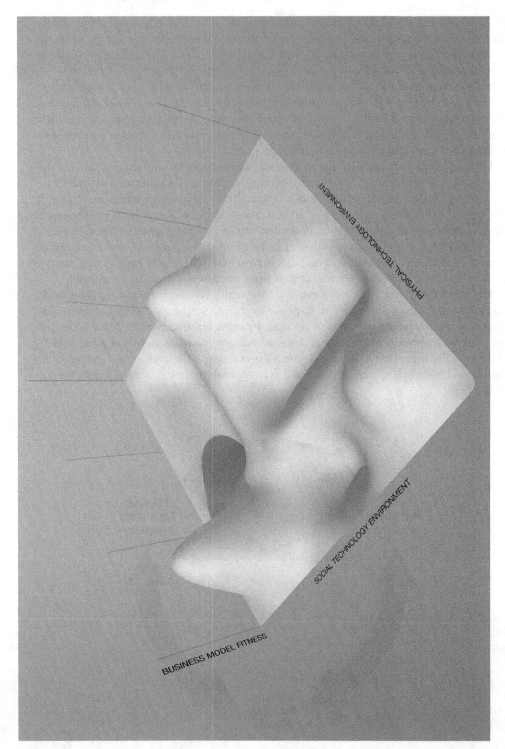

Figure 5.3 An example fitness landscape

In reality, even this three-way adaptation is a simplification of reality. Sub-components of each environment and business model, such as social and professional preferences for care pathway, economic resources, political policy and many other issues, all conflate to drive even a relatively simply change in one therapy area. If we expand our thinking to include all of the different diagnostic, therapy and care pathways in a modern healthcare system, then the applicability of the term 'complex adaptive system' and Darwin's metaphor of the entangled bank become clearer and more pertinent than ever.

After social and technological environments and co-evolution, there is one more idea to introduce before we begin to apply evolutionary economics to our industry. This is the concept of the fitness landscape. This is an evolutionary biologist's tool, introduced by Sewall Wright in 1931 (16), which can be adapted for use in evolutionary economics. In essence, it is a three dimensional data plot in which two horizontal axes represent variation in the social and technological environments whilst the vertical axis represents the fit of a particular business model. In biological evolution, fit corresponds to reproductive capability. In its economic application, fit is more accurately correlated to financial success, such as risk-adjusted return on capital at risk. Figure 5.3 is a generic fitness landscape in which a number of different social and physical environments come together and in which the success of a hypothetical business model varies in the different contexts.

Fitness landscapes help us to understand industry evolution in a number of ways that are perhaps best understood through biological analogy. If we begin with a collection of very different but co-existing biological species and observe that sloths, piranhas and capybaras all share an environment (i.e. the Amazonian rain forest), we can imply that, in that shared environment there must be a number of different ecological habitats that we might, for simplicity, call the tree canopy, the ground and the river. Conversely, if we begin with those three habitats, we might predict the very different traits of those species. In the same way, we can look at past and current business models and infer the history and development of the various habitats in the same business environment. Alternatively, we can look at the forces shaping and changing those habitats and predict the business models that will evolve to fit those habitats. In our hypothetical Figure 5.3, each peak represents a business model well adapted to its habitat. In turn, each habitat is shaped by different combinations of social and technological conditions. If we knew the nature of those business models, we could infer a lot about the business habitats in which they thrive and we could compare and contrast the strategies, structures and capabilities those habitats select for. We might also use the fitness landscape to predict and explain negative outcomes. In Figure 5.3, we might predict that the deep valleys represent combinations of physical and social environments in which there is no well adapted business model.

6 Explaining the industry's past

The fitness landscape, representing as it does the co-evolution of industry business models with their social and technological environments, comes to life when we use it to explain the history of the pharmaceutical industry. The year 1870 is a good starting point for two reasons. First, it is the date that historians usually use for the beginning of the second industrial revolution, also known as the technological revolution, which dramatically changed the pharmaceutical industry and many others (17). Second, prior to that time the business model for the industry, what we might call the apothecary business model, had remained largely unchanged for centuries.

If we landed a time machine in 1870 and asked to be shown the industry that invented and made medicines, we would have been taken first to an apothecary because what we now call pharmaceutical companies did not exist in their current form, although their ancestors did. The key characteristics of the apothecary business model were that it was local, small scale and based on technologies that had existed for centuries. The in-house prepared, unproven and largely ineffective products they sold would have been very familiar to apothecaries from previous centuries. As different as it was from today's pharma company, it was the phenotype of the pharmaceutical business model at that time. Before we make the mistake of dismissing the apothecary model, let's remember that this was a very successful business model. It dominated its environment for about 600 years because it was perfectly adapted to a social and technological environment that had changed little in that time. The local, small-scale and low technology model was perfectly adapted to a world in which travel and communication was difficult, where economies of scale were impossible and pharmaceutical science had progressed little since the Dark Ages. This is graphically represented in the fitness landscape shown in Figure 6.1, which shows one well adapted business model. This is of course a simplification to make a point but not an oversimplification.

Figure 6.1 shows a simple fitness landscape in which there was only one significant habitat, characterised by primitive technology, narrow geographical scope, limited legal constraints and dominance of what we now call self-funded consumers. Starting from about this time, however, the relative stability of the industry's environment was transformed by a number of fundamental and far-reaching changes in both the social and physical technological environments. These are discussed in more detail in *The Future of Pharma*, but the most important of them are summarised in Figure 6.2. Some of these factors, such as germ theory and the emergence of early healthcare systems, will be familiar and obvious in their impact on the industry. However, less obvious influences, like early forms of what we now call globalisation and communications technology, were just as important in their impact. It's important to appreciate that, whilst these changes would have been perceived as a series of unconnected, gradual and incremental changes happening as society grew and developed, their cumulative effect over a quite short period of time was much more

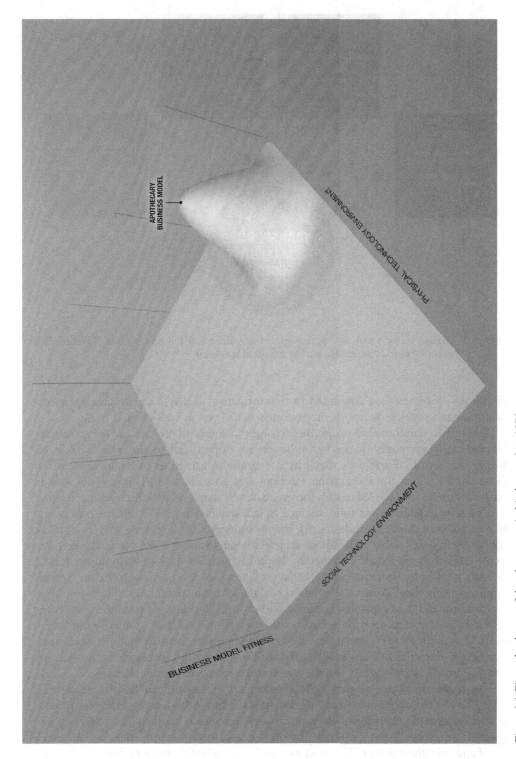

APOTHECARY
BUSINESS MODEL

PHYSICAL TECHNOLOGY ENVIRONMENT

SOCIAL TECHNOLOGY ENVIRONMENT

BUSINESS MODEL FITNESS

Figure 6.1 Fitness landscape of the pharmaceutical industry, circa 1870

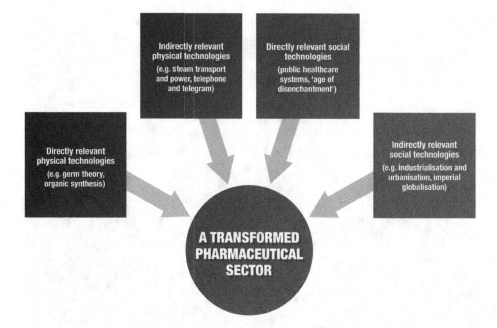

Figure 6.2 Changes in the social and technological environments of the pharmaceutical and medical
technology sector during the second industrial revolution

significant. Together, they amounted to transformative, relatively abrupt changes in the
environment to which the apothecary business model was so well adapted.

Despite their transformative nature, these changes took time to play out and the apothecary
business model eventually mutated into the retailers of packaged goods we now recognise.
Whilst they remain distributors, they play no significant part in the invention and manufacture of medicines. But these changes did not only act to push apothecaries back into an
ecological niche, they also led to the emergence of new species of pharmaceutical company.

If we now travelled in our time machine to half way between 1870 and the present and
asked again to be shown the industry that invents and makes medicines, we see very different
entities. A knowledgeable contemporaneous guide might ask us if we wanted to be taken
to the research-based industry, typified by Bayer or Merck or the over-the-counter (OTC)
industry, typified by Beechams, Parke-Davis or Johnson & Johnson. Both of these 'species'
of pharmaceutical company were clearly very different from apothecaries. They were large,
international and their capabilities differed both from each other and from the apothecary.
Research-based companies such as Bayer owed their position to their distinctive capabilities
in R&D, whilst their OTC cousins excelled in branding and distribution. Of course, sometimes these distinctive business models lived within separate silos within the same company,
but that doesn't negate the fact that they were and are very different animals.

This transformation is explained by evolutionary economics. In the years following
1870, the changes shown in Figure 6.2 reshaped the fitness landscape of the pharmaceutical industry and created new ecological niches for which apothecaries were not well
adapted. Into these spaces grew the first great pharmaceutical companies, both research
based and over-the-counter. This is shown in the simplified form, in Figure 6.3.

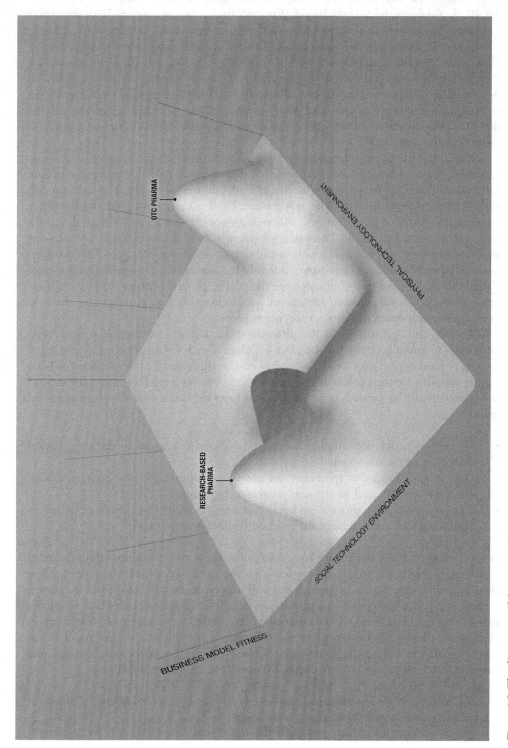

Figure 6.3 The divergence of the research-based and over-the-counter pharmaceutical sectors, circa 1930

Of course, the changes in the social and technological environments didn't stop in the 1930s, although the Second World War did cause a discontinuity in both social and technological environments. In the post-war years, at least in the western world, change accelerated. In the social environment, social healthcare systems become dominant even in the US, and regulation and clinical trial harmonisation placed new selection pressures on the existing business models. And commercial law changes, such as the Hatch-Waxman Act enabling generics and patent limitations, changed the competitive environment. In technology, the industry experienced what has become known as the therapeutic revolution (18) with an unprecedented flow of new technologies in both pharmaceutical and medical technology.

Just as in the late nineteenth and early twentieth centuries, these changes further fragmented the fitness landscape. And, as I hope is now becoming clear, the emergence of new habitats in a fitness landscape almost inevitably leads to more speciation of business models as they adapt to those habitats. This is represented in Figure 6.4, which shows the pharmaceutical industry of the recent past, although it's not difficult to see close parallels with the medical technology sector. These new species may show their origins in their pre-war ancestors but they have quite different capabilities, structures and strategies. The modern research-based pharma giant has quite a different business model from its ancestor, even if it might share the same historical corporate name. The generic pharma and biotech business models, which are arguably parasitic or symbiotic to research pharma, have emerged from the research-based model via a speciation process.

Obviously, this explanation of the pharmaceutical industry's evolution is necessarily simplified. It would be more accurate, but less clear, if each fitness peak was portrayed as clusters of smaller peaks, for example. And of course, this simplified description has been further simplified in this précis of my earlier work. Notwithstanding that, three important points should be prominent in the previous brief explanation of the pharmaceutical industry's past:

- The industry did not simply change; it co-evolved with its social and physical technological environments.
- This co-evolution led to speciation, the emergence of multiple new business models that were well adapted to the new market environment.
- This co-evolutionary process can be extrapolated to predict the future of the pharmaceutical and, more widely, the medical technology industries.

Before I summarise my work from *The Future of Pharma* that discusses the extrapolation of evolutionary trends, it is worth taking a few lines to clear up a point of terminology. To be clear, what has happened, is happening and will happen in the pharmaceutical industry is evolution. It is not *like* evolution, and I am not using evolution as a metaphor for how the industry is changing. What we are observing is the variation, selection and amplification of replicators, leading to the emergence of new categories of interactors, and that *is* evolution. The fact that the replicators are organisational routines, not genes, and the interactors are firms, not organisms, is a mere detail. To quote J Stanley Metcalfe (19):

> *Evolutionary theory is a manner of reasoning in its own right, quite independent of the use made of it by biologists. They simply got there first.*

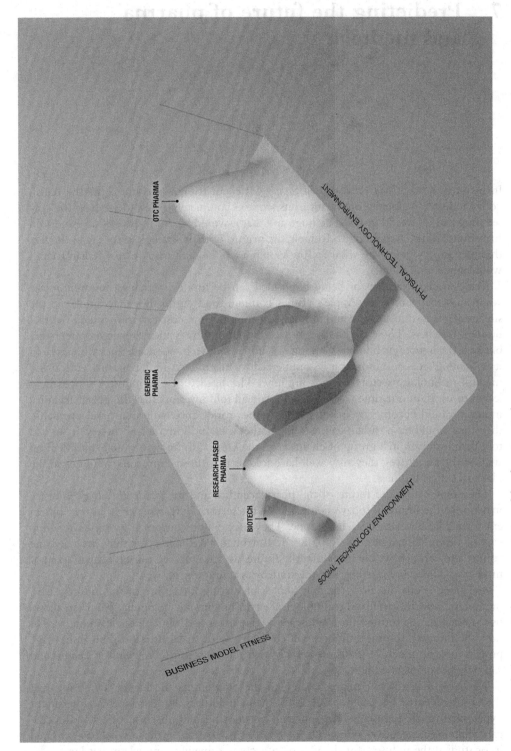

BIOTECH

RESEARCH-BASED PHARMA

GENERIC PHARMA

OTC PHARMA

BUSINESS MODEL FITNESS

SOCIAL TECHNOLOGY ENVIRONMENT

PHYSICAL TECHNOLOGY ENVIRONMENT

Figure 6.4 The late twentieth century speciation of the pharmaceutical sector

7   Predicting the future of pharma and medtech

In his great book, *Good Strategy, Bad Strategy*, Richard Rumelt recounts how the Italian coffee industry – globally dominant in its sector – completely failed to see how the coffee shop market would grow to be huge and that it would be dominated by an American firm from Seattle. According to Rumelt, the origins of their strategic error lay in the fact that they simply didn't see what Starbucks sells as coffee (and many of my Italian friends would agree with them!).

Many similar examples of being blindsided can be found in strategy research: music companies that didn't see Apple's iTunes coming; food companies that didn't see the supermarkets as direct rivals; and airlines that thought low cost carriers wouldn't attract business travellers. These are all case studies illustrating how senior executives often wear blinkers. Such strategic blindness among executives, known by the academics who research it as 'framing', is as common as it is commercially dangerous. And the pharmaceutical and medical technology sectors are not immune. The history of our industry should be a lesson to us. If, in our time travel to 1870, we had told investors that the pharmaceutical industry would become, by many standards, the world's most important and profitable, then they would have rushed to invest in apothecaries and lost a lot of money. If we had told them to invest in a group of chemists on the Upper Rhine who were experimenting with coal tar and dyes, they may well have told us that those companies were not in the pharmaceutical business.

The point is that the future of the pharmaceutical and medical technology industry may not be the future of today's companies in the sector. They may persist in very different form, like Bayer or GSK have done. They may exist as historical footnotes forming part of future companies, like Upjohn or Burroughs-Wellcome. Or they may become extinct altogether. If we are to predict the future, we have to keep ourselves open to all of those possibilities and not 'beg the question' by assuming the answer.

As I hope is obvious now, the first step in predicting the future of the industry is to understand how its social and technological environments are changing. This then allows us to anticipate the future fitness landscape of the sector and, with all due caution, predict how the industry's business models will co-evolve to fit that landscape. This three-stage process took up much of the three years of research in writing *The Future of Pharma* and can only be summarised here.

We have to begin our understanding of the environmental changes by seeing past the unsubstantiated hype about our sector. Most industries are pervaded by a persistent hyperbole that the industry is dynamic and fast moving; and pharmaceuticals and medical technology executives often talk in those terms. However, those who have worked in or studied the industry for decades have become somewhat inured to that hyperbole, recognising that the industry has been broadly one of constant, important but gradual rather than transformative change. This is only to be expected in a sector characterised by stabilising factors such as long development cycles, conservative regulation regimes, high barriers to new entrants and institutional customers who are often slow to innovate. In reality, pharmaceuticals and medical technology have been slow moving in comparison to many other sectors. In the terminology of Stephen Jay Gould, the sector appears to have been in a period of equilibrium, in which relatively slow, incremental and continuous change is preceded and followed by 'punctuations' of rapid, transformative and discontinuous change.

But if it is true that we have been in a period of equilibrium, many who work in or study the pharmaceutical and medical technology industry perceive that just such a punctuation is underway. Academic research and industry leaders report that the number, magnitude and conjunction of market changing trends acting on the sector is something unusual in historical terms, perhaps preceding a discontinuous change in industry structure that occurs very rarely. Those changes are summarised in Figure 7.1, divided into direct and indirect social and technological changes.

It takes little insight to see that this convergence of change is reminiscent of the changes summarised in Figure 6.2. Those earlier changes presaged a fundamental change in the industry's business models, and it seems realistic to expect that the result of the current set of trends will be as fundamental as those of the second industrial revolution that created the industry as we know it.

Trying to predict the likely course of these future changes was the core of *The Future of Pharma* and the findings emerged from my earlier research in three stages, each building

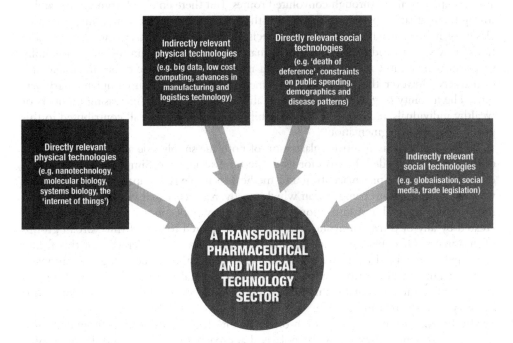

Figure 7.1 Changes in the social and technological environments of the pharmaceutical sector in the early twenty-first century

on the other: first, the implications of changes in the social and technological environments; second, the nature of the fitness landscape created by those changes; and finally, the predicted business models that would emerge to fit that landscape.

My first finding was that, in adapting to the availability of new physical technologies, the industry was polarising in the ways it was creating value. Traditionally, the bulk of the value creation in our sector could be attributed to research and development, with operations, supply chain, marketing and other parts of the value chain playing important but supporting roles. However, my research revealed a strong theme that adaptation to changes in the technological environment was leading to three classes of habitat in which value creation by innovation, operational efficiency and customer understanding were, respectively, the dominant modes of value creation. This was not a wholly surprising finding. The polarisation of approaches to value creation is the core of Porter's 'generic strategies' concept and is an idea well accepted in strategic management. The mechanism for this seems to be that changes in a firm's value chain tend to conflict with each other, at least in part. For example, adaptations in the supply chain to take advantage of lean manufacturing technologies may reduce a firm's ability to tailor its products to specific customers, at least relative to a less-lean competitor. Similarly, a firm's adaptation to new immunotherapy science in oncology is likely to reduce its ability to compete on price with rivals using older technology. Overall, the adaptation to new technological environments pushes firms to either product excellence or operational excellence or customer intimacy, to use Treacy and Wiersema's terms for this polarisation phenomenon (20).

My second finding was something of a mirror image of my first. It was that the customers of our industry are polarising into three groups. For most of the post-war period, pharmaceuticals and medical technologies were largely paid for by governments or insurance companies, albeit through convoluted routes. But there emerged from my research a strong theme that adaptation to changes in the social environment were leading to three classes of habitat in which the purchase decision was primarily made either by institutions or by wealthy individuals or by mass market individuals. Again this was not wholly surprising, since most research literature on market maturation describes fragmentation of markets. However, this phenomenon seemed to have at least four complementary origins. The inability of governments to fund all possible treatments, increasing numbers of wealthy individuals, increasing self-responsibility and globalisation all contributed to this profound market fragmentation.

Taken together, this adaptive polarisation of both the supply side and the demand side of the industry provided the basis for its future fitness landscape. Simply put, the ecological system in which pharmaceutical and medical technology companies were operating was fragmenting. From being one in which mostly-research-based value was delivered to mostly governmental and institutional customers, it was becoming one in which value created by any of three dominant modes could be offered to any of three broad groups of customers. Of course, it is necessary to recognise that some elements of this future landscape have existed for many years – for example, low cost generics as operationally excellent but not innovative companies – but the general picture of a broadening and fragmenting industry habitat is a useful first step in understanding the co-evolution of our industry with its environment.

This broadening and fragmentation of the sector's habitat is shown in simplified form in Figure 7.2, which shows how the polarised approaches to creating and defining value in this market are defining the basic future structure of the market.

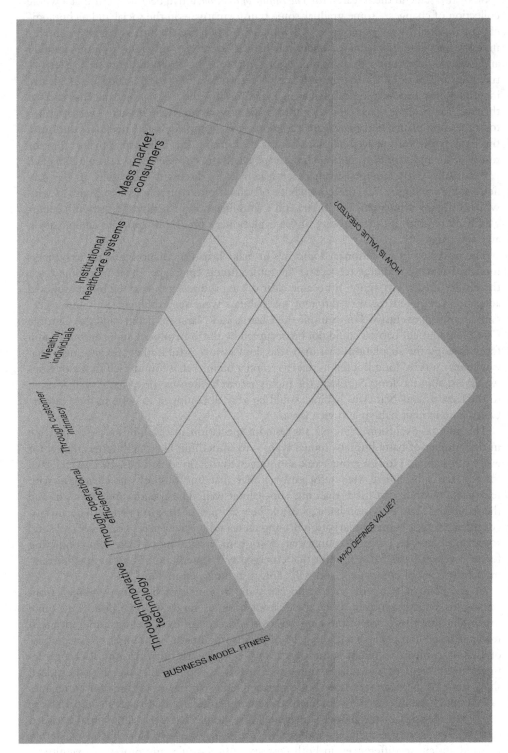

Figure 7.2 The fragmentation of the fitness landscape for pharmaceuticals and medical technology in the early to mid–twenty–first century

So by this stage in the research for *The Future of Pharma*, it had become clear that a whole collection of changes – some gradual, some transformative – in the social and technological environments were combining to fragment and polarise the fitness landscape for the industry into nine sub-habitats. These sub-habitats were very different from one another and each would require a business model different from the others either in strategy, structure, capabilities or all those things. It was, to return to a biological analogy, as if we had identified nine basic ecological niches in a rain forest – the tree canopy, the land surface, the river, for example – and identified three basic ways of surviving in each – perhaps photosynthesising plants, herbivores and carnivores, for example. As our research continued, this basic framework proved helpful as a way of thinking, but it became obvious that the reality of the industry's future fitness landscape was more complex than a simple 3×3 grid.

Eventually, what emerged from the research (as is discussed more fully in the earlier book) was Figure 7.3, the complexity of which often surprises the executives with which I discuss it but which is in fact still a simplification of reality. As Darwin's entangled bank reminds us, the capacity of the evolutionary process to generate complexity is awe-inspiring.

The next step of evolutionary logic was to make broad predictions about the business models that would emerge to occupy the future fitness landscape. Indeed, in some cases, these were already emerging. It became clear during the research that the business model adaptations required for very different sub-habitats were very different and almost certainly mutually exclusive. For example the Lazarus and Narcissus habitat and the Chronic Cost Containment habitat could not be occupied by the same model. In terms of our rain forest analogy, the adaptations that made the sloth so successful in the trees also mean that it wouldn't survive long if it fell in the river; and a piranha that found itself in the treetops would last about as long. Similarly, the highly research intensive firm that is well adapted to the Lazarus and Narcissus habitat would be very ill equipped to cope in the Chronic Cost Containment habitat and vice versa.

This mutual exclusion principle suggested a speciation in the industry – an increase in the number of basic business model types – to something like one business model for every sub-habitat. However, our work also suggested that, in some cases, the traits selected for by each sub-habitat were sufficiently similar that one business model might, with reasonable flexibility, fit more than one sub-habitat well. The Lazarus and Narcissus and the Advanced State Provision habitats would be examples of this. In essence, there are two conflicting forces: habitat polarisation driving increased speciation; economies of scale and scope and synergies pushing against that. As our understanding of these two conflicting forces developed, the balance point that emerged was a prediction of seven new business models, 'species' of company if you will. This is summarised in Table 7.1.

At this point it is worth once again clarifying a point that has often emerged from discussions with executives about these seven business models. Some point out, quite understandably, that some of these models exist already. For example, our most advanced research-based companies such as Roche or Medtronic might be thought of as examples of Genius companies, whilst some of the low cost generic pharmaceutical companies might be thought of as Monster Imitators. To this I would argue that they do indeed show some of the necessary traits but that true Genius and Monster Imitator companies will be much more extreme versions of these companies and that today's companies are merely antecedents of the models I suggest. For example, the price differential between today's most expensive therapies and generic drugs may be very large but in the future I would anticipate differences, in both cost and efficacy, of many orders of magnitude.

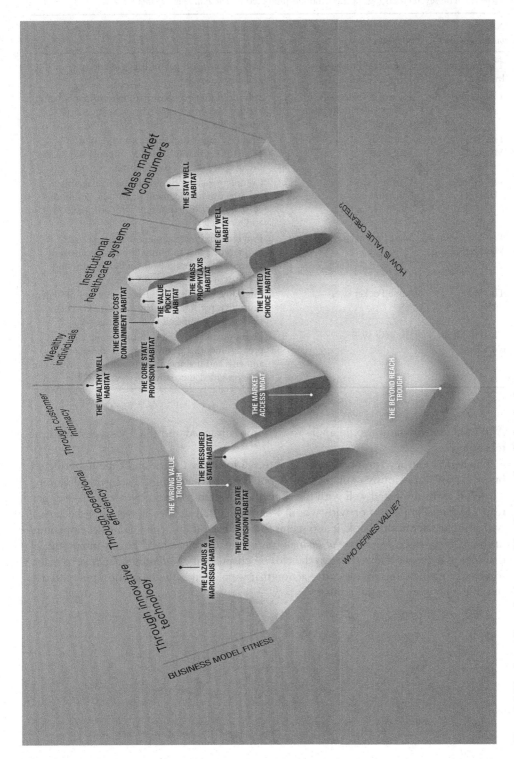

Figure 7.3 The future fitness landscape of the pharma and medical technology sectors

Table 7.1 The seven emerging business models predicted in *The Future of Pharma*

Name of business model	Habitat(s) to which it is adapted	Nature of value proposition
The Monster Imitator	Core State Provision Limited Choice	Very low cost, off patent drugs at adequate quality and service levels
The Genius	Lazarus & Narcissus Advanced State Provision Pressured State	Advanced therapies that have demonstrably better clinical outcome than very low cost generic alternatives
The Trust Manager	Get Well Stay Well	Trusted drugs, nutraceuticals and related programmes that treat minor ailments and enable the maintenance of good health
The Disease Manager	Chronic Cost Containment	Complete therapy provision and management for the effective management of chronic conditions at the lowest cost consistent with adequate quality and service levels
The Lifestyle Manager	Mass Prophylaxis	Provision and management of therapies and programmes that minimise the development of more serious conditions at the lowest cost and adequate quality and service levels
The Value Picker	Value Pocket	Innovative new drugs and adaptations of off patent drugs that provide comparative context-specific value when compared to low cost generics
The Health Concierge	Wealthy Well	Provision and management of therapy and programmes that resolve non–life-threatening ailments and maintain health more effectively than state provided alternatives

And of course the same would apply to the most advanced and the lowest cost medical technologies.

The logical journey from environmental trends to future fitness landscape to predicted business models obviously contains many approximations and high-level generalisations. That said, it has resonated well with the thousands of industry executives who have either read *The Future of Pharma* or with whom I have discussed it since it was published. As I will examine later in this book, it also seems to be borne out in principle by developments in the industry since *The Future of Pharma* was originally researched. This is important, as that logical sequence allowed me, in the closing chapters of *The Future of Pharma*, to make some recommendations for executive action that were intended to be of most practical use to those who worked in the industry.

8 Practical implications for an evolving industry

As is famously carved on Karl Marx's tombstone in Highgate Cemetery, philosophers have only interpreted the world in various ways; the point is to change it. Predicting the future business models of the sector has value only if it allows executives to influence or direct the evolution of their business. In *The Future of Pharma*, I attempted to contribute to this by suggesting that such direction needed to proceed in four stages, summarised in the following paragraphs.

The first step in directing the evolution of a firm is to select the sub-habitat or habitats that the firm wishes to occupy. In discussion of this point with many of the industry's senior executives, two important issues emerge. The first is the reluctance to choose a habitat and, therefore, potentially restrict market potential. The corporate level strategy of many of the pharmaceutical industry's largest firms currently includes both research-based models (heading towards Genius) and generic (heading towards Monster Imitator). Yet there is reason to believe that these may be transitional forms that will eventually resolve into more pure play companies. In particular, members of the investment community who were interviewed for my earlier research pointed out such hybrid models would always suffer from a 'conglomerate discount'. Essentially, investors believed that the same board could not extract maximum value from two or more very different businesses and that, in any case, it was the job of investors and analysts to allocate resources across a portfolio of businesses, not that of the board.

The second point to emerge from the discussion of habitat selection was that many firms instinctively saw their future as Genius companies whilst relatively few seriously considered other options. Again, there are reasons to believe that this is unlikely to be a viable choice for all of the firms who make it. Most important of those reasons is that there is unlikely to be space in the Lazarus and Narcissus and adjacent habitats for many companies of significant size. Although it will be very profitable, the proportion by volume of the pharmaceutical and medical technology markets that will be held by very expensive, very effective products is likely to be small and unable to sustain many large companies. A second, also important reason that many aspirant Genius companies may not fulfil their ambitions is risk. Being a Genius will be a high stakes, very high risk, very high return game and, for many companies and their boards, it will be preferable to opt for less risky strategies.

Discussions with industry executives since the publication of *The Future of Pharma* suggest that even the first step of guiding one's own evolution by choosing a habitat will not come easily to many firms. However, if we assume that some firms will jump – or be pushed over – this hurdle, then their second decision concerns strategy.

Even with a clear choice of habitat and therefore an outline idea of business model, a firm still has to make strategic decisions – that is, choices about where to allocate resources – at several levels. These will include choices between therapy areas, core technologies, geographies, the nature of their value proposition and target segments.

Given a clear choice of habitats and resource allocation pattern, the third step in deliberate evolutionary guidance implied by my research is the active cultivation of the capability profile for the new business model. An important discovery made during the research was that the capabilities of pharmaceutical and medical technology firms that characterised each business model fell into three broad categories:

- Hygiene capabilities: those capabilities essential just to operate within the market but which do not confer any competitive advantage. Being able to compile and submit appropriate regulatory submissions may be an example of a core capability.
- Differentiating capabilities: those capabilities that, if relatively superior to the same capabilities in competitors, confer competitive advantage. Being able to develop differentiated value propositions may be an example of differentiating capability.
- Dynamic capabilities: those capabilities that act to reshape or transform other capabilities and so allow the firm to adapt to a changing environment. Being able to generate market insight may be an example of that.

Importantly, whilst core and dynamic capabilities are likely to be common to all future business models, differentiating capabilities are likely to be business model specific.

As Table 7.1 implies, the range of capabilities required by any of the new business models is both wider and more developed than the capability set that currently characterises most pharmaceutical and medical technology companies. This has two important practical implications. First, evolving from today's business model to a future one, whichever is chosen, necessarily requires the acquisition of significant new capabilities. Second, gaining and holding a competitively superior position in any habitat will depend on acquiring those capabilities both more quickly and more extensively than other firms that are trying to capture the same habitat. This requirement to out-evolve rivals by rapid, effective capability acquisition has important ramifications for the structure of the firm, since building capabilities organically is a relatively slow process. It follows that another important step in steering a firm's evolution is to make choices concerning the boundaries and governance structure of the firm. In other words, what capabilities the firm itself will develop, which it will capture by acquisition and, to the extent that it will require capabilities from outside the firm, what relationships structures it will build with other entities in order to access those external capabilities. In *The Future of Pharma*, I predicted the emergence of symbiotic network structures, which I later called holobionts (21). I predicted that these would become important and perhaps dominant organisational structures in future and that building and managing them would be a further hygiene capability required by most firms in the sector.

9   Watching the future unfold

In this chapter, I have reprised the ideas and thinking that went into *The Future of Pharma*, extending those ideas beyond pharma to medtech and, in places, clarifying issues that have emerged from discussing my work with thousands of industry executives and other experts. I hope it's not immodest to say that this work has been very well received, with glowing reviews and, importantly for me, enthusiastic endorsements from people who know the industry well.

But, as the English idiom has it, the proof of the pudding is in the eating. It's not enough to simply predict the future and, since writing *The Future of Pharma*, I have spent my time gathering information about how the sector is evolving. My goals have been to test my own predictions and the theories that underpin them but also to provide further practical guidance for those who work in the sector. In the following chapters, I am going to look at how the trends in the social and physical technological environments are developing, how this is shaping the industry's fitness landscape, how firms in the sector and around it are adapting to their new world and how we might better manage that evolutionary process. In doing so I hope to contribute to the survival and success of what may well be the world's most important industry.

Part 2

An immeasurably superior power

But Natural Selection, as we shall hereafter see, is a power incessantly ready for action, and is immeasurably superior to man's feeble efforts, as the works of Nature are to those of Art.

Charles Darwin, *The Origin of Species*

10 Introduction

The emergent pressures of selection

In the preceding pages of this book, I argued that an industry is part of a complex adaptive system in which its business models co-evolve with its social and technological environments. In Part 1, I summarised the work from *The Future of Pharma*, which applied the concepts of evolutionary economics to the pharmaceutical sector and examined the complex changes taking place in its co-evolving environments. This in turn led to my conclusion about the shape of the sector's fitness landscape and the various new business models that are emerging to populate that landscape.

But our sector is broader than pharmaceuticals alone. It also includes medical devices and technology, diagnostics and imaging, biotechnology and innumerable other sub-sectors that overlap, interconnect and influence each other. Consequently, the rather arbitrary, product-based, sub-divisions we apply are not always helpful when we try to understand how the industry as a whole is evolving. By analogy, we would not get very far in understanding the ecology of rain forest if we only considered mammals, reptiles or insects alone. We are better to consider all of the industry sub-sectors as one heterogeneous but connected sector and examine its evolution as a whole. That is the approach I will take for the rest of this book, referring to the entire industry as the life sciences industry.

If we are to understand, predict and manage how the massive and complicated life sciences industry evolves, we need to extend and deepen our analysis of its social and technological environment in three ways. First, we need to ensure that we consider social and technological factors that shape all of the sub-sectors, not only pharma. Second, we need to ensure that our collection and synthesis of these factors is up to date. Finally, and most importantly, we need to better understand how those environmental factors shape business models. In particular, since the mechanism of evolution rests on selection, we need to understand how changes in the social and technological environment change the selection pressures that act upon business models.

There are, of course, a myriad of possible factors to consider in both the social and technological environments. Every day brings news of new scientific developments, changes to regulatory systems, pricing controls, disease patterns or other changes that have a direct or indirect bearing on the industry. This blizzard of change makes work for those many consultancies that collate and repackage information about new trends in everything from big data and immunotherapies to social media and emerging markets. The intuitive and typical way to make sense of these torrents of information is to collate, sort and extrapolate from them, with the goal of understanding their impact and predicting the future implications of the most important. This is indeed what almost all industry reports do.

But although it is necessary and useful, this 'collate, sort and extrapolate' approach is not sufficient for the difficult task of understanding how the industry will evolve. That is because a 'collate and extrapolate' methodology is built on the implicit assumption that the industry behaves in a linear, simple manner. It assumes relatively simple causal links between changes in, for example, information technology and payer systems and the way that businesses structure themselves and the strategies they follow. This is a false, simplistic assumption; it neglects the complex adaptive nature of the industry and of economic systems in general. If we are dealing with a complex adaptive system, then extrapolation and prediction, however sophisticated, is unlikely to provide a reliable guide to the future because such systems don't behave in a linear manner. For an entertaining and informative description of why this is so, you are recommended to read *Forecast* by Mark Buchanan (22); but, in short, complex adaptive systems demonstrate something called emergent properties. These are patterns of behaviour, often unexpected and impossible to predict, that result from the non-linear interaction of all the many component parts of the system. In fact, emergent properties are so hard to predict that a better approach seems to be to identify these properties as early in their emergence as possible, then judge what they imply and adapt to them as quickly as possible. That 'identify, judge and suggest adaptation' approach is the one I take in this second part of the book. It will seem alien and frustratingly qualitative for readers who, like me, were trained as physical scientists, but I ask you to be tolerant. We have not yet developed the science to predict the behaviour of complex adaptive systems in the quantified manner that we can for a relatively simple physical or chemical system.

Fortunately, for our purposes, we don't need to completely characterise all of the system interactions and all of the emergent properties of the entire complex adaptive system that is the life sciences industry and its social and technological environments. That, in any case, would be an impossible task. Instead, it is sufficient for our purposes to understand the most important changes taking place, the interactions between them and the major emergent properties that result from those interactions. Then, having identified as early as possible the major emergent properties of the system, we need to understand how those properties create conditions that favour or prejudice particular business model characteristics. In the language of evolutionary biology, we need to know what selection pressures are arising from the complex adaptive system that is the healthcare environment. It is those selection pressures that shape the industry's adaptive landscape; and it is that adaptive landscape into which new business models evolve. This line of thought is summarised in Figure 10.1, but if a historical parallel helps, I refer you back to Chapter 6, 'Explaining the Industry's Past'. The second industrial revolution, with its mass of changes in the social and technological environment, was a beautiful illustration of the emergence of selection pressures that led to the consequent evolution of the research-based pharmaceutical company.

So this section of the book will look again at the changes that are happening in our industry's social and technological environments. In particular, it will look at the changes since the research for *The Future of Pharma* and the changes that influence not only pharma but the life sciences industry more generally. My goal is to identify the emergent properties of our industry's system, to understand the selection pressures and anticipate the shape of the industry's fitness landscape in a more detailed way than in my earlier work. Using that understanding, I will look again, in Part 3 of the book, at the speciation and emergence of business models in our sector. This allows me in Part 4 to prescribe ways that firms might manage and accelerate the evolution of their own business models.

The central challenge, of course, is to organise what information we have to achieve clarity without oversimplification; to simplify as far as possible but no further as Einstein is

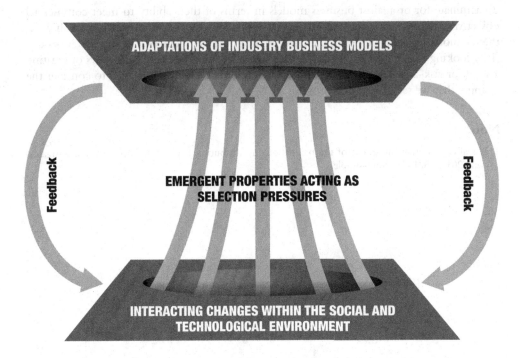

Figure 10.1 The emergence of selection pressures from the market environment

often paraphrased.[1] To begin with, I have used Nelson and Winter's division of social and technological environments as a good, if imperfect, starting point to organise my observations. In each of these two divisions, I will argue that what is emerging from the complexity is a small number of important emergent properties: shifts in those environments that create selection pressures, shape the landscape and allow us to predict, in broad terms, the evolution of business models in the sector.

However, before we do, there's one further point to make about the parallel between biological and economic evolution. In biology, fitness is a function of reproduction. When we say an organism (that is, an interactor) is better adapted to its environment, we actually mean it does a better job at facilitating the spread of its genes (that is, its replicators). In economic evolution, organisations are the interactors and organisational routines the replicators, and the same definition of better adapted applies: successful organisations are those that enable their organisational routines to be spread. In the case of commercial organisations operating in capitalist (or pseudo-capitalist) economies, the replication of routines is closely related to the firm's longevity and success. In simple terms, firms that survive tend to spread their organisational routines either by growth or by being copied. Motorola and Six Sigma, Ford and the production line and Procter & Gamble and Brand Management are all examples of this. Of course, history does not record the origins of those organisational routines whose originating firms died before their routines could be copied. So when we talk about selection pressures in an economic environment, we mean those environmental forces that favour or prejudice a firm's success and growth and hence the spread of its routines. In commercial organisations, this means that selection pressures discriminate for or against business models in terms of their ability to meet commercial objectives, such as risk-adjusted return on investment (ROI). When we look at shifts in the technological and sociological environment of the life sciences industry, we are essentially looking for emerging properties that favour or prejudice particular ways of creating a superior risk-adjusted rate of return. It's through that lens that we need to consider the changes that we see going on around us.

Note

1 A really interesting discussion of the origins of this attribution is given at http://quoteinvestigator. com/2011/05/13/einstein-simple/.

11 Selection pressures emerging from the social environment

When considering the social environment in which the life sciences industry sector operates, it helps to appreciate a distinctive characteristic of the sector, namely its multiple, varied and very strong connections to society as a whole. Whilst all industries operate within their societal context, our sector is especially strongly connected to society by both institutional systems (such as laws, regulations and state-funded healthcare) and by non-institutional factors (such as demographics, social attitudes and lifestyle trends). Many other sectors share some of these connections but none are so tightly woven into their societal context as is the life sciences industry. Like the life sciences sector, the financial services sector is highly regulated; and some others, such as the arms industry and the civil engineering sector, count governments as their major customer. Others, such as the construction industry and

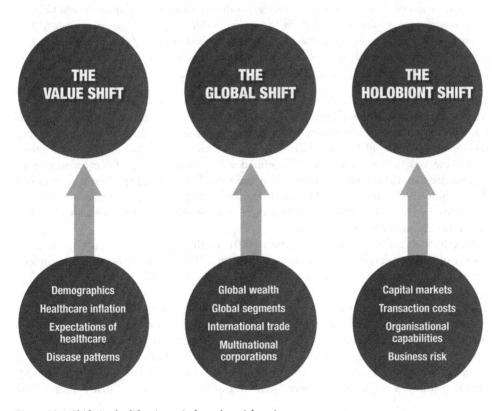

Figure 11.1 Shifts in the life science industry's social environment

the fashion sector are, like life sciences, influenced heavily by the demands that flow from lifestyle and demographics. But it is hard to think of another industry that is so closely connected to its societal base in so many ways. Our sector is connected to society by regulation, government customers and the impact of lifestyle and demographics, as well as many other societal factors, such as wealth distribution and globalisation. Just as importantly, we are connected to society by our links to academic, healthcare and other societally-embedded systems. And each of these connections is bidirectional; our industry helps societies age, supports academic research, enables healthcare system design, shapes regulation and influences lifestyles. In return, each of those aspects of society influences the industry more or less directly. These bilateral links, and the way they interconnect into a complex web, mean that, perhaps more than any other, this industry both shapes and is shaped by society.

Understanding how the social environment is shaping the industry was one of the primary objectives of the research behind this book. From the mass of data in that research, a number of fundamental shifts in our industry's social environment emerge. Each of these shifts creates a selection pressure that shapes the industry's fitness landscape. These are summarised in Figure 11.1 and discussed in the following sections.

The value shift

Box 11.1   The value shift

An emergent property of the healthcare system in which the definition of the value of treatments, interventions and associated products and services is changing from a relatively simple and ubiquitous definition of value as improved clinical outcome, as defined by healthcare professionals, to a much more complex, context-specific definition of value defined in terms of clinical, economic and other factors by some combination of healthcare professionals, payers and patients or their proxies.

The defining characteristics of any market are the people and organisations who decide what is valuable and how they choose to define value. When those two parameters of value definition change, the nature of the industry that delivers that value will inevitably also change. We are all familiar with how this has happened in the computing market. First, there was fragmentation of who defined value, with a change from companies to individuals; then the definition of value changed to include not only processing power but also mobility and connectivity. The consequence of that shift is what makes the famous prediction by IBM's Thomas Watson, that there was a global market for perhaps a handful of computers, so amusing to us today.

Exactly such a shift in value definition began in the life sciences sector around the middle of the first decade of the twenty-first century. Whilst still uneven and incomplete, it is reshaping the industry in a fundamental way. The value shift (see Box 11.1 and Figure 11.2) is an emergent property of this market, characterised by two factors. First, there is a fragmentation in who decides what is worth paying for and, second, a shift in the criteria upon which they base their choices. It is a shift that is clearly visible in pharmaceuticals, medical technology and almost all other sub-sectors of the industry.

Like all emergent properties, the value shift cannot be attributed directly to a small number of discrete factors; that is not the way complex adaptive systems behave. Instead, the value shift is a behavioural pattern borne out of the interaction of many intertwined

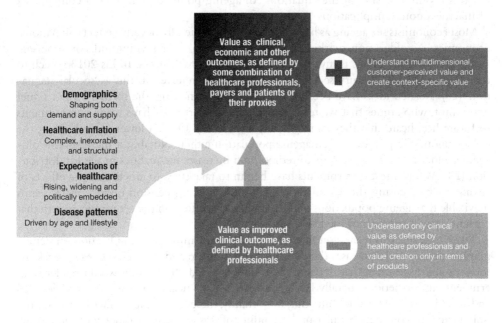

Figure 11.2 The value shift

factors. In the following sections, I describe what emerged from my research as the four most important factors driving the value shift. The reader should remember that this list is a simplification to aid thinking and should not be mistaken for a comprehensive catalogue of all the factors involved.

Demographics: shaping both demand and supply

Arguably the most fundamental factor contributing to the value shift is that of population demographics; birth rates are declining and populations are ageing. This is not simply a western phenomenon but a global one; the number of people over sixty-five in the world is expected to increase from 600 million to 1.1 billion in the next twenty years (23). An optimistically-titled UN report in 2012, *A Celebration and a Challenge*, described how two people celebrate their sixtieth birthday every second (24). Cumulatively, the proportion of the population over sixty is expected to rise from 1 in 9 today to 1 in 5 by 2050. At present, only Japan has an older population of more than 30 percent of the total. However, by 2050, sixty-four countries are expected to join Japan in having a third of their population in that older age group. The healthcare impact of this global ageing is well described in a US Department of State report, which describes how non-communicable diseases primarily associated with age, such as heart disease, cancers and diabetes will, by 2030, come to represent 54 percent of the disease burden in low to middle income countries and 89 percent in high income countries (25). Such well known data are often simplistically associated with higher demand for healthcare as if this were the only factor driving the value shift. It is true that older people generally have greater healthcare needs and place a greater relative demand on healthcare systems, but this is only one side of the equation. An ageing population also has a complex set of macroeconomic implications.

Most economists see ageing as having complex but generally negative effects on national economies. As older, non-working people draw down their savings and consume less, share prices decline as less is invested and economic growth slows. In his 2013 speech to the IMF, former US treasury secretary Larry Summers referred to this as 'secular stagnation' (26). Related ideas have been described by Stephen King, the former HSBC Chief Economist, who argues that western governments in particular have made commitments to future healthcare that they can't possibly afford (27). Overall lower growth is not the only economic implication of an ageing population either. Notably, it increases the 'old-age dependency' ratio of workers to retirees, and increases inequalities in wealth distribution (28). Whilst most governments have begun to take steps to ameliorate the effects of ageing, such as raising the age of retirement and reducing pension obligations, it seems inevitable that ageing populations will have a negative effect on the economic growth that currently pays for much of the healthcare we receive.

Taken together, this related set of economic and epidemiological implications of demographic change both increases the demand for healthcare and reduces, relatively speaking, society's ability to meet that demand. This double-sided effect alone would render governments and societies generally less able to pay for the healthcare their citizens demand and would lead to the value shift. But, importantly, these demographic factors are not the only factors to consider. A fuller understanding of this emerging property of the healthcare system comes from an appreciation that demography interacts with three other major factors: healthcare inflation, healthcare expectations and disease patterns.

Healthcare inflation: complex, inexorable and structural

Even without the double-sided effects of demographics, inflation in healthcare expenditures would still be a significant issue. The rate of inflation in healthcare expenditures has slowed recently but still remains far ahead of normal consumer inflation (29). Critics of the life sciences industry often equate this to the unreasonable cost of drugs and other products, based on a much-cited work by Joseph Newhouse (30), but this view is both discredited and unhelpful (31). Healthcare inflation is multifactorial and about much more than the cost of medical technology. The causes of the problem have been studied extensively and, as a review of the research literature by Martin and others expressed it:

> No single pattern of results is clearly identified. Among the 20 articles, four consider income to be the principal determinant of healthcare expenditure, two of them jointly with population ageing. Six highlight population ageing, as against six others that emphasize the proximity to death. The remaining six do not focus on a specific variable, or focus on another variable, e.g. technological progress or territorial decentralization.
>
> (32)

To an experienced researcher, such a conclusion is a clear indication that healthcare inflation is a multifactorial problem. But even Martin's review misses what some see as the most important reason that healthcare costs are rising faster than governments' ability to pay for them. The economist William Baumol has described how labour intensive services such as healthcare and teaching have a tendency to fall into a 'stagnation trap' in which labour costs rise faster than productivity, driving inflation higher than the standard rate (33). The only cure for this, as Erixson and van der Marel have noted, is major productivity reforms, which are very difficult in practice (34).

So, healthcare inflation is multifactorial, probably embedded in the system and, failing major structural reform of healthcare systems, almost certainly likely to continue. It is undoubtedly a real phenomenon that in isolation would lead to the emergence of the value shift and is reinforced by rather than ameliorated by its interaction with demographics. However, even these two powerful factors are not solely responsible for the value shift. Expectations and disease patterns also play their part.

Expectations of healthcare: rising, widening and politically embedded

Demographics and inflation alone might be considered sufficient drivers for the emergence of the value shift even if society's expectations were static, but they are not. At national, supranational and individual levels, our expectations of healthcare systems are growing. The global expression of this could be seen at the UN in December 2012, when the General Assembly passed a resolution urging all governments to 'move towards providing all people with access to affordable, quality healthcare services'. And this was not a one-off piece of political posturing. To quote the World Health Organization (WHO) website:

> This concept [Universal Health Coverage] has been increasingly recognized in international fora since WHO published the World Health Report 2010, entitled Health systems financing: the path to universal coverage. These include the Mexico City Political Declaration on Universal Health Coverage adopted in April 2012, the Bangkok Statement on Universal Health Coverage in January 2012, and the Tunis Declaration on Value for Money, Sustainability and Accountability in the Health Sector, adopted in July 2012.

At a national level, rising expectations for the provision of healthcare are driving policy decisions in both developed and emerging markets. This is exemplified in the US Affordable Care Act, China's innovations in healthcare insurance (35) and what the BBC called 'Indonesia's Humongous Healthcare Plan' (36), all of which are attempts to meet rising public expectations for healthcare provision. In these and other examples all over the world, government policy is reflecting a strong and increasing public demand for better access to better quality healthcare.

At the root of these global and national expansions of provision lie individual expectations. The King's Fund, a greatly respected UK think tank, wrote in 2012:

> It is a common belief in healthcare circles that expectations of health services are rising rapidly – patients are less deferential, empowered by the availability of more information, particularly over the web, and are demanding more and more.
>
> (37)

Such rising expectations of individuals are not new and are a by-product of consumer culture, as neatly summarised in a 2008 WHO report:

> Health systems are also a reflection of a globalizing consumer culture As societies modernize and become more affluent and knowledgeable, what people consider to be desirable ways of living as individuals and as members of societies, i.e. what people value, changes. People tend to regard health services more as a commodity today, but they also have other, rising expectations regarding

> *health and healthcare. They expect their families and communities to be protected from risks and*
> *dangers to health. They want healthcare that deals with people as individuals with rights and*
> *not as mere targets for programmes or beneficiaries of charity. They are willing to respect health*
> *professionals but want to be respected in turn, in a climate of mutual trust.*
>
> (38)

Driven by rising levels of income, education and access to media, then expressed through government policy and supranational bodies, the rising expectations of people in both developed and emerging economies would alone lead to price pressures in the healthcare system. Interacting with the effects of demographics and inflation, expectations contribute significantly to the emergence of the value shift.

Disease patterns: driven by age and lifestyle

The fourth major trend in the social and technological environments of the life sciences industry is a fundamental and far-reaching change in the diseases we suffer from and that we ask healthcare systems to manage. It is a trend that is partly driven by the other three and, in the manner of complex adaptive systems, also shapes demographics, inflation and expectations.

That the types, prevalence and virulence of diseases and conditions are related to a society's structure, behaviour and wealth is not a new idea. Demographers have long referred to an 'epidemiological transition' from pre-industrial patterns of epidemic infectious diseases to modern patterns of death from chronic diseases (39). That shift, which occurred in the nineteenth and twentieth centuries in the west and is occurring now in the developing world, was in part facilitated by the life sciences sector but also in large part by public health measures such as sanitation and education. To some extent, this shift is an aspect of demographic ageing, already discussed earlier. As populations age, some particular diseases – in particular neurological diseases such as Parkinson's, Alzheimer's and various other forms of dementia – stand out in their prevalence. Olesen and Leonardi (40) attribute 35 percent of the disease burden in Europe to brain disorders of one kind or another. This epidemiological transition alone would add a significant burden to healthcare budgets and would contribute to the value shift; but we can perhaps resign ourselves to it as the unavoidable consequence of longer lives. The same cannot be said for the other facet of changing disease patterns, those attributable to lifestyle.

By contrast to the epidemiological transition, what we observe today in developed and increasingly in emerging markets is a challenge that has been called 'The New Public Health' (41). This challenge is not simply one of ageing; it is the consequence of how we choose to spend those longer lives. As Pedro Carrera-Bastos and his colleagues described it, we are faced with the 'diseases of civilisation'. To quote their paper:

> *It is increasingly recognized that certain fundamental changes in diet and lifestyle that occurred*
> *after the Neolithic Revolution, and especially after the Industrial Revolution and the Modern*
> *Age, are too recent, on an evolutionary time scale, for the human genome to have completely*
> *adapted. This mismatch between our ancient physiology and the western diet and lifestyle*
> *underlies many so-called diseases of civilization, including coronary heart disease, obesity, hyper-*
> *tension, type 2 diabetes, epithelial cell cancers, autoimmune disease, and osteoporosis, which are*
> *rare or virtually absent in hunter–gatherers and other non-westernized populations.*
>
> (42)

Whilst some years ago lifestyle diseases were considered a purely western phenomenon, that is no longer the case. Writing in 2008, Rachel Nugent pointed out:

> *Chronic diseases are increasing in global prevalence and seriously threaten developing nations'*
> *ability to improve the health of their populations. Although often associated with developed*
> *nations, the presence of chronic disease has become the dominant health burden in many devel-*
> *oping countries. The rise of lifestyle-related chronic disease in poor countries is the result of a*
> *complex constellation of social, economic, and behavioural factors. Variability in the prevalence*
> *of chronic disease is found both at the country level and within countries as differences in risk*
> *factors are observed. This upward trend is forecast to continue as epidemiologic profiles and age*
> *structures of developing countries further shift.*
>
> *(43)*

This shift in disease patterns has many implications, but it is the economic implications that drive the value shift. The Milliken Institute predicts that, by mid-century, the burden of chronic diseases will cost the US $6 trillion each year in direct and indirect costs. Nugent (op. cit.) found that chronic diseases were responsible for 50 percent of the disease cost burden in developing countries and predicted that these diseases will cost those countries $84 billion by 2015 if nothing is done to slow their growth.

Different value, different valuers, different selection pressures

In short, our modern lifestyles and the diseases they lead to may be sufficient cause for the great value shift. But, woven together with demographics, inflation and rising expectations, they form an inexorable force shaping our society as well as the life sciences industry that is so closely connected to it. Of course, to point to these four prominent factors is to not to dismiss the others. Other factors and interactions in the social environment also emerged in my research. Patient empowerment, the industry's poor public reputation and state indebtedness, especially in the wake of the financial crisis, were among those factors that seem to play a subsidiary part to the four main drivers of the value shift discussed here. Whatever the factors and their relative contribution, there is no doubt that the great value shift is a fundamentally important emerging property of the system that will shape the industry's fitness landscape.

It is important to remember that the value shift is not simply the same customers being more concerned about price. It is also a shift in which customers determine what is valuable. We can see evidence of both aspects emerging every day in the industry press. The spread of bodies to assess health economic value, the so-called health technology assessment bodies, is an obvious indicator, as are the those clinically effective products that they refuse market access on the grounds of lacking cost benefits. The shift to generics and the increasing use of professional purchasers for medical devices are also examples of the increasing importance of health-economic outcome. Equally important is the shift in who is determining what good value is. We see this in computerised prescribing protocols and the shift in decision making power from physicians to purchasers. Less obvious but growing in importance is the role of the patient, or their proxy, in the choice of drugs and devices. We see this in increasing co-payments, cross-border on-line purchasing and, in some cases, patient specification of some medical appliances for ease of use or cosmetic reasons.

Hence the value shift has many drivers and is exemplified in many ways. But, for all its many drivers and facets, the core implication of this emerging property is relatively straightforward; it resolves into a fundamental far-reaching change in the selection pressure on the industry's business models. To be specific, the value shift applies a selection pressure in favour of business models that can understand what multidimensional, multi-customer, customer-perceived value is and create that context-specific value through its combination of product, services and pricing. At the same time, the value shift creates a selection pressure against business models that continue to understand value only in terms of clinical outcomes as defined by healthcare professionals and value creation only in terms of products. This is summarised in Figure 11.3.

On first read, this may not seem a great shift from the recent past. For years, firms have claimed value and differentiation for their brands, based on small clinical difference, levels of service and a vague implication of quality beyond that specified by regulatory standards. However, in the past, many premium products and services have been 'me too' or 'me slightly better' products that, contrary to their positioning by marketers, did not create real customer value. In many mature sectors of the industry, competition was between very similar products whose differentiation was only visible, if at all, under the microscope of detailing and, arguably, skewed trial data.

That this 'me too' model of product development survived, and even thrived in many parts of the industry, is an indication of different selection pressures in the past. The

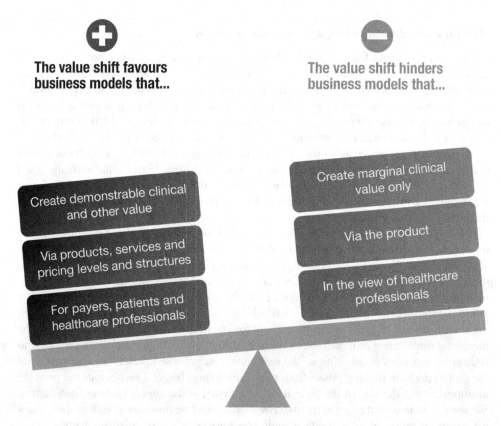

Figure 11.3 Selection pressure implications of the value shift

former market environment, in which healthcare professionals made decisions under a blizzard of marketing activity and favoured 'me too' products supported by large marketing and sales resources. In the present and emerging future market, the failure of many products to gain HTA approval, the relatively reduced role of healthcare professionals in product choice and the growth of generic or low cost versions of drugs and devices are all evidence that the environment has changed. This shift, which is in fact a reversion by healthcare markets towards the behaviour of most other markets, is a fundamental force shaping the industry landscape.

The value shift, therefore, is a major change in the selection pressures acting on the industry's business models. From the perspective of the research-based companies in the industry, it is arguably the most important change to which they must adapt. But it is not the only change in the selection pressures facing the life sciences industry. If we are to understand the evolution of the life sciences industry fully, we need to identify any other emerging properties of our social and technological environments and the selection pressures they imply.

The global shift

Box 11.2   The global shift

An emergent property of the healthcare system in which the demand for treatments, interventions and associated products and services is changing from one which is geographically focused on developed economies and in which demand heterogeneity is limited and based mostly on differing clinical requirements, to one in which demand has a global geographic spread and is very heterogeneous along multiple dimensions of clinical requirements, payer preferences and patient needs, both clinical and otherwise.

If the defining characteristic of a market is who defines value and how they do so, as discussed in the section concerning the value shift, then it is also important where that value is created, defined and accessed. All value, perhaps especially health value, is both created and delivered in a physical location and also in a distinctive local legal and cultural context. Since this context shapes both value creation and value definition, it is an important shaper of the fitness landscape.

At the beginning of my working lifetime, many companies in the life sciences sector could justifiably argue that their market was geographically restricted to the US, Western Europe and Japan. Any other territories could be, and were, grouped as 'rest of world' and were considered trivial as both commercial opportunities and, for the most part, as sources of competitors. Few of us can have failed to notice rapid change from this situation in most product and many service markets; from Lenovo laptops and Samsung phones to Tata steel and Emirates airlines, the globalisation of markets seems as relentless as it is unstoppable. Importantly, the corollary to these global brands is the rise of transnational segments in consumer goods, air travel, automobiles, entertainment and many other sectors. It was the inevitability of globalisation that led the British politician Clare Short to say 'People have accused me of being in favour of globalisation. This is equivalent to accusing me of being in favour of the sun rising in the morning.' That Ms Short is a left-wing politician makes her observation all the more telling.

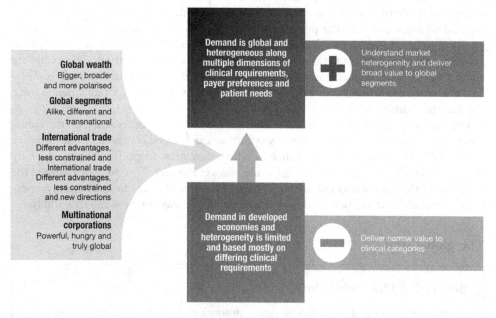

Figure 11.4 The global shift

Exactly such a shift in the geographical location of customers and competitors is occurring in the life sciences industry, albeit with a high degree of variation between the industry's sub-categories. Like the value shift, the global shift (see Box 11.2 and Figure 11.4) is an emergent property of the market characterised by two factors. There is both a spread of demand and supply outwards from the west to emerging markets and also the rise of segments that not only cross borders but, increasingly, lack correlation to national or regional boundaries. The first of these factors is more visible and well recognised but the second may prove to be more important.

Consistent with its emergent nature, the global shift cannot be said to be caused directly by a number of specific factors. In the manner of complex adaptive systems, the global shift is a phenomenon resulting from the combined effect of many separate but related factors. In the following paragraphs, I describe what emerged from the research as the four most important factors that are driving the global shift. Again, however, the reader should remember that the list is a simplification to aid thinking and not a comprehensive catalogue of all the factors involved.

Global wealth: bigger, broader and more polarised

Globalisation is both a cause and an effect of changes in the world's productivity and wealth. It is the habit of economists to discuss and dissect the data endlessly, yet there are three high-level trends upon which they agree in principle, if not in detail. The first of these is the long term trend towards increasing global wealth. The Organisation for Economic Co-operation and Development (OECD) estimated that the long term future growth trend in global product per capita is about 3 percent (44). This broad trend masks sub-trends of industrialisation and post-industrial economic development but the point remains that the world economy has grown significantly faster than even its population.

The second point of economists' consensus is that the global distribution of wealth between nations is shifting from the north and west to the south and east. In a fascinating paper, Danny Quah of the London School of Economics describes how the world's centre of economic gravity has shifted in the past thirty years from a point west of London to about 1800 km deep inside the Earth as economic power has shifted away from the developed economies of North America and Western Europe (45). This global shift in wealth has been accompanied by a significant decrease in the number of people living in absolute poverty (46) and the rise of middle classes in middle income countries (47).

Finally, most economists concur that, at least in capitalist systems, increasing wealth is correlated to increased inequalities in wealth between rich and poor. This last issue is perhaps the most contentious of the three points. As this book is being written, the bestselling book on the Amazon chart is *Capital in the 21st-Century* by Thomas Piketty (47) which, notwithstanding the predictable quibbles over its data, methodology and prescriptions, makes clear the way that economic growth is correlated to increasing inequality. To quote Piketty:

> *When the rate of return on capital exceeds the rate of growth of output and income, as it did in the nineteenth century and seems quite likely to do again in the twenty-first, capitalism automatically generates arbitrary and unsustainable inequalities that radically undermine the meritocratic values on which democratic societies are based.*

Whatever the political and policy implications of these three great trends, it seems clear that the world's wealth is bigger than it was, more evenly spread across the world and more unevenly spread between the rich and the poor. Further, it seems likely that these trends will continue to a greater or lesser degree. This globalisation of the economy is one of the factors that, combined in a complex manner with other factors, leads to the emerging property of the global shift in the life sciences market.

Global segments: alike, different and transnational

Market segments are groups of customers within a market who, whilst sharing the same basic need, differ in the specifics of their needs. Importantly, customers within a market segment have the same specific needs and behave similarly to other customers in the same segment. Their needs and behaviour differ from those customers in other market segments. Since the early years of globalisation, academics have observed that, particularly in consumer markets, market segments have transcended national boundaries. An examination of, for example, the premium segments in markets such as automobiles, watches, alcoholic drinks or fashion reveals that customers in these segments have more in common with customers in the same segment in other countries than they do with customers from another segment in the same country. In many markets, transnational segments are taken as a given and imply segment-specific, global marketing strategies (48).

Traditionally, the life sciences market has followed this pattern in only a limited way, distorted by its unusual decision making processes, narrow value propositions and the importance of governments as payers. As discussed earlier in the section covering the great value shift, the needs of healthcare systems historically were largely defined by healthcare professionals and in terms of clinical needs. This resulted in a market where global segmentation was very simple and strongly aligned to national wealth. It is only a slight simplification to say that all customers in rich countries were considered to be one, up-market segment and all customers in poor countries were placed in another, down-market and neglected segment. In medical marketing, segments have generally been defined in terms of products or simple customer categories and not in the needs-based manner of consumer companies (49).

The convergence of the shifts in value definition and the three trends in global wealth is leading to a shift in the segmentation patterns of the life sciences market in two ways. First, markets are segmenting according to both clinical and non-clinical needs, such as market access conditions (50). Second, those segments are now much less well correlated to national boundaries. Premium and mid-market market segments now exist for pharmaceuticals and medical technology in emerging markets previously considered only to be generic or low cost markets. To quote from a McKinsey report:

> Global pharma companies are missing a chance to serve Brazil's increasingly prosperous and growing middle class. Although wealthier segments spend more on drugs per capita, the scale of the underserved middle-class market is almost twice as big.

(51)

This rise of relatively high priced segments in traditionally low priced markets is only one side of this change. The other is the rise of low cost segments in traditionally high priced markets. This is most commonly seen in generic products in both off-patent pharmaceuticals and relatively low tech consumable medical devices, but it is another example of the way that segments no longer align with national boundaries.

This twin change in the segmentation of life sciences markets – from clinically-defined, geographically bounded segments to segments defined by a wide range of needs that transcend borders – is another of the factors that, combined with others in the complex adaptive system of healthcare, is leading to the emerging property of the global shift.

International trade: different advantages, less constrained and new directions

Macroeconomic trends may create the conditions for the global shift; they also enable firms to address it. For the demand side of the market to be addressed by the supply side, it requires international trade by companies to be possible and profitable. The factors that make it so are part of the complex adaptive system into which the life sciences industry is embedded.

At the root of international trade lie the differential advantages of nations, the idea that some countries are better at some things than others. Academics discuss the origins and nature of such national advantages. For example, Michael Porter's seminal *The Competitive Advantage of Nations*, which argues that sustained national advantages depend on the capacity of a country's industry to innovate and upgrade (52). Whilst the details of this concept may be up for debate, there seems little doubt that, for the present at least, US companies have some differential advantage in knowledge intensive areas whilst India, for example, has similar differential advantage in labour intensive areas. It is this gradient of capability that creates the potential for international trade in life sciences as well as other sectors. Importantly, most views of differential advantage see it not as inherited or embedded in a country's natural resources but as dynamic and changing and the result of many factors in both the private and state parts of the economy. The US's technological leadership in many aspects of biotechnology is attributed to a cluster of factors ranging from the financial infrastructure and government funding to intellectual property law and industry/university relations (53). Increasingly, however industrial policies have attempted to create or sustain national advantages. For example, India's policies on intellectual property rights is an attempt to create a national advantage (54), and such policies have led to a more variegated world in terms of differential advantages in the life sciences sector. At the same time, there is a broad trend to reduce trade barriers, especially non-tariff barriers such as those implied by regulatory frameworks through multilateral treaties such as the Trans-Pacific Partnership, The Transatlantic Trade and Investment Partnership and the Comprehensive Economic and Trade Agreement (55).

The net result of the changes in national advantages and barriers to international trade has not only been an increase the proportion of goods and services that are traded across, rather than within, borders but also a shift in the pattern of international trade. Now, more than half of developing market trade is with other emerging economies rather than with the rich world (56). The life sciences industry is part of this general if uneven trend although, by some measures, our industry is a laggard in its degree of internationalisation when compared to sectors such as IT and automobiles (57).

Overall, the picture that emerges is of a steady increase and diversification of international trade, driven by differential advantage and enabled by a reduction in barriers, of which the life science sector is an important part. That growth and spread, along with the global macroeconomic trends and global segments, contribute to the emerging global shift in the sector.

Multinational corporations: powerful, hungry and truly global

The final component of the global shift is both reinforced by and reinforcing of economic trends, global segmentation and the spread of global trading. This component is the rise of the multinational corporation (MNC). MNCs differ from companies that are merely international in that, whereas the latter may merely sell their wares in many countries, MNCs by definition typically carry out research and development, manufacturing and distribution in many countries outside their 'home' market.

MNCs are playing an increasingly important role in the global economy generally, acting as conduits for capital, knowledge and capabilities. In the life sciences sector, MNCs are not a new phenomenon. Large US and European companies such as Johnson & Johnson, Medtronic, GSK and Novartis have long used this operating model. However, the pattern of MNC operation does appear to be changing in breadth, scale and direction. The breadth of direction can be seen in the expansion of, for example, product development into emerging markets. Medtronic's development work in both China and India are examples of this, as is the increasing spread of pharmaceutical trials into emerging markets. The scale of MNC operation is also significantly larger than in the past. Investment into emerging markets, whether by direct operations, acquisition or partnerships, has become central to the growth plans of all life science companies of any significant size. Nor is this trend only represented by the spread of western companies to the east. Professor Ka Zeng at the University of Arkansas points to the globalisation of China's life sciences sector as a future disruptive force in the sector (58). The forces behind the increased ambition of MNCs are the need to grow faster than is possible by relying on mature, slow growth western markets and the desire to spread risk exposure across markets at different stages of development. Growing in this way, however, life science MNCs also become more powerful in relation to individual customers, regulators and governments.

Hence the final major component factor contributing to the global shift is the growth in importance of the multinational company. Their capabilities, resources and goals both depend upon and contribute to the emerging global shift in the sector.

A bigger, more diverse market of global segments

As with the value shift, the global shift resolves into a fundamental, pervasive change in the selection pressure on the industry's business models. The global shift applies a selection pressure in favour of business models that can understand the heterogeneity of their market, which use that understanding to select which parts of the market to focus upon and can deliver value to targeted customers on a global basis. At the same time, the global shift creates a selection pressure against business models that continue to view market heterogeneity only in simple, clinical terms, those unable to focus their resources appropriately and those which cannot deliver customer-specific value globally. This is summarised in Figure 11.5.

Again, it would be easy to misinterpret the global shift as a limited, incremental development of the international markets we have known for decades but that would be a mistake. In the past, markets outside the developed west were relatively trivial. Differences

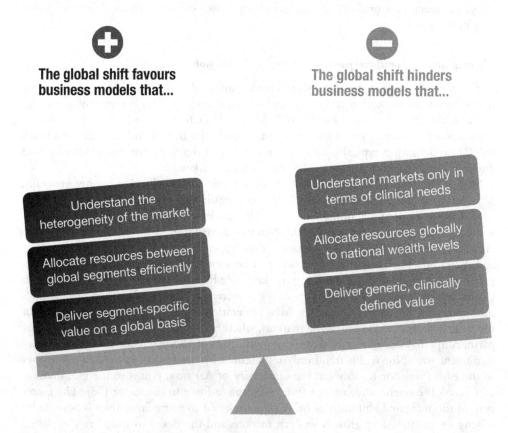

The global shift favours business models that...

The global shift hinders business models that...

Understand the heterogeneity of the market

Allocate resources between global segments efficiently

Deliver segment-specific value on a global basis

Understand markets only in terms of clinical needs

Allocate resources globally to national wealth levels

Deliver generic, clinically defined value

Figure 11.5 Selection pressure implications of the global shift

between the developed markets, beyond important operational details, were relatively small and market heterogeneity could be understood reasonably well in clinical terms such as disease stage or procedure type. Even when non-clinical differences between markets were acknowledged, they could be characterised quite simply, for example as advanced markets vs. low cost markets. By and large, advanced markets and developing markets were similar to their peers and distinct from each other. As a result, a single value proposition could be addressed to the vast majority of the market's profit pool, with relatively superficial localisation. The remaining, low cost part of the market could be addressed, if at all, with a low cost variant that met similar clinical needs more cheaply. The world was a simpler place.

The global shift involves three important differences from that former situation. First, the market is geographically much more evenly spread. Second, differences between purchasing and usage contexts are no longer based only on clinical factors but also on payer preferences and patient drivers such as cost, ease of use and even fashion. Finally, market heterogeneity is transnational, with all segments present to some significant degree in all national markets. The rise of healthcare systems in huge markets like China and Indonesia, the fragmentation of payer systems in countries such as the US and the convergent needs of urbanised middle classes across the globe are all evidence of this.

The global shift is therefore another major change in the selection pressures acting on the industry's business models. It overlays and compounds the value shift. To understand how our industry's fitness landscape will change, it is important to grasp that it is not a simple internationalisation of markets but a global segmentation of the market. It is also important to appreciate that the value and global shifts are only two of the emerging, interacting properties of the healthcare system.

The holobiont shift

Box 11.3   The holobiont shift

An emergent property of the healthcare system is one in which the dominant form of economic entity is changing from organisations with predominant centres and well defined, stable boundaries and scope to polycentric networks with fluid, ill-defined boundaries and scope.

Both the value shift and the global shift are emerging properties of the life sciences complex adaptive system that have their most visible effects on the demand side of the market – the patients, payers and healthcare professionals that purchase and consume medicines, devices, services and so on. But to consider only the changes in the demand side of the market would be simplistic; the supply side of the system is also important, and changes in it also create new selection pressures for and against industry business models.

The single most important characteristic of the supply side of the market is the way that the life science industry organises itself. By this, I mean the way that all of the industry's economic activities – the invention, manufacture and marketing of products and services – are sub-divided between different organisational entities and how those entities connect with each other.

The study of the organisation of the supply side of the market has a long history, reaching right back to 1776 and Adam Smith's *Wealth of Nations* with its discussions of British pin factories. In essence, the question that industrial economists explore is one of organisational boundaries: how much economic activity to perform inside the firm and how much to source from other, external organisations? This is known colloquially as the 'make or buy' decision and the choice firms make between these options is, unsurprisingly, contingent upon many factors. Historically, integration (making most things, buying relatively little) was the dominant model, with Ford's River Rouge Complex held up as the historical archetype. Integrated organisations think that they can get the best combination of cost, risk, flexibility and control by directly managing most of their operations. By contrast, disintegrated organisations (those which buy most things and make relatively little) believe the opposite. Disintegration is common in industries like construction and in entertainment. Hollywood is the supreme example of economic activity being carried out by an interdependent network of specialised firms rather than a single large corporation. When you watch the opening credits of a movie, with their acknowledgement of four or five partner organisations, you are watching an example of a disintegrated, networked organisation that was assembled to make that movie and whose parts will afterwards reorganise into another network to make the next movie.

The make or buy choice is not as binary as it sounds. Between the extremes of integration and disintegration lie every possible shade of grey, every possible combination of make or buy. And there is no single best choice between make or buy: it depends on the business environment.

Historically, the life sciences sector has been relatively integrated, developing, making and marketing its own products and services. And, despite more recent trends of outsourcing and partnering, the typical large pharma or medtech company is still involved in inventing, making and selling its products. However, a shift in the way economic activity is organised is underway that is, like the value and global shifts, reshaping the life sciences industry in a fundamental way. The holobiont shift (see Box 11.3 and Figure 11.6) is an

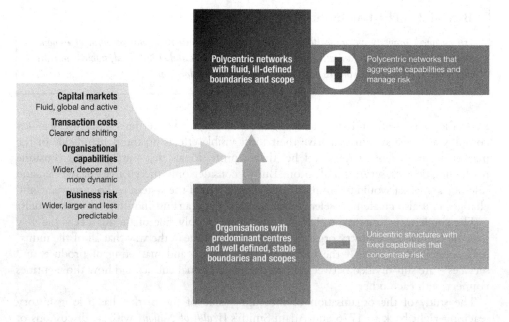

Figure 11.6 The holobiont shift

emergent property of this market, characterised by two factors: a disintegration of economic activity across a network of partners and an increasing fluidity and complexity in what entities carry out which activities. It takes its name from a close biological analogue. In 1991, Lynn Margullis coined the term to describe coral reefs, which are symbiotic collections of many different organisms (59). Since then, many organisms we used to think of as discrete entities have become better understood as holobionts. For example, humans and their extensive and essential collection of microbes in the gut and elsewhere are a form of holobiont. In my work, I have researched and written about holobionts emerging as a competitive entity in the life sciences sector (21).

Like all emergent properties that are characteristic of complex adaptive systems, the holobiont shift cannot be attributed directly to a small number of discrete factors. Instead, the holobiont shift is an organisational pattern born out of the interaction of many intertwined factors. In the following paragraphs, I describe what emerged from my research as the four most important factors that are driving the holobiont shift. As with the other shifts, the reader should remember that the list is a simplification to aid thinking and not a comprehensive catalogue of all the factors involved.

Capital markets: fluid, global and active

For the most part, life science companies are part of the same capital market as any other type of company. Certainly, there are companies in the sector that are not publicly traded and are, to some degree, shielded from the capital markets; but even these private firms compare their returns to their publicly traded counterparts. In that respect, life science companies are connected to the financial markets in the same way as any other company. The capital markets, however, have themselves evolved significantly in the last couple of decades. It is beyond the scope of this book to discuss the detail of that evolution, but its broad trends and their implications for life science companies are important to the emergence of the holobiont shift.

Partly driven by information and communications technology, partly by national and international legislation and partly driven by complex innovation in financial products, capital markets have become more fluid, more global and more active. More than ever before in history, capital now flows freely between firms and sectors, between asset classes and across. In simple terms, this increases the efficiency of capital markets and, from a company perspective, the pressure from investors and their analysts. This pressure increases the requirement for boards to improve and demonstrate their risk-adjusted rate of return. In short, the investment environment has become less cosy and more competitive (60, 61).

This increased investor pressure has different implications for different life science companies. But from a start-up raising funds for development, to an IPO candidate with a promising, developed technology to a large, mature company seeking to acquire or resist acquisition, the increased and increasing pressure to manage and meet investor expectations translates into a requirement for the most efficient and effective organisational form possible. In effect, this forces boards to constantly re-evaluate the boundaries of their organisation and the concomitant 'make or buy' decisions. A firm making the wrong decisions about where its boundaries lie might have higher costs or less-mitigated risks than is possible and investors will punish that.

Changes in the capital markets, especially the way in which greater capital fluidity places increased pressures on boards to demonstrate efficacy, is one of the factors driving the holobiont shift. But it is not the only factor pushing in that direction.

Transaction costs: clearer and shifting

Transaction costs are quite simply the costs associated with any economic transaction, whether that is measured in time, money or anything else. When I buy a book, for instance, it costs me not only its price but also the time spent looking for it. And these additional costs apply to any transaction, whether it is between a buyer and a seller or between two colleagues in adjacent offices. Just think of the time costs when, for example, R&D hands over a new product to manufacturing. The communication and coordinating costs of a complex company, much of it in time-hungry meetings, are huge.

The concept of transaction costs was introduced by Ronald Coase in the 1930s (62) but today is more associated with Oliver Williamson (63). It is an indication of the importance of the idea that both men have been awarded Nobel Prizes for their work. At the risk of oversimplifying, transaction cost economics considers the issue of 'make or buy' and organisational boundaries in terms of the transactions that have to take place in any economic system. These can be internal transaction costs, as when a company 'makes' a new product by funding its own R&D department, or external transaction costs, as when the company 'buys' a new product by licensing it from another company. Which of these is the most efficient approach varies with context. From a transaction cost point of view, the best structure for any economic activity (such as inventing, making and selling a new medical technology) is the one with the lowest combined transaction costs. And so whether that activity takes place in an integrated company, a disintegrated holobiont or something in-between is a context-dependent choice. The contextual factors that influence transaction costs and therefore organisational boundaries are many and varied. They range, on the external side, from the costs of finding an external partner and managing the relationship to, on the internal side, poor utilisation of fixed, sometimes inflexible assets and the inefficiencies of internal customer relationships.

For life science companies, many of the factors that influence transaction costs are changing. Information technology makes finding and communicating with partners much easier, even across continental distances. The ubiquity of the English language in business, the prevalence of international contract law, the standardisation of software systems and convergent approaches to research and regulation all make the barriers between organisations less costly to cross. Similarly, the growth of as specialist consultancies facilitates partnering. By contrast, larger, integrated organisations are made less attractive because of a variety of factors including labour protection laws, the global spread of companies and the rapidly evolving complexity of medical technology. Many decisions that would historically have been 'make', such as discovery phase research, active ingredient or key component manufacture or selling, are now seen as 'buy' decisions, either for reasons of efficacy or efficiency or both.

For life science companies, this means that they must constantly compare their organisational effectiveness not only to clearly defined competitors with integrated structures but also to fluid, ill-defined holobionts of organisational partners that, in aggregate, constitute competitors. It also means, of course, that their own options for organising themselves now extend from fully integrated to fully disintegrated, with innumerable options between these extreme.

So changes in the balance between internal and external transaction costs are another factor which, alloyed with increased capital flows and investor pressure, contributes to the emergent property of the holobiont shift. But even these two strong factors are not the only ones leading to a change in the way that economic activity is organised in the sector.

Organisational capabilities: wider, deeper and more dynamic

Whether organisations are integrated, 'making' most of what they do, or disintegrated, 'buying' everything they can, they exist for a reason. As Adam Smith noted, the reason that organisations replaced cottage workers is that they are mechanisms by which to assemble and coordinate capabilities. The fact that modern economic organisations such as the large company evolved at the same time as technologically complex processes and elaborate investment infrastructure is not a coincidence; the industrial revolution was a co-evolution of organisational form and the technological complexity of the tasks they had to perform. A cottage worker can make a cotton bandage and sell it to her neighbours but it takes a corporation to develop, make, market and then globally distribute an adhesive dressing, made from a composite polymer construction with high moisture vapour permeability and impregnated with antimicrobials.

Importantly for the evolution of the industry, the capabilities needed by life science companies are not static. The 1930s life science company, either in pharma or medical technology, evolved by developing capabilities in research and development that were unknown in the nineteenth century. Today's life science companies require highly developed capabilities in many areas that would have been unknown to their 1930s ancestors, with regulatory compliance being the most obvious. And today's companies are as different from their 1930s forebears as those companies were from the apothecaries. It follows, therefore, that if the necessary capabilities to compete in the future life sciences market change significantly, then the organisational form adopted by future life sciences companies, particularly their organisational boundaries, will change too.

Such a change in necessary competitive capabilities is observable in my research, and we can classify it according to three dimensions: widening, deepening, dynamism. As already mentioned, necessary capabilities are widening. The most obvious example is market access. Market access capability is a term that took on its current meaning (adapted from international trade negotiations) only in the mid-1990s. We might similarly argue that capabilities in digital media, corporate social responsibility and managing emerging markets are capabilities that have become necessary only in recent years and that will become more important in the future. The deepening of necessary capabilities is also noticeable across the industry's value chain. The technologies used in research and development, operations and supply chain and are all advancing, rendering it necessary for life sciences companies to become ever more expert and specialised. An obvious example is data analysis, which is not new in the life sciences industry but which is becoming so specialised and advanced as to be unrecognisable from what was called data analysis twenty years ago. The same could be said of capabilities in licensing and partnering agreements, pharmacovigilance and compliant manufacturing. In short, today's companies need to be much more capable than their forebears.

The relentless widening and deepening in the capabilities needed by life science companies adds another consideration, that of how to change capabilities. Academics often class capabilities as first order or operational, meaning the ability to do routine things, and second order or dynamic, meaning the ability to reconfigure resources to create new capabilities (64). As markets develop and more and better first order capabilities are necessary to operate in the market, the need for second order, dynamic capabilities increases too. These include the ability to create market insight, create differentiated strategy, acquire new knowledge and restructure the organisation: in short, the ability to change.

So if we consider that organisations such as life science companies exist to assemble and apply capabilities, their task is becoming ever harder as their requisite portfolio of capabilities widens, deepens and becomes more dynamic. The difficulty of understanding and directing such a diverse and complex set of competences obviously challenges the span of control and comprehension of leadership teams. It is for this reason that conglomerates such as GE, Johnson & Johnson and Procter & Gamble divisionalise into smaller units. It is also the reason that, increasingly, large pharma and medtech companies outsource many specialist functions to smaller, expert partners, from basic research to specialised manufacturing.

The growth of necessary capabilities is the third factor, alongside capital flows and transaction costs, contributing to the emergence of the holobiont shift as an emergent property of the life sciences market. These three factors combine with a fourth to shape the holobiont shift.

Business risk: wider, larger and less predictable

Central to capitalist economic organisations is the idea of capital at risk; the resources invested into a venture that may add to or subtract from that investment. Industries vary along a spectrum of capital intensity but, by most reckoning, life sciences companies, especially research-oriented firms, sit at the capital-intensive end of the range. This would, in any case, make life sciences companies more aware of the need to manage commercial risk but, exacerbating the capital intensity issue, life sciences companies typically operate in areas where scientific knowledge is imperfect, and likely downsides include the death or disability to large numbers of people. Thalidomide and Vioxx have become bywords for unforeseen risk in pharma and both medical device (65) and pharma (66) product recalls have increased in recent years. Such recalls are of products that have already reached the market. Pre-launch failures, especially at late stages of development, are common in the industry and are a very large source of commercial risk. Failures during development and after launch are increasing as regulators tighten control and vigilance procedures become more stringent. As a result, the business risk attributable to one (or more) of several possible technological factors becomes greater each year. Furthermore, these factors are amplified for companies operating in particularly innovative areas, such as biologics or implantable technology.

This increase in technologically-based business risk is compounded by a broadening of risk sources. To the technological risks already mentioned must be added commercial risks, including market access risk, regulatory risk and intellectual property risk. Recent years have seen many examples of drugs that have achieved regulatory approval (which traditionally involves the three hurdles of quality, efficacy and safety) but which have fallen at the fourth hurdle of cost effectiveness, when they are refused market access by health technology assessment bodies. Market access mechanisms and processes work differently in medical devices, diagnostics and other sub-sectors of the industry, but the challenges of reimbursement and coverage are directly analogous. Similarly, the revenue stream may be put at risk by some legal or political issue, as recent bribery and corruption cases involving pharma companies in emerging markets have shown. In short, investors considering the risk to their investment must now consider not only the failure to develop a safe and effective product but also the risk that even a good product may not be granted access to its target market, or may fall foul of an unpredictable legal dispute.

The combination of increased technological and commercial risk has an additive, synergistic effect. As legal, regulatory and health economic assessments evolve, they become more complex and harder to anticipate. This means that business risk in life sciences, always a major issue, has become not only larger and more diverse but also less amenable to forecasting and calculation. Taken together, this change in the scale and nature of business risk has pushed life sciences companies to place risk management high in their list of considerations when designing their organisational structure. Disintegrated structures, including licensing, joint ventures and distribution partnerships have a number of benefits. However, a primary driver of these interfirm relationships is often that they mitigate risk. In the case of licensing products late in their development, for example, the company buys the rights to a product at a stage when risk is lower and more predictable. In the case of a joint venture, the risk may not be mitigated but the capital at risk is shared and effectively reduced. In addition, as the preceding section on organisational capabilities implies, disintegrated arrangements may also reduce risk by effectively importing knowledge or capabilities into the organisation.

Increasing concern about risk, together with more powerful investor forces, changing transaction costs and the need for a wider, deeper capability set add together to create the holobiont shift.

Organisational forms for a more challenging and less forgiving world

As with the other emergent properties, to point to a number prominent factors contributing to the holobiont shift is to not to say there are no others. Although in analysing my research I tried to clarify and classify in order to reduce complexity, other factors and interactions in the social environment also emerged from the data. Activist shareholders, ambitious venture capitalists, economic protectionism and a developing culture of partnering in all parts of the value chain were among those factors that seem to play a subsidiary part to the four main drivers of the holobiont shift discussed here. Whatever the factors and their relative contribution, there is no doubt that the holobiont shift is a fundamental and important emerging property of the system that will shape the industry's fitness landscape.

As with the value and global shifts, the holobiont shift represents a change in the selection pressure on the industry's business models, one that is perhaps less obvious but no less important than the first two. The holobiont shift applies a selection pressure in favour of business models that can build and manage dynamic, symbiotic networks of different organisational entities and use that structure to create better returns, manage risk or some combination of the two across any part of the value chain. At the same time, the holobiont shift creates a selection pressure against business models that persist in unicentric structures that fail to optimise returns and risk across any part of the value chain. This is summarised in Figure 11.7.

It would be easy to misinterpret smaller changes in the way the industry operates, obviously visible today, as evidence that holobionts are already the dominant structure in the life science industry. All industries involve interfirm relationships, ranging from outsourcing through licensing to joint ventures and wholly owned subsidiaries. In recent years, pharmaceutical and medical technology industries have been especially active in this respect. However, these current relationship models differ markedly from organisational patterns selected for by the holobiont shift. The current model of organisation usually retains a well-defined centre in which a central, predominant company draws on the resources of one or more partners. In such a unicentric company, both risk and returns are heavily concentrated in the centre and so, accordingly, is decision making power. In current models, the power relationships typically make it clear who is the lead and who is the

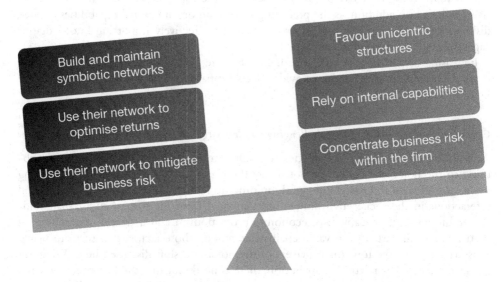

The holobiont shift favours business models that...

Build and maintain symbiotic networks

Use their network to optimise returns

Use their network to mitigate business risk

The holobiont shift hinders business models that...

Favour unicentric structures

Rely on internal capabilities

Concentrate business risk within the firm

Figure 11.7 Selection pressure implications of the holobiont shift

follower entity and the limits of the commercial arrangement are typically fixed around a given project area.

By contrast, in a truly holobiont arrangement, many partners engage with each other through multiple relationships, rendering the concept of 'leader' irrelevant. These multivalent relationships make it hard to define the boundaries of the holobiont's activity. Most importantly, risk, return and decision making power are spread and allocated to where they can best be managed. In short, holobionts take the idea of co-specialised partnering, in which each partner does what it does best, to its logical conclusion of a widely dispersed, virtual organisation in which many specialised entities perform the large number of different activities that make up the value chain. Holobionts are to simple partnering relationships as extended families are to childless couples; bigger, more complex, harder to understand and describe but, potentially, much more rewarding.

The holobiont shift is therefore another major change in the selection pressures acting on the industry's business models. It adds another factor, in addition to the value shift and global shift, to the social environment factors shaping the fitness landscape. However, our understanding of the emerging properties acting as selection pressures on the life science sector is only half complete if we consider only the social environment. We must also consider those pressures emerging from technological environment and that is what we will do next.

12 Selection pressures emerging from the technological environment

Just as the life sciences industry shapes and is shaped by its social environment, it interacts in a similarly complex manner with its technological environment. And the technological environment itself is a tangled web of interacting developments. It includes those technologies with both direct, immediate impact on the sector (for example, developments in biological and materials sciences) and those with indirect, implicit impact (information technology and supply chain technology are both examples of this). It is those interactions that I will examine in this section.

Arguably the relationship between the industry's business models and the technological environment is even more complex and difficult to understand than that with its social environment. This is because, whilst the whole industry operates in the same, healthcare

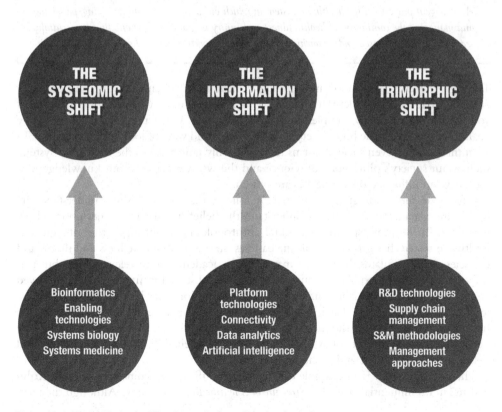

Figure 12.1 The shifts in the life sciences industry's technological environment

related parts of the social environment, the most important facets of the technologi-cal environment vary greatly between, for example, specialised pharma and consumable medical devices. For instance, whilst the value shift, the global shift and the holobiont shift impact similarly across the whole breadth of the sector, the same cannot be said of many technological developments. This is illustrated by 3D printing. Whilst it may be a significant factor in shaping the market for some medical devices, its impact on most parts of the pharmaceutical market is much less obvious. Similarly, the great advances in systems biology look set to change the way we develop and use drugs but their impact on, say, trauma reconstruction in orthopaedics is much more oblique.

Notwithstanding the heterogeneous pattern of interaction between the sector and its technological environment, we can still look for and identify emergent properties of that system. As with the emergent properties of the social environment, we can imply the shifts in the selection pressures acting on the industry's business models. Just as with the social environment, my research on the technological environment identified three major shifts that will favour some business models and discriminate against others. These shifts and the parts of the technological environment that are most important to their emergence are summarised in Figure 12.1 and discussed in the next three sections.

The systeomic shift

Box 12.1   The systeomic shift

An emergent property of the healthcare system in which our approach to understanding, perceiving and managing the continuum of health, illness and injury is changing from one that is essentially reactive, population-based and hierarchical to one that is proactive, personalised and participatory.

Through the eyes of a social anthropologist, healthcare systems are just one of many cultural artefacts of a society. It is a visible manifestation, part of the superstructure if you will, of our massively complex human social system. Underpinning and shaping any healthcare system are the host society's norms, beliefs and ways of looking at the world. To an anthropologist, even societal norms that seem only tangential to the healthcare system, such as our society's philosophy of science and the way we partition our knowledge into silos, have an influence on the healthcare system.

From that anthropological perspective, it follows that, if we wish to understand the healthcare system, we need first to understand the belief systems and values upon which it is built. To be more specific, a cultural anthropologist might argue that our current healthcare system has grown out of our basic assumptions about wellness and illness and the science that explains them. This may seem an academic and irrelevant aside but it is important because it explains an emergent property observed in my research. I observed an emerging but recognisable shift in the basic assumptions that have shaped we way we look at healthcare, a shift that is having and will have fundamental implications for the healthcare system and for the life sciences industry that is part of it. Greatly inspired by Leroy Hood of the Institute of Systems Biology (67), I labelled this the 'systeomic shift' and defined it as in Box 12.1 and as shown in Figure 12.2.

The systeomic shift is an example of a paradigm shift, a term coined by Thomas Kuhn in 1962 in his influential book *The Structure of Scientific Revolutions* (68). Although the term

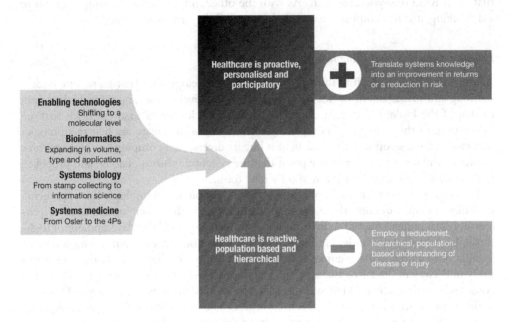

Figure 12.2 The systeomic shift

has been somewhat debased by its overuse in recent years, Kuhn's concept of the paradigm shift retains great value as a description of what is currently occurring in both the science and technology of medicine. Because Kuhn's work concerned the scientific community and the nature of scientific revolutions, it applies perfectly to the implications of the technological environment for medicine and healthcare. In Kuhn's terms, a paradigm shift is a change in the set of basic assumptions held by a community, which leads to a fundamental change in the way that community behaves. Oft-quoted examples include those from Ptolemaic (earth-centred) to Copernican (sun-centred) cosmology and from miasmas to germ theory in the explanation of infectious diseases. So Kuhn's term refers to something of a very fundamental nature that has important and wide ranging effects. Those readers used to hearing the term 'paradigm shift' applied, as Larry Trask has said, 'with wearisome frequency to almost any change in policy or fashion' (69), should appreciate that when I talk about a paradigm shift in medicine, I am using it in Kuhn's original, fundamental and far-reaching sense.

In the life sciences industry and the technological environment with which it is co-evolving, we are observing the early but unmistakable signs of a true paradigm shift in the basic assumptions that shape our approach and attitudes to wellness and illness. The systeomic shift is an emergent property of this market, relating not simply to how we diagnose, treat and monitor illness and injury but also to how we understand and manage wellness and illness as part of the same continuum.

Like the emergent properties in the social environment described earlier, the systeomic shift cannot be attributed directly and simply to a small number of discrete, independent factors. It is a pattern arising from a large number of complex interactions. In the following pages, I describe what emerged from my research as the four most important of factors that are driving the systeomic shift. As with the other shifts, this list is a simplification to aid thinking; it is not comprehensive catalogue of all the factors involved.

Enabling technologies: shifting to a molecular level

At the root of the systeomic shift lie technological developments that allow our understanding and management of disease to shift from the level of the organism or the organ to that of the biological system, and the cell. It is developments in these fields that are interacting, in the manner of complex adaptive systems, to create applied technologies that enable the systeomic shift. This field is hugely diverse and complex but perhaps three examples will serve to illustrate the point that the systeomic shift is enabled and propelled not simply by new knowledge but also by new tools.

The first and most obvious example is the explosion in technology for sequencing genomes and subsequently the emerging technology for the other 'omics, such as proteomics. The sequencing of the first human genome has spurred the development of high-throughput, parallel methods. Those methods allow fast and low cost sequencing and make feasible both individual screening and whole population studies such as the innovative study underway in the Faroe Islands (70). The improvement in sequencing capabilities and costs has been dramatic (71) but was more eloquently described by Dame Joyce Thornton at the 2014 Bernal Lecture at Birkbeck College, London. The cost of a genome sequence in 2003, she told the audience, was equivalent to the price of a large London house; but by 2013 the same result, achieved much faster, cost the same as an Arsenal Football Club season ticket. Taking their lead from genomics, the complementary technologies to study the role and function of other important biological molecules are also advancing rapidly. These are anticipated, in the case of proteomics for example, to 'soon be studied at a similar level of dynamic resolution as has been the norm for transcriptomes' (72).

A second example is the rapidly developing field of biomarkers, the various definitions of which overlap around measurable, molecular level indicators of biological processes (73). Relatively simple biomarkers have been used for some time, for example in the case of lipid levels as a predictor of cardiovascular disease or prostate specific antigens as a diagnostic aid for prostate cancer. But the breadth of applications of biomarkers for prediction, screening and other uses is expanding very rapidly. Troponin as a test for myocardial damage (74), proteases in wound healing (75) and cytokines in orthopaedics (76) are all current examples from the research literature. Importantly, biomarkers play several roles: in understanding disease mechanisms, in developing therapies and in managing treatment at an individual level. Like genomics and the other 'omics, they are a molecular level enabling technology that allows medicine to move to proactive, personalised and preventive approach.

A third example of enabling tools lies in the broad area of gene manipulation and synthetic biology. Genetic modulation techniques, such as stable transfection, are becoming developing quickly. CRISPR-Cas systems are beginning to be described as mainstream for genome editing (77). Routine gene synthesis, which may eventually lead to routine genome synthesis, is now enabled through the rapid decrease in cost and increased availability of synthetic oligonucleotides. Synthetic biology, with its potential for 'de novo' engineering of genetic pathways, offers apparently limitless applications (78). Already, it has been used to screen tuberculosis drugs, in vaccine production and in drug synthesis (79). In medical devices, a good example of likely future trends in this area is the work at Freiburg University using synthetic biology tools to develop smart biomaterials that respond to external stimuli by the release of therapeutic substances (80).

These three examples are just a small sample of the many ways that molecular level technologies are enabling the shift away from traditional, reductionist medicine and towards a systeomic approach to wellness and disease. Their impact on the life sciences industry, however, is complex and typically manifested via the other drivers of the systeomic shift, which I discuss in the following paragraphs.

Bioinformatics: expanding in volume, type and application

Bioinformatics, the discipline of gathering and using biological data, is one of the most striking examples of a phenomenon emerging from the complex adaptive system that is the life sciences sector. Its remarkable expansion is a good example of what happens when several different technological developments interact. Bioinformatics is the direct result of our ability to sequence genomes and analyse biological processes combined with the growth of computing power and the development of data analysis methods. Without any one of these three, bioinformatics would be a much less significant field than it is now becoming.

As previously mentioned, Dame Janet Thornton, director of EMBL-EBI, gave an erudite and entertaining account of the history, future and implications of the bioinformatics revolution at her Bernal Lecture at Birkbeck College, London in March 2014 (81). Her lecture, which drew on many sources, pointed to the way that bioinformatics would inform first prevention, by leading to a better understanding of the genetic and molecular basis of disease, second personalisation, by identification of genotypic variation, and finally therapy, by radically improving our understanding of drug targeting. These and other benefits of bioinformatics are clearly drivers of the systeomic shift; they come not only from the massive expansion in the volume of data but also in the scope of the information now used in bioinformatics: proteomics, metabolomics, lipidomics and transcriptomics, to list a few. Interestingly, Dame Janet also pointed out that, in order to realise the benefits of bioinformatics, health systems would need to address issues ranging from data storage capacity and data security to skill shortages in making sense of bioinformatic data. Although she didn't use the term, those issues are a good example of the co-evolutionary tensions that occur when enabling technologies advance faster than their potential users.

It is beyond the scope of this book to discuss the bioinformatic discipline in any detail. The important point to grasp is that the explosion in bioinformatic technology is one of the most important factors contributing to the systeomic shift. And, just as bioinformatics has is enabled by the technologies mentioned in the previous section, it is itself an enabler of systems biology, which we discuss next.

Systems biology: from stamp collecting to information science

Ernest Rutherford, often called the father of nuclear physics, is quoted as saying that all science is either physics or stamp collecting. This disparaging remark may have had some basis when it was made in the early twentieth century; biology as a science then mimicked physics' reductionism but lacked its quantitative rigour. However, such a criticism has long since become less valid as biological sciences have become quantitative. What is more, in the last decade or so, biology has moved even further along this trajectory with the emergence of systems biology.

It is hard to locate a single origin for systems biology. Although it has become a distinct discipline only in the twenty-first century, it has its origins in the mid-twentieth century in the work of Ludwig von Bertalanffy's General Systems Theory and of Hodgkin and

Huxley's work on quantifying cellular function. These and other developments led eventually to what is often seen as the birth of systems biology in 1966, when Mihajlo Mesarovic organised the first symposium on the topic. However, for the following three decades, the approach seemed to promise much but deliver little, either academically or practically. Only very recently has the availability of large amounts of biological data and cheap processing power allowed systems biology to come of age and begin to change the way we understand health and illness as 'perturbations' of biological systems. Like many young disciplines, systems biology has not yet developed a single, agreed definition. However, the various overlapping attempts at definition concur around its principal characteristic of holism (as opposed to reductionism) and that it is essentially an informational science (82) that attempts to 'address the missing links between molecules and physiology' (83).

The applications of systems biology are widespread and growing at a very fast pace. Recent work has discussed everything from understanding neurological disease (84) to nutrition (85) and from bioprocess development (86) to epidemiology (87). Among the rapidly growing literature in this area, systems biology seems to offer ways to discover biomarkers (88) and how wounds heal (89). Indeed, the nature of systems biology, as an approach rather than a specific, applied technique, suggests that it will change the way we look at most biological questions.

The systems biology approach is also informed by the discipline of nanotechnology (90). Both areas are concerned with molecular level processes and are fundamental approaches with wide application. Nanotechnology seems to offer most immediate applications in drug delivery, where it can enable development and commercialisation of entirely new classes of macromolecules that need precise intracellular delivery for their bioactivity (91). However, nanotechnology also has potential to change drug discovery, biomaterials and many other areas of medicine. Like systems biology before it, nanotechnology is slowly fumbling towards maturity but seems certain to have practical implications that are both fundamental and far reaching.

As with enabling technologies and bioinformatics, systems biology and nanotechnology are perhaps best understood not through their short term, direct application. It is through their indirect implications and interaction with each other that they will have the most impact on the life sciences sector. Thought of this way, enabling technologies, bioinformatics, systems biology and nanotechnology are foundation stones for a systems medicine approach, as I will discuss next.

Systems medicine: from Osler to the 4Ps

The current, dominant paradigm in medicine is sometimes referred to as Oslerian, after the nineteenth century Canadian physician William Osler (and one of the founders of Johns Hopkins Hospital) who is sometimes called 'the father of modern medicine' (92). This appellation is a simplification of course; not only does medical practice have many, intertwined origins but the Oslerian tradition has many meanings (93). Notwithstanding its simplification, it is reasonable shorthand for the way of understanding disease and, by extension, health and wellness, that has dominated since Osler's time. Loscalzo and Barabasi describe this traditional approach and criticise its limitations thus:

> *The Oslerian formalism for human disease links clinical presentation with pathological findings. As a result, disease is defined on the basis of the principal organ system in which symptoms and signs are manifest, and in which gross anatomic pathology and histopathology are correlated.*

In using this sorely outdated approach to defining human disease, we construct nosological silos that focus exclusively on end-stage pathological processes in a single organ largely driven by late-appearing, generic end-stage mechanisms rather than true disease specific susceptibility determinants viewed in their holistic, systems-based complexity.

(94)

The point is therefore well made that, whilst respecting the great, historical contributions made by a traditional view of medicine, what we today call 'modern medicine' is still rooted in an era when gross pathology and histology were the best tools available. Unsurprisingly, the implications of enabling technologies, the bioinformatics revolution and systems biology, are leading to the replacement of the Oslerian tradition with what has been labelled P4 medicine. This term refers to the convergence of technologies that would allow medicine to become personalised, predictive, preventive and participatory, in contrast to traditional approaches that were population based, reactive and hierarchical (67).

In truth, the shift from the traditional, Oslerian approach to P4 medicine is only at its earliest stages, and it is hard to find many examples of its application. What is emerging promises to reshape medical understanding, prevention and treatment. In the understanding of disease and wellness, work on so-called 'disease modules', a group of network components that contribute to the phenotype, is developing into a study of the interdependence of those modules and thus the creation of a 'disease-ome' that helps to explain the interconnectivity of diseases (94).

Similarly, the systems approach is allowing some researchers to develop genome-scale metabolic models that offer ways of understanding complex disease areas such as cancer, cardiovascular or neurodegeneration (95). At a preventative level, systems medicine offers better ways to anticipate and avoid cardiovascular disease (96), diabetes (97) and even alcoholism (98). All of these and other developments point to the eventual reshaping of healthcare by systems medicine, a harbinger of which can be seen at Ohio State University Medical Center and its cooperation with the Institute of Systems Biology. Here, 55,000 employees are involved in a large-scale experiment in the value of P4 medicine. To quote Clay B Marsh, Director of the Center for Personalized Medicine:

Ohio State has an integrated, closed system. We are the employer, payer, and provider of healthcare to our employee base. This gives us an opportunity to test whether different types of approaches to healthcare and wellness-based care can lower costs and improve outcomes.

(99)

That systems medicine is not rapidly overtaking the Oslerian tradition can partly be attributed to its technological complexity but also perhaps to co-evolutionary dynamics. The translation of systems biology into systems medicine requires the adaptation of professional education and healthcare processes and such adaptation acts as a barrier to the uptake of P4 medicine. But, whilst such barriers may slow its impact, they seem unlikely to stop it.

In common with the other emerging properties, the various factors that lead to the systeomic shift combine to create a clear and important change in the selection pressures facing the life sciences industry. Since it represents a fundamental change in our knowledge base, the systeomic shift applies a selection pressure in favour of business models that can translate that knowledge into an improvement in returns or a reduction in risk at any point in their value chain. The counterpoint to this is that the systeomic shift creates a selection pressure against business models that remain based on a reductionist, hierarchical,

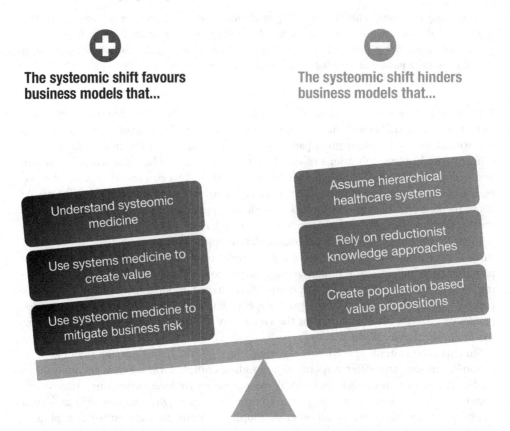

Figure 12.3 Selection pressure implications of the systeomic shift

population-based understanding of disease or injury and the ways we manage them. This is summarised in Figure 12.3.

A once in a century opportunity

As with the other shifts, it would be easy to see the systeomic shift as a continuation of trends that are already adapted to by the industry, but again this would be a misreading of the situation. Whilst it is true that the industry has continuously recognised, contributed to and adapted to change in medical practice for most of the past century, what we are seeing now seems to be quite different both qualitatively and quantitatively. The rate of change in fundamental knowledge is of a different order of magnitude even from the advances of the second half of the twentieth century. In addition, those earlier advances depended to a large degree on a core methodology that was reductionist and population based, epitomised by the 'gold standard' of the double-blind, randomised clinical trial. By comparison, today we see a convergence towards individual and holistic approaches characterised by the combination of data analysis and stratified, if not individualised, therapies.

The systeomic shift is a major change in the selection pressures acting on the industry's business models. It represents an opportunity to create value in prevention, diagnosis, treatment and therapy and favours business models that can identify and exploit those opportunities. However, its impact can be understood only in the context of the other selection pressures emerging from the technological environment, the information shift and the trimorphic shift, which we will discuss in the next two sections.

The information shift

Box 12.2   The information shift

An emergent property of the healthcare system in which the collection, storage, use and communication of information is shifting from small-scale, fragmented, unidirectional and deductive to large-scale, integrated, pervasive and inductive.

For most of economic history, we have lived in societies in which the economic resources we value are mostly tangible – labour, materials and capital being the most obvious and important. By the second half of the twentieth century, economists began to consider that information was an important, perhaps the most important, economic resource. The seminal work of this period that epitomised this shift in thinking was Fritz Machlup's book, *The Production and Distribution of Knowledge in the United States*, published in 1962 and from which we gained the phrase 'information society' (100). Since then, various estimates have been made of how quickly we are moving to an information society, or knowledge economy as it is sometimes rephrased. Some estimates suggest a 25 percent per annum growth in the information we can store, so that the global stored information per person has grown from less than one CD worth in 1986 to sixty CDs' worth in 2007. Other estimates suggest that computers have grown our information processing capacity by 60 percent per annum over the last couple of decades (101). Such estimates are both difficult and necessarily inexact. What seems clear is that the world we live in is increasingly driven less by our ability to use labour to shape materials and more by our ability to gather data and transform it into information and knowledge.

In my research for this book, the impact of this growth in information gathering, processing and usage arose repeatedly as a very important factor shaping the industry. Its indirect and direct effects were mentioned at least as often as the more obviously relevant technological developments in biological and material sciences. What became clear were not only large, quantitative changes in the volume of data usage and the speed of its processing but also qualitative changes in where the data came from and how it was translated into information, knowledge and insight. I have designated this manifestation of a wider global trend in the life sciences sector as the information shift, as defined in Box 12.2 and Figure 12.4.

Even more than the other shifts, it is tempting to see the information shift as the result of a single major factor, such as processing power or the growth of internet access. But this would be to forget the principles that underlie complex adaptive systems. Like the value, global, holobiont and systeomic shifts, the information shift cannot be attributed in a simple, direct manner to one or even a small number of discrete factors. Like the other emerging properties of this complex adaptive system, it is a pattern arising from a large number of complex interactions. Following the pattern of the earlier sections, I next describe what emerged from my research as the four most important factors driving

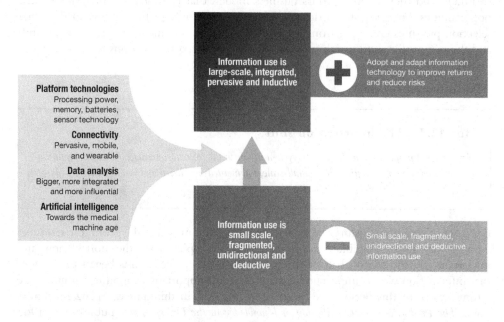

Figure 12.4 The information shift

the information shift. As before, I ask you to remember that the list is a simplification to aid thinking that should not be mistaken for a comprehensive catalogue of all the factors involved.

Platform technologies: foundations of the future

The foundations of the information shift lie in a set of disparate technologies that impact not only the life sciences but also many other sectors. As platform technologies, they do this not by direct, stand-alone application but by enabling other information and communications technologies. Any summary of the vast breadth and speed of these platform-technology developments can only be imperfect, but there are perhaps four key trends that are most important to the evolution of the life sciences sector.

Increasing processing power

In 1965, Gordon Moore's paper about cramming more components onto integrated circuits has become one of the sacred texts of the information age (102). In recent years, the familiar projections of continuous rapid improvements in processing power known as Moore's Law have begun to be challenged (103). It does seem, however, that in the medium term, processing power will continue to increase for some years, until silicon technology reaches natural limits imposed by the laws of physics. That is unlikely to result in a levelling out in processing speeds, however. Advances in chip design, such as parallelisation, will provide some additional scope for increased speed. Beyond that, more advanced ideas, such as carbon nanotube computers (104) and eventually quantum computing (105) offer potential for ever more powerful computers. Furthermore, speed is not the only important trend in processor design. Firms such as ARM, Qualcomm and Intel are competing in areas like power consumption to make great leaps in processing power for mobile devices.

Advances in memory technology

Memory ranks alongside processing speed as a key determinant of any computer's effectiveness. Both memory capacity and the speed with which data can be input and output are important factors in memory performance and, hence, the capability of any information technology. In particular, faster data access is important to allow real-time processing of data. Historically, most computers used spinning magnetic or optical discs. Increasingly, however, this is being replaced with other technologies such as random access memory (RAM), which speeds data access by up to 20,000 times, is better able to handle data of varying structures and has lower power consumption. Dominated by three large manufacturers, RAM technology is also falling in price (106). As with processing power, these developments make information technology both more powerful and more widely applicable in contexts ranging from large data centres to wearable devices.

Developments in battery technology

Many applications or potential applications of information technology rely on mobile power supplies that are reliable, lightweight and long lasting. Advances in mobile technology during the last decade or so have been enabled in large part by the development of better battery technology, in particular the lithium ion battery. Conversely, the relatively slower development of battery technology, compared to other platform technologies, is sometimes seen as a brake on the development of information technology. But developments in battery technology now appear to offer significant advances in parameters such as energy density and recharging cycles (107). These include improving lithium ion batteries with nanotechnology (108) but also new battery chemistry, such as lithium sulphur and lithium oxygen, or even successors to lithium, such as magnesium. If, as seems likely, the promise of these developments is realised then they will enable ever wider application of mobile and wearable medical technology.

Expansion of sensor technology

By definition, information technology involves the use of data and, ultimately, it is the nature and quality of this data that determines its usefulness. Since much data is provided by sensors of some kind, advances in sensor technology influence how information technology is applied in the life sciences. It is a field of rapid and varied developments, characterised by advances in the efficacy of sensors, their size and the range of phenomena they can now measure (109). From their current, limited applications for intermittent testing for simple molecules, such as blood sugar, technologies such protein microarrays offer the potential for continuous monitoring of a wide range of biomarkers using wearable 'biochips' (110).

Similarly, the combination of motion sensing technology with extant technologies for heart rate, blood oxygen and other indicators offer not only individually important data but, through wireless connectivity, potentially huge data sources. An early example of this is the joint project of the Michael J Fox Foundation, a Parkinson's disease charity, and Intel (111). This increase in data from wearable sources is, arguably, one of the most exciting areas of technological development in life sciences; it promises to allow continuous, easy gathering of a huge variety of data. This will have profound implications at two levels. For individuals, it will enable the proactive, personalised and participatory medicine discussed earlier. At a population level, it will provide the raw material for the big data approaches I will discuss later.

The development of the platform technologies that enable the information shift could be a book in itself but that is not my purpose here. It is sufficient to recognise that these technologies and other, less prominent, enabling technologies are part of the complex adaptive system that includes the life sciences industry. The interaction and adaptation to each other of these technologies enables the connectivity, artificial intelligence and data analysis I will discuss next and together they combine and lead to the emergence of the information shift.

Connectivity: pervasive, mobile, and wearable

The information shift is not just about crunching more data more quickly. Compared to the recent past, it involves different types of data, from many more sources, analysed and synthesised in different ways. Together, this allows more and better information and knowledge to be created and communicated. Central to this is how information technology has transformed. No longer mostly restricted to fixed devices and with limited connectivity, it is now mobile and permanently connected to an ocean of other data. This pervasiveness of information will have an enormous impact on what data can be gathered and how it can be used at all stages in the value chain, from research and development to manufacturing and operations to sales and marketing. There are three main factors contributing to the increasing connectivity of information technology:

Wireless and other telecommunications infrastructure

Self-evidently, connectivity requires a connection to the world's telecommunication network, whether by mobile phone signal, landline, Wi-Fi or some other technology. The number of people having access in this way has grown very rapidly. The World Bank estimates that between 2000 and 2012, the number of mobile phone subscriptions grew from 1 billion to 6 billion, 5 billion of which were in developing countries. The same report estimates that 75 percent of the world's population were then (in 2012) within reach of a mobile phone signal and that, as an indication of the future, in Latin America that figure was 98 percent (112). There is parallel growth in access to and speeds of Wi-Fi and fixed broadband (113). Just as significant is the growth in access to and use of mobile devices (114). Although growth in access rates varies between countries, the trend would suggest that, in the near future, almost everyone who can afford it will be able to connect to the rest of the world electronically. And every one of these people will have an interest or need for healthcare in some way.

The internet of things

The growth in the connection of human beings to each other via the internet is only half the story of the growth in connectivity; the less obvious but perhaps more significant factor is the growth in machine-to-machine connections, the internet of things. In 2014, market research estimates were that 1.9 billion devices, from car monitors to home appliances, were connected to the internet. More strikingly still, the same research estimated that by 2018 the internet of things would include 9 billion devices, roughly equal to the number of smartphones, tablets, PCs and wearable computers combined (115). Of course, not all of the internet of things is related to the life sciences sector, but growth in our sector reflects these wider trends (116). The early and most reported applications seem to be in integrating data that was already being collected and sharing it more effectively. For example, Microsoft's case study in patient information management at Henry Mayo Memorial Hospital, Valencia, California (117). But such cases are the low hanging fruit, as it were, enabling integration of data that is already available and obviously complementary. Perhaps more exciting is the prospect of data from disparate sources with no obvious relationships yielding value that we cannot yet imagine. But that next step will almost certainly involve advanced analytics and probably artificial intelligence, the two components of the information shift I will discuss in the next two paragraphs.

Wearable technology

Currently less advanced and ubiquitous than mobile phone technology and the internet of things is the development of wearable health technology. As with many technological developments, early steps down this path are gimmicky and restricted to small, technologically innovative segments. As I labour away on this book, my wrist-worn activity tracker is recording me as being idle. But Apple, Samsung and others are already developing more advanced devices that monitor not just movement but also pulse rate, blood oxygen and other vital signs; the range of what can be monitored will only increase. Google's prototypes of glucose-monitoring contact lenses, recently licensed to Novartis, are an example of this (118). 'Hard' technology such as wrist bands and contact lenses are the first manifestation of wearable technology, but a second wave of 'soft' sensors is under development. Research in this area is looking at incorporating monitoring technology into clothing via so-called fabric-circuit boards that are stretchable and can be machine washed and dried. Again, early applications look likely to be specialised, such as detecting bullet wounds for soldiers, but such technologies are likely to diffuse into wider use so that monitoring will become routine without wearing dedicated devices (119). Similar soft technology built into clothing can measure heart rate and brain activity and how hard muscles are working (120). The long term potential of wearable technology has been recognised by the European Union funded MyHeart project, which seeks to prevent cardiovascular disease by monitoring and early diagnosis. Perhaps even more than mobile phone technology and the internet of things, wearable technology points towards the pervasive connectivity that will help shape the future of our sector.

Building on the enabling technologies discussed earlier, the connectivity implied by wireless technology, the internet of things and wearable technology combine to completely reshape the quantity and type of data the life sciences industry can work with and the uses we can make of it. However, data are only raw materials. Translating it into tangible benefits and profitable products and services requires that the data be analysed and synthesised into information and knowledge. In an interesting example of co-evolution, the technologies and methodologies behind this are developing as quickly as those for gathering the data, as we will discuss next.

Data analysis: bigger, more integrated and more influential

In my research for this book, one of the common themes that emerged was that gathering data was perceived as less of a problem than managing it. The bigger challenge is to turn data into information, information into knowledge and to identify what knowledge, if any, is sufficiently rare and valuable to constitute an insight. This challenge is leading to two trends in data analysis that are important factors in the emergence of the information shift:

Integration of multiple, diverse data sources

I have already discussed how the pervasive connectedness of information technology would provide many more sources of much more varied data, whether from machines, via the internet of things or from people via mobile phones and wearable sensors. To this, we can also add the greater availability of clinical trial data, part of the trend of companies to share their data and the emergence of 'real world data', a trend driven by increasing regulatory vigilance and the need to demonstrate health economic outcomes (121). Alongside this growth of data sources, the technology to integrate them has developed and become more powerful. These range from approaches to integrating electronic health records, such as the Athena Health patient portal, to multi-use open source software such as Hadoop, which allows processing of large data sets from many sources. These developments, enabled by ideas like the semantic web (122), mean that the increasing amount of health data can be organised to allow analysis and synthesis.

The expansion of algorithm technology

Banning Garrett of the Atlantic Council think tank has calculated that between 1988 and 2003, whilst processor performance grew a thousand fold, algorithm performance has grown by a factor of 43,000. Garrett correctly sees big data, as it has become known, at the confluence of other trends:

> Algorithms are a critical factor enabling the era of big data, which also has been made possible by virtually unlimited computer processing power and storage, both of which are trending toward 'free'.
>
> (123)

In the context of the life sciences sector, it is more helpful to see algorithms as an important factor among many leading to the information shift.

In both the primary research interviews and the secondary research of analysing others' prior research, data analytics was a constantly recurring theme. Importantly, the impact of data analysis is not limited to any one part of the life sciences value chain. Most of the early applications and publications concern its application in R&D. McKinsey, for example, describes its uses in drug discovery and clinical trial management (124). In medical technology, Boston Scientific sees the future as a convergence of 'devices and informatics'. However, the applications of algorithm-driven use of big data in life sciences also extend to operations and sales and marketing activities. Merck's use of production data to enhance vaccine production is a good example of this (125), but data analytics are becoming increasing important in operational activities, such as supply chain management and regulatory compliance. In sales and marketing, we are beginning to use data analytics to predict market behaviour (126), improve patient compliance (127) and manage sales teams (128), to name just a few applications.

Data analytics, made necessary and possible by proliferating data and more powerful algorithms, is therefore affecting the life science industry's entire value chain in multiple complex ways. It is easy to get lost in this complexity, but it is also important not to. The important point to draw from these developments is that data analytics is contributing to a larger, more fundamental shift in the way we use information. In doing so, it is contributing to the change in selection pressures acting on the industry's business models. That said, even big data has its limits. In essence, it relies on spotting correlations that aren't visible by traditional methods and, as every researcher knows, correlation does not equal causation. An example of the limitations of big data was given in February 2013, when Google Flu Trends made large errors in predicting the doctor visits for influenza-like illness (129). The use of big data is only as good as the underlying science and the models we have to explain relationships. As useful as it is, big data's practical application still depends on thinking, learning intelligence as distinct from powerful but essentially 'stupid' algorithmic logic. Such intelligence has been the preserve of human beings but, as I will discuss in the next section, changes in that part of the technological environment are another contributor to the information shift.

Artificial intelligence: towards the medical machine age

Although the term was first coined in 1956 by John McCarthy at MIT, definitions of artificial intelligence are problematic. They revolve around a consensus about how its outcomes differ from non-intelligent processes: visual perception, speech recognition, learning ability and other human-like capabilities. But they tend to shy away from descriptions of how its mechanism differs from sophisticated but inherently dumb algorithms. Despite this inexactness of meaning, we are clearly moving towards something more powerful than even complex algorithms. The combination of ideas like fuzzy logic, natural language processing and knowledge representation, together with huge amounts of processing power, are leading to the evolution of capabilities that differ markedly from data analytics alone. They are taking us, in the words of Erik Brynjolfsson and Andrew McAfee, towards a second machine age in which many of the tasks that currently require human intelligence will be carried out by artificial intelligence.

The poor definition of artificial intelligence (AI) confuses attempts to describe its application. Researchers talk about an AI effect: the discounting of AI applications as mere computing when they lose their novelty. Even if it is not always possible to point to examples of AI application, it is certainly true to say that artificial intelligence is less advanced than data analytics as an applied discipline but that its application has begun with relatively simple tasks and that it is developing quickly.

In the clinical setting, the application of artificial intelligence can probably be said to have begun in the 1960s with clinical decision support systems (130). Despite that early start, only recently have truly intelligent systems begun to be adopted. The use of IBM's Watson in oncology is the most obvious example of this (131), and artificial intelligence has also been applied in the interpretation of medical images (132). The impact of artificial intelligence in the life sciences industry is more recent and less developed but, like data analytics, seems to be starting in research and development and slowly spreading to other parts of the value chain. In drug discovery, the development of BPM 31510, an oncology drug 'designed' using artificial intelligence by Berg, is an early example of this (133). If Berg's early results are an indication of the future, artificial intelligence looks like it may drastically reduce drug development times and costs. In medical technology, artificial intelligence is enabling the development of diagnostic devices that can be used by consumers, encouraged by Qualcomm's $10m XPrize (134). Other examples of early AI applications support physicians' diagnoses by giving them access to a larger data set (135).

In manufacturing and operations, artificial intelligence systems are beginning to be applied to increase both efficiency and flexibility. For example, Universal Robotic's Neocortex software, combined with 3D imaging, has been used in medical device assembly (136). In pharmaceutical manufacturing, artificial intelligence has been applied to improve performance and quality in tablet production (137). And, in supply chain design, it is being used to optimise distribution routes (138) and to improve demand forecasting (139).

In the sales and marketing part of the value chain, artificial intelligence seems yet to make a significant impact on the life sciences sector. This may partly be due to the onerous compliance and regulatory constraints placed on pharmaceutical and medical technology marketing. But developments outside the sector seem likely to percolate into the industry with important implications. There are perhaps three areas where this is most likely to happen. The first is the enhancement of predictive modelling of markets, discussed in the data analytics section of this book. This will fundamentally change the current practice in assessing market potential and preparing business plans. The second is in the control of sales and marketing resources. Despite the recent vogue for marketing accountability, the allocation of these often large spends is, at best, a skilled craft rather than a science. We might expect artificial intelligence, acting on data about what works and what doesn't, to make the process much less subjective. The third is in the management of the customer interaction process. In most parts of the sector, 'dumb' media such as websites and promotional materials and 'smart' human sales forces are still the basis of sales and marketing effort. Even when dressed up as continuing medical education, the methods are essentially unchanged from a generation ago. Artificial intelligence offers new ways to interact with the customer, whether physician, patient or payer, that is more effective, more compliant and less costly. In all three cases, the imperfections of the current approaches are likely to create opportunities for artificial intelligence.

The contribution of artificial intelligence to the information shift is perhaps the most speculative of the four factors I have discussed here. It is some way behind the well-established trends in enabling technology, connectivity and data analytics. However, it may be that, combined with those factors, it makes the biggest contribution of all to the information shift. If so, that will be because how we currently use information is both enabled and constrained by our human intelligence. Whatever its other merits, human intelligence wasn't designed to handle the relationships within the vast amounts of data we now have to work with. Faced with complex tasks, humans fall back on heuristics and other cognitive short cuts that, as the statistics on misdiagnosis tell us, make for more haste and less speed. Artificial intelligence is the only foreseeable solution to that limitation.

As with the other shifts, it would be easy to underestimate the importance of the information shift. Superficially, we could view it as no more than a continuation of the rapid growth of information technology of the last twenty or thirty years. That long term trend has changed the industry in very significant ways but such a linear view would not allow for the convergence of information and communication technologies that we are now observing. The step-change in capabilities across the value chain is qualitatively different from even the stunning advances in information technology that we have seen in the last working lifetime.

In particular, the scale and breadth of the data we will be able to gather and the pervasiveness and manner in which we will be able to translate it into information is quite different from what we have in the past, perhaps prematurely, called the information revolution.

Swimming in a sea of information

In exactly the same way that the various developments in life sciences technology combine to create the systeomic shift, developments in information and communications technology add up to the information shift which, like the systeomic shift, is a clear and important change in the selection pressures facing the industry. As another fundamental change in our environment, the information shift applies a selection pressure in favour of business models that adopt and adapt that technology to create an improvement in returns or a reduction in risk. As with the systeomic shift, business models may adapt to the information shift in how they invent products or service, how they make and deliver them or how they manage customer relationships. The obverse to this positive selection pressure is that the information shift creates a selection pressure against business models that remain based on the use of information in a small-scale, fragmented, unidirectional and deductive manner. This is summarised in Figure 12.5.

At the risk of stressing the point too much, the information shift does not operate in isolation from the other selection pressures. Its impact must be considered in the context

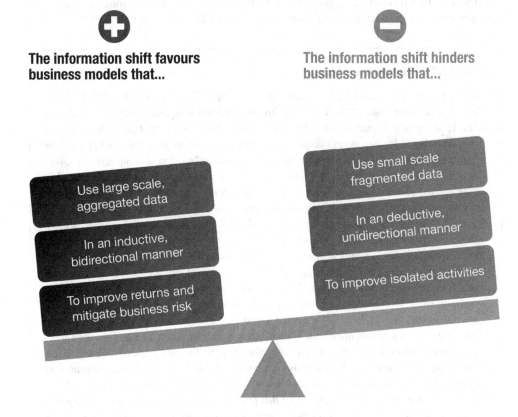

Figure 12.5 Selection pressure implications of the information shift

of the value, global, network and systeomic shifts, as well as the trimorphic shift, which I will discuss next.

The trimorphic shift

Box 12.3   The trimorphic shift

An emergent property of the healthcare system in which the focus of supply side economic activity is changing from organisations that are relatively similar in how they distribute effort across their value chain to one in which supply side economic activity is based on organisations that are strongly focused on either customer intimacy, operational excellence or product excellence.

In simple terms, trimorphic means the existence of three distinct forms. In the history of biological evolution, for example, it is often associated with Wallace's discovery that the females of certain Malaysian butterflies appear in three distinct forms. In our research, it refers to the analogous observation that life science companies appear to be differentiating into three broad, distinct forms, each with a focus on a different part of the value chain.

This three-way polarisation is not unique to the life sciences sector. The same trend is seen in most sectors, although how the polarisation plays out is sector specific. It is explained by two different management ideas, the value chain and the industry life cycle. If you're not familiar with these, they are introduced in Box 12.4 and Box 12.5.

Box 12.4   The value chain

The value chain concept was crystallised from earlier ideas by Michael Porter in 1985, in his book, Competitive Advantage *(140). It is a simplification of Porter's important and influential piece of work, to say that he had two big ideas: one obvious, the other less so. Porter's first idea was that, essentially, all business organisations do three things: they invent, they make and they sell. In saying this, it's important to know that a 'business organisation' could be a single firm or a collection of allied firms, and that what they invent, make or sell may be products, services or both. His second and less obvious idea, sometimes labelled Generic Strategies, was that firms create competitive advantage by focusing their resources on only one of these three activities (invention, making or selling). They aim to be demonstrably superior, relative to their competitors, in the focus activity and allocate sufficient resources to the other two activities to be just good enough. Underpinning Porter's second idea was a wealth of industrial economics research that revealed first, that firms have limited resources and, second, that creating a clear, distinctive superiority (i.e. excellence) in any one of the three activities is very expensive. This is especially so in mature markets with good, strong competitors when 'good enough' is already very good and 'excellent' is a very high standard. Porter warned that firms that do not focus but instead spread their resources more or less evenly across the three value chain steps would usually fail to develop competitive advantage in any of the three areas. This is because competence is related to resource allocation. So the evenly spread company would be better than good enough at all three things but not superior (relative to a focused competitor) at any one thing. Translated into a life sciences industry context, firms that focus on inventing things are our innovative, research-based firms; those that focus on making are our low cost, generic firms; and those that focus on selling are those that compete either by brand strength or by customising the product or service. Later, Treacy and Wiersema repackaged Porter's ideas in their book* The Discipline of Market Leaders *(Ibid.), in which they provided examples from many sectors. In their work, they usefully re-labelled the focus of research-based companies as 'product excellence', low cost firms as striving for 'operational excellence', and firms focused on selling as seeking 'customer intimacy'. The terms are clearer than Porter's, but the fundamental ideas are essentially the same.*

Box 12.5   The industry life cycle

The industry life cycle concept has a longer and less clear history than the value chain (see for example [2–4]). It is also less of a theory (that is, an explanation of a phenomenon) than a generalised observation, what management theorists call 'law like generalisation' (141). According to the industry life cycle concept, the number firms in a sector changes over time, as does how they choose to compete. At the beginning of an industry, many firms appear and they often have very different products and ways of doing business. Over time, firms exit and merge leading to share consolidation, with typically a few firms having the majority of market share. Where industry life cycle theory meets the value chain concept is in the observation that, as industries mature, the merging and consolidation typically leads to three groups of firms, known as competitive sets, each focused on either inventing, making or selling. Hence we see the emergence of a competitive set of research-based innovators, focusing their resources on inventing clearly superior products and content with being good enough in operational efficiency and customer relationship management. These fit well into Treacy and Wiersema's product excellence category. Alongside these innovators and, in some ways complementary to them, emerge cost leaders, focused on having the lowest possible cost base, happy to be imitators rather than innovators and eschewing inefficient product tailoring and specialisation. These are the operationally excellent firms. Finally, there may emerge companies who focus resources on understanding the variation in customer needs and adapting their product or service (or more often a combination of both) to the specific needs of customer sub-groups. This final group may innovate in customisation and service, but rarely in product technology, and will aim to have acceptable, rather than superior, costs. These are the customer intimate companies. Thus, industry life cycle is really a description of how the value chain and generic strategy concepts play out over time. Its value lies in predicting the future. By considering factors such as the current distribution of market share, levels of product differentiation and growth rates, we can make a reasonable estimate of where we are in an industry's life cycle and predict what will happen to industry structure.

Applying these two ideas to life sciences reveals an industry that is maturing but not yet mature. Between 2007 and 2012, the market share of the ten largest pharma companies increased to 43 percent, still far from concentrated (142). However, we can see clear differences in allocation of resources between, for example, research-based pharma, where R&D spend is 15 to 20 percent of sales, and generic pharma, where it is a fraction of that. A less developed but similar picture is seen in medical technology, where generic devices are beginning to make inroads into simpler device categories and in emerging markets (143). Historically, more complex drugs and devices typically have a high service and customisation element to their value proposition. Until recently, we have not seen the emergence of a complementary 'low service' model; however, in orthopaedics we can now observe the beginning of a polarisation between high service and low service firms (144).

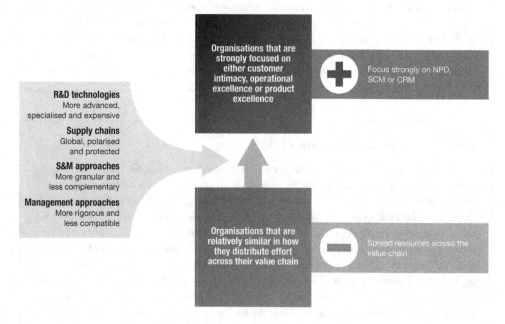

Figure 12.6 The trimorphic shift

These observations suggest a prognosis that the business models of the life sciences industry are likely to polarise in the future. We should expect to see transition from a group of firms that are not very different from each other to an industry of three distinct competitive sets (the product excellent, the operationally excellent and the customer intimate) that are fundamentally different in their capabilities and almost incomparable in their resource allocation patterns. This is exactly the emerging property of the sector that I observed in my research and I have labelled the trimorphic shift as defined in Box 12.3 and shown in Figure 12.6. This shift has not yet fully emerged (for example, there is little in the way of a generic medical device sector as yet and personalised pharmaceutical therapies are still in their infancy), suggesting that the necessary evolutionary conditions have not yet existed. In the following paragraphs, I will describe how these conditions are now beginning to emerge and are driving the trimorphic shift. Again, I remind the reader that this is a descriptive, selective list of factors and not a comprehensive catalogue of contributing points.

Product excellence technologies: ever more advanced, specialised and expensive

The technology employed in the research, discovery and development stages of the life sciences industry is hugely varied and is advancing across all stages of the process. In pharmaceuticals, a number of new technologies, from microfluidic PCR to high-throughput mass spectrometry are improving the way that therapeutic targets are validated and candidate molecules are screened (145). Similar technological advances are improving the development pathways of medical devices, especially with implantable devices (146). New materials, such as graphene (144) and new development technologies, such as additive manufacturing (also known as 3D printing) of prototypes (147) also enhance the ability of firms to become product excellent. Similarly, in molecular diagnostics, advances in the systeomic shift are enabling the development of monitoring, screening and diagnostic technology both in vivo and in vitro (148). And across all parts of the life science sector, the integration of information technology is both enhancing product design and changing the way products are developed. This ranges from wireless communication (e.g. chips in implants, equipment and pills) to the use of social media (e.g. to recruit trial patients) to the use of big data and real world data to test safety and efficacy. At the same time as information technology is enhancing the R&D process in life sciences, it is also allowing the augmentation of core products. Connectivity of patient monitoring devices, new drug formulation and delivery technologies and the miniaturisation of diagnostic tests are all examples of this.

The influence of technology on firms' ability to invent and develop new products is large, growing and near impossible to summarise effectively. The more important point to grasp is that many of these technologies for enhancing R&D are as specialised and expensive as they are advanced. Unlike enabling platform technologies, which tend to impact a whole sector, specialised technologies tend by nature to have an impact that is limited largely to firms developing complex, advanced products, being much less relevant for firms who, for example, make relatively simple products very cheaply or whose advantage comes from customer intimacy. Furthermore, the use of such technologies (or more specifically, the integration of these technologies into advanced R&D processes) is increasingly becoming a source of implicit intellectual property that is more defensible than the explicit knowledge that might be publicised in patents. The net result is that such technological developments are not only making innovative firms more innovative, they are also making these firms more different from those firms who see their competitive advantage as resting on operational excellence or product intimacy.

Operational excellence technologies: polarising between global and shared and protected and specialised

Just as innumerable individual technologies are enabling product excellent firms to innovate more, faster and better, we might expect an analogous technological impact on the operational supply chains and this is indeed what emerged from my research.

From this part of my work, the overarching theme is the emergence of global and significantly shared supply chains as outsourcing has become a near-default position for many firms (149, 150). In the upstream supply chain, this trend is most obvious for base materials, such as active ingredient manufacture in pharma and medical grade polymers in medical devices, but the trend seems to include any part of the supply chain that does not include proprietary technology or a mission-critical, customer-facing activity. In the downstream stages of the supply chain, physical product distribution is similarly becoming ever more outsourced and shared as logistics chains consolidate (151, 152).

Running alongside this development of a global and shared supply chain is a great leap forward in the efficiency of life sciences supply chains, enabled by technologies in both manufacturing and logistics. In pharma, the shift away from traditional batch manufacturing and scale up, towards continuous production and 'in series' manufacturing methods is well advanced (153). In medtech, the huge variety of products and manufacturing methods makes it harder to define manufacturing trends, but it also appears to be moving away from traditional manufacturing towards very efficient, just in time manufacturing (154, 155). In both pharma and medtech, enabling technologies such as cloud storage of information, tracking technologies, enterprise resource planning software and other technologies are making supply chain management much more efficient (156, 157).

Running counter to this overarching trend towards global and shared supply chains is a much smaller trend in the opposite direction. This occurs when the supply chain represents a source of distinctive competitive advantage. Thus, when firms make very complex products (such as in gene therapy biologics, some implants and some patient-specific devices), when there is a great risk of loss of tacit intellectual property (158) or when the supply chain creates some specific value-add (for example, customised medical devices [159]), they are less able and often less willing to take advantage of a shared supply chain.

So, as with R&D technologies, it seems that the various technologies that can enhance the efficiency of the life sciences industry are not leading to an even increase in efficiency across the industry. Instead, they seem to have a polarising effect. They enable operationally excellent companies to become much more efficient but have less impact on product excellent or customer intimate companies. By contrast, those companies are enabled to become more specialised and more responsive but at the opportunity cost of not becoming hyper-efficient.

Customer intimate technologies: enabling understanding, personalisation and integration

Just as various technologies are enhancing the ability of some companies to become even more product excellent and some are enabling others to become even more operationally excellent, we can observe a cluster of technologies that are enabling customer intimacy to a much greater level than before. These technologies seem to cluster into three emerging and complementary trends: customer segmentation, value proposition customisation and value chain integration.

Customer segmentation – understanding the heterogeneity of customers' needs and motivations – is a characteristic of effective marketing in all mature markets. Traditionally, life science companies have been weak in this area, often mistaking categories like disease stages or injury types for true customer segments (49). But technological changes, including those discussed in the information shift earlier, are enabling life science companies to uncover customer segments more effectively. The increasing availability of data from patients (160, 161), healthcare professionals and payers (162, 50) is allowing firms to identify segments among all three groups and to synthesise them into contextual segments when all three play a part in the choice of treatment or therapy (163).

Complementing customer segmentation is the ability to adjust the value proposition to particular segments and customers. The most discussed examples of this are in 'personalised' products, such as genotype-specific drugs or made-on-demand implants. Clearly, these are possible only as a result of developments in product technology. However, equally important are customised pricing plans that reflect payers' risk tolerance (164), tailored support programmes for new products in surgery and specifically targeted promotional campaigns for some aesthetic products. All of these are examples of adapting the offer to customer segments and are made possible only by technologies that allow customer segments to be understood and the offer made to them to be adapted.

Both customer segmentation and personalisation of the offer reach their ultimate expression when life science companies integrate their activities closely into their customers' value chain. We see this already in areas such as medical nutrition, dialysis and, increasingly, chronic diseases such as asthma, diabetes and COPD. It necessarily involves both a very detailed understanding of an individual customer organisation (e.g. a hospital or primary care provider) and the ability to build an extensive subset of the firm's activities around that customer's needs. This is only possible as a result of information and communication technology, such as with the internet of things approach, that some medical equipment manufacturers are adopting in areas like diagnostics and imaging.

As with technologies that enable product excellence and operational excellence, technologies that enable customer intimacy tend not to benefit all companies equally. Instead, they enable customer intimate companies to be still more intimate and therefore more different from product excellent and operationally excellent companies.

Advancing in three distinctly different directions

As with the systeomic shift, the information shift and the three shifts emerging from the social environment, it is tempting to see the trimorphic shift as no more than an incremental continuation of historical trends, the maturing of the life sciences industry as suggested by industry life cycle theory. But this would be to underestimate the importance of what is happening, which is more than simply industry consolidation. The trimorphic

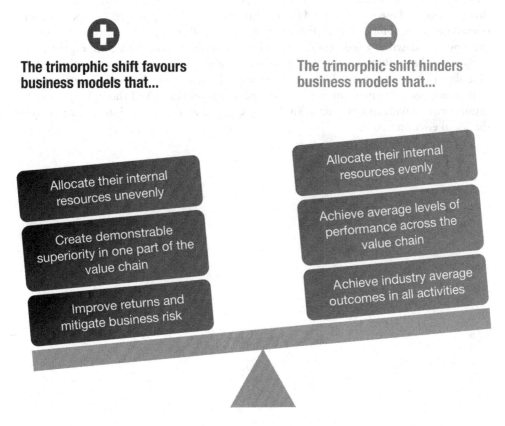

The trimorphic shift favours business models that...

Allocate their internal resources unevenly

Create demonstrable superiority in one part of the value chain

Improve returns and mitigate business risk

The trimorphic shift hinders business models that...

Allocate their internal resources evenly

Achieve average levels of performance across the value chain

Achieve industry average outcomes in all activities

Figure 12.7 Selection pressure implications of the trimorphic shift

shift will probably lead to the traditional outcomes of industry maturation, such as market share concentration and industry shake-out via merger and acquisition, and those trends will change the industry significantly. However, a more important implication of the trimorphic shift is likely to be extreme differentiation. Product excellent firms will be extreme versions of today's research-based firms. Operationally excellent firms will make today's generic companies appear inefficient and expensive. And current levels of segmentation and customisation will look very crude indeed in comparison with future customer intimate firms. The differences between these three competitive sets will make the differences between, for example, today's research led companies and today's generic companies look relatively small. Indeed, the three competitive sets will be so different from each other that they will barely see each other as competitors, since their targeted customers and value propositions will be so different.

This polarisation in how firms create competitive advantage is clearly a change in the selection pressures facing the industry's business models. The trimorphic shift applies a selection pressure in favour of business models that focus on creating value by product excellence, operational excellence or customer intimacy and by targeting the parts of the global market that will respond to such an offer. Similarly, the trimorphic shift will apply a selection pressure against firms that do not focus their resources and which adopt a strategy that straddles across the three approaches. Such firms, that may have good products *and* efficient operations *and* effective sales and marketing processes, will find themselves at a disadvantage to those more focused firms with either excellent products *or* hyper-efficient operations *or* the ability to identify and satisfy very small and specific customer segments, perhaps even down to a segment of one. These pressures are summarised in Figure 12.7.

By now, I hope my final point in this section is predictable. As important as the trimorphic shift is, it acts not alone but in concert with the systeomic shift and the information shift which also emerge from the technological environment. And those three shifts act simultaneously with and interact with the value, global and network shifts emerging from the social environment.

13 Asking the right questions

The scientist is not a person who gives the right answers, he's one who asks the right questions.
Claude Lévi-Strauss

We have now reached the end of Part 2 of *Darwin's Medicine*. In Part 1, I reprised the content of *The Future of Pharma*. I began with the two fundamental ideas of my work: first, that industries are complex adaptive systems and, second, that evolutionary theory, with its variation, selection and amplification mechanism, is the best science we have to explain and perhaps predict such systems.

Using evolutionary theory as a guide, I then synthesised historical observations and data about pharma and wider life science industry and its social and technological environments. That led to an explanation of the industry's history as one of a fragmenting fitness landscape and the corollary of speciating business models. Building on those ideas, I used research data to predict further fragmentation of the fitness landscape and even more speciation of industry business models. In *The Future of Pharma*, I used those predictions to suggest the capabilities and traits that companies operating in that market would need. These began with 'hygiene' capabilities, necessary just to exist in the market and very similar regardless of chosen habitat. Perhaps of more interest are the differentiating and dynamic capabilities, necessary to thrive in the market, rather than just survive. Importantly, those traits and capabilities vary depending on which habitat or habitats the company chooses to compete in.

The Future of Pharma was very well received by its target market of industry executives. The book sold well, was critically acclaimed and inspired a lot of very flattering emails. The same strong theme of positive comment arose from the hundreds of presentations and workshops I have given since. But the discussion about the topic at presentations and meetings, usually with clever people who are very knowledgeable about the industry, is a more informative channel of feedback than book reviews and emails; and that is because of one small word. Almost always, direct, face to face feedback about *The Future of Pharma* began with high praise, followed by the word 'but', as executives built on my ideas to ask more questions. Although they were extremely varied and often indicative of the questioner's personal position, these hundreds of 'but . . . ' statements coalesced into three coherent themes. Here they are, simplified for clarity:

- What about the sector outside pharmaceuticals, including medical technology, medical devices, diagnostics and the dozens of sub-sectors that intertwine to make the life sciences sector?

- What about the sub-species, meaning all of the variants of business models within the seven generalised business models suggested in *The Future of Pharma*?
- What can we learn for practice, meaning what generalised findings can we turn into normative, directive recommendations about how to compete in this market?

These statements challenged and inspired me. The first was a clear gap in my work, made all the more pressing by obvious convergence of the industry sub-sectors and the blurring of traditional boundaries between them. Such a gap is relatively easy to fill by extending the scope of my research and doesn't require any extension to theoretical models or the kind of data collected. However, the other two questions were more problematic. First, as my challengers had implied, it was apparent that my 'seven species of future business model' finding was only a first approximation to reality. To revert to a biological metaphor, my model was more like one of seven genera or families of business models and, within each of these, there were likely to evolve multiple distinctive species. My previous work had not explored that in much detail. Second, whilst *The Future of Pharma* had dedicated quite a lot of its content to the sort of normative, directive recommendations that executives seek, it clearly wasn't sufficient. On reflection, it seemed clear to me that improved recommendations for practice would need more than simply understanding the seven genera in more detail. They were likely to need a study of emerging species and their differences. In other words, a careful look at who is doing what and how.

Challenging questions from knowledgeable executives are extremely valuable to inspire further work but they are only the beginning of designing rigorous research. For that, management science academics are taught ways of defining precise research questions that challenge current thinking and make a contribution to knowledge and practice (see [165] pages 11–12). In this case, the challenges made by executives translated into two further research questions.

Research question 1:
How are the changes in the social and technological environment of the life sciences industry translating into selection pressures that shape its fitness landscape?

This question arose from two fundamental ideas of evolutionary theory. First, changes in the social and technological environments create selection pressures that shape habitats and sub-habitats in the fitness landscape. Second, genera and species evolve to fill habitats and sub-habitats in the fitness landscape. At a fundamental level, therefore, the weaknesses in *The Future of Pharma* flowed from an insufficiently deep examination of how environmental changes were creating selection pressures and shaping the fitness landscape. Add to that the need to expand the research across the whole industry and to update it from its 2010–2011 base, and the first question, which is a clear guide for research, is formed. This is the question that I have addressed in Part 2 of this book. The exploration of social and technological environment changes and, more importantly, how they translate into selection pressures that favour or disfavour any given business model is much deeper and wider than in *The Future of Pharma*.

Research question 2:
How are firms adapting to these selection pressures and the new fitness landscape?

This question arose from the nature of the industry. As a complex adaptive system, it is not predictable in a linear sense; one cannot say, 'This will definitely happen.' Nor can one even say, 'This is happening now and it extrapolates to a specific outcome in the future.' All one can do is make a great number of observations and use ideas from evolutionary theory to interpret them as early, weak signals of the emergent properties of the system. When researching *The Future of Pharma*, some early signals could be detected. The limitations of small molecule innovation and the rise of generics were two salient examples of this. Those and many other observations supported the predictions of the seven new business models in that book. But even the many observations made in that research were too weak and too few to allow insight into the finer grained structure of the landscape and its corresponding species. More work was needed. Since then, the dynamic nature of the industry has meant that those weak signals of its emerging properties have become ever stronger and more frequent. Add again the need to expand the research across the whole industry and the second question, which is also a clear guide for research, is formed.

With its corresponding research, this second question forms the basis of Part 3 of *Darwin's Medicine*. I begin by organising and structuring a huge number of observations of what life science companies are doing. Based on primary research interviews, secondary research by others and analysis of mountains of public domain data, I look at how companies are responding to the selection pressures described in Part 2. Doing so allows us to detect early adaptations to the environment and to better understand the nature of new business models. This in turn allows me to go much further in understanding the mechanisms of adaptation and making recommendations for how life science companies may direct their own evolution.

Part 3

Evolution is cleverer than you are

One general law, leading to the advancement of all organic beings, namely, multiply, vary, let the strongest live and the weakest die.

Charles Darwin, *The Origin of Species*

14 Introduction

Orgel's Second Law

In all my reading about evolutionary theory, perhaps my favourite anecdote is that about Orgel's Second Law. Leslie Orgel was an eminent British chemist-turned-evolutionary-biologist who was among the first people to see Watson and Crick's double helix model and who later went on to do important work on the origins of life. By all accounts, he was also a man with a wry sense of humour. When challenged that there was insufficient evidence that evolution could be responsible for the complexity of life, apparently he responded with the pithy retort: 'Evolution is cleverer than you are,' a phrase that has entered the folklore of evolutionary scientists and is now known, slightly flippantly, as Orgel's Second Law. Flippant or not, Orgel's intent was surely to remind us that billions of years of variation, selection and amplification by untold numbers of replicators and inter-actors is far more likely to find solutions to the problems of survival than is our limited human imagination.

Orgel's Second Law and the implied limitations of human predictive powers apply to socio-economic systems just as much as they do to biology. In the case of the life sciences industry, the complex and dynamic interactions between the industry's business models and the six great shifts mean that it is just too difficult to predict in the simplistic, extrapo-lative, forecasting sense of that term. Many authors do attempt prediction of course but, in the face of such complexity, their work is often much closer to speculation than to science. If we want to peer into the future with any degree of rigour, we need a different approach – an evolutionary approach.

Evolutionary biologists have debated the predictive, as opposed to explanatory, power of evolutionary theory for decades. In general, they are reserved or sceptical about our ability to predict evolutionary outcomes. As Stephen Jay Gould explained in his book *Wonderful Life*, if we re-wound and re-ran a tape of life's history on Earth, it is doubtful that it would ever turn out the same way twice (166). There are just too many interactions that might easily have happened differently and changed the course of life on Earth. However, more recently, biologists have shifted to that idea that, if we understand the situation and the selection pressures well enough, we may be able to predict evolutionary trajectories to a limited extent (167). Their work, with species as varied as E.coli, Caribbean lizards and fish from African lakes, is leading evolutionary biologists towards the idea that Darwin's idea might eventually have some of the predictive power of the theories we use in physical sciences. Indeed, some researchers are already using these ideas to predict the evolution of antibiotic-resistant bacteria and of flu strains (168).

In this third part of *Darwin's Medicine*, I describe my work that paralleled that of the predictive evolutionary biologists as I looked for – and found – the industry's emerging

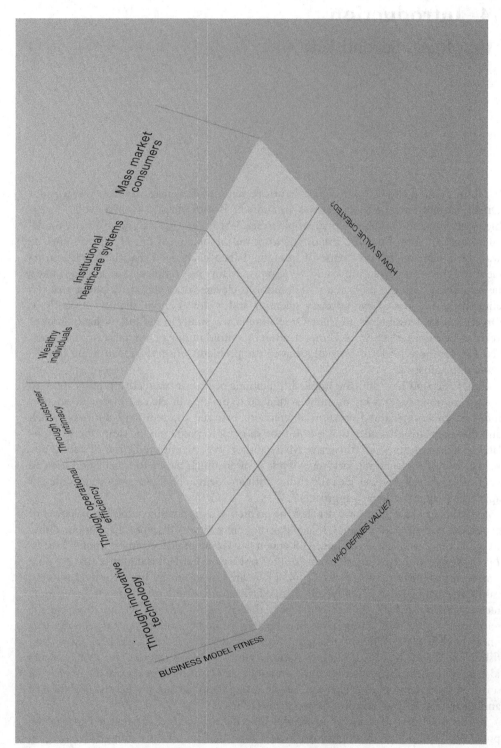

Figure 14.1 The habitats of the life science fitness landscape

patterns of responses to the six great shifts. Although my starting point is the fitness landscape derived in *The Future of Pharma* (see Figure 1.12 in Section 1.7), I will go much deeper and expand from purely pharma to the life science industry generally, including medical technology, diagnostics and other sectors. Eschewing a simplistic forecasting approach, my methodology was to gather large amounts of mixed data. My sources range from interviews with senior executives, secondary sources such as market research reports and, most importantly, a large collection of industry data, such as press releases and news reports, about what firms are doing as they attempt to adapt to their environment. This last data set included everything from mergers and alliances to product launches to restructuring and new market entries and many other activities. To analyse this varied mass of data, I collated, organised, re-arranged and re-categorised it until there emerged the sort of patterns in the data that reveal the emergent properties of the system. What emerged is what I now describe in Part 3, specifically two sequential evolutionary choices by firms: the choice of habitat in which to compete followed by the choice of how to compete within that habitat. As already identified in *The Future of Pharma* and summarised in Figure 14.1, the choice of habitat in which to compete involved two component choices: whether to compete on technological innovation, operational excellence or customer intimacy and whether to compete for the preference of government payers, affluent consumers or mass market consumers. These choices led to the nine basic habitats shown in Figure 14.1.

From the second evolutionary choice, about how to survive and thrive within a chosen habitat, there emerged a fitness landscape that was fragmenting under the pressures of the six great shifts and, correspondingly, a population of life science firms that was speciating into a large variety of diverse business models. The parallels with Darwin's discoveries – such as the speciation of finches on the Galapagos Islands – became very clear.

The outcomes of this part of my research were complicated and so I have used the habitat structure of Figure 14.1 to clarify and structure my findings. This is just as one might describe the fauna of Africa by describing separately those animals that live in the rain forest, desert or savannah. In each habitat, I have described the various evolutionary choices that firms are making and the business models that are evolving as a result of those choices. And, just as that metaphor implies, the complexity that emerges is both fascinating and informative.

15 Technological innovator species emerging in the government payer habitat

It is not difficult to see the individual, case-specific ways that life science companies are trying to adapt to the selection pressures created by the six shifts. Every product launch, investment, alliance and restructuring is routinely announced and this mass of data streams across my desktop every day. The challenge for management scientists is to see a pattern in this huge diversity of adaptations.

Making sense of diversity is arguably the oldest scientific problem of all. We see it in the Ancient Greeks' categorisation of matter as the four elements earth, air, fire or water, and it is the underlying aim of what we now call big data analytics. Almost every language has an idiom equivalent to the English 'seeing the wood (or forest) for the trees'.

More relevant to the life sciences industry is the work of Linnaeus, the eighteenth century Swedish scientist, who faced the same problems when he tried to make sense of biological diversity. His work gave the world the taxonomy on which we still largely rely. His great contribution was to identify similarities and differences (for example mammary glands or spines), which could be used to group and classify living things in meaningful, useful ways.

Management scientists can learn from Linnaeus's biological taxonomy because making sense of the baffling, muddled variation in life science business models requires an approach that is similar in principle to that which he took. His approach was to look for important, relevant variations between different examples and use those differences to create a framework for useful aggregation and differentiation.

Applying this to our industry, what differences between business models might be useful? In fact, the biological analogue gives us a strong clue about what to look for. In evolutionary biology, the 'choice' of how to give birth is driven by whatever increases biological fitness. Consider, for example, the difference between oviparous (egg-laying) and viviparous (delivers live young) animals. Evolution 'chooses' between oviparous and viviparous (and other phenotypic traits) depending on what optimises the chances of reproductive capacity and survival rates. Following that approach implies that we need to consider what the analogous choices would be in the evolutionary context of the life sciences industry. In other words, what is the business equivalent of reproductive success, and what are the choices that life science companies make in order to optimise that?

As I have described earlier in this book, just as the principal indicator of biological fitness is reproductive capacity, the principal indicator of business model fitness is risk-adjusted rate of return. Just as we can understand biological diversity as different ways of optimising offspring, we can understand business model fitness as different ways of optimising that economic goal. This is an important concept, and it is difficult to make sense of the many variations in business models unless one first realises that they are all attempts to maximise return, minimise risk or (more usually) achieve the optimal balance between the two. So, if you're skim reading at this point, pause for a moment to give some thought to this idea. Every business model is an attempt to optimise risk-adjusted return on investment. This is most clearly true in publicly owned companies but, even in family owned or not-for-profit organisations, it remains true that the owners, whoever they are, are trying to get the best return on their money after considering the risk involved. In the technological innovator space, this guiding idea is especially important because both the capital at risk and the risks taken are typically higher in this space than in others.

In our analogous, Linnaean taxonomy, the major divisions rest on fundamental differences, such as the having or not having membrane-bound nuclei, having or not having spines, having or not having live young. By and large, such fundamental, structural differences aren't visible among technologically innovative life science companies. True, there is variation in size, ownership structure and funding models, but no clear pattern emerges in that variation. Instead, those variations seem to be the idiosyncratic results of history. To relate it back to our biological analogue, when we look at technologically innovative life science companies, it is as if we have already discarded all the plants, invertebrates, mammals, reptiles and others and focused on, say, birds. And, if we want to understand the differences between members of a family of animals such as birds, then common features (such as spines, wings and egg laying) are less useful than the more variable adaptations in either behaviour or physical features – hence why Darwin classified Galapagos finches according to beak shape.

In my research, the challenge was to search through the diversity of adaptive responses by life science companies and look for commonalities and differences analogous to those Linnaeus observed in biology. In particular, I was looking for emerging differences in traits between business models that are, to the casual observer, very similar. The difference being that I was not looking for variation in physical traits intended to increase reproductive capacity but for variation in strategies, capabilities, structures and other organisational traits that are intended to optimise risk-adjusted ROI.

This sense making process involved collecting and studying a confusing, hugely diverse mass of business model adaptations. This was true even among the subset of life science businesses focused on technological innovation rather than (as in other parts of the fitness landscape) operational excellence or customer intimacy. But with repeated examination, sorting and re-sorting of the examples, three differentiating variables emerged, three diverging approaches to optimising risk-adjusted ROI, that were analogous to the choices between physical traits made by biological evolution. At the risk of overusing my Darwinian metaphor, the data suggested that the different kinds of 'birds' I was looking at varied in three important ways.

In the following paragraphs, I will first draw out those three key variables and discuss the business models they suggest. Then I will look at the data, the real world examples that support or qualify these emerging business models. Do bear in mind, however, that this 'model first, data second' structure is, in fact, the reverse of how my research progressed. In reality, these ideas and models emerged from the data, not the other way around.

Three evolutionary choices

Firms make choices about how to survive and thrive in the market. The choices they make differ from those of some competitors and have similarities with the choices of other competitors. Sometimes even within the same firm, business units make choices that differ from or resemble the choices made by sibling business units, whilst at the same time those choices may be similar to or different from competitors' choices. Across the whole life sciences industry, these choices vary hugely. Even within the subset of the industry where governments are payers and the company has made the choice to compete through technological innovation, there is scope for these adaptive choices to differ. In my research, many such differences emerged. Among other things, choice of geography, extent of vertical integration, ownership structure and governance arrangements all vary across this sub-habitat within the industry landscape, as well as, of course, choice of the medical needs to be met. To revert to my biological metaphor, the industry contains a large variety of birds of different size, shape and colour. In biology, some trait variations are more significant than others and provide more clarity in differentiating between species; in the same way, some business model choices emerged as more relevant and more useful for identifying the way that technological innovator business models were speciating. In particular, three choices emerged.

Incremental vs. discontinuous innovation

> *The life sciences industry has a habit of incremental innovation aimed at long term management of a disease. Many firms are continuing down that path, but some are focusing on discontinuous innovation aimed at curing the condition.*
>
> **Richard Klausner, Illumina**

For technological innovators, a key determinant of risk-adjusted rate of return is technological risk. In other words, what matters most for these firms is the probability that their technological innovation will come to fruition and deliver the promised benefits and profits. In general, smaller, incremental innovations, being based on relatively well understood extant technologies, carry lower levels of technological risk than innovations based on new, less well understood, technology. Incremental innovations also typically require relatively lower levels of investment. Hence, when compared to attempting radical, discontinuous innovation, opting for incremental innovation is a way of reducing both risk and the amount of capital at risk. Incremental innovation can therefore be a way to optimise the viability of the business model in terms of risk-adjusted rate of return.

The trade off is that, in most cases, incremental innovation also offers only incremental benefits to the customer and so often commands only incrementally larger market share, prices and margins when compared to discontinuous innovation. In addition, incremental innovation is often imitated more easily and quickly than more radical innovation, shortening exclusivity times. These factors usually translate to lower prices, margins and shorter life cycles and thus reduced overall returns than for a discontinuous innovation.

Hence, the choice between incremental and discontinuous innovation is a trade off between risk and return. Firms always talk up their strategies as being highly innovative, but in reality they make a choice: low risk baby steps to modest return, or high risk leaps in the hope of a big pay-off. Only a lucky few manage to avoid that trade off.

This choice creates a useful way of understanding the variety of adaptations of business models in the life sciences sector. Either choice may optimise risk-adjusted rate of return, depending on the particular circumstances of the situation, or it may be possible for a business model to choose anywhere along the incremental–discontinuous innovation spectrum. In practice, as we will see, business models tend to polarise into one approach or the other.

Technology integration vs. technology focus

> *One of the biggest things that we are driving across our business is the value that comes from systems think-*
> *ing and integrating technologies from an end-to-end perspective.*
>
> **Michael Swinford, GE Healthcare**

In addition to the degree of innovation, from incremental to discontinuous, a business model also involves a choice of technology focus. On this continuum, a firm may choose to create value by developing a single technological approach or by integrating two or more different but complementary technologies. The first approach aims to realise the potential value from a single technology, the second seeks to do the same from the complementarities between different technologies.

In any given market situation, either approach has a certain level of technological risk. Equally, either approach offers a certain level of differentiation, customer benefit, resistance to imitation and, hence, level of return. Typically, focus on a single technology might carry less risk than integrating multiple technologies, each of which carries risk, because of the additional risk associated with combining technologies. Conversely, an integrated technology may address a larger pool of potential profit than a single technology focus. As they attempt to optimise the viability of their business model, firms choose which to do, based on their perception of risk and return in their particular business context.

This means that the choice of focusing resources on developing a particular technology or on integrating complementary technologies is another risk vs. return choice. There is no single best choice, but there may be a best choice for any given market situation. This makes the technology focus vs. integration choice a second useful way of understanding the variety of adaptations of business models in the life sciences sector. As with the choice between incremental or discontinuous innovation, either may optimise risk-adjusted rate of return. Or, again, it may be possible for a business model to choose anywhere along the focus–integration spectrum, although, in practice, business models tend to polarise at one or other end of that spectrum.

Small target population vs. large target population

> *A particularly prominent trend in the industry is the focus on smaller patient groups, as you see in rare*
> *diseases. Quite understandably, payers will find the resources to make a significant improvement to the lives*
> *of a small patient group.*
>
> **Per-Olof Attinger, Roche**

The nature of the target market is perhaps the biggest single factor influencing the possible returns on an investment. Obviously, the size of the market is central to this but it is far from a simple 'bigger is better' correlation. Larger markets usually attract higher levels of competition than smaller markets; and more competition means smaller share and more margin pressure. At the extremes, small markets may allow niche strategies, in which competition is effectively excluded and profit margins can be very high. This is especially true in technologically innovative markets where the entry costs may be very large, relative to the size of the market.

Return and risk are therefore related to market size and associated factors, such as entry/ exit barriers and level of competitive intensity. This means that the choice of attacking a large market or a small one is another risk vs. return choice that, like the technological focus choice, is context dependent.

This makes the choice of market size a third useful way of understanding and differentiating between the variety of business model adaptations in the life sciences sector. Either choice may optimise the business model's risk-adjusted rate of return, depending on the particular circumstances of the situation. As with the other two choices, it may be possible to choose a business model that sits anywhere along the large–small market continuum. And again, as with the other two choices, in practice we see a tendency towards polarisation.

Undoubtedly, there are other choices determining the risk-adjusted rate of return of a technological innovator business model that could serve as differentiating traits to help us understand and categorise emerging business models. A number of other factors did indeed emerge from my work; but these three stood out as the dominant, salient differentiating traits. Like the length, width and shape of Darwin's finches' beaks, these are criteria against which the multitude of observable adaptations can be usefully assessed and categorised.

To a large degree, these three adaptations are largely independent of each other; there seems to be little correlation between one choice and another. This means that they can be combined to form a taxonomy of theoretically possible business models, as shown in Figure 15.1.

When considering Figure 15.1, it is important to remember three things. First, this applies only to the technological innovators in the government payer habitat because the observations and evidence of the three business model variations come only from that habitat. I will address variations observed in other habitats later in the book. Second, the set of eight choices are theoretical predictions; they are what we might expect to see, but it does not mean that all eight business models have yet been observed, fully evolved, in practice. Third, this taxonomy implies eight homogeneous and distinct models, with no overlap between them. In practice, like all taxonomies, we should expect the boundaries

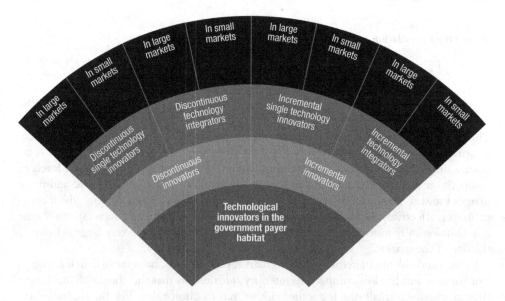

Figure 15.1 A taxonomy of technological innovators in the government payer habitat

between them to be blurred. We should not be surprised to find some business models that don't fit easily into any one category. In other words, we might expect to find business model analogues of the warm-blooded, web-footed, egg-laying, furry duck-billed platypus! As in biology, the existence of these apparently anomalous business models doesn't mean that the taxonomy is incorrect. It only means that, like all taxonomies, Figure 15.1 is an approximation.

Even with those caveats, this model is a useful aid to our understanding of industry evolution. It allows us to compare, contrast and make sense of the myriad variations in business models that we observe in practice, in the same way that Linnaeus's work allows us to makes sense of the bewildering variety of biological species. Each of these eight categories is analogous to a 'species' of technological innovator that might occupy the government payer habitat. It reveals a level of speciation that lies within the broad 'genius' genera that I identified in *The Future of Pharma* and is more detailed and more accurate than that earlier work, but it does not contradict it. As with biological taxonomy, each of the eight predicted species of business model might be expected to share much in common with its seven technologically innovative cousins, whilst also being differentiated by some important variations in how it has chosen to optimise its evolutionary fitness.

In biology, our understanding of similarities and differences between species helps us to understand how their various adaptations, their evolutionary choices, have allowed them to survive in their ecological habitat. In the same way, this more accurate taxonomy of technological innovators gives us a way of understanding the business model traits, capabilities and organisational routines that allow firms to thrive in their habitat. In short, this model gives us a way of observing the cacophony of changes in this part of the market and allows us to make out the coherent pattern that emerges. And making out the pattern is the essential prerequisite to learning from those changes.

As I have already said, my work did not flow from concepts to models to data. The three salient evolutionary choices emerged gradually *from* the data; the empirical evidence was not structured to fit predefined conceptual dimensions. To explain this further, I will discuss some of the evidence and how it illustrates and qualifies the eight species of technological innovator model shown in Figure 15.1. I will then move on to what we can learn from this taxonomic model.

Incremental innovators

All firms are attempting to optimise their evolutionary fitness by some combination of reducing risk and maximising return. In this section, we are considering those firms that have chosen to compete in the government payer habitat and via incremental rather than discontinuous innovation.

The evolutionary strategy of the four incremental innovator business models involves betting that lower risk will more than offset the limited returns possible relative to the alternative of more radical, discontinuous innovation that will be chosen by their more adventurous competitors. This is a justified belief; innovating in relatively small steps, in familiar areas, with well understood science, usually has more chance of succeeding technically. Complementing this reduced technical risk, it also is also more likely to succeed organisationally as it requires less change of people, skills, structure and habits. As outlined earlier and in Figure 15.1, all incremental innovators share their choice of lower risk for lower returns but vary in their choice of target market size and technology focus. This leads us to the prediction of four different incremental innovator models, as follows.

The Traditional Blockbuster model

In some senses, the way in which we compete has not changed much. Our new Eylea product is an incremental innovation, but it meets an unmet need that is recognised by payers, patients and prescribers.

Andreas Fibig, Bayer

This approach is characterised by a focus on a large market with a potential for large returns but the likelihood of intense and comparable competition. It is also marked by a focus on a single, relatively well understood technology, which mitigates technical and organisational risk. If it is successful, this model offers high fitness since it optimises both the numerator and denominator of the risk-adjusted rate of return calculation.

It is fair to call this the life science industry's 'traditional' model since, for most of the past couple of decades, much of the industry's innovation has not been radical or discontinuous; it has been based on single technologies, aimed at larger markets. Blockbuster drugs, such as the statins (e.g. Lipitor) and proton pump inhibitors (e.g. Nexium), and the major classes of medical implants, such as vascular stents and grafts and orthopaedic implants, such as hips and knees, are all examples of this.

When we look at what life science companies are currently doing to optimise their fitness, it is not surprising that much of what we observe is merely 'doubling down', a re-emphasis of this traditional model. We can see this in many of the successful strategies in both pharma and medtech markets. Part of Bayer's current focus in pharma is built on molecules such as Eylea and Xarelto, whose basic science was discovered in the 1980s and 1950s respectively. The battle for the massive asthma and COPD markets, currently being fought between companies such as GSK and AstraZeneca among others, is based on incremental extension of products to include single, double and triple active ingredients and incremental improvements in delivery technology. Both of these are incremental innovations with a narrow technological focus but aimed at large markets. The picture is similar in medical technology, although the technologies and market sizes are very different. In cardiology medical devices, the extension of transcatheter aortic valve implantation, led by Medtronic and Edwards, and the development of leadless pacemakers, from companies like Medtronic, Boston Scientific and St Jude Medical, are examples of incremental innovations with a narrow technological focus but aimed at relatively large markets. Even some apparently market changing business models are, in fact, examples of this approach. For instance, Celgene's Revlimid has revolutionised treatment of multiple myeloma, but it is a development of an old molecule, the infamous thalidomide. Equally, the developments in ultrasound, CT scanning and fMRI have done the same in those areas but are incremental improvements on established technology. All are examples of the industry's Traditional Blockbuster model based on incremental, relatively low risk innovation aimed at large, lucrative markets.

Describing the model as traditional is not meant to be pejorative; this model has been responsible for many of the industry's great contributions to our society and our economy. It's also likely that this model will, in some contexts, continue to create much value in the future. As I write, results for Novartis's LCZ696 (now named Entresto), another example product of the traditional model, looks as if it may become a 'mega blockbuster' in hypertension and heart failure. But it is worth noting that the six great shifts do place some particular selection pressures on this business model. The value shift demands that the model create real health economic value, something that was never really asked of its twentieth century antecedent. The value shift and global shift together fragment the large, homogeneous markets that the traditional model assumes. The holobiont shift enables smaller, networked competitors to compete with the large, integrated company structures with which the Traditional Blockbuster model is usually associated. The systeomic shift further fragments the patient population and creates the threat of radically innovative competitors that are much more effective. The information shift, via real world big data, promises to illuminate where blockbuster products do and do not create value. The trimorphic shift threatens the rise of very cheap imitative products from rivals focused on cost leadership. Taken as a whole, the Traditional Blockbuster model seems at once the dominant model in the technologically innovative, government payer habitat and, at the same time, the model most at threat from changes in the environment.

The Life Cycle Exploitation model

> *Micra is a superb example of improving existing technology with miniaturisation, battery technology and communications. It's a much more compelling proposition that the technology it replaces.*
> **Angelo De Rosa, Medtronic**

Like the Traditional Blockbuster model, this approach is characterised by the incremental innovation in a focused area of existing technology. Where it differs is that it focuses on the exploitation of small, contiguous sub-markets or cannibalisation and protection of current markets. In both cases, the potential returns are less than the Traditional Blockbuster model. But they are still significant. Furthermore, the risk associated with this model is smaller than incremental new product development because it usually involves even smaller technological steps in markets that are already well understood. So this model, if successful, also offers a high level of fitness by optimising both risk and return.

The Life Cycle Exploitation model has long complemented the Traditional Blockbuster model, representing a way for an innovator to squeeze extra returns from sunk costs, to leverage existing brand reputation and make use of market knowledge and sales channels they have already acquired. These advantages are open to companies exploiting the life cycle of their own products. Also, by mimicking technology and building on market knowledge and customer acceptance that has already been created, follower competitors are able to 'draft' behind a market leader, much like a racing cyclist in a peloton.

We might therefore expect the Life Cycle Exploitation model to thrive in a market environment where even incremental innovation has become more costly and more risky and investors more demanding, just as I described in Part 2 of this book. Indeed, this is a model that we see becoming more common. In pharma, for example, we can see this in the way that AstraZeneca is attempting to extend its Brilinta drug for acute coronary syndrome. Their strategy depends on trial data that demonstrates the product can be used as a preventative therapy, not only as a treatment. Another example is AbbVie's extension of the indications for their Humira anti-inflammatory product, in anticipation of biosimilar copy-cat competitors. In medical devices, development of mammography into 3D imaging by Siemens and others is also typical life cycle exploitation. So, too, is Cochlear's Baha 5 Sound Processor, which extends their bone conduction technology in order to exploit sub-segments in that market. All of these are examples of incremental innovation in a focused area of existing technology that focuses on the exploitation of small, contiguous sub-markets or cannibalisation and protection of current markets.

It is easy to see Life Cycle Exploitation models as somehow secondary to the Traditional Blockbuster business models but in fact such models probably account for a large part of the value realised by innovative companies. As innovation becomes harder and more costly, this is likely to remain true. As with the Traditional Blockbuster model, however, the six great shifts change the selection pressures acting on this business model, although they appear to be a more even balance of positive and negative. Together, the value and global shifts fragment the market, creating opportunities for variations on core technology, so long as those variations create value. The holobiont and trimorphic shifts enable the accessing of external, complementary capabilities that enable the extension of the core technology. Cochlear and other hearing device companies, as mentioned earlier, do this partly via smartphones, for example, whilst 'smart' inhalers offer the possibility to do this for respiratory drugs. The information shift creates great opportunities for products to be extended via the information they create, as Quest Diagnostics are doing with sharing of BRCA gene data. At the same time, by enabling radical innovation, the systeomic shift threatens to dramatically shorten the life cycle of some incremental innovations and so shorten life cycles and obviate minor product variations. The rapid changes in patient stratification in oncology are an example of this, rapidly rendering some non-stratified approaches irrelevant. Looked at in context, the Life Cycle Exploitation model can be seen as both favoured by the selection pressures in the environment but also strongly dependent on the vulnerable blockbuster model.

The Value Fracking model

> *A lot of routine issues around judgments of dosing and the whole interplay between food intake, exercise and insulin could be better handled by Artificial Intelligence that can draw on a much broader source of data. That is what computers typically do well.*

Jakob Riis, Novo Nordisk

Like the Traditional Blockbuster and Life Cycle Exploitation models, this approach is characterised by incremental, rather than discontinuous, innovation. Like the Traditional Blockbuster model, but unlike the Life Cycle Exploitation model, it also chooses to exploit relatively large markets. But it differs from both of these in that the value it seeks to create comes from integration of previously distinct technologies. In effect, this kind of business model releases value that is trapped in the structure of healthcare systems by breaking down barriers between functional and process silos. For this reason, the 'fracking' label is useful, because of the analogy to a technology that has transformed the oil and gas sector. Like the Traditional Blockbuster model, the Value Fracking model offers large potential returns for relatively low risk. Successful implementation of this model provides a high level of evolutionary fitness by optimising both the numerator (return) and denominator (risk) of the risk-adjusted rate of return calculation.

This model is has emerged more recently and, so far, to a lesser degree in the life sciences sector than either the Traditional Blockbuster or Life Cycle Exploitation models. In part at least, this is because the industry has historically been able to create value by exploiting relatively narrow, self-contained technologies. For example, the management of chronic conditions such as hypertension or diabetes requires both therapeutic and diagnostic technologies, but the business models addressing these two parts of the treatment process have traditionally been separate. However, this historical approach can also be understood as an artefact of the often product led culture of life science companies, which creates a bias towards narrow technology focus. Increasingly, value is inaccessible to business models with a narrow technological focus because, first, the technology is mature with its most obvious benefits already commoditised and, second, the value lies less in the performance of the core product and more in how it fits into the healthcare system's network of inter-related activities.

We might therefore expect the Value Fracking model to thrive in situations where the core technology is mature and the current healthcare process has structural inefficiencies. This is the case in many parts of the life science market. As a result, we see this model becoming more important, although it is clearly less advanced than the two previously discussed models with a narrower technological focus. The Value Fracking model is most clearly illustrated in the approach taken by health information technology companies, such as GE Healthcare and Siemens. Siemens' IHE (Integrating the Healthcare Enter-prise), for example, involves building on existing technologies to improve connectivity and interoperability between healthcare IT systems. If successful, this releases the value currently locked up by lack of clinician access to data and inefficient clinical workflows. Importantly, IHE and other approaches involve working across the whole of a hospital and, sometimes, its secondary care context. Its intent is to optimise the efficiency of the 70 percent or so of a hospital's costs spent on labour so that the potential value, and cor-responding revenue, that could be released is very large indeed. In pharmaceuticals, we see examples that appear to be technologically very different but in fact are fundamentally the same Value Fracking model. For example, a huge amount of value is locked away in patient non-compliance, so the integration of technologies to release this value is an obvious way for pharmaceutical companies to create value. This is the rationale behind Proteus Medical's cooperation with a number of pharmaceutical companies. Its 'chip in a pill' technology, for example, has been licensed by Novartis for use in immunosuppression, oncology and cardiovascular therapy areas. Similarly, the use of telemedicine by Merck and others to complement the use of their drugs is intended to release value that is locked up in current treatment processes, rather than improve directly the effectiveness of the drugs used. All of these are examples of incremental innovation, since none of the technologies are, in themselves, radically new science. They all aim to release large amounts of value in large markets. They are all based on integration of multiple, disparate technologies. As different as these different companies' approaches may appear, they are all Value Fracking models.

As these examples show, the potential fitness of Value Fracking models lies in releasing large amounts of value (and so revenue) from innovation that is relatively low risk. As core product innovation becomes harder, riskier and more costly and the need to release value in healthcare systems becomes greater, Value Fracking is likely to become a common business model. But as with the other models, the six great shifts place both negative and positive selection pressures on this business model. The value shift creates a strong pressure to release the value available by pooling information and re-designing clinical workflow. The global shift will raise the importance of rural and other geographically-dispersed market segments that could benefit from Value Fracking. But it also provides the oppor-tunity of emerging markets that wish to 'leapfrog' inefficient western healthcare systems and design more integrated systems from scratch. This is analogous to what has happened with mobile, cellular phone technology in some emerging markets that have skipped over widespread use of landlines.

The holobiont shift favours Value Fracking because it makes it possible to access a wider range of technologies and distribution channels without the firm having to develop a wholly new set of resources from scratch. Without a holobiont, this would be a barrier for firms that were, previously, tightly focused on a single technology class. The cooperation between pharmacies, such as Walgreens, and point of care diagnostics companies is an example of this. For the same reason, the holobiont shift also makes it easier for new entrants, from the IT sector for example, to enter healthcare markets as new competitors. The information shift obviously favours those Value Fracking models in which medical technology is fused with information technology, as with Siemens and GE. Similarly, the systeomic shift provides more sources of information and knowledge to be integrated so as to release value. Large population and neonatal genetic screening, for example, will eventually be able to guide an individual patient's treatment regime. And, when systems medicine approaches change existing treatment regimes, as we see in oncology and other areas of stratified medicine, it coincidentally favours Value Fracking models by helping to fracture traditional silos in medical practice. Meanwhile, the trimorphic shift – in which differently-focused companies either provide new technologies to integrate or drive down the costs of the component technology – also favours Value Fracking models.

For the most part, the Value Fracking model appears to be favoured by the six great shifts. However, if anything, the shifts favour new entrants into the healthcare market and threaten traditional life science companies that do not partner with them in holobionts.

The Speciality Domination model

> *At Boston Scientific, we are a medical device company but many of our businesses, before solutions became more the buzzword, have been very active in providing services and solutions within their business unit. We do have a capability at Boston Scientific called Advantix. We have a number of solutions within our Advantix portfolio, but they are aimed toward logical services or productivity benefits that are tied to our products.*
> **Mike Mahoney, Boston Scientific**

Like the three models previously discussed, the Speciality Domination approach is characterised by incremental, rather than discontinuous, innovation. And, like the Life Cycle Exploitation model, but unlike the Traditional Blockbuster and Value Fracking models, it also chooses to exploit relatively smaller and often contiguous market opportunities. But it differs from the Life Cycle Exploitation model in that the value it seeks to create comes from the combination of previously distinct technologies. Instead, like Value Fracking, this business model releases value that is inaccessible to single product or single technology approaches by breaking down barriers between connected needs. This combination of focusing on smaller, related markets with a range of technologies typically implies that the model concentrates on a closely related set of treatments or customer needs. Since, in life sciences, related needs are typically clustered within a clinical speciality and the firm usually aims to achieve a dominant position in that space, the Speciality Domination model is a reasonable shorthand description of this model.

Like the Life Cycle Exploitation model, the Speciality Domination model offsets smaller potential returns against relatively low risk. Even more than in Life Cycle Exploitation, this risk mitigation arises from both technical and commercial considerations. Technical risk is mitigated by the focus on incremental innovation and commercial risk is mitigated by the focus on a number of products or technologies that share the same customers.

When, as often happens, this focus also releases external synergies, risk is mitigated still further. By external synergies, I mean that a set of externally-oriented resources, such as sales team, market research and marketing communications, which are focused on one customer set, is typically more effective than the same resources spread over multiple, disparate customer groups. If successful, this model offers a high level of fitness, in terms of risk-adjusted return on investment, by offering a relatively lower level of risk, even if the returns involved are relatively small.

The Speciality Domination model is more developed in medical technology, where usage of different products is more closely interconnected, than in pharmaceuticals. Overall, it appears to have emerged less than either the Traditional Blockbuster or Life Cycle Exploitation models but rather more than the Value Fracking model. Again, this is partly explained by the industry's historic ability to create value by exploiting relatively narrow technologies. But Speciality Domination appears to have been less constrained than Value Fracking by the culture of life science companies. This seems to be because it is more congruent with a product led culture than the speciality-spanning Value Fracking model. In addition, the Speciality Domination model is favoured by two market trends: increasing technological connectivity of products within specialities and the marketing and compliance costs involved in managing customers. Done well, Speciality Domination creates value from product connectivity and reduces the costs of compliant marketing.

We might therefore expect the Speciality Domination model to thrive in situations where multiple, related products were used together and where the user group – the community of practice, in academic jargon – was well defined. These two conditions apply more in some parts of the life science market than others, and we do indeed see this model emerging in those areas. Hence the Speciality Domination model is most clearly illustrated in very specialised, relatively self-contained communities of practice, such as in pathology labs, operating departments, cardiology or urology. Roche Centralized Diagnostics is an example in the former area, where they integrate a wide range of diagnostic technologies, along with automation technologies, to create value in this well-defined market. Philips, with very different technologies and customers, adopt a similar model in operating theatres. In single use medical devices, Mallinckrodt in critical care, Boston Scientific in cardiology and Bard in urology, are each attempting to dominate their chosen specialities, although these cases involve both the integration of products and the integration of support around the products.

In all of these cases, the key to the business model is being dominant in the speciality and being a minor player is likely to be an untenable position. This is well illustrated by GE's decision to exit electronic medical records when they failed to achieve a dominant position. In pharmaceutical markets, where the Speciality Domination model is less well developed than in medical technology, we still see it in specialised areas where the Traditional Blockbuster model is less easy to execute. We see it with Baxter in dialysis or Nutricia in clinical nutrition but perhaps more interesting are examples of mainstream pharmaceutical companies attempting to develop the model in some clinical specialities. Novo Nordisk, attempting to carve out a dominant position in a set of conditions related to obesity, is an example of this model emerging from their diabetes business.

Despite their significant visible differences, all of these are these cases have the characteristics of Speciality Domination models. They all involve incremental rather than radical innovation. They all target relatively small, contiguous pockets of value, rather than blockbuster markets, and they are all based on creating value from integration of multiple product technologies with, in some cases, service model innovation too. As different as they appear, they are all Speciality Domination models.

These, and many other examples uncovered in my research, suggest that Speciality Domination is emerging as a common adaptation to market conditions. Like all business model adaptations, it seeks to optimise evolutionary fitness in the form of risk-adjusted rate of return. In areas where discontinuous innovation is becoming harder, riskier and more costly, this model and its three incremental innovation cousins are likely to become more common. The synergies and economies of scope made possible by focusing on a speciality will also drive this model's growth. But, as with the other models, the six great shifts place both negative and positive selection pressures on the Speciality Dominator business model. The value shift creates a strong pressure to release any value available by integrating activity within specialities, just as the Value Fracking model does on a larger scale across healthcare systems. The global shift creates global segments that are likely to be relatively homogeneous at a speciality level, offering economies of scale. This is analogous to what has happened in some specialised information systems, such as Enterprise Resource Planning and Customer Relationship Management, in which the value sought is similar across the globe. The holobiont shift makes it possible to create Speciality Domination without it being necessary to develop or acquire all of the necessary product or technology types in-house. Philips's cooperation with Mount Sinai to develop a digital pathology database is an example of this, as are innumerable examples of in-licensing and joint ventures for technology acquisition. As for the larger scale Value Frackers, the information shift obviously favours those Speciality Domination models in which medical technology is integrated with information technology, as in the Roche Diagnostic Systems example. Similarly, the systeomic shift promises to identify technologies that can be integrated to dominate a speciality. Our growing knowledge of the genetic, lifestyle and microbiome causes of obesity is an example of that. It seems likely in future, for example, that obesity management and treatment of the related metabolic syndrome will depend on integrating diabetes management with knowledge from genomics and the microbiomics, both areas of systems medicine. And the trimorphic shift will favour Speciality Domination models by raising the product performance and barriers to entry in any given speciality, increasing the likelihood that each will become a two or three horse race, as we already see in areas such as cardiology and vaccines.

Like some of the other incremental innovation models, therefore, the Speciality Dominator appears to be generally favoured by the six great shifts. However, if anything, the shifts favour not the emergence of a small number of giant, Multi-Speciality Dominators but two or three for each of a large number of specialities, pointing towards a large number of fundamentally similar business models that focus on different specialities.

A species flock of incremental innovators in the government payer habitat

This part of the life sciences fitness landscape, in which firms compete by innovating and trying to sell that innovation to governments, is the habitat that is most familiar to the majority of today's pharma and life science companies. It is, after all, the habitat that they have been adapting to since the Second World War and, whether or not it is commercially sensible to do so, their deeply embedded and persistent company cultures make them look to this habitat first. More than that, if we look beyond the investor relations spin, we can see that the choice of many, perhaps most, companies is not radical (and hence risky) innovation but instead incremental, relatively low risk innovation. This seems to be a more recent adaptation that began perhaps in the 1980s, following the post-war therapeutic revolution. We shouldn't judge this choice too harshly. Even if it does not sound as glamorous as radical, discontinuous innovation, the prevalence of this evo-lutionary choice to avoid risk tells us something important: it is a good way to increase fitness, or at least it has been in the recent evolutionary history of the sector. As we have discussed in the preceding sections, incremental innovation can be used to exploit larger, newer markets or smaller, adjacent markets and by using single technologies or by com-bining technologies. Each of these sets of evolutionary choices confer levels of risk and return that vary with the market situation and, for any given combination of firm and market context, one of these is the optimum choice. That is to say, one of them optimises risk-adjusted rate of return.

These optimising choices within incremental innovation are leading to the evolution of four species we have discussed so far. In their similarities and differences, they are analo-gous to what biologists call a species flock or species complex – a number of similar spe-cies living in the same habitat but employing different traits to optimise their fitness. These complexes of species are often found in nature – in bird populations, for example, where it is thought that their complementary mixture of behaviours might help to construct their own ecological niche. It is not hard to see an analogous niche construction mechanism in the life science industry. Within one habitat, the range of similar but different business models helps exploit both large and small markets and both simple and complex technolo-gies. Hence, it offers investors a wide range of risk and return options. Looked at from that perspective, a species flock of business models appears to be a much better way of exploit-ing the environment than a single species, no matter how well that species is adapted. As industries evolve we should then expect to see species flocks of business models emerge to fit the environment better and so displace single dominant species.

The 'species flock as habitat shaper' is another biological analogue that helps us to understand what is happening in the life sciences industry. From our discussion of the technological innovator/government payer habitat, we can see a pattern of these four different species emerging in response to the selection pressures created by the six great shifts. The Traditional Blockbuster, the most dominant form currently, would seem to be in relative decline. Whilst we can always point to successful examples of this model, the relative dominance of the blockbusters based on incremental innovation – Nexium or Lipitor in pharmaceuticals, for example, or Opsite, Vicryl or Adapta in medical devices – appears to be in decline. This is what we would expect, given the role of the six great shifts as selection pressures on this model discussed earlier. Those same selection pressures also explain the relative increase in Life Cycle Exploitation models, as can be seen in Johnson & Johnson's recent plans for no fewer than twenty-five line extensions compared to ten new product applications. This trend is even more pronounced in medical technology, where 510(k) applications (which claim equivalence to an existing product) are far more common than regulatory applications for wholly new technology. We can also see the increasing relative importance of the technology integrating models of Value Fracking and Speciality Dominator. This is most obvious in device/IT integration but, as discussed earlier, we can also see it in the combination of technologies around specialities.

My work suggests, then, that the six great shifts are acting on the technological inno-vator/government habitat to favour the emergence of four business models, based on

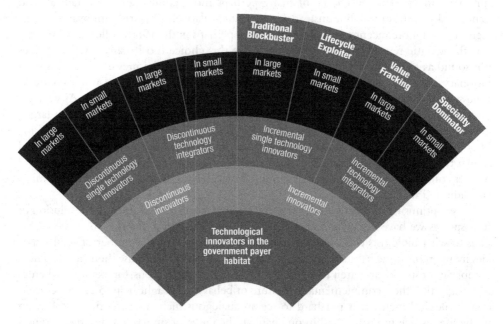

Figure 15.2 The emergence of incremental innovator models in the government payer habitat

incremental innovation, as summarised in Figure 15.2 and Figure 15.3. In the next part of our discussion, I will look at the parallel emergence of business models when firms make the riskier, higher return discontinuous innovation choice.

Discontinuous innovators

Despite their different evolutionary choices, incremental and discontinuous innovators share the same goal. They are both attempting to optimise their evolutionary fitness via some combination of reducing risk and maximising return. The difference between the two approaches lies in the trade off they choose. The evolutionary strategy of discontinuous innovators is a bet that higher return will more than offset higher risks compared to the less risky incremental innovation made by their more cautious competitors. This is a reasonable belief; innovating in big, bold steps in unfamiliar areas with poorly understood science may be less likely to succeed but when it does it is more likely to create distinctive, differentiated value and commensurately high returns. Furthermore, complementing these higher returns, the organisation is also more likely to create spin-off benefits as it develops fundamental capabilities, establishes a strong reputation and so creates a more sustainable competitive advantage. Just as the four incremental innovation models described earlier choose a lesser level of technological risk, all of the discontinuous innovators choose to take a relatively higher risk. That is not to imply that these four models are identical because, like their incremental cousins, they vary in their choice of target market size and technology focus. As with the incremental innovators species flock, this leads us to the prediction of four different kinds of discontinuous innovators, shown in Figure 15.1. We will examine these in this section, but first it's worth considering some historical context to this evolutionary choice.

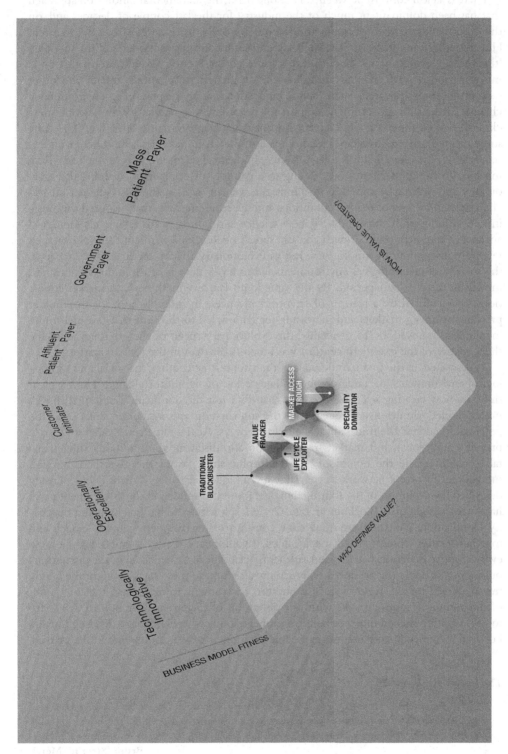

Figure 15.3 The emerging fitness landscape of incremental innovator models in the government payer habitat

There is a clear contrast between, on the one hand, the incremental innovation approach that has been dominant in much of the industry for the last couple of decades and, on the other hand, the discontinuous innovation approach that emerges from the research. However, there are many similarities between the discontinuous model and the so-called 'therapeutic revolution' in the period that followed the Second World War. In that optimistic period, a wave of innovations such as antihypertensive, antidepressant and other new drug classes appeared. Such radical innovation was an adaptation to environmental changes of the time: government support for research, loose regulatory frameworks, new clinical trials methodology and advances in pharmacology, to name but a few. The same surge of innovative technology, based on electronics, materials science and better understanding of physiology, led to similar advances in medical technology, from the heart–lung machine to the modern wound dressing to a panoply of implants in orthopaedics, cardiology and other specialities. With hindsight, we can see that the post-war period was characterised by a set of market conditions and selection pressures that favoured this surge in radical innovation. Not only did new science and unmet needs favour technological advances, rapid economic growth and the spread of socialised medicine also encouraged relatively discontinuous innovation. Just as evolutionary theory predicts, this change in the social and technological environments led to an evolution of the industry's business models in the post-war period. By the same logic, late twentieth century market conditions, characterised by a plateau of scientific advances, an intensification of shareholder pressure, maturing markets and increasing regulation, led to the shift that favoured more incremental innovation. To generalise, the evolutionary speed of the life sciences in the third quarter of the twentieth century was much faster than in the fourth quarter.

As described, in the first two decades of the twenty-first century, the social and technological environments are undergoing another period of significant change. The six great shifts are now creating selection pressures that disfavour the dominant Traditional Blockbuster model. Unmet needs remain but the information and systeomic shifts offer the potential to address them in radically innovative ways. At the same time, value shift price pressures and global shift market fragmentation also disfavour the traditional, incremental blockbuster, and the holobiont and trimorphic shifts favour the growth of business models that involve a network of specialised, symbiotic networks of firms. I have already described the evolution of the four incremental innovator models in the government payer habitat: the Traditional Blockbuster, Life Cycle Exploitation, Value Fracking and Speciality Domination. But these are quite close cousins to later twentieth century models and together form a closely related species flock. Evolutionary theory predicts that, because every adaptive direction will be tried, further speciation can be expected in the discontinuous innovator direction. So now I will turn my attention to the other branch of the family tree predicted for the technological innovator/government payer habitat, the four kinds of discontinuous innovator. As with our discussion of incremental innovators, I will try to avoid getting sucked into a semantic argument about where the fuzzy dividing line lies between incremental and discontinuous and focus on what we can observe in the market.

The Budget Buster model

We've seen the rise of companies focused on a single therapy area, such as Celgene and Gilead, and now we're seeing that level of focus arise in previously more disparate companies, as with GSK and Novartis's asset swap. It a corollary of the research intensiveness needed at the leading edge of fields such as oncology and virology.
Bruno Strigini, Merck

This discontinuous innovation approach is characterised by a focus on a large market with the potential for large returns and corresponding likelihood of intense competition. But it is also marked by a focus on a single technology that is a discontinuous step from current knowledge, which somewhat mitigates the threat of competition. If it is successful, this model offers high fitness by creating a very large numerator (return) whilst accepting a substantial denominator (risk) in the risk-adjusted rate of return calculation.

When we look for the emergence of this model, we need to be careful. We shouldn't expect the evidence to be as clear for this new model, resulting from very recent pressures, as it is for the Traditional Blockbuster model, which emerged in the last thirty or forty years. We also have to be careful to distinguish the fuzzy boundary between incremental and discontinuous innovation. Even with those caveats, we can see clear signs of the model being well on the way to emergence as a distinct entity. This is most obvious in some areas of pharmaceuticals, where large biological molecules are displacing small molecule therapies. AbbVie's Humira was an obvious early example of this model, both as a discontinuous innovation and a very large market (rheumatoid arthritis). But, in the future, Humira is likely to be seen as a mere harbinger of many more developments in this field. Merck, Bristol-Myers Squibb and others immunotherapy in oncology; Amgen, Regeneron and others with PCSK9 therapies for cardiology; Biogen and others in multiple sclerosis – all are companies that have taken the high risk/high return choice. And although biologics are the most prominent example of discontinuous, single technology pharmaceutical innovation, there are others, such as Pfizer's work on antibody drug conjugates, that are also better described as discontinuous rather than incremental innovations.

The Budget Buster model is less fully emerged in medical technology. This is partly due to less direct impact of the systeomic shift in this area but also the result of medtech firms' tradition of incremental innovation. However, examples of discontinuous, single technology focus are visible in the most advanced areas of medical technology. Myriad Genetics RNA-expression Prolaris test is a discontinuous advance from conventional pathology in the huge market for prostate cancer detection. GSK's investment in neuromodulation, with applications in epilepsy and other conditions, is another example meeting the same criteria. The same company is also considering applications in asthma and diabetes. At an earlier, pre-market stage of evolution, molecular diagnostics, nanotechnology and attempts to develop synthetic body parts such as the cornea and pancreas are all signs of this new, more innovative model emerging. As different as these businesses appear, they all involve discontinuous innovation aimed at large markets. They all represent the same kind of evolutionary high risk/high return strategy.

The principal characteristics of this model – discontinuous technology, large markets, significant advances over existing approaches – combine to create another defining feature that is common to most, if not all examples of this model: their impact on budgets is often enormous. The cost of developing such products, the need for risk-justifying returns and the application to large patient numbers add up to budget impacts that are, in many cases, quite staggering. In addition, the high level of differentiation implied by a successful model of this type reduces direct competition and hence price pressure. Often, this model delivers patient benefits that easily justify the cost at an individual patient level, but this still leaves the issue of enormous budgetary implications at a population health level. It is some comfort for a payer or government health department to know that their patients are receiving better treatment for multiple sclerosis or some form of cancer than ever before. But the payer also has to face the issue that, as the costs of new, innovative diagnostics and therapies combine with large patient numbers, they create the dilemma of rationing care or ignoring budget restrictions. It is for this reason that I label this model the Budget Buster model.

As with all other business models, the six great shifts create selection pressures that favour and disfavour the Budget Buster model. The systeomic shift favours it by creating a torrent of new knowledge that is the ultimate and necessary foundation of this model. The information shift does the same, including by creating enabling technologies in research and development. The trimorphic and holobiont shifts enable firms to exploit this advanced knowledge by removing the need to build the necessary organisational capabilities from scratch but also by sharing some of the risk involved. The global shift creates global segments in both developed market and in emerging markets for this model to exploit. The only negative selection pressure is the value shift, which disfavours more expensive treatments. In particular, the value shift selects against variants of this model have a net negative impact on treatment costs. The value shift also fragments the market according to how value is perceived, assessed and compared to other approaches. Such fragmentation creates the need for Budget Buster models to understand and manage this payer complexity. Overall though, the selection pressures seem to favour those variants of the Budget Buster model that can demonstrate health economic value against the heterogeneous standards of fragmented national payers.

The Obligation Exploitation model

In rare diseases and similar cases, there is something like a moral obligation, a solidarity within society. Society looks at these unfortunate people whose lives have been severely damaged and, rightly, does not apply the same judgement criteria as it does for larger scale but less debilitating conditions.

Per-Olof Attinger, Roche

Like the Budget Buster model, this approach is characterised by discontinuous innovation in a focused area of new technology. Where it differs from the Budget Buster is that it focuses on relatively small markets. This would seem to be a poor adaptive choice; high investment for smaller returns would normally lead to low evolutionary fitness. But closer examination of this model reveals that, as Orgel said, evolution is very clever. First, discontinuous innovation offers greater benefits, differentiation and hence margins. Second, the choice of smaller market offers reduced competitive intensity, reinforcing the margin advantage of this choice. These are adaptive advantages we have already seen in the Life Cycle Exploitation model. But finally and perhaps most significantly, this adaptation offers some particular advantages arising from the nature of the market chosen. In the Obligation Exploitation model, the chosen market is typically one where the clinical need is compelling and often highly emotive. Consequently, the societal pressures to meet those needs are disproportionately high. The combination of patient groups, media attention and political pressures leads to some conditions being regarded as more worthy of healthcare budget than others. These societal pressures lead to the development of specific, anomalous market conditions that allow higher prices and sometimes lower costs. For example, different market access conditions and lower regulatory hurdles often characterise these markets. This model relies on the exploitation of society's sense of moral obligation, some might say guilt, in a way that is quite different from other models – hence the Obligation Exploitation label I have applied to it. Like the other models, the Obligation Exploitation model is an adaptation to optimise risk-adjusted return on investment. When successful, it leads to evolutionary fitness by extracting unusually high returns from a relatively small market, by adaptation to market conditions that are determined socially, politically and emotively, rather than economically and rationally.

When we look at the data we see the Obligation Exploitation model thriving as expected in market conditions where social obligation is high. Typically, these conditions include significant, often distressing, unmet clinical need in a population that is seen as especially deserving and is so small that it can be treated as economically exceptional. These conditions lead via political processes to the favourable market conditions, such as support for development, willingness to fund at a higher level or unusual ease of regulatory access, in which the Obligation Exploitation model thrives. Typically, we see such conditions only in relatively small, specialised markets in developed countries or in grossly underserved markets in developing countries. For example, the US Centers for Disease Control and Prevention classes Ebola as a rare disease. However, the most obvious and established examples of the Obligation Exploitation model are in the pharmaceutical categories known as orphan drugs or rare diseases. Once a tiny, neglected area, legal changes mean that the category now extends to 468 indications and 373 approved drugs. As a result, this model is spreading from rare disease specialist companies, such as Shire, Sobi and Recordati, to be the model for divisions of larger pharmaceutical companies. We see this exemplified in companies like Sanofi via its acquisition of Genzyme, and Roche via its acquisition of Genentech. The Obligation Exploitation model is perhaps less prominent in medical technology, but that is not to say it does not exist. The market conditions still apply although the innovation is generally less radical than in pharmaceuticals, which is consistent with the traditions and culture of medtech. For example, Synthes markets a device, the VEPTR, for babies with congenital deformities that prevent normal breathing. In a direct analogue with the Orphan Drug Act, the VEPTR was approved under the FDA's Humanitarian Device Exemption programme. Kaneka's Liposorber system, intended for children with primary focal segmental glomerulosclerosis (FSGS) is another example of the Obligation Exploitation model in medtech. Perhaps the most salient example is in interventional radiology, where discontinuous innovation in robotics is transforming procedures in this specialism. This does not seem to be an example of exploiting obligations until one recognises that, in this case, the obligation is to healthcare professionals rather than the patient. Robotic systems like Hansen's Magellan greatly reduce their exposure to radiation and our society's view of safety issues, along with our litigious environment, create exactly the conditions for this model to be viable.

It would be easy to see Obligation Exploitation models as essentially niche and commercially less attractive than their much larger volume Budget Buster cousins. But that would be to miss the point. A business model creating a high risk-adjusted return on investment in a relatively small market is more viable and sustainable than one creating a meagre risk-adjusted return in a large market. Besides, the combination of high margins and, in some cases, quite significant global volume, makes many Obligation Exploitation models far from small in absolute terms. In addition, some variants of this model, like Hansen's, have the ability to spread risk and extract return from multiple niches that share similar needs and utilise the same intellectual property assets.

As with all other models, the six great shifts apply positive and negative selection pressures to the Obligation Exploitation model. The systeomic and information shifts favour it, as these shifts provide the knowledge and enabling technology upon which the model is dependent. The trimorphic shift favours the required research intensity and the holobiont shift allows firms to spread risk and acquire new capabilities easily through partners. The global shift spreads the cultural values that create societal obligations and creates global segments beyond developed markets. The value shift is the only one that would appear to disfavour Obligation Exploitation. But this is where we see how clever evolution is and the wisdom of Orgel's words. On closer consideration, we can see that this model is an adaptation intended to negate, or at least mitigate, the value shift by 'trumping' economic factors with moral, political and social considerations. By finding markets where the value shift is less relevant, this model is analogous to an animal that has learned to survive in the fierce desert sun by living underground. Looking at the sum of the selection pressures, the Obligation Exploitation model can be seen as strongly favoured by the six great shifts, which of course explains why it is thriving.

The Secular Grail model

> One of the big shifts we see is that from purely product innovation to procedural innovation. Surgery has to move more towards a centre of excellence model, where procedures are standardised and optimised, more like pit crews than artists. That's a major shift we see.
>
> **Kevin Lobo, Stryker**

In our consideration of business models emerging in the technological innovator/government payer habitat, we have so far looked at six quite different approaches, varying in the continuity of their innovation, the nature of the target markets and the scope of their technological focus. As different as they are, these models share a common feature: they are limited in their ambitions. The Traditional Blockbuster, the Life Cycle Exploitation, the Budget Buster and the Obligation Exploitation share a narrow technological focus. The Value Fracking and the Speciality Domination models, both technology integrators, have a wider technological focus, but are limited to incremental innovation and, in the latter case, relatively smaller markets. When we look for the emergence of a model without any of these limitations, a model that achieves evolutionary fitness through discontinuous innovation across multiple technologies applied to large markets, we are looking for a model of much greater ambitions. Such a model would, if successful, create very high risk-adjusted return on investment and we might expect it to dominate and transform the market. The Secular Grail label I have given this model, prompted by the Arthurian legend, would seem to fit both its desirability and the difficulty in finding it.

It seems fair to say that this model has not yet fully emerged in the life sciences sector. As with the other technology integrator models this is because, in part at least, the industry has historically been able to create value by exploiting relatively narrow, self-contained technologies. As a result, organisational structures have been relative siloed along product lines. Even in firms like Johnson & Johnson, where multiple technologies are exploited, technology silos remain strong. Product led, rather than market led, cultures also play a part in hindering the emergence of the Secular Grail model. But the 'pull' of latent value (to both the customer and supplying company) and the 'push' of new technologies are slowly leading, if not to the emergence of this model, then to the early signs of its antecedents. In the diabetes market, for example, Lilly and others are experimenting with combining information technology, drug delivery technology and pharmaceutical technology to continuously monitor blood sugar and manage insulin levels. Novo Nordisk and IBM are combining AI and pharmaceuticals in the same market. A huge market, addressed by integrating several technologies in a discontinuous manner, these are the sort of things we might expect to lead to the Secular Grail model. In medical devices, we can see an analogous adaptation by Stryker who acquired Mako for its robotic technology. Stryker sees robotics as a 'game changer' in the orthopaedics market, which is otherwise at risk of commoditisation and price pressure. Again, it is a very large market being addressed by discontinuous innovation that integrates different technologies.

However, perhaps the largest and most obvious example lies in the combination of pharmaceutical therapies with diagnostic technologies – companion diagnostics, as the field has become known. This began with Roche's Herceptin in breast cancer in 1998, and Novartis's Gleevec is the other notable example. But the field has grown rapidly to include many therapeutic areas and, looking at products in the pipeline, its growth looks set to continue (169, 170). More recently, the FDA approved a companion diagnostic genetic test to select patients with metastatic colorectal cancer for treatment with the drug Vectibix. Most frequently, the Secular Grail model is conflated with the whole idea of personalised or stratified medicine, but that conflation unhelpfully narrows our understanding of this model. Drug/diagnostic combinations, robotic orthopaedics and continuous management of insulin are all examples of integrating technologies to create discontinuous innovation and release the value in large markets. They represent at least early forms of a Secular Grail business model.

Superficially, we might wonder why the Secular Grail model has not emerged further and faster than it has. But it takes only a little thought to see the simultaneous difficulties involved. To do so requires the development of discontinuous technology, its integration with other technologies (that may also be novel) and commercialising these in a large market, in the face of many (often low cost) incumbents. This combination of factors creates a high level of risk that, to be viable, must be offset by a very large return. We might, therefore, see it emerging in areas where the market need is very large and current approaches are far from ideal. In particular, we should expect to see the Secular Grail model emerge where the value is found less in the core product (the drug, the device or the diagnostic test, for example) than in the gaps or connections in their use. This is exactly what our limited examples suggest. In large part, the challenges of managing diabetes lie not in the effectiveness of the monitoring or treatment per se but in fitting these into real life. It is increasingly hard to improve orthopaedic implants significantly, but there is much benefit to be found in improving their implantation procedure. The nature of many diseases, especially many cancers, means that improving the effectiveness of treatment across an entire population is near impossible but improved targeting of treatments promises better outcomes, both clinically and economically.

Looking for the emergence of the Secular Grail model is reminiscent of those archaeologists who, on their hands and knees, crawl over the East African rift valley looking for evidence of the early hominids who presaged the evolution of *Homo Sapiens*. Just as they find bone fragments that indicate a larger skull or an upright posture but associated with older, ape-like characteristics, our evidence suggests parts of a business model that is not yet fully evolved. As important as companion diagnostics are, for example, we are still at the beginning of a journey where drugs are prescribed only to patients that we know will benefit, rather than those we hope will benefit. We are even less far along the evolutionary path of releasing value by eliminating user error or improving patient compliance. But the early signs we *can* see suggest that the fully-developed Secular Grail model where we combine multiple discontinuous technologies to release significant value from huge markets will be as large an advance on our current business models as you readers are upon your Australopithecine ancestors!

The potential fitness of the Secular Grail model lies in releasing large amounts of value (and so revenue) by virtue of greatly improved outcomes across a large market. If it works, models of this type create enough return to offset the relatively high capital at risk when developing them and bringing them to market. But, as with the other models, the six great shifts place both negative and positive selection pressures on this business model. The effect of these pressures is similar to that on the Value Fracking model but applied to larger markets. For example, the value shift creates a strong pressure to release the value found in the connectivity of diagnosis, treatment and management. The global shift will both extend target segments from the developed world but also, potentially, open up clinical segments based on racial genotypes (such as in sickle cell anaemia) or regionally dominant diseases, such a malaria. The global shift again provides the opportunity of emerging markets that wish to leapfrog inefficient western healthcare systems and design more effective systems from scratch but via more discontinuous innovation than Value Fracking models. The holobiont shift favours the Secular Grail model, perhaps even more than the Value Fracker, because it makes it possible to access a wider range of technologies and reduces innovation barriers for firms that are tightly focused on a single technology class.

The cooperation between drug and diagnostic companies is an example of this, as is the cooperation between drug companies and IT companies. However, the most intriguing holobionts of all are being formed by new entrants into health – Qualcomm, 23andMe and various mobile telecoms companies fall into this category. The information shift favours such new entrants and the formation of holobionts that include IT players. The systeomic shift is perhaps the most powerful pressure acting on the Secular Grail model, favouring the use of systeomic medicine based on bioinformatics, genomics and so on. And the trimorphic shift, in which differently-focused companies either provide new technologies to integrate or drive down the costs of the component technology, also favours the Secular Grail model, just as it favours Value Fracking models but perhaps playing an even more important role by enabling discontinuous innovation.

The Secular Grail model, then, appears for the most part to be favoured by the six great shifts, which is why we see its emergence in the face of huge technical difficulty and business risk. However, the shifts seem to favour models that overcome those barriers by holobiont building and focusing on large markets with latent, interstitial value.

The Market Creator model

> *The final approval of Glybera marks a major step forward in making gene therapies available . . . for a large number of rare diseases with very high unmet medical need. It is a fair price to pay for a therapy that restores body function and is not just a short-term fix.*
>
> **Jörn Aldag, uniQure**

Like the Budget Buster, Obligation Exploitation and Secular Grail models, the Market Creator model is characterised by the choice to attempt discontinuous rather than incremental innovation. Like the Obligation Exploitation model, but unlike the Budget Buster and Secular Grail models, it also chooses to exploit relatively smaller market opportunities. However, it differs from the Obligation Exploitation model in that the value it seeks to create comes from a combination of otherwise distinct technologies rather than focusing on one technology. Like Speciality Domination, the Market Creator business model releases value that is inaccessible to single product or single technology approaches by addressing connected needs. In doing so, it typically falls outside existing product categories and exploits opportunities that were previously latent and unexploited. For that reason, I have given it the Market Creator label.

Like the Obligation Exploitation model, superficially the Market Creator appears to be a mistake, a choice in the direction of *reduced* evolutionary fitness. The combination of discontinuous innovation across more than one technology implies high risk. The choice of relatively small markets implies lower returns. The choice to reduce the numerator and increase the denominator in the risk/return calculation seems counter intuitive. But, like the Obligation Exploitation model, the Market Creator illustrates the truth of Orgel's Second Law. First, discontinuous innovation that releases latent value offers greater differentiation and hence margins. Second, the choice of smaller market offers reduced competitive intensity, reinforcing the margin advantage of this choice. These are adaptive advantages we have already seen in the Life Cycle Exploitation and Obligation Exploitation models. In some cases, the Market Creator model may also exploit some of the latter's societal pressure advantages. But perhaps the most important advantage the Market Creator model has is that, if executed appropriately, the combination of discontinuous innovation across technologies may create the high barriers to entry that lead to a niche market. Niche is a much abused word but, in this case, I use it to mean a market that has high barriers to entry, relative to market size, making it not worth the effort for a market follower.

Like all other models, the Market Creator model is an adaptation to optimise risk-adjusted return on investment. When successful, it leads to evolutionary fitness by extracting unusually high returns from a relatively small market by releasing value from the connection of unmet needs that are both economically and, sometimes, socially determined. In that sense, it combines the characteristics of both the Speciality Dominator and the Obligation Exploiter.

This view of the Market Creator suggests two things. First, we should see it being slower to emerge than technically easier and lower risk models. Second, we should see it emerge first in areas of high unmet need, perhaps with social obligation, where small market volumes allow very high prices to be tolerated by payers and where only integrated technologies can address that need. As with its single technology focus cousin, the Obligation Exploitation model, we usually see such conditions only in relatively small, specialised markets in developed countries. The most obvious example of a Market Creator model is gene therapy, a leading example of which is the Chiesi/uniQure product Glybera for lipoprotein lipase deficiency. Other examples are likely to emerge in the near future for SCID (severe combined immune deficiency) and perhaps even HIV and haemophilia. The characteristic thing about gene therapy (and the related germ line therapy) is that it combines multiple technologies in a discontinuous manner. Genomic screening, viral vectors and even complex supply chain technologies are all necessary to implement the treatment. Although the details of the technologies involved differ somewhat, cell therapy, particularly stem cell therapy, also fits this model of combining multiple technologies in a disruptive, discontinuous manner. Holocar, approved in 2015 for blindness due to burning and also marketed by Chiesi, is an example of such a model. Such leading edge, almost science fiction, therapies also hint at another characteristic of the Market Creator model – increasingly, they blur our traditional sector definitions of pharmaceuticals, medical technology and biotechnology that we have used for decades.

This is also well illustrated in the application of nanotechnology, where it is being applied to drug delivery, diagnostics and imaging. Similarly, additive or 3D printing applied to medical devices combines technologies to create tailor made implants, 3D printed pills with patient-specific active ingredients and replacement body parts in cases of trauma are all Market Creators. The superficial differences between these businesses – from gene therapy to personalised replacement noses – disguise their important underlying similarities as business models. They each use discontinuous innovation, woven together from several technologies, to create value in a relatively small market. In doing so, they create, or hope to create, a numerator of unusually high returns that more than compensates for the high denominator of risk involved. As different as the technologies and applications are, these disparate businesses are making similar choices to optimise evolutionary fitness.

As with the Obligation Exploitation model, it would be easy to see the Market Creator model as essentially niche and commercially less attractive than the much larger volume Budget Buster and Secular Grail models. But that would miss the point. A business model creating a high risk-adjusted return on investment in a relatively small market can be a viable one and will emerge if the selection pressures favour it in that market context. Despite the specialised target markets, those conditions may include significant global volume. In addition, some variants of this model, such as 3M's investment in drug delivery nanotechnology, have the ability to spread risk and extract return across multiple niches that share similar needs and utilise the same intellectual property assets.

As with the other models, the six great shifts apply both positive and negative selection pressures to the Market Creator model. It is the systeomic and information shifts that favour Market Creators most, by providing the knowledge and enabling technology upon which the model is dependent. The trimorphic shift allows the research intensity, and the holobiont shift the risk-spreading and new capabilities that all of the discontinuous models require, although they also disfavour the single company, non-holobiont Market Creator. The global shift creates global segments beyond developed markets that may make a clinical indication viable but also make globalisation essential. The value shift disfavours high prices and reduces the influence of clinicians in selecting products. But even the value shift may favour the Market Creator model if the perceived unmet need and the value created by the model are sufficiently high. Furthermore, the smaller volume of these markets and, in some cases, societal pressures allows them some protection from value shift, compared to the Budget Buster and Traditional Blockbuster models, which attract most payers' attention.

The Market Creator model therefore looks set, as the six great shifts gradually select for its traits, to be favoured by the changing environment, which is why we see its gradual emergence in the face of great technical difficulty and business risk. However, as with the Secular Grail, the shifts seem to particularly favour those models that adjust to the selection pressures by holobiont building, focusing on unusually large returns and high barriers to entry and of course doing so on a global basis.

A species flock of discontinuous innovators in the government payer habitat

I am still exploring the habitat that is familiar to most of today's pharma and life science companies: that part of the landscape where firms compete by innovating and trying to sell innovation to governments buying on behalf of their citizens. This is the habitat that most companies have adapted to in the last seventy years or so and, in doing so, they have developed company cultures that are, in Peter Drucker's words, persistent and pervasive. But unlike the incremental innovators, the four adaptive strategies I have just described each involve a choice of more radical, discontinuous innovation. Again, we need to look beyond the investor relations spin of incremental innovators to appreciate that what the Budget Buster, Secular Grail, Obligation Exploitation and Market Creator models are

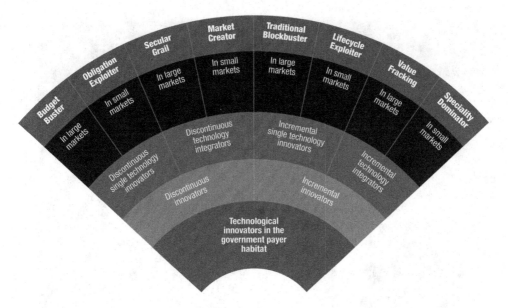

Figure 15.4 The emergence of discontinuous innovator models in the government payer habitat

doing amounts to truly discontinuous innovation, analogous to the great therapeutic revolution of the 1940s and 1950s. Interestingly, these four models are emerging in both large and small companies, in pharmaceuticals, medical technology and all other parts of the innovators' habitat. Their varied choices of how and where to be discontinuous innovators each have different levels of risk and return and, for any given firm and market context, one of these choices is the optimum. That is to say that, in any part of the technological innovator/government payer habitat, one of these models optimises risk-adjusted rate of return and evolutionary fitness.

The selection by the market environment of these choices within discontinuous innovation is leading to the evolution of four species we have discussed as summarised in Figure 15.4 and Figure 15.5.

Just as with their incremental cousins, the similarities and differences between discontinuous innovators mean that they are a species flock or species complex – a number of similar species living in the same habitat but employing different traits to optimise their fitness. As we have discussed, their complementary mixture of behaviours can be seen as helping to construct their own ecological niche. Combined with incremental innovator models, this range of discontinuous innovator business models helps to exploit large and small markets, simple and complex technologies and offers investors a complete range of risk and return options to suit their appetite. This means that, together, two flocks of discontinuous and incremental innovator species are a much better way of exploiting the government payer habitat via technological innovation than a single species or even single flock. Looked at as whole, our evidence and examples point to these two species flocks emerging to both shape and exploit the technological innovator/government payer habitat, as summarised in Figure 15.6.

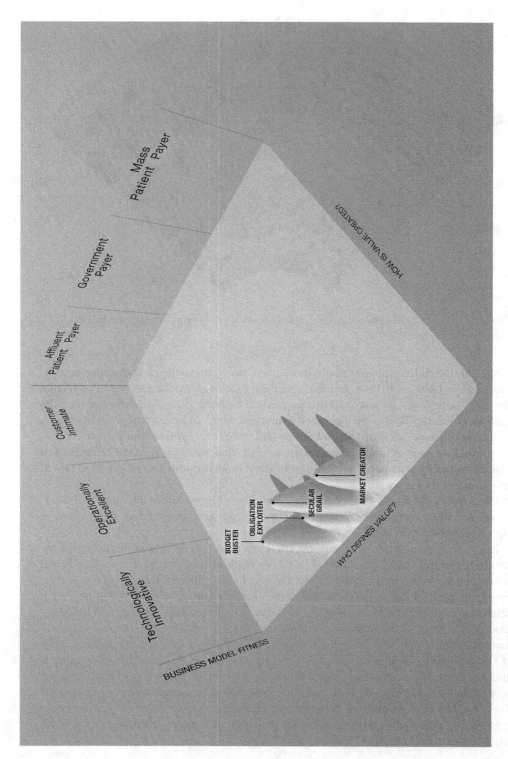

Figure 15.5 The emerging fitness landscape of discontinuous innovator models in the government payer habitat

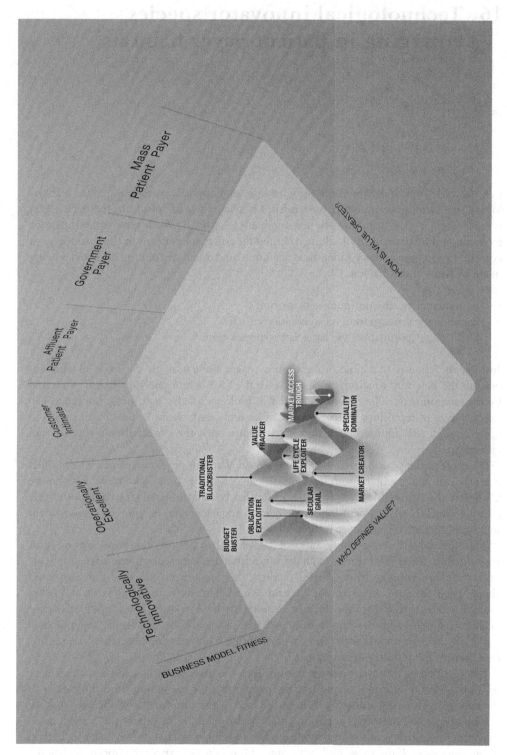

Figure 15.6 The emerging fitness landscape of incremental and discontinuous innovator models in the government payer habitat

16 Technological innovator species emerging in patient payer habitats

In Chapter 15, which discussed the eight business models that are emerging in the techno-logical innovator/government payer habitat, I restricted my discussion to the habitat that is most familiar to existing life science companies – that in which governments pay for technological innovation. By looking carefully for emergent patterns in the cacophony of companies' strategic choices, I identified the three fundamental evolutionary choices being made by firms in this habitat:

• Incremental vs. discontinuous innovation
• Technological integration vs. technology focus
• Small target population vs. large target population

Just like the 'choices' that biological evolution makes, these strategic decisions all represent bets on the best way to survive and thrive in the face of the selection pressures created by the environment. The difference is that in biology 'survive and thrive' means to live long enough to reproduce so that genes can be replicated, whilst in business it means to make enough risk-adjusted return on investment so that the organisational routines can be replicated.

For most of the period since the Second World War, this government payer habitat has been the one about which innovative life science companies have cared most. Even in the US before the Affordable Care Act, the market has been dominated by payer systems that are either directly government funded (Medicare and Medicaid) or indirectly government supported (private or employer insurance).

This focus has been entirely rational because, directly or otherwise, governments accounted for the large majority of all the innovative medicines, diagnostic tests and medi-cal technology bought. In developed markets, this remains largely true but this hasn't always been the case. Prior to the Second World War, most drugs, devices and other medical products were paid for directly or indirectly by the patient. It was only socialised healthcare systems and mass health insurance that changed that. Even today, self-purchase (especially in emerging markets) and co-payment (in many developed markets) are signifi-cant parts of the industry environment.

As described in Chapter 6, in the period since the emergence of a life sciences indus-try in the second industrial revolution, the principal payer has swung from the patient to institutions such as governments. But, in the face of the transformative changes that we can observe in the industry's environment, it would be naïve to expect the current over-whelming dominance of the institutional payer to remain unchanged. As we touched on in our discussion of the value shift in Chapter 11, we should expect the importance of the patient payer (or payer influencer) to grow in both developed and developing markets. It would be easy, especially for firms well adapted to the government payer environment, to mistake patient power as a secondary issue. That would be a mistake, and it is worth taking a moment to consider why the patient payer is an emerging property of our complex adaptive healthcare system, an inevitable and inexorable consequence of the six great shifts in the social and technological environments.

The patient payer gap

> *One major theme is the consumerisation of healthcare. Ten years ago, if you asked someone which knee replacement they received, they would have had no idea. They didn't care because they weren't paying. But as soon as they start putting their own money towards something, they suddenly care a lot. Speaking to the patients is going to be massively important in the future. It's early days but it's going to spread and be everywhere in the world.*

Kevin Lobo, Stryker

Consider for a moment the big picture of what is happening in the technological environment. Developments which we discussed under the systeomic, information and tri-morphic shifts in Part 2 are expanding what is technologically possible at an almost dizzyingly rapid rate. We take for granted that today's diagnostics, medicines, devices and other medical technologies allow us to diagnose, treat, cure and manage many more conditions than we could in even the recent past. Even so, all the indications are that today's technological possibilities are less than those of tomorrow. This expansion in technological capability, combined with demand expansion created by demographics and lifestyles, means that, if resources permitted, the amount of money governments could spend on healthcare is growing at an enormous rate and has no conceivable boundaries. As far as my research has been able to find, no-one has estimated this notional and elastic growth rate; it would be extremely difficult to do so with any accuracy. But considering both the demand side and supply side factors strongly suggests that the growth rate of possible spend is surely in double percentage figures. As the industry and its environment co-evolve, the amount of healthcare it will be possible to buy (if resources allow) will be almost limitless.

Consider next what is happening in the social environment, especially the economic and political areas. Developments here, discussed in the value and global shifts in Part 2, are constraining the amount of money that governments and other payers have available to spend on healthcare. That growth in healthcare spending is limited by four principal factors:

- The growth rate of national economies,
- The political ability of governments to raise taxes from those economies,
- The other, non-healthcare demands on government spending,
- Governments' political willingness to allocate money to healthcare.

As a result of the combination of these and other factors, the increases in nominal healthcare spending per head is rising at about 4 percent per annum, albeit with large inter-country variations. Even if we make conservative assumptions about the growth in potential healthcare spending and optimistic assumptions about future government health spending, there is a large difference between the two. What governments can spend will grow more slowly, perhaps much more slowly, than the expansion in the healthcare that governments could buy if their resources allowed.

This disparity between what governments could buy and what they can afford to buy creates a latent market: healthcare that people want but which their government cannot or will not provide for them. This gap between clinical needs and technological possibilities on the one hand and economic feasibility on the other is growing as a fast growth rate in the former outpaces the slow growth of the latter. To this latent market we can introduce other elements of the environment that I have already discussed: the growing inequalities of wealth, the decline in deference for governments and healthcare professionals, the availability of information, the growth of e-commerce, the ease of physical travel and other factors. Together, these both oblige and enable patients and their families to purchase their own healthcare outside the government payer habitat. Consequently, it becomes more likely that this latent market is transformed into an actual one, where patient payers (or carer-payers) become significant purchasers of the diagnostics, therapeutics and medical technology for which their governments cannot or will not pay. This is illustrated in Figure 16.1.

If governments and other institutions have to make choices between what they will and will not pay for, what will those choices be? The choices will obviously vary greatly between contexts and be subject to all kinds of political and often irrational influences. But, at a high level, it is not difficult to anticipate the healthcare needs that governments will refuse to fund or will demand that patients contribute to. Indeed past and current practice suggests that these unfunded needs will fall into a hierarchy. First, technology that enhances beauty or non-essential physical performance is likely to be among

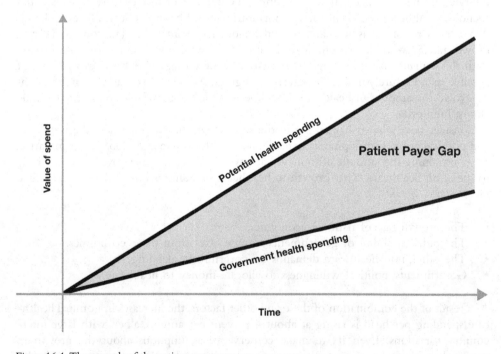

Figure 16.1 The growth of the patient payer gap

the first to sit outside the government payer habitat, as we see already with areas like cosmetic surgery and some sports medicine. Then, as pressure on government budgets grows, we can expect to see the restriction of spending on medical technologies and therapies that offer benefits only in convenience or aesthetics, as we see in areas such as sports injuries, hearing loss, dentistry, eyewear and prosthetics. Beyond this come more contentious areas of real clinical need that are not life threatening, such as fertility treatment, contraception and sexual dysfunction. In many markets already, these are either not paid for by governments or are viewed as controversial. Still further out, we can imagine limitations on the funding of treatments that enhance life beyond what is considered normal, by increasing longevity, vitality or physical performance. For example, in situations where governments struggle to fund the healthcare that maintains normal life in their working age citizens, it is not hard to see governments perceiving life extension beyond 100 as an inappropriate use of taxpayers' money, especially if that life extension is of poor quality. Such rationing of healthcare is already implicit in many socialised healthcare systems and, influenced by the ethics of end-of-life care, will grow in importance as a healthcare funding issue.

It is these spaces then – starting with beauty and extending to prolonging the life of centenarians – in which we already and increasingly will see the withdrawal of the government payer. And as governments withdraw, we should expect to see the opening up of new habitats for life science companies in which the patient, not the government, is the primary payer and, hence, the customer. Indeed, we can already see the adaptation of firms to this habitat in some market access schemes aimed at the middle classes of emerging economies.

The picture I have just painted, in which governments or insurers used to provide almost all the healthcare that was technically possible but are now outpaced by a rapidly expanding universe of technological possibilities, hence opening up the 'patient as customer' habitat, is a very western view of the world. Indeed, it is a very socialised medical system view. It is a better description of the UK, France, Canada, Australia and other countries with similar healthcare systems, than it is of the US. And it is a very poor description of many emerging markets, where state provision has little history of providing anything but basic care. However, socialised, insurance-based and emerging markets are all heading to same conclusion from different starting points.

The patient payer habitat is opening up in the social healthcare systems typical of Western Europe as their provision contracts, relative to what is technologically possible. The same habitat, already more prevalent in the US, is opening up as a complement to Medicare and Medicaid state provision and the insurance markets shaped by the Affordable Care Act. In emerging markets, the patient payer is already the norm and will remain a large part of the environment even as countries like China, Indonesia and others expand basic state provision to their massive populations. Whilst their populations have the same healthcare aspirations as westerners, the governments of emerging markets do not seem to aspire to the same level of universal state provision of advanced healthcare that developed nations are struggling to sustain. Whether the patient payer habitat is a creation of relatively shrinking state provision or the result of expanding but constrained state provision, it will become a more important habitat of the life sciences sector than it is today. Historically, patient payers have occupied a place in the industry's attention a long way behind the traditional payers of governments and insurers. But their relative importance will change for most companies and, for some firms, the patient payer habitat will become more important than the government payer habitat.

However, as Figure 7.3 in Part 1 of this book illustrates, the patient payer habitat is not homogeneous. It ranges from those living in absolute poverty through the middle classes to the very wealthy indeed. It includes all imaginable levels of discretionary income and healthcare purchasing power. As I examined in our discussion of the global, value and other shifts, these wealth defined categories of patient payers are no longer synonymous with the wealthy west and the poor rest. Whilst national differences in wealth still exist, the wealthy, the middle classes and the poor co-exist in most countries, albeit in different proportions and according to differing local definitions. I began to unravel this complexity in *The Future of Pharma*, where my first level of approximation was simply to divide patient payers as wealthy and mass market, but it is quite obvious that the patient payer habitat is much more granular than that, with many different levels of ability to self-fund healthcare. However, in the context of technologically innovative firms, we can consider only one simple but important division, that between those who can afford to pay for innovative healthcare and those who cannot. The line between these two groups is ill defined and varies between geographies and product categories but, for life science companies, the middle class or wealthy patient, western or otherwise, is a potential customer for technologically innovative therapies whilst the poor patient is either not a potential customer or can be reached only via government or other institutional payers.

To all intents and purposes then, that part of the fitness landscape where innovative technology meets those with no means to pay for it is a fitness trough. In this situation, business models that combine both truly innovative technology and the necessary low pricing are not viable. I appreciate that some readers will argue with this view, pointing to examples of low cost models in the life science sector. But my argument is that such models are either not technologically innovative (although they may be innovative in supply chain or service design) or are aimed at government payers. In all of my research, I did not find a business model that was truly technologically innovative *and* truly low cost. The Beyond Reach trough, as I labelled it in *The Future of Pharma*, seems very real.

This leaves the habitat characterised by technological innovation and relatively wealthy patient payers. This is not a small space. In 2011, the Economist reported that globally there were over 24 million people with a net worth of over $1 million – more than the total number of Australians. The OECD predicts that the global middle class will be 4.9 billion people by 2030. These are not the super-rich but, when their life or the life of their children is under threat, they may be able to afford some of the healthcare that is deemed unaffordable by their governments. The question is, what business models will evolve into this affluent patient payer habitat? In *The Future of Pharma*, I suggested a 'Lazarus and Narcissus' fitness peak that would be occupied by the same genius business model that would occupy the advanced state and pressured state peaks. My research since then suggests that this is too simple a view and that a species flock of business models is emerging to occupy the technologically innovative/patient payer habitat.

Two evolutionary choices

If, as a consequence of the six great shifts, a habitat is emerging in which some patient payers want and can afford innovative medical technologies that their government will not or cannot pay for, then it seems inevitable that business models will evolve to occupy that space. That raises the question of what those models will look like and to what extent we can see them emerging in the data, that is the pattern of activity of today's companies.

Those questions are similar in nature to the one we addressed for technological innovators in the government habitat. We should anticipate that the answer might have similarities with that more familiar habitat, since we are again looking for mutations in the technological innovator family of business models. We should also anticipate some differences, since we are looking at adaptations to a quite different group of customers. In any case we might expect the business models in this patient payer habitat to be less emerged and less diverged from existing models because their habitat is more recent than the government payer habitat. Whatever the similarities and differences, we should still expect to see evolutionary choices that represent alternative ways of optimising risk-adjusted return on investment because that driver is the same in all of the industry's habitats. Just like all species seek to replicate their genes by reproductive success, all business models seek to replicate their organisational routines by optimising risk-adjusted return on investment.

As with the previous discussion about the three evolutionary choices made in the government payer habitat, it is worth remembering that the following description is presented back-to-front. Although it may seem like I am imposing concepts onto the data, in fact the observations emerged from the data and the resulting concepts were then used to structure it. What emerges from the data is not dissimilar from but a little simpler than in the government payer space. In particular, two evolutionary choices emerge as important.

Incremental vs. discontinuous innovation

> In medicine, it's always been the wealthy who have funded innovation because they wanted to live longer. The first cases of bypass surgery in the 1960s would have been the richest people on earth who were travelling to South Africa and Brazil to have this done so they could live longer. They were, if you will, the gilded guinea pigs that helped the initial surgical teams really understand how to do it and how to do it better, how to incrementally improve it. And then after about four- or five thousand cases it broke out into the United States. Within five years it became the standard of care and tens of thousands of people benefitted from this from all walks of society.

Daniel Carlin, WorldClinic

Technological innovators trying to sell their innovations to wealthy consumers face the same fundamental choice as those selling to governments. Since a key determinant of risk-adjusted rate of return remains technological risk, what still matters most is the probability that their technological innovation will deliver the promised benefits and returns. Hence, they face the same choice between incremental, lower risk innovations offering smaller potential returns and discontinuous, higher risk innovation offering larger potential returns. Although the market characteristics and dynamics may be very different from those in the government payer habitat, the choice between incremental and discontinuous innovation remains a trade off between risk and return and remains a fundamental choice influencing the viability of the business model.

Holistic vs. symptomatic benefits

> We move from the treatment of symptoms to getting to the molecular cause of disease and, more importantly, we use our understanding of baseline risk to delay or eliminate the incidence of that. So that's a very different world.

Steve Burrill, Burrill LLC

In the patient payer habitat, the other two evolutionary choices made in the government payer habitat appear conflated into one. Instead of options to choose large or small markets and narrow or broad technological focus, the evolutionary choice seems to be either to address single conditions symptomatically or manage overall health more holistically. This conflation arises from two specific characteristics of the patient payer habitat. First is the small size of all markets in this habitat, relative to the government payer habitat. Second is the broad correlation between clinical outcomes and technology breadth. By that I mean that, as a generalisation, the complexity of biology means that all approaches to holistic or predictive healthcare involve combinations of technology and are resistant to single technology approaches. This correlation is not perfect, as I will show in a moment, but it is broadly true.

Taken together, these two evolutionary choices suggest the emergence of a species flock of four business models in the technological innovator/patient payer habitat, as shown in Figure 16.2.

When considering this model, it is again important to bear in mind that the same caveats apply as in the government payer habitat. It applies only to the patient payer habitat as the observations and evidence come only from that space. Also, the four models are theoretical predictions; they are what we might expect to see, but it does not mean that all four of these business models yet exist in fully-fledged form. Third, this model implies four discrete models with no overlap between them. In practice, we might again anticipate some business models that do not fit easily into any one category, as in my previous

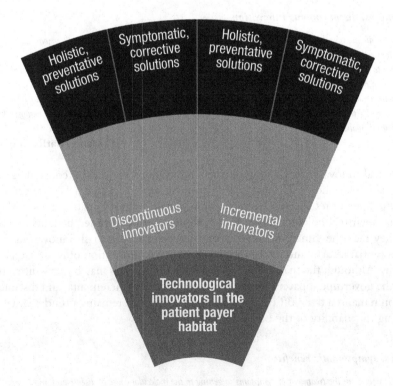

Figure 16.2 A taxonomy of technological innovators in the patient payer habitat

reference to the duck-billed platypus. Figure 16.2 is an approximation like its government payer equivalent (Figure 15.1) and all other taxonomies.

Those caveats accepted, this model is a useful aid to our understanding of the evolution of technologically innovative business models in the patient payer habitat. It allows us to makes sense of the confusing variety of different approaches that technological innovators might take in this habitat. In doing so, it reveals a level of speciation within the broad Lazarus and Narcissus fitness peak that I identified in *The Future of Pharma*. It is therefore a more detailed and informative picture, whilst still being consistent with those early ideas.

As I have already said, these two salient evolutionary choices are emergent properties of this part of our complex adaptive system. They emerged from the data rather than the evidence being structured to fit two theoretical dimensions. In the following sections, I will give some examples of the evidence and how that illustrates and qualifies the four species of model shown in Figure 16.2. I will then move on to what we can learn from it.

Discontinuous innovators

The Methuselah model

> Age is the number one risk factor for every disease, but it's not treated as a disease on its own. To crack the question of aging, we need to connect layers of information that have never been put together, starting with the entire human genome and then layering in the genetic code of the microbes, in addition to measuring proteins and chemicals. We're trying to get the whole picture and create a database that can actually become really predictive of what's associated with disease and what's associated with health.
>
> **J. Craig Venter, Human Longevity Inc.**

This approach is characterised by its ambition to improve human health and wellness in a holistic, rather than symptomatic, manner. It is also defined by its application of discontinuous rather than incremental technological innovation. As such, it is a 'bet big' model, since it is a choice to accept high technological risk in return for high potential returns. In evolutionary terms, this model is viable only if in execution the return compensates for the risk. In that sense, it is closely related to the Secular Grail and Budget Buster models in the government payer habitat. Where it differs from those models is that its goal is to create clinical outcomes that the patient will pay for, even when their governments deem them unaffordable. For example, many of the examples of this model's emergence involve a promise of longevity extended beyond what society sees as typical. It was for this reason that, as it emerged from the data, I labelled it the Methuselah model.

Predictably, given its dependence on the most advanced technologies and non-government payers, the Methuselah model is not well advanced in its development compared to other models that are closer to those traditionally employed by the life science industry. But it does appear to be emerging with remarkable rapidity. The archetype of the Methuselah model is J. Craig Venter's Human Longevity Inc., with its stated goal: 'to extend and enhance the healthy, high-performance lifespan and change the face of aging'. Cisco's healthcare venture Calico similarly aims 'to harness advanced technologies to increase our understanding of the biology that controls lifespan'. As well as their holistic aims, both companies are based around the application of multiple technologies, both life science and information technology, to achieve discontinuous leaps in what is possible. They are also interesting from the point of view of organisational structure and boundaries because, as yet, none of these firms have shown any interest in a fully-integrated commercial model spanning the whole value chain from discovery through operations to sales and marketing. Instead, Human Longevity Inc., Calico and other firms look likely to work as part of a holobiont with more traditional pharmaceutical and medical technology companies, health service providers and non-profit organisations. It is an interesting aspect of this habitat that non-profits, such as the Alliance for Aging Research and the Institute for Aging Research at Albert Einstein College of Medicine, seem to play an especially important part. Both holobiont structures and the prominence of non-profits seem to be adaptations to the high levels of risk involved, suggesting that very high risk selects against traditional, integrated for-profit business model structures.

This Methuselah model's focus on discontinuous, relatively risky research involving the combination of multiple technological fields, from genomics and bioinformatics to microbiomics and stem cell therapies, also applies to the Marvel model, discussed later. What distinguishes the former from the latter is that Methuselah models have very broad goals that are not related to curing or managing a specific disease or injury. This means that the benefits Methuselahs aim to provide, such as a longer, more healthy life, are highly desirable to individuals but are very likely to fit into one of the categories that financially constrained and value-seeking governments will not pay for. For example, life extending therapies, such as promised by Calico's NAMP inhibitors or Human Longevity's stem cell therapies are likely to be expensive and low priorities even for generous governments. Governments will be pressured to pay for them of course but, faced with a choice between enabling sixty year olds to live to seventy or paying for 100 year olds to reach 110, longevity is likely to become an optional, payable extra, like attractive spectacles or white teeth.

Of course, the essence of the Methuselah model and its three cousins in the patient payer habitat is that they will not be dependent on the reimbursement and market access issues that shape the government payer habitat. Hence, the selection pressures created by the value shift help the patient payer habitat and favour rather than disfavour the Methuselah model. At the same time, the global shift creates a large, widespread market among the affluent classes that now exist in significant numbers in many countries and not just in developed economies. Simultaneously, the holobiont shift favours the multiple-capability, risk-dispersing networked organisations necessary to deliver the Methuselah model, whilst the trimorphic shift also supports the research intensive nature of this model and reduces the costs of non-core activities. Of course, the Methuselah model, along with other discontinuous innovation models, is favoured by and largely predicated upon the technological developments that I have discussed as part of the systeomic and information shifts. Hence, the combined effects of the six great shifts not only create the patient payer habitat but also favour the emergence into that habitat of the Methuselah model. Indeed, it is clear that this model has become viable only because of the selection pressures created by those shifts.

The Marvel model

I grew up in the 1970s watching 'The $6 Million Man' and that definitely piqued my interest. In fact, probably the reason I got into biomedical engineering in general was that television show and the idea that you could not only restore body parts but actually create a better human. There were many of us at the company who were influenced by that show in particular. Our challenge did turn out to be a very significant *challenge. There are lots of folks around the world trying to do similar things, but it turned out to be a more significant task than we had anticipated. It took us more than twenty years and more than $200 million in investment to solve the various problems.*

Dr Robert Greenberg, Second Sight Inc.

Like the Methuselah model, this approach is characterised by its application of relatively advanced technologies. But it is more focused in its goals, aiming to provide solutions to specific conditions, diseases or injuries. It is therefore a slightly smaller bet than the Methuselah model, since it is a choice of lower technological risk in return for lower potential returns, compared to that model. Bear in mind, however, that all of these risk and return assessments are relative to each other and the technological risk of the Marvel model is still higher than, say, the Life Cycle Exploitation model. And this model, like the others, is viable only when execution leads to returns that outweigh the still considerable risk. Like its three cousins in this patient payer habitat, the Marvel model's goal is to create clinical outcomes for which patient payers will pay when their governments will not. For example, some of the cases of this model's emergence involve a promise of improving physical capabilities beyond those of a normal human being. It was for this reason, and inspired by my daughter's love of superhero movies, that I labelled it the Marvel model.

The Marvel model's requirement for advanced technologies and dependence on non-government payers means that, like the Methuselah model, it is only beginning to emerge. Marvel models are complementary to Methuselah models within firms like Calico and Human Longevity Inc. where their research offers potential therapies for diseases associated specifically with ageing. Calico and AbbVie's collaboration is an example of the Marvel model emerging in this context. So, too, is the development of so-called 'germ line engineering', in which the DNA of eggs is edited, for instance to remove a predisposition to breast cancer. The Marvel model is also exemplified by developments in medical technology that have, with a nod to science fiction, been labelled bionics. Examples of this include Touch Bionic's i-limb™ ultra-prosthetic hand, Second Sight's Argus retinal implants and, of course, the prosthetic legs that allow para-athletes to compete against their able bodied counterparts. These examples use discontinuous innovation to counter the effects of illness or injury but, further out, we can see the emergence of examples where the aim is to enhance the healthy human body. The US army's exoskeleton project, enabling super-human strength and endurance, is a forerunner of this. Developments are also taking place to enhance the senses, to provide superior memory and to enhance many other human capabilities via gene therapy. Many of these sound like science fiction, far from reality, but the technology is advancing very rapidly towards commercial applications.

Like the Methuselah model, the Marvel model focuses on discontinuous, relatively risky research involving the combination of multiple technological fields that often make the traditional medical technology/pharmaceutical boundary meaningless. Unlike Methuselah, however, the Marvel model has more limited or focused aims of curing or managing a specific disease or injury, or of augmenting specific natural abilities. The benefits the Marvel model aims to provide – correcting conditions that until now have been considered incurable, or improving our naturally-limited capabilities – are highly desirable to individuals but may well be so expensive that they fit into one of the categories that value-seeking governments won't pay for. Adrianne Haslet-Davis, a dancer who lost one of her feet in the 2013 Boston Marathon bombing, is an example of this. The prosthetic she now uses, made by BiOM, is so advanced that it allows her to dance but it is not available through Medicare. The development of advanced but very expensive solutions such as these raises the likelihood, if not the certainty, that society will be divided between those who can afford treatment or augmentation (or both) and those who cannot.

To stress the point, the Marvel model and its three patient payer cousins will not be dependent on the government payer. Taken overall, the selection pressures created by the six great shifts will favour this model. They will negate or mitigate government payer pressures, open up accessible global segments, enable innovative, risk-dispersing business structures and provide the technological advances upon which the Marvel model is built. From an evolutionary perspective, the Marvel model is an almost inevitable adaptation to the selection pressures arising from the industry's changing social and technological environments.

Incremental innovators

The Midas model

We are already treating ageing. We have been doing ageing research all along but we didn't know it.
Professor Brian K. Kennedy,
Buck Institute for Research on Aging

The Midas model is distinguished from the Methuselah and Marvel models in that it aims to create value from incremental innovation, whilst still aiming to deliver holistic rather than symptomatic solutions. It is therefore a medium-sized bet: a choice of lower technological risk in return for large potential returns that may be at risk of technological imitation and therefore competition. This set of risk/return choices makes it analogous to the Traditional Blockbuster model but in the patient payer habitat. Its success depends on being able to convince patient payers that a relatively small technological step offers unexpectedly high benefits. Many of the examples of this are technologies that are well known, almost mundane, but which may offer previously unrealised benefits that are the stuff of dreams, such as extended life. During my research, these models suggested to me a classical metaphor, hence the Midas model label. The most interesting thing about this model is the difficulty of proving that the claimed benefits are real to the standards required by regulatory authorities. The cost and difficulty of doing this is leading some companies to simply bypass the regulatory approval of claims, going for a consumer marketing rather than regulatory approved approach.

At first sight, the Midas model's lack of clinical evidence might make it seem more related to areas such as traditional folk medicine, homeopathy or other models that many see as 'snake oil'. But there is an important difference between those models and what is now emerging. Unlike many 'snake oil' companies, there is technological innovation behind the Midas business models and there is significant justification for some of the claims they make, albeit by proxy. Faced with an environment in the government payer habitat that demands very high standards of evidence for efficacy and cost-effectiveness claims, Midas model companies simply adapt by shifting to the less demanding patient payer habitat. There are numerous examples of this model emerging. Elysium Health, for example, positions its products as dietary supplements to mitigate regulatory barriers; but its product, Basis, contains active ingredients that have the intent to reduce ageing by the same mechanism that is observed in very low calorie diets. The same biology lies behind Novartis's work with everolimus and other rapalogs that appear to inhibit ageing. The anti-ageing effects of metaformin, a common type-2 diabetes medicine, and aspirin are also encouraging the development of Midas model companies. As much as these may sound like snake oil, the firms and individuals behind them are not ones we would associate with that label. It seems likely that medications, and perhaps devices, that sidestep regulation to make or imply wide health benefits from incremental technological innovation will be the basis for Midas model businesses.

The Midas model therefore shares with the Methuselah model the promise of wide, holistic benefits, but based on incremental, rather than discontinuous technological innovation. This approach makes the more evidence demanding government payer habitat unwelcoming and pushes firms towards the patient payer habitat. Unless, strongly against current trends, it becomes easier to prove clinical and health-economic benefits, the benefits of longer healthier lives that the Midas model aims to provide are unlikely to gain government reimbursement. Elysium Health, whose technological credentials are very impressive, are an illustration of this and seems to be an early signal of an emerging trend.

Elysium Health is also an illustration that companies in the patient payer habitat choose not to be dependent on the government payer. As with all the models in this habitat, the selection pressures created by the six great shifts will favour the Midas model. They will open up the patient payer gap across global markets, enable holobiont business structures that can both innovate technologically and reach consumer-like health markets. The systeomic and information shifts, although acting with perhaps less force than on the discontinuous innovator models of Methuselah and Marvel, will still favour Midas's incremental innovation. The cumulative, interacting effects of the six great shifts therefore seem likely to favour the Midas model along with the other patient payer models.

The Mender model

We're going to be developing new techniques and instruments for less-invasive treatments for knee, shoulder and hip replacements. That means that we will utilise our experience in terms of reducing the surgery time and recovery for patients where total joint replacement can be performed in an outpatient setting.
Reinhold Schmieding, Arthrex

The fourth species that is predicted to emerge in the technological innovator/patient payer habitat is the Mender model. Like the Midas model, this approach is characterised by its application of incremental technological innovation but, like the Marvel model, it is more focused in its goals, aiming to provide solutions to specific conditions, diseases or injuries. It is therefore the most cautious bet in this technological innovator/patient payer habitat and, in that respect, it is similar to the Speciality Domination model in the government payer habitat. Like the three preceding patient payer models, the Mender model's goal is to create clinical outcomes where governments' reluctance to pay is negated by the buying preferences of patient payers. Most examples of this approach involve promises to correct the ravages of life, caused by either normal wear and tear or else caused by and limiting of sporting activity. It was for this reason that I labelled it the Mender model.

The Mender model's requirements for relatively incremental technological advance and appeal to well established human vanity mean that it is the most emerged of the four species in the patient payer habitat. The archetype is Allergan, with its Botox product and its acquisition of Kythera, which points to a further commitment to this habitat. Other firms, such as Nestlé, are trying to capture this habitat and there are a multitude of similar attempts to address this vanity driven market with incremental technological innovation.

The therapies and equipment targeted at the cosmetic surgery market, so-called 'cognitive enhancement drugs' and laser surgery to remove the need for wearing spectacles are contrasting and superficially different models but share the same fundamental evolutionary choices about risk and return in the patient payer habitat. In medical devices, the shift of orthopaedic companies towards higher-margin sports injury or reconstructive surgery products are examples of this. Smith and Nephew's acquisition of ArthroCare and Stryker's of Pivot Medical are both examples of a step towards the Mender model and away from their legacy, lower-margin, hip and knee reconstruction businesses, which are Traditional Blockbuster business models. In these examples, we can see these large, well established companies evolving incrementally from Traditional Blockbuster models towards the Mender model. We might expect this to be a relatively easier transition than the one to more discontinuous innovation models, since it does not require the acquisition of genes (that is, organisational routines) for radical innovation. However, it does require the acquisition of genes for managing patient payers rather than healthcare professionals and government payers, which is a far from easy mutation.

The selection pressures of the six great shifts act collectively to favour the Mender model as much as its cousins. Like all the models in this space, it is favoured by the combination of the value and global shifts transforming the latent patient payer market into a significant and real opportunity in both developed and developing geographies. Equally, the polarisation of the trimorphic shift and the networking of the holobiont shift favour the acquisition of the necessary new consumer marketing capabilities. The risk mitigation those two shifts enable is still important, although less than in discontinuous innovation. And the pressures arising from the systeomic and information shifts, whilst present, are probably less significant here than in the other three patient payer models.

A species flock of technological innovators in the patient payer habitat

In the preceding discussion, I explored a habitat that has, for decades, been of secondary importance to technologically innovative life science companies: that part of the landscape where firms compete by innovating and trying to sell that innovation to patients who have to pay for themselves. Although it has some superficial similarities to over-the-counter markets, it differs in that it involves new innovation rather than 'milking' old innovation by, for example, extending off-patent products into consumer markets. Importantly, this is a mostly new habitat, opened up by the different growth rates of economic and technological possibilities, as shown in Figure 16.1.

Into this habitat are evolving new species that are making evolutionary choices about how to achieve the best balance of risk and return. As in the government payer habitat,

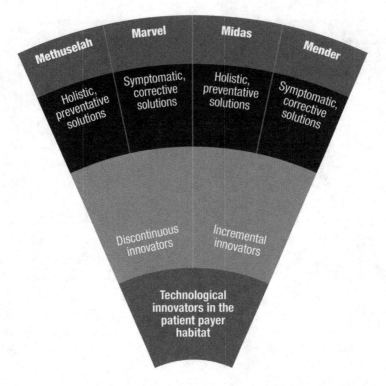

Figure 16.3 The emergence of technological innovator models in the patient payer habitat

they are choosing between discontinuous and incremental innovation. In addition, they are choosing between, on the one hand, limited ambitions to solve specific problems and, on the other, bold aspirations to extend life and wellbeing. These choices are leading to the emergence, at varying speeds and to varying degrees, of the four new business models I have described. Together, these offer investors a complete range of risk and return options to suit their varying appetites and ambitions. In another example of species helping to create their own ecological niche, the resulting inflow of investment helps to create the patient payer habitat. They are shown again, now with their model names, in Figure 16.3 and Figure 16.4.

At this point, having completed our exploration of the technological innovator part of the industry's fitness landscape, it is worth pausing to consider the species we have seen evolving into it. In *The Future of Pharma*, I was able to discern only one technologically innovative business model, the Genius, which might occupy both the patient payer and government payer habitats. That earlier work suggested that this single species, character-ised by its technological innovation capabilities, might occupy the three fitness peaks of Lazarus and Narcissus, Pressured State and Advanced State. The work I have done since then shows that this picture, whilst not wrong, was only an approximation. Evolution, as Orgel said, is cleverer than I am. Faced with the single challenge of optimising risk-adjusted rate of return, technological innovators appear to be evolving into no fewer than twelve business models, each occupying a different peak in the fitness landscape. This is shown in Figure 16.5.

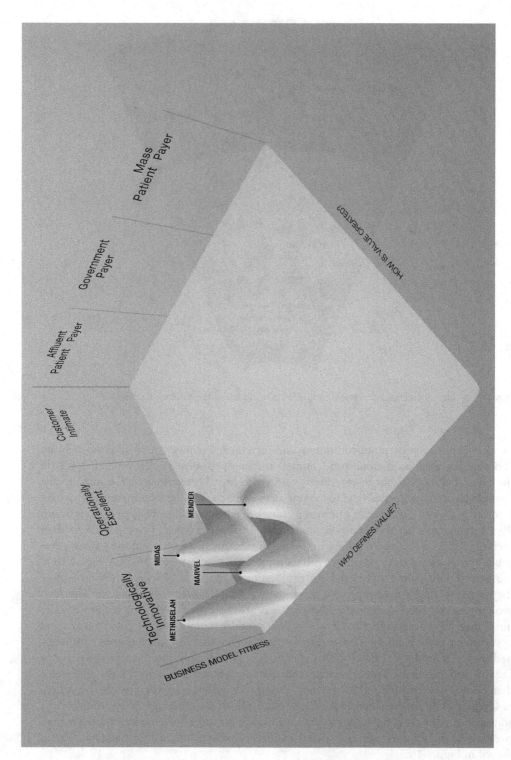

Figure 16.4 The emerging fitness landscape of technological innovator models in the patient payer habitat

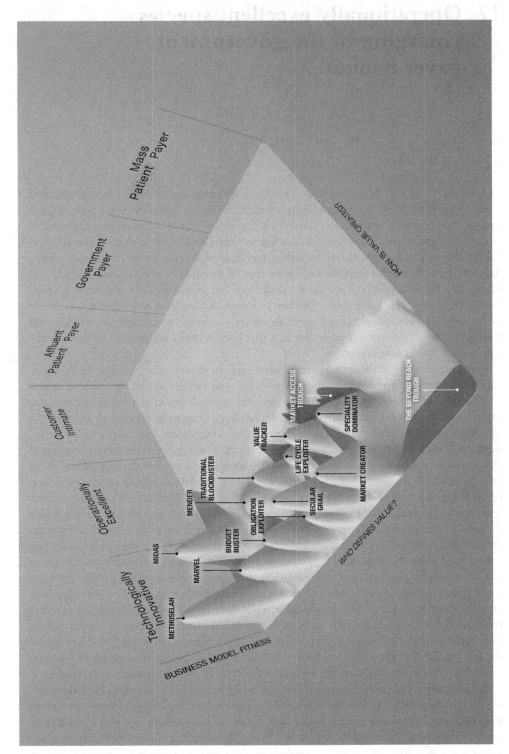

Figure 16.5 The speciation of technologically innovative business models

17 Operationally excellent species emerging in the government payer habitat

I began this third part of the book by looking at business model evolution in the habitat with which most life science companies are familiar and to which they are best adapted, namely that in which companies choose to compete by selling technological innovations to government payers. Then, in the following section, I moved on to explore the adjacent habitat where firms might thrive by selling technological innovations to affluent patient payers. I argued that this hitherto negligible part of the market was growing quickly and inexorably because our technological capabilities are growing faster than our governments' capability to pay for them. Further, I argued that business models that were truly technologically innovative would probably never compete significantly in the Beyond Reach trough of poor patient payers because that habitat could not provide sufficient risk-adjusted return on investment.

In my exploration of these two parts of the fitness landscape where technological innovators will thrive, I avoided the temptation to become tangled in the vast web of inventions and developments that are the most obvious and well reported evidence of industry evolution. These developments, from nanotechnology to immunotherapy to the internet of things, are very important, but their profusion, complexity, variation and interconnectedness make it hard to see any emergent pattern. Further, focus on this technological environment would disproportionately amplify its role and neglect the role of the social environment. To understand the evolution of business models, as opposed to the evolution of the technology, I found I needed to look wider than technological developments. I drew lessons from the father of biological taxonomy Carl Linnaeus and looked for the major differences and similarities between the decisions that firms are making in these habitats. To reiterate, I did not try to impose any pre-supposed order on the data that I collected; I tried to identify the order that was emerging from this complex adaptive system. From this inductive process emerged the realisation that there is an important parallel between evolutionary fitness in organisms and in organisations. Both organisms and organisations are interactors that act as vehicles for their replicators (genes and organisational routines respectively). The fitness of each corresponds to being around for long enough to allow their replicators to be replicated. For organisms, fitness is broadly the same thing as reproductive success. For organisations, fitness correlates to risk-adjusted return on investment, since that leads to their persistence and the replication of their organisational routines.

Realisation of this parallel between business and biology led to another. In biology, we observe evolutionary 'choices' such as having a spine or not, laying eggs or live young and having or not having cell nuclei. In my data about the life sciences industry, I was able to identify the analogous evolutionary choices that technologically innovative firms are making, such as degree of innovation, technological focus and market size. Using these choices as a predictive framework, I identified the emergence, to varying degrees, of two species flocks of technologically innovative business models: eight species in the government payer habitat and four in the affluent patient payer habitat. The identification of these emergent species, evidenced by the real world examples from the data, represents a development of the Genius model discussed in *The Future of Pharma*, which now seems more like a genera containing these two flocks and twelve species of technologically innovative models.

In this section, I am going to move on from technologically innovative species to explore that part of the industry landscape where competitive advantage arises from operational excellence. That is, firms whose competitive advantages arise mostly from organisational routines that reside in the supply chain management part of their value chain. This is also sometimes called Operations and is distinct from, but of course connected to, the new product development (NPD) and customer relationship management (CRM) parts of the value chain. In my experience, executives often confuse operational excellence with mere operational proficiency, so it is worth a brief reiteration here to avoid misunderstanding.

Operationally excellent companies compete usually by offering the same or lower price than their competitors but having lower costs and thus higher returns. In contrast to technologically innovative models, they cannot claim truly superior product efficacy or performance and, in contrast to customer intimate models, they do not claim to create value by meeting customer needs more closely than their rivals. To reiterate the ideas discussed in the technological innovator section, operationally excellent companies do not of course ignore NPD or CRM parts of their value chain; they must work hard to remain acceptable to their customers in these activities. But operationally excellent firms do not attempt to be superior to their competitors in NPD or CRM. How they differ from their rivals, where they create their competitive advantage, lies in their operational activity of making and providing their products and services to the customer. Of course, the lines between these three approaches to competition are often blurred and even more often are hard to discern, but the basic premise remains as Michael Porter first identified it: there are three fundamental types of company, just as the domains of Archaea, Eubacteria, and Eukaryote are fundamental types of living organism.

In exploring how operationally excellent business models are evolving, I will again begin with the habitat that is most familiar to today's companies, the government payer habitat. Traditionally, this is the habitat occupied by generics companies in pharma and their equivalents in medical technology, the low cost imitative manufacturers. After that, I will discuss the habitats that include both affluent and poor patient payers. In each habitat, the first question we need to answer is the same as we asked of technologically innovative business models: what pattern of evolutionary choices can we see emerging from the innumerable decisions made by firms operating in this habitat?

Two evolutionary choices

In *The Future of Pharma*, I predicted the emergence of a single species of operationally excellent company called the Monster Imitator. In a sense, this was the simplest of the seven models that emerged from that earlier research. It was huge (in order to have economies of scales and market power) and excelled in both the identification of opportunities to imitate and their exploitation. As with my prediction of the Genius model in technological innovators, my subsequent work shows that I was too simplistic; once again, evolution has been cleverer than I ever could be. My original prediction was based on firms making a simple, binary choice: to be operationally excellent or not. In fact, life science firms in this habitat seem to be making two related choices: how much to be operationally excellent and, if not driven purely by the objective of low cost, in what way to differentiate.

Undifferentiated vs. differentiated

> *In my space we're not seeing it yet. But it doesn't mean it's not starting to happen. Cardiac stents I think is a good example, where there are a lot of players and you have low prices. I think glucose monitoring is another area, as are trauma extremities products. But other companies have tried to genericise devices, with hips and knees for example, and they've had miserable failings. Until you de-skill the procedure you cannot have generics. The hips and knees procedures are so complicated to do, that the hospitals need our people and our service there helping them.*

Kevin Lobo, Stryker

For operationally excellent companies, the key determinant of risk-adjusted rate of return is achievable profit margin. In other words, what matters most for these firms is the probability that their operational excellence will deliver the promised cost that will allow the necessary margin in a market where price competition is intense. Textbook theory in this area, such as the work of Porter and Treacy and Wiersema, suggests that this is a binary choice between being lowest cost or strongly differentiated, via either technological innovation or customer intimacy. There can only be one lowest cost competitor, so the theory goes, and trying to be both low cost and differentiated leads to a straddling position that is uncompetitive. From my data, a more nuanced picture emerges. It appears that whilst there is, as theory predicts, a clear divide between operationally excellent firms on the one hand and technologically innovative or customer intimate models on the other, there is gradation and granularity within operationally excellent models. Again, what we observe is explained in terms of risk and return. A 'pure' choice to be the lowest cost business model offers the potential for a high return relative to rivals that are low cost but not lowest cost. But the pure lowest cost model is also relatively high risk, although the risk is not of the same kind faced by technological innovators. Partly, risk for operationally excellent companies arises from the investment needed to be the industry cost leader; this position typically demands investment in a very capital-intensive supply chain, so increasing capital at risk. Partly, it arises from the binary choice: if you fail to be lowest cost then your focus means you cannot compete on any other basis and you may lose not incrementally but spectacularly.

Faced with this relatively high risk/high return situation, it is possible to trade off risk and return by attempting to differentiate to some limited degree without trying to be a fully-fledged technological innovator or customer intimate. Such limited differentiation can take many forms, from technology to branding to service levels, but it inevitably increases costs with the hope of increasing customer preference and hence price, share or both. In some contexts, this limited differentiation may offer a different and preferable balance of risk and return, compared to a pure play operationally excellent model. This is because it has different investment requirements and a less precipitous risk profile. As with other evolutionary choices, choosing between lowest cost and or some limited degree of differentiation are both possible ways to optimise fitness and commercial viability. Like the choices made by technological innovators discussed previously, this choice gives us a way to understand how business models are emerging in this area.

Older technology vs. newer technology

> *There are significant hurdles to overcome in the successful development and commercialisation of biosimilars. The evolving regulatory environment and uncertainty remains one of the most important challenges we are facing at the moment. This is especially the case in the US market. The development of biosimilars is also a very complex process and requires in-depth understanding of biotechnology as well as the specific therapeutic*

areas. Biosimilar development also requires significant investment. According to current estimates, it costs
between $100 to $250 million to develop a biosimilar and takes between seven and nine years.
Steffen Wagner, Sandoz

Operationally excellent companies are necessarily technology followers, in the sense they have chosen not to compete on new product development. But technological innovation and its adoption by healthcare systems do not happen instantaneously. Rather it happens in a wave as innovation diffuses through the market. Hence, for any technological innovation, there is a leading edge of this technology adoption wave, involving the newest technology, followed by established technology and then the oldest, obsolescent technology.

Whilst a technological innovator must, by definition, fight to maintain a position at the leading edge of this technology wave, technology followers can choose how closely behind the innovators they follow. For operationally excellent firms, desperate to optimise margin, where they choose to ride in this technology wave is important. They can choose to be fast followers, trying to mimic leaders as soon as they can get around intellectual property protection, or technology laggards, trying to extract value from the long tail of obsolescent products. Again, it is important to remember that fast followers are not trying to compete on the same basis as technological innovators; they are seeking out the competitive space that lies between those innovators and slow imitators. Yet again, their choice can be understood as a risk/return trade off. The technical and market risk for a fast follower is higher than for a slower imitator (but less than for a true innovator) but the potential returns are also higher (although again, less than for an innovator). Either choice can be a way to optimise fitness and commercial viability. Like the choice of whether to differentiate or not, the choice of how quickly to chase innovators gives us a way to understand how business models are emerging in this area.

These two evolutionary choices, emergent as they are, may not be the only differentiating traits that help us understand and categorise emerging business models in this operationally excellent, government payer habitat. As with technological innovators, a number of other factors did indeed emerge from my work. Scale, product specialism and geographical focus were examples of these. But the choices of how much and how to differentiate stood out as the dominant, salient evolutionary alternatives. They provide criteria against which the multitude of observable adaptations can be usefully assessed and categorised. They are, to a large degree, independent of each other and can be combined into a taxonomy of theoretically possible business models in this habitat, as shown in Figure 17.1.

When we look at Figure 17.1, it is important to remember the same caveats apply here as in my examination of the technological innovator habitats. First, this taxonomy applies only to the operationally excellent companies in the government payer habitat because the observations and evidence of the business model variations come only from that part of the fitness landscape. I have already addressed the taxonomy of technological innovators, and I will address the variations observed in other habitats later in this part of the book. Second, Figure 17.1 is a predictive model; it suggests what we might expect to see, but it does not mean that all four of these business models have yet been observed, fully evolved in practice. Finally, this model implies four homogeneous and distinct models with no variation within them and no overlap between them. In practice, like all taxonomies, we should expect some intra-model variation and the boundaries between them to be blurred. Remembering the duck-billed platypus, we need to remember that, as in biology, the existence of apparently anomalous business models doesn't mean that the

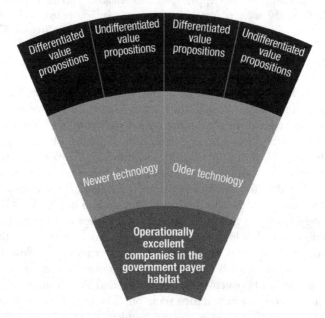

Figure 17.1 A taxonomy of operationally excellent business models in the government payer habitat

taxonomy is fundamentally incorrect. It only means that, like all taxonomies, Figure 17.1 is an approximation with fuzzy boundaries and may need subsequent refinement. Readers with a biological training will recall that the micro-organism Euglena, which was found to have some characteristics of plants, animals and bacteria, led to the creation of a fifth kingdom, the protoctista.

Just as Figure 15.1 and Figure 16.2 did for the technologically innovative habitats, the model in Figure 17.1 guides our understanding of the evolution of operationally excellent business models. It allows us to structure and make sense of the innumerable, individual choices that we see companies making in this part of the industry. As in the other habitats, each of these four categories represents a 'species' of operationally excellent company that might occupy the government payer space. This model predicts a level of speciation that is more detailed than the broad Monster Imitator model identified in *The Future of Pharma*. Like the Genius model of technological innovator, the Monster Imitator now looks more like a genera than a species. This revised prediction emerges from newer research and uses data that were not available to the previous book; it is more detailed and more accurate but builds upon rather than contradicts the earlier model.

As in biological taxonomy, each of the four species of business model in Figure 17.1 is likely to share much of its DNA – that is to say its organisational routines – with its operationally excellent cousins. For example, all four must have the routines that enable efficiency and lack those that enable advanced product innovation capabilities. Equally, the four will differ, in particular with respect to the routines for technology choice and how much and how to differentiate. Just as when biologists differentiate between, say, different species of mammals or reptiles, this more accurate taxonomy helps us to understand the differences between operationally excellent business models. In particular, it gives us a way of understanding the business model traits, capabilities and organisational routines that allow operationally excellent firms to thrive in the crowded and intensely competitive government payer habitat.

The value of a predictive model like Figure 17.1 is that it tells us where to look for evidence of speciation. In this section, I will now discuss some of that evidence and how it illustrates and qualifies the four species model shown in Figure 17.1. I will then move on to what we can learn from it.

Older technology models

The Cost Leader model

When we announced the [Ranbaxy merger] we said that the focus of the merger was to accelerate the growth of both the companies. India is a large market where our focus will be to grow faster than the market and add a few percentage points to our market share every year. The US is the largest market and the focus will to be see how we can bring back many of the Ranbaxy products which are not in the market and improve market share, and strengthen our branded business. We want to focus on growing the business faster than historical growth rates.

Dilip Shanghvi, Sun Pharmaceutical

The purest form of operationally excellent business model is, self-evidently, one which thrives by being operationally excellent and nothing else. This model I have christened the Cost Leader, with due acknowledgement to Porter's work. The Cost Leader model is perhaps closest to the Monster Imitator model described in *The Future of Pharma*, although it seems clear that versions of this model will exist in both pharma and medtech markets. The Cost Leader model is characterised by a focus on mature technology with no form of technical or clinical differentiation. In this model, competitive advantage comes only from operational efficiency. This model offers high evolutionary fitness when a cost base lower than that of all other competitors creates superior returns, even at prices below that of the competition, and when these returns outweigh the commercial risk of achieving that low cost base.

The pure play form of this model, in which cost is everything, is unlike most historical or current life science business models, most of which have focused on technological innovation. Current evidence suggests that the Cost Leader model has not yet fully emerged in the sector. Generic Medical Devices Inc. attempted this model but failed in 2012. At present, the nearest thing to a generic medical technology model can be seen only in very low tech products that are used in a medical setting but which barely merit the label medical technology – cardboard bedpans and disposable wipes are examples of this. In pharma, the nearest we have to Cost Leaders are generic companies like Sun Pharmaceutical. But Sun, like the generic divisions of the research-based pharma companies, is not yet a true Cost Leader in the sense that it would still appear to 'straddle' strategies (in Porter's terms) by attempting some level of brand or technological differentiation. Although it is a relatively low cost manufacturer, without a single-minded focus on cost, Sun and similar companies do not truly meet the criteria of a Cost Leader.

The true Cost Leader model is likely to emerge from one or both of two ancestor models. The most likely antecedents are companies like Sun and its Chinese equivalents like Guangzhou or Xiuzheng. With strong operations in emerging markets and no legacy of high cost cultures, these companies are likely to grow in scale to become Cost Leaders. Indeed, this seems the only way they are likely to compete with the western, branded companies that currently dominate the generic sectors of even emerging markets. The consolidation of this part of the industry, including Sun's acquisition of Ranbaxy among others, seems to point to this growth and evolution. So would the growth by acquisition of the Chinese medical technology firm Sinocare which attempted to acquire Bayer's diabetes device business before acquiring the smaller PTS Diagnostics. The other possible antecedent of a Cost

Leader company is the aggregation and streamlining of existing, usually western, technological innovators whose products are no longer at the leading edge. This seems to be part of the strategy of Valeant, which has been vigorous in its rationalisation of acquisitions. However, it is hard to imagine western companies being able to transform themselves into true Cost Leaders, which would involve a radical transformation of their organisational routines. More likely is that firms like Valeant represent an adaptation towards other, limited differentiation species of operationally excellent companies, as discussed in the following sections.

It is almost tautological to say that the Cost Leader model is an adaptation favoured by the value shift, but it would be simplistic to see it only as that. The Cost Leader model is also strongly favoured in both developed and emerging markets by the growth of global segments that are focused on price and little else; such segments are part of the global shift. The Cost Leader model is also enabled by the disintegrated business structures and focused value chains favoured by the holobiont and trimorphic shifts. Less direct but also significant are the pressures on healthcare budgets by the systeomic shift, whose expensive innovations demand cost reduction elsewhere. Similarly, the efficiency and management improvements to supply chain technologies, enabled by the information shift, also favour the Cost Leader model. As with the previously discussed technological innovator business models, it is the net influence of the selection pressures that we need to consider and these seem to favour the eventual emergence of the Cost Leader model. But that is not to say the Cost Leader will be the only or dominant operationally excellent model. In fact, it seems likely to share this habitat with its cousins, as I will discuss next.

The Trust Leader model

> *The globalisation of the market has moved faster than many companies' ability to manage their supply chain securely. This led to complex, often poorly understood supply chains as well as issues such as counterfeiting. Either of these can and has led to situations where people have died and been seriously injured. Governments, especially in developed markets, have responded with steps like the Falsified Medicines Directive but such things have limited effectiveness. As customers learn this, then a secure, well managed and trustworthy supply chain will become more and more of a competitive advantage.*
>
> **Hedley Rees, Pharmaflow**

This model is characterised by a focus on mature technology that is differentiated either by brand reputation, added value services, some marginal technical differences or some combination thereof. In the examples I observed, brand differentiation was typically associated with higher service levels and vice versa. In pharmaceuticals, it also covered so-called 'super generics', a contentious term, not universally recognised, that refers to new formulations and other minor technical advances. This model offers high evolutionary fitness when it creates superior returns from an investment in minor differentiation, such as branding, service levels or small technological innovations. In all of the examples seen in my research, the basis for differentiation from very similar but much cheaper Cost Leader equivalents was principally trust placed in the supplier. This focus on trust and its implied value as the basis of competitive advantage led me to dub this the Trust Leader model. Other models involve trusted brands of course; but they do not rely on it as the principal source of competitive advantage.

The Trust Leader model is already well established in both pharmaceutical and medical technology sectors, where it is used to prolong the life of products that were once considered innovative but are no longer leading edge. The most salient examples are seen in companies such as Sandoz, Pfizer, Abbott and others, with divisions that are dedicated to established or mature products. In medical technology, we see the same approach, especially in mature single-use products like sutures, gloves, syringes and so on. In these and many other examples, once the marketing spin is removed, there is very little, if any, difference in technical performance between the branded product, such as Aspirin or Vicryl, and its lower cost equivalent. Yet in many markets, even with supposedly rational, value-seeking government payers, the branded product has significant market share and an even greater share of the market's profit pool.

It is tempting to attribute this apparently irrational buyer behaviour to weaknesses in procurement processes, and this may indeed be part of the explanation. But, in the context of intense pressure to reduce costs, the persistence of the Trust Leader model suggests that there is more to it than this. It is clear that, in paying a premium over lowest cost alternative, payers are seeking to satisfy some need that they regard as important and that they perceive not to be met by lowest cost, unbranded equivalents. Close examination of the business models in this area seem to point to this. Companies such as Becton Dickinson and Johnson & Johnson, both of whom operate successfully in many mature categories of the medical device market, manage to dominate their categories without strong technological advantages. Their combination of a trusted brand, service levels and product range advantages allow them to stand apart from lower cost rivals. The same result is achieved with similar methods by pharmaceutical generic companies such as Sandoz, Teva and Mylan, who dominate this part of the market, despite not being the lowest cost competitor.

Like the other models, Trust Leadership is a result of the selection pressures created by the six great shifts. At first sight it appears to survive despite being disfavoured by the great value shift. Superficially, we might expect these pressures to select against products that cost more for no significant benefit in clinical outcome. Closer consideration demonstrates that the net effect of the shifts actually favours the model. In particular, globalisation has created two selection pressures that favour Trust Leaders. The first globalisation effect is the growth of emerging market middle classes that are large markets for affordable, adequate products. The second globalisation effect is the growth of issues such as counterfeiting and doubtful quality standards of products made in some emerging markets. Together, these two aspects of globalisation create the 'affordable, trusted brand' market segment for which the Trust Leader competes. Paradoxically, the value shift also favours business models that can reduce the costs and risks to healthcare providers by wrapping their essentially commodity products in a thin layer of added value service. In other words, Trust Leader models are also creating value via a small amount of customer intimacy. Add to this the indirect effect of the trimorphic and holobiont shifts, allowing firms like Becton Dickinson or Sandoz to reduce costs by outsourcing, and the habitat for the Trust Leader, sitting between the lowest cost business models and the much higher priced, truly innovative models, becomes evident. Taken as a whole, the Trust Leader model seems favoured by the selection pressures and likely to persist.

Newer technology models

The Fast Follower model

> *We aim to expand our research and development capabilities and strengthen partnership with government authorities to offer Chinese patients cutting edge products at more accessible prices. For example, we are very likely to offer simplified or entry level versions of our insulin pump.*
>
> **Hooman Hakami, Medtronic**

Both the Cost Leader and Trust Leader models involve the evolutionary choice of focusing on mature technology, a choice that chooses lower returns for lower risk. By contrast, both of the newer technology and operationally excellent models involve choosing younger technology (just behind the leading edge) and accepting a higher risk in the hope of a higher return. These models try to find a space where competitive advantage comes from offering lower prices than technological innovators but better outcomes than the Trust Leader or Cost Leader models. As with their two older technology cousins, the two newer technology models differ in their decision to differentiate or not via brand and service levels. Of these two operationally excellent models focused on newer technology, the first to emerge appears to be the branded, differentiated model, which I have labelled the Fast Follower model.

The Fast Follower model offers high evolutionary fitness when two conditions are met. First, when superior returns can be generated on the increased investment required to follow closely behind the technological innovators and to offer a level of branding and service differentiation. Second, when those returns outweigh the increased technological risk of this model compared to the Cost Leader or Trust Leader models. By definition, the emergence of this model is contingent on the existence of innovative technologies that can be imitated. In pharmaceuticals, the Fast Follower is best exemplified by the rise of biosimilars, which are to biological therapies what generic pharmaceuticals are to small molecule therapies. In early 2015, the FDA approved Sandoz's Zarxio (a biosimilar version of Amgen's Neupogen), marking a milestone in the emergence of the Fast Follower model. In Europe, around twenty biosimilars are already approved for use but, at the time of writing, it is the imminent Fast Followers of blockbuster biologics such as Remicade, Humira and Herceptin that provide clear evidence of the emergence of this model. Market research reports predict that, between 2013 and 2019, the global biosimilar market will grow from $2.4 billion to $23 billion. This is evidence of both the adoption of the model and the selection pressures in its favour.

In medical technology, the emergence of the Fast Follower model is observable, if perhaps less obvious and more fragmented. Product development and intellectual property rights are much more incremental than in pharmaceuticals and yet the demand for good but lower cost products in medical technology is unlikely to be less than in medicines. An early indication of a Fast Follower in medtech lies in the globalisation strategies of leading western companies, which mirror the branded biosimilar strategies of the leading pharmaceutical companies. For example, Philips's emerging market strategy includes the digital x-ray system MobileDiagnost Opta, which is manufactured in India and aimed at global markets. This is a Fast Follower of their own leading technology to provide good, lower cost but not very innovative, products. Similarly, Medtronic's innovation centre in Shanghai, tasked with developing products for the Chinese and other emerging markets, complements its 'value product' strategy to acquire low cost emerging market manufacturers. In the same way, GE Healthcare is investing heavily into India to produce low cost, Fast Follower products in categories such as PET-CT, MRI and ventilation. However, note that in both pharmaceuticals and in medical devices, the Fast Follower still involves a brand and significant added value support. Lower cost is part of this model but lowest cost is not the focus of the model. In these examples we see the newer technology equivalent of the Trust Leader, not the Cost Leader.

As with the other models, the emergence of the Fast Follower model cannot be explained as the result of only one selection pressure. It shows the net result of all of the selection pressures acting simultaneously and to varying degrees. As with the other operationally excellent models, the value shift and global shift favour the Fast Follower by creating a large market for these good but cheaper products. At the same time, the global shift enables both innovation and manufacture in emerging markets, something that would not have been contemplated until relatively recently. The focusing and disintegration of the trimorphic and holobiont shifts enable firms to simultaneously combine the necessary level of innovation and low cost in a way that would be difficult for an integrated firm. The information and systeomic shifts play an indirect role, driving forward the innovative wave, providing a stream of new technologies to be imitated, at the same time increasing budget pressures that grow the 'value segment' in all markets. Considered holistically, the six great shifts and their selection pressures make the emergence of Fast Followers seem inevitable.

The Frugal Follower model

> On the original innovation front, we have commercialised the first novel biologic in India, an Anti-EGFR monoclonal antibody, Nimotuzamab, for head and neck cancer, which has benefited over six thousand patients since its launch in 2006. Most recently, we have commercialised our second novel biologic, Itolizumab, for Psoriasis. This drug has an enormous potential to address a number of unmet needs of multiple autoimmune diseases like Multiple Sclerosis, Sjogren's Disease, Lupus etc. We also have a very exciting oral insulin development program which can transform insulin therapy for diabetic patients. It has also been my unfulfilled aspiration to deliver a global blockbuster from Biocon, with a 'made in India' label.
>
> **Dr Kiran Mazumdar-Shaw, Biocon**

The last, and I will argue least emerged, of the four operationally excellent models is the newer technology equivalent of the Cost Leader. Like the Fast Follower, this model is characterised by a focus on newer technology and promises better outcomes than the Cost or Trust Leader models. Also like the Fast Follower, this model offers no clinical advantage over the leading edge innovation. In contrast to the Fast Follower, however, this model offers no added value in brand reputation, added value services or some combination of both. Like the Cost Leader, its competitive advantage arises from lower prices and its success depends on having lower costs than any of its competitors. This focus on low cost following as the basis of competitive advantage is the reason I called this the Frugal Follower model.

The Frugal Follower model offers high evolutionary fitness under conditions similar to the Fast Follower. First, if the investment in following close behind the technological innovators creates superior returns on the required investment. Second, if those returns outweigh the risk of the model, which are higher than its less innovative cousins. With the Frugal Follower, the risk is both technological and commercial because its strategy involves the same binary, win–or–lose risk structure as the Cost Leader. And, like the Fast Follower, the emergence of this model is contingent on the maturation of innovative technologies that can be imitated.

At first it seems self-evident that there is a market for the benefits of newer technology at the lowest possible cost. Yet the Frugal Follower model seems the least emerged of the four models in this operational excellence/government payer habitat. There are early, weak signals of emergence but they are much less obvious than for the Fast Follower. In this, the Frugal Follower shows parallels with the Cost Leader model, which is less developed than the Trust Leader. Currently, the most advanced indication of a Frugal Follower model can be seen in Samsung Bioepis, which has a number of biosimilars in late-stage development and is clearly focused on following innovators such AbbVie. However, Samsung Bioepis looks just as likely to develop into a Fast Follower with brand differentiation. Perhaps more indicative of Frugal Followers is the growth of biosimilar companies in emerging markets. Companies such as Axis Biotec (Brazil), 3S Bio (China) and Biocon (India) are emerging, often with government encouragement, to address domestic demand. In particular, their focus is often on high value monoclonal antibodies, which are demanding increasingly large slices of those countries' national healthcare budgets. At this stage, these companies show little interest in global markets, but it seems inconceivable that they would not spread from their domestic markets, once they have mastered the technological difficulties of making such products. When they do, it is hard to imagine them succeeding in direct competition against western innovators and Fast Followers unless they adopt the Frugal Follower model.

As with the Fast Follower model, the emergence of Frugal Followers is harder to discern in medical technology markets but early signs can still be seen, particularly in emerging markets. Indicative of this model is Microport, a Chinese manufacturer of cardiovascular stents, whose fast following undercuts western companies by about 40 percent. Similarly, China's largest medical device manufacturer, Mindray, is now becoming a significant player in areas such as patient monitoring, imaging and diagnostics. Its Indian equivalent, Trivitron, can make similar claims in similar areas. These and other examples all look like the emergence of Frugal Followers.

The emergence of the Frugal Follower model again shows the combined, cumulative result of all the selection pressures acting at once. To a large extent, the selection pressures favouring the Frugal Follower are similar to those favouring the Fast Follower. However, the reasons for the more rapid emergence of the latter over the former (which echoes that of the Trust Leader over the Cost Leader) are not yet clear. It could be that the selection pressures favour the two more differentiated models or that some selection pressure is disfavouring the more pure play lowest cost models or some combination of both factors. Alternatively, and in my view more likely, it is simply a matter of timing, exacerbated by the market imperfections of the life science market. Despite this difference in speed of emergence, the evidence suggests that the Frugal Follower model will emerge strongly in due course.

A species flock of operationally excellent models in the government payer habitat

In this part of the book, I have explored the habitat where firms compete by being operationally excellent and selling the benefits (usually lower prices) to governments buying on behalf of their citizens. This habitat has always existed to some extent in the life sciences industry but, until recently, it has been of secondary importance when compared to the more profitable technological innovator approach. When one reads the annual reports of pharmaceutical and medical technology companies, the dominant theme remains pride in technological innovation rather than in operational excellence. The six great shifts and the selection pressures that flow from them are, if not reversing that relative importance, rebalancing the relative significance of these two approaches.

Whilst my work for *The Future of Pharma* suggested that a single Monster Imitator model would emerge, my newer research suggests a more detailed, interesting picture. Once again, this is evidence that evolution is cleverer than I am. The evidence of firms' evolutionary choices suggests that a pure play commodity approach of cost leadership, as predicted by Porter, is unattractively high risk to life science companies. The immediate reason for this is path dependence, the academic term for the legacy of historical decisions. Most life science companies, whose history and culture make them unsuited to cost leadership, seem to be shying away from the binary, winner-takes-all outcomes of a lowest cost strategy. Instead, they are trying to find a fitness peak that lies between lowest cost and technological innovation or customer intimacy. Hence, the Trust Leader model, the organisational routines of which were already present in innovative companies in order to eke out the life cycles of mature products, has emerged first. Scientific advances and financial pressures are leading to the rapid emergence of its more technologically advanced cousin, the Fast Follower.

The slower emergence of the pure play Cost Leader can also be attributed to lagging effects of the selection pressures. The pressures of the value shift, as intense as they seem to technological innovators, are building slowly. They have not yet forced all governments to focus entirely on price. Furthermore, the opportunities provided by the global shift are still masked, to a degree, by concerns over quality and veracity and by issues of intellectual property protection and trade agreements. This is a transitional state, however. As the value shift and global shift continue and as they are amplified by the price pressures of the systeomic shift and reinforced by the holobiont and trimorphic shifts, it seems inevitable that all four of these models will emerge strongly. Indeed, in the examples I have cited we can already see their antecedents. As in the technological innovator habitat, this range of different operationally excellent business models offers investors a broader range of risk and return options than a single model. This will attract more investment, creating a positive feedback loop that helps expand the habitat.

Taken as a whole, our evidence and examples point to this species flock, shown in Figure 17.2 and Figure 17.3, emerging to both shape and exploit the operational excellence/government payer habitat.

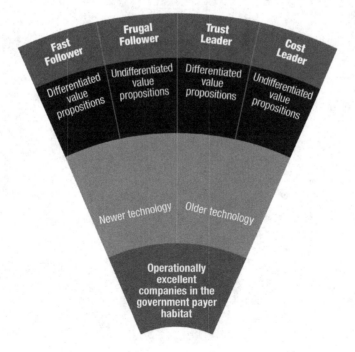

Figure 17.2 The emergence of operationally excellent models in the government payer habitat

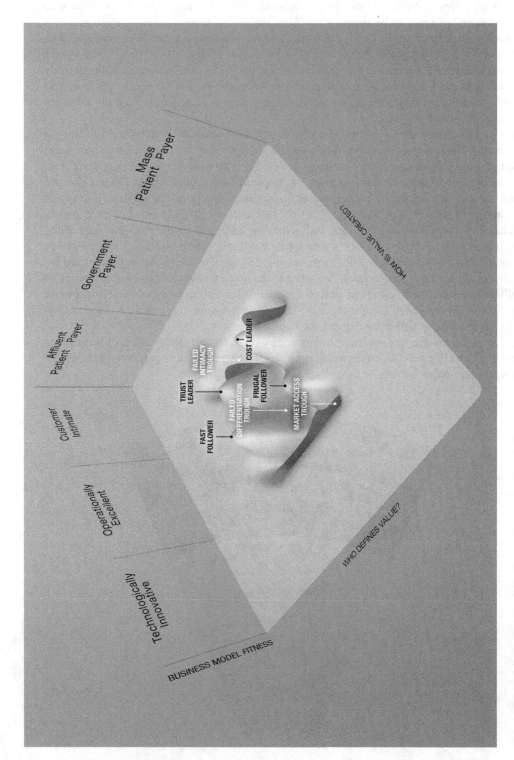

Figure 17.3 The emerging fitness landscape of operationally excellent companies in the government payer habitat

18 Operationally excellent species emerging in patient payer habitats

In this section, I will continue to explore that part of the life sciences industry landscape where competitive advantage arises from operational excellence. That is, as I began in the preceding section, I am going to explore the evolutionary choices of firms whose competitive advantages arise mostly from organisational routines that reside in their supply chain management. Having already explored the habitat where the government is the payer, I am now going to look at where the patient is the payer. By referring back to Figure 14.1, you will see that I am exploring the habitat adjacent to the operationally excellent/government payer habitat and the Beyond Reach trough.

I have already looked at other habitats where patients self-fund some or all of their medical treatment. In the technological innovator/patient payer habitat, I described four species of technological innovator emerging to meet the needs of affluent patient payers; these were the Methuselah, Marvel, Midas and Mender models. I have also described the Beyond Reach trough, where business models that attempt to sell truly innovative technology to poor patient payers are unlikely to be viable. In contrast, I will now discuss the habitats where operationally excellent business models address patient payers.

As discussed in Chapter 16, patient payer habitats formed mostly because what was technologically possible expanded beyond the ability of governments to pay. As a result, it became necessary that patients pay for some products and treatments, either partly or wholly (Figure 16.1). At the same time, inequality of wealth distribution led to an increase in the number of very affluent patients and thus created a market of patients able to pay for advanced technologies.

In the operationally excellent part of the landscape, the patient payer habitat is mostly attributable to two slightly different factors. First, as a result of demographics and lifestyles, growing volume of demand is outstripping the ability of governments to pay. Second, the rise of global middle classes, not very affluent but with some discretionary spending power, creates a market for affordable healthcare. As in the technological innovation/patient payer habitats, there is a large and growing part of the market where the patient is the customer rather than government. In contrast to the technologically innovative habitats, the patient payer customer of operationally excellent companies has much smaller discretionary spending power and cannot be described as rich. So whilst, in my earlier description, I discussed how the four technologically innovative models are evolving to occupy the habitat of affluent patient payers, in this section I will discuss how operationally excellent models are evolving to meet the fill the habitat of poorer, mass market patient payers. Before I do, however, it's worth a reminder that, as a result of the six great shifts, the patient payer transcends borders and traditional market categories. Just as affluent patients now exist in emerging markets, less affluent and poor patient payers now exist in developed markets. In the US, for example, the growth of internet pharmacies, grey markets and parallel trading is evidence of that.

As with all of the other habitats, the key to understanding speciation of business models in the operational excellence/patient payer habitat is to remember that business models represent a set of evolutionary choices aimed at optimising risk-adjusted return on investment. From the plethora of choices that my research catalogued, two distinct patterns emerged. The first is that operationally excellent companies are not choosing to target the most affluent patient payers. In simple terms, the value represented by operationally excellent firms (adequate efficacy at low cost) does not appeal to the most affluent of patient payers. Like all of us, they want the best healthcare that they can afford but, unlike many of us, the richest, most affluent patient payers can afford the very best, most innovative healthcare. This pattern was first observed in *The Future of Pharma* and, after extending my research both in time and across sectors, the evidence still supports this conclusion. I can see no evidence of life science business models aiming to compete on the basis of operational excellence for the most affluent consumers. Due to the preferences of affluent patient payers, such a model would appear to have low evolutionary fitness. In *The Future of Pharma* I labelled this the Wrong Kind of Value trough and that label remains apposite. In this trough, we can see the mirror image of its Beyond Reach counterpart. In both, the distinctive traits of the business model are a poor adaptive fit to the dominant needs of the habitat (high efficacy and low costs respectively).

If the nexus of operational excellence and very affluent patient payers represents a fitness trough, then the intersection of that low cost approach with less affluent and poor payers seems an obviously better adaptation. However, the heterogeneity of this huge group of patients also infers that there will be more than one fitness peak and more than one business model is likely to emerge. I searched for these possible adaptations by asking the same question as I did for the previously discussed habitats: what pattern of evolutionary choices can we see emerging from the decisions made by firms operating in this habitat?

The answer to that question was that two distinct choices were and are being made.

Two evolutionary choices

In *The Future of Pharma*, I identified only one possible fitness peak in this patient payer/ operationally excellent part of the landscape, which I labelled Limited Choice. I predicted that this habitat would be relatively homogenous, since all patients would be driven by the need for low costs. Reflecting my belief in a homogenous market environment, I predicted that the Monster Imitator business model would dominate this habitat in the same way as it would reign over the similarly price conscious habitat where government payers sought low cost products. But, as with my earlier predictions in other habitats, my research for this book has revealed that, compared to evolution, I am a dunce. My original prediction was based on two premises. First, influenced by Porter, I presumed that firms in this habitat would make a clear cut choice to be the lowest cost producer. Second, I adopted the premise that all non-affluent patient payers were similarly price oriented in their purchasing motivations. The evidence points to both these premises being false or at least inaccurate. As in earlier sections, my new work improved rather than replaced my earlier research. It caused me to revisit my assumptions and, as a result, two salient evolutionary choices emerged in this habitat.

The middle classes or the poor

> *As more and more of the world's population becomes middle class and you move big waves of the global population from poverty to middle class, they're more educated, they've got more access to information via the internet and mobile devices. Even the corporations like GE where we're self-insured with a quarter of a million employees and their family members we've shifted to more of a co-pay, a co-insurance programme where people are more accountable. And when people are more accountable they want to have more of a say in the healthcare that they seek.*
>
> **Michael Swinford, GE Healthcare**

> *We thought [Africa] would be the next Asia, but we have realised the middle class here in the region is extremely small and it is not really growing.*
>
> **Cornel Krummenacher, Nestlé**

The billions of less than affluent patient payers vary greatly in their discretionary income. Some have significant money to spend on healthcare, in particular the middle classes and those whose healthcare purchasing power is supported by their governments. Others, in particular the very poor in less developed markets, have little or no spending power beyond subsistence. Although many balk at the ethical implications, in practice, money means choice. If they wish, the middle classes can choose to pay more for products that are differentiated by brand, service, technology or otherwise. Their poorer neighbours do not have this choice, and their healthcare purchasing choices are dictated by the need for the lowest possible price. This heterogeneity among patient payers gives firms in this habitat a choice with important evolutionary implications. Just as in the government payer habitat, operationally excellent firms in this less than affluent patient payer habitat make a risk versus return trade off decision about whether to differentiate or not. As before, a 'pure' choice to be the lowest cost business model, targeting the poorest patients, offers the potential for high return, because volumes are large; but it comes at relatively high risk, as a result of the binary market outcomes of this decision. Choosing to be the lowest cost producer and not invest in any form of non-cost differentiation (like the Cost Leader and Frugal Follower models in the government payer habitat), means betting on being the winner in a winner-takes-all competition. By contrast, an alternative approach to this risk leads some firms to attempt limited differentiation, like the Trust Leader and Fast Follower models in the government payer habitat.

Demanding or undemanding conditions

> *I think there are a lot of things that point to the fact that the role of the consumer will continue to increase and the importance of the physician will diminish, not just for minor conditions. And I think that will have a pretty significant impact very soon. This is driven by the fact that people are much more informed nowadays and because it's very easy to find information about almost any disease topic pretty quickly and actually be more informed than the prescriber.*
>
> **Marc Sluijs, Oracle**

Just as less than affluent patient payers vary in their discretionary income, they also vary in the nature of their healthcare requirements. Some seek treatments that are easily within the capabilities of modern technology. Examples include most non-resistant bacterial infections, minor and moderate injuries, less severe congenital deformities and some chronic diseases associated with ageing or lifestyle, such as rheumatoid arthritis and hyperlipidaemia. Some, however, require treatments that place much greater demands on technology – many cancers, degenerative diseases, major traumatic injury and the multiple co-morbidities typical of old age fall into this category.

Like the differences in patients' discretionary spending power, these differences in clinical needs provide life science companies with a choice that trades risk against return and so has evolutionary implications. A business model can choose to address more demanding clinical needs, usually implying less competition and higher margins but also threatening lower volumes and greater commercial risk. Alternatively, a business model can choose to address less clinically demanding needs, implying large volumes but increased competition and lower margins.

As ever, no single trade off decision is optimal in all cases; there is only an optimal choice for a given company in a given market. This decision is closely analogous to that in the government payer habitat between following close behind the leading technology, like a Fast Follower or Frugal Follower, or focusing on mature technology, like a Trust Leader or Cost Leader. These parallels with the government payer habitat are very clear to see. It is a phenomenon known in evolutionary biology as convergence in which species facing similar challenges make similar evolutionary choices. For example, frogs, aardvarks and anteaters, faced with the challenges of eating elusive insects, have all developed sticky tongues. Similarly, business models trying to capture price-sensitive customers – whether governments or patient payers – are likely to evolve similar traits of operational excellence, limited differentiation and focus on lucrative technologies or clinical needs.

The patterns emerging in this part of the industry landscape therefore predict four species that are similar to those in the government payer space, as shown in Figure 18.1.

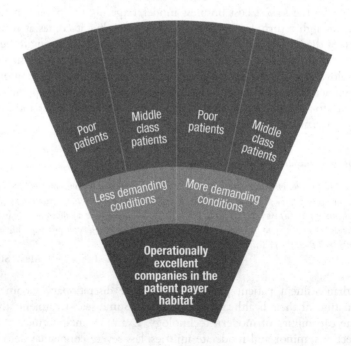

Figure 18.1 A taxonomy of operationally excellent companies in the patient payer habitat

Just as for its analogues in other habitats, when we look at Figure 18.1 it is important to remember the caveats that apply. It applies only in this habitat; it is predictive, not necessarily descriptive; and it is, like any taxonomy, an approximation of reality. Despite these qualifications, the model in Figure 18.1 guides our understanding of the evolution of operationally excellent business models in the habitat where patient is the payer. It helps us look for emerging models among all the noise of market activity. And, as in the other habitats, it suggests that we might be looking for something more complex and varied than a single business model. In particular, it suggests we are looking for a species flock that shares organisational routines for operational excellence with its cousins in the government payer habitat; however, importantly, they have different organisational routines for finding and managing customers. In fact, this taxonomy suggests that we are looking for four close cousins of the four models seen in the government payer space. Like the overlap between the genomes of you and your cousins, these models should share some, but not all, of their routines with their cousins. For example, they would differ in the replacement of government payer routines (for example, routines that enable contract compliance, tendering and market access) with patient payer routines (for example, ones that enable consumer marketing and retail distribution).

This predictive taxonomy is especially useful in this habitat because we expect some of these species to be barely emerged. The relatively recent development of global middle classes and of poor patients who can aspire to modern healthcare mean that business models have had little time to adapt. We should therefore expect only early signs of this species flock, but there is some evidence that the four species shown in Figure 18.1 exist, as I will now discuss.

Models for less demanding conditions

The Consumer Brand Leader model

> *The vision was a very simple one; we saw a material opportunity for ongoing, long-term growth, it's an appealing sector. Self-served consumer healthcare in a global environment, where demographics are changing, you have the emerging middle-class. You've got governments under pressure in terms of funding and prescription healthcare.*
>
> **Emma Walmsley, GSK**

Similar to its Trust Leader cousin adapted for the government payer habitat, the Consumer Brand Leader model is characterised by a focus on using mature technology that offers no clinical advantage over the alternatives but which, in the eyes of its middle class patients, is differentiated by its brand reputation. Hence the Consumer Brand Leader label. For both cousins, high evolutionary fitness is achieved when the model creates superior returns from an investment in branding and service levels. The major and important difference between the two cousins is that, whilst both models depend on their ability to create customer preference, their customers are quite different. This means that the organisational routines needed are also different. By way of example, consider the different routines needed for dealing with a health authority purchasing committee versus those for managing retail promotions.

Just as the Trust Leader model is already well established as a way to extend the life of both pharmaceutical and medical technology products, an antecedent to its Consumer Brand Leader cousin is already well established in the form of consumer healthcare companies. The most developed examples of this lie in the products for minor conditions such as painkillers and first aid dressings. Some of these models reside in the consumer products divisions of life science companies, such as Bayer, GSK and Johnson & Johnson. In these cases the blurred boundaries and synergies between prescription and consumer markets, especially in emerging markets, mean that it is relatively easy and attractive for traditional pharma and medtech companies to develop Consumer Brand Leader models. The joint venture of GSK and Novartis, and Bayer's acquisition of Merck's consumer business are indications that they are doing just this. In medical technology, Philips's consumer connected health strategy is another example, as are devices for blood glucose monitoring, blood pressure monitoring, pregnancy testing and so on. In many large market sectors, branded products from these consumer health companies already dominate the category even in the face of low cost own brand or unbranded competition.

In the case of the Consumer Brand Leader, it is perhaps a little easier to see how a strong brand can create customer preference than it is in the government payer habitat. The lack of a formal, cost-focused buying process and the role of the brand as shorthand to communicate quality and provenance explain why the capability to create and sustain a strong brand is so important. The possession of that capability also explains why western consumer health companies like those mentioned previously currently dominate this habitat. However, the importance of brand capabilities would also point to the origin of new entrants. For example, this habitat is exactly where one would expect consumer goods companies to enter the healthcare market. The healthcare divisions of Procter & Gamble and Unilever are examples of this and, although they do not operate significantly in pharmaceutical or medical technology categories now, the growth of this habitat is likely to tempt them to enter in some form.

However, they face strong competition from the existing consumer health companies. In a habitat where emerging markets are increasingly important, a more likely evolution can already be seen in the adaptation of western consumer healthcare companies to better address consumers in emerging markets. Taken together, these examples are evidence of the growth of the habitat and the evolution of the Consumer Brand Leader model.

Like all emerging business models, the Consumer Brand Leader model is being shaped by the selection pressures created by the six great shifts. Unlike its government payer cousin, it is favoured by the value shift, an artefact of which is to push costs onto patients and therefore involve them in the purchase decision (for example, by limiting government funded treatment for minor conditions). The similarity of the Consumer Brand Leader with its government cousin means that the pressures created by the global shift, such as emerging market middle classes and concerns about quality and provenance, favour both Trust Leader and Consumer Brand Leader business models. Even more than for government payers, middle class patient payers seek an affordable, trusted brand. The polarisation effects of the trimorphic and holobiont shifts allow firms to acquire and employ the wide range of capabilities needed – technical, commercial and operational – to operate in this habitat without having to build a large company. The information shift, through the internet, social media and data analytics, enables the brand management and channel management necessary for this model. And the systeomic shift, whilst only indirectly influential, places demands on government payers and increases the size of the patient payer habitat. Hence the Consumer Brand Leader, even more than its government payer cousin, is favoured by the selection pressures of the industry's social and technological environments.

The White Labeller model

> *The rapidly ageing global population, together with the associated increase in the demand for healthcare-related devices, has influenced growth in the market for medical device outsourcing in recent years. The widespread increase in prevalence of conditions such as cancer and cardiovascular disease will fuel the demand for cardiovascular and monitoring equipments. Medical device companies are rapidly adopting the use of contract manufacturers as a strategic means of staying ahead of the intensifying competition in the market place. As medical devices get increasingly complex, electronic manufacturing services in particular will offer great opportunities for market growth over the next few years. The rapidly improving protection of intellectual property in emerging markets such as China and India should also act as a catalyst for growth in these markets as more OEMs choose to partner with CMOs in the region in order to take advantage of the lower cost base offered.*

Moses Akintomide-Akinwamide, Visiongain

Similar to its Cost Leader cousin adapted for the government payer habitat, the White Labeller model is a pure play model characterised by a focus on undemanding conditions in poor patients and using mature technology that offers no clinical advantage over the competition. In both of these lowest cost models, competitive advantage comes only from price competition, and high evolutionary fitness is achieved only when two conditions are met. First, when investment in achieving the industry's lowest cost base allows it to create superior returns, even at prices below that of the competition. Second, when these returns outweigh the commercial risk of the model. The major and important difference between these lowest cost cousins is that their customers are quite different. This means that the organisational routines needed to manage customers are somewhat different. The limited differences are therefore most likely to lie in those routines for minimising the costs and maximising the margins in their very different distribution channels. The dominant importance of the distribution channel to the consumer version of the Cost Leader and the likelihood that it would operate largely through retail channels, often as own label products, led me to give it the White Labeller epithet.

Just like the government payer Cost Leader, the White Labeller has not emerged to anything like the same extent as its differentiated, branded relation. Of course there are own label versions of simple medicines and medical devices and price is an important component of competition, but this is not the same as Cost Leadership. Many generic drug companies, such as Sun, have significant consumer drug portfolios but, again, these are typically closer to Trust Leader models. The undeveloped state of the generic medical technology field means that the White Labeller model has not emerged there yet to any significant degree.

In reality, the most likely antecedents of the White Labeller model that we can currently observe are those same companies that I cited as examples the government payer Cost Leader models. Those emerging market generic pharma companies and low cost medtech companies are likely first to cross the boundary between the government and patient payer habitats, which is especially fuzzy in their home markets. Then, as their government markets mature and become even less profitable, they will probably focus more deliberately on consumer markets. Since the organisational routines they will need to adapt to consumer markets are mostly those around retail distribution chains, it is very likely that they will form holobionts with consumer Cost Leaders, such as Walmart, perhaps operating as contract manufacturers. As with the possible new Trust Leader entrants, it is also possible, in theory, that White Labellers may emerge from the streamlining of current consumer health companies but there is no sign of that in the data. Those companies face much larger cultural and path dependency barriers than companies with a Cost Leader heritage. Wherever they emerge from, it is likely that, as the aspirations of poor patients for modern healthcare grow, the White Labeller model will emerge as an adaptive response to that demand.

Like its government payer cousin, the White Labeller model is an adaptation favoured not only by the obvious, direct pressures of the value shift but also by the growth of global poor consumer segments in both developed and emerging markets. Both lowest cost models are enabled by the disintegrated business structures and focused value chains favoured by the holobiont and trimorphic shifts. Both are favoured by the demands made on healthcare budgets by the systeomic shift and the efficiency and management improvements enabled by the information shift. Overall, the net influence of these selection pressures seems to favour the emergence of lowest cost models in both patient payer and government payer habitats. How significant the White Labeller will be will depend largely on how many poor patients will exist between the middle classes and the very poor, who are beyond reach of any business model.

Models for more demanding conditions

The Patient Demander model

> Cipla has always brought accessible and affordable medicines to fight against diseases like AIDS and Hepatitis B. Hence, Cipla has made it a priority to bring Hepcvir to patients in India as well as the other developing nations.
>
> **Subhanu Saxena, Cipla**

Similar to its Fast Follower cousin that is adapted to the government payer habitat, the Patient Demander model is a differentiated model characterised by a focus on more demanding conditions in middle class patients. It focuses on technology that is just behind the leading edge, with the aim of offering clinical advantage over mature technology competitors. This model is driven by the existence of relatively well informed patients who demand greater efficacy than that offered by older products, hence the Patient Demander description. Like its government payer cousin, the Fast Follower, the Patient Demander model achieves evolutionary fitness only when two conditions are met. First, when investment made in following close behind the leading edge creates customer preference and superior returns. Second, when those superior returns outweigh the commercial and technical risks of the model. The major and important difference between the two models is that their customers are quite different. This means that the organisational routines needed to manage customers are likely to be somewhat different. In particular, the Fast Follower and Patient Demander models will probably differ in those organisational routines employed in creating customer preference, such as those involved in segmentation, targeting and proposition development.

From looking at how other models are emerging, it is no surprise that the Patient Demander model is much less emerged than its relation the Consumer Brand Leader. This is presumably because healthcare systems and professionals still control the treatment of more demanding conditions much more than they do less demanding conditions. The evidence for the emergence of Patient Demanders is still scant, but what there is intriguing. For example, Gilead is partnering with generic companies in emerging markets to make available a generic version of Sovaldi, its very effective Hepatitis C treatment. This seems aimed at both government payers and middle class patients, making it a step towards a Patient Demander model. Another example can be found in Roche's partnering with insurance companies in China to make Herceptin available to patient payers. Again, this targeting of middle class patients with an advanced, but ageing, treatment points to the emergence of a Patient Demander model. In vaccines, the increasing trend for middle class grandparents to gift vaccines to their descendants is another example of the same model, since the vaccines often complement state provision. In medical devices, the evidence for Patient Demander models comes from the development of technology that is easier to use and has lower power demands, as required in some emerging markets. Demands by patient and their carers for non-routine treatments such as proton beam therapy point to a latent Patient Demander fitness peak. The slow emergence of this model reflects the involvement and control of healthcare professionals in the use of more advanced medical technologies. However, in some areas, such as cosmetically or ergonomically advanced prosthetics or in sports injury treatment, there are early signs that companies are targeting middle class consumers with technology that is only just behind the leading edge. It is in these early signals that we detect the emergence of the Patient Demander in both pharmaceuticals and medical technology.

The emergence of the Patient Demander model, nascent as it is, is the aggregate result of selection pressures acting simultaneously and to varying degrees. As with the other operationally excellent models, the value shift and global shift favour the Patient Demander by creating a large global market for these premium consumer products. The global shift also enables both innovation and manufacture in emerging markets, where a large proportion of this market lies. The trimorphic and holobiont shifts enable firms to simultaneously combine the necessary level of innovation and low cost operations. Again, the information and systeomic shifts play an indirect role by feeding the Patient Demander model with new technologies to be imitated. An overall consideration of the six great shifts and their selection pressures therefore makes the emergence of the Patient Demander seem inevitable, even if that emergence is slowed by the role of healthcare professionals in managing more demanding conditions.

The Canny Consumer model

> *A cottage industry of drug distributors, medical tourism agencies and consultants is emerging to offer patients in the US and other developed countries cheap copies of Sovaldi from countries where it is sold for one percent of the US price.*
>
> **Shannon Pettypiece and Ketaki Gokhale, Bloomberg**

Mirroring its Frugal Follower cousin that is adapted to the government payer habitat, the Canny Consumer model is a pure play model that offers no clinical advantage over the competition. It is characterised by a focus on more demanding conditions in poor patients and using more advanced, but not leading, technology.

The target customer for this model demands efficacy but requires low prices, which prompted the Canny Consumer label, 'canny' being used in the sense of being careful or discerning. As with its Frugal Follower cousin, competitive advantage for the Canny Consumer model comes only from price competition and high evolutionary fitness is achieved only when two conditions are met. First, the investment required to achieve the lowest cost base among its competitor set must create superior returns, even at prices below that of the differentiated competition. Second, these superior returns must outweigh the risk of following close behind innovators. The major and important difference between the two frugal cousins is that their customers are quite different. This points to the organisational routines of the two closely related models being very similar but differing importantly with respect to customer management. Given the basis of their competitive advantage, the Canny Consumer model's most distinctive routines are likely to be those for minimising the cost and maximising the margins in their very different distribution channels.

For many of the same reasons as its government payer cousin, the Canny Consumer is the least emerged member of its species flock. Although the emerging market of bio-similar companies and low cost medical technology companies discussed earlier are Frugal Followers in the government payer habitats, they have not yet crossed into patient payer habitats. However, they will inevitably see their government markets mature and become less profitable and this will lead them to focus on consumer markets, evolving into Canny Consumer models. To get the organisational routines and capabilities they need, they may form holobionts with consumer Cost Leaders in retail channels. The evidence reveals few signs of other possible antecedents to the Canny Consumer model although medical tourism and grey markets (from low cost to high cost markets) point to the latent demand. The constraints of culture and path dependence probably mean that only these emerging market companies could follow this model and that no other model is likely to be viable for them.

The Canny Consumer model is favoured by the selection pressures all of the six great shifts. The cost pressures of the value shift; the growth globally of poor consumers disinte-grated, holobiont business structures; focused, trimorphic value chains; and new, systeomic technologies to imitate – these all favour the emergence of this model. That it is not yet clearly emerging seems to be the result of a number of factors, some transient and others less so. The relatively recent nature of many of the six great shifts is part of the reason this model has not fully emerged; their concomitant selection pressures have not yet had time to shape the market in this habitat. More persistent is the fact that demanding conditions, managed by healthcare professionals, give less of a role to patients, even when they are paying. Taken together, these considerations suggest that the Canny Consumer model will emerge; but it will do so more slowly and perhaps never with the same prominence as its cousins.

A species flock of operationally excellent models in the patient payer habitat

In this part of the book, I have explored the habitat where firms compete by being operationally excellent and trying to sell the benefits (usually lower prices) to patient payers. Like the adjacent habitat where the government is the payer, this habitat has always existed to some extent in the life sciences industry. However, until recently it has been of secondary importance when compared to the more profitable technological innovator habitats. The six great shifts and the selection pressures that flow from them are changing the relative importance of those habitats in both developed and emerging markets.

In *The Future of Pharma* I suggested a single operationally excellent model, the Monster Imitator, bestriding both government payer and patient payer habitats. My newer research suggests that four species will emerge in each habitat. These two species flocks will be very similar, with a great deal of commonality in their 'routineomes'. All eight models will have well developed routines for operational excellence. Their genes for product develop-ment will differ, depending on what conditions they focus upon. Similarly, their genes for

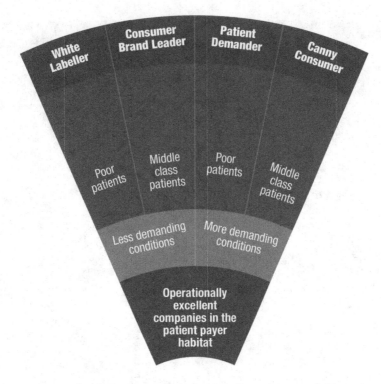

Figure 18.2 The emergence of operationally excellent models in the patient payer habitat

customer management, depending on which customers they target. In both government and patient payer species flocks, we see the species emerging at different rates. This is partly the differential effects of selection pressures and partly cultural and path dependency effects. For those species closest to existing business models, such as the Consumer Brand Leader, the evidence is plentiful and strong. For those that are a greater evolutionary distance from current business models, such as the Canny Consumer, the evidence is currently scant and weak. Yet it is perhaps these predicted but little-emerged models that have the most potential to change the industry. A Frugal Follower, for example, could disrupt much of the industry in this habitat and beyond. Both separately and together, the two operationally excellent species flocks offer investors a broad portfolio of risk and return options, attracting investment and so helping to expand their own habitats.

Looked at as whole, our evidence and examples point to this species flock, shown in Figure 18.2 and Figure 18.3, emerging to both shape and exploit the operational excellence/patient payer space.

Life on the entangled bank

At this point, having completed our exploration of both the technologically innovative and operationally excellent parts of the industry fitness landscape, it is worth pausing to consider the species we have seen evolving during our exploration. In *The Future of Pharma*, I was able to discern only two business models that might occupy these varied habitats; I called them the Genius and the Monster Imitator. That earlier work suggested

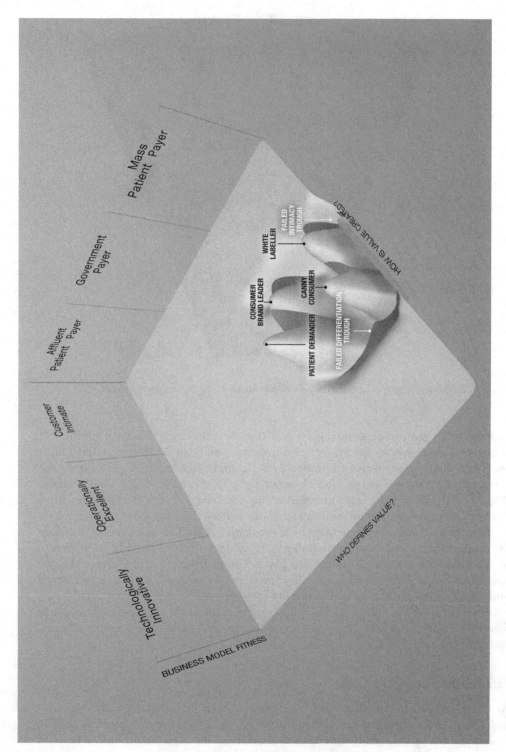

Figure 18.3 The emerging fitness landscape of operationally excellent companies in the patient payer habitat

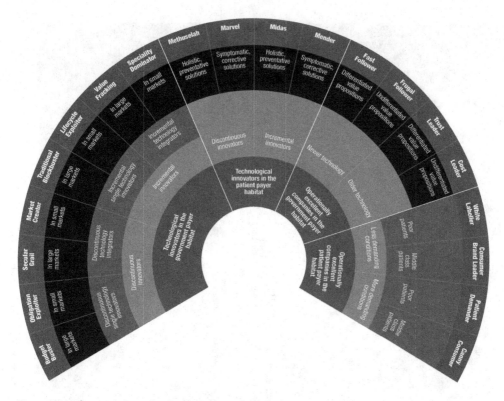

Figure 18.4 The speciation of technological innovator and operationally excellent models

that together these two species would occupy the fitness peaks of Lazarus and Narcissus, Pressure State, Advanced State, Core State Provision and Limited Choice.

The extensive work I have done since shows that this picture was only an approximation and has confirmed Orgel's observation that evolution is cleverer than I am. The Genius and the Monster Imitator now appear to be genera, not species. In the context of the six great shifts, whose selection pressures determine the survival implications of each evolutionary choice, two related species flocks of operationally excellent models are emerging, each with four discernible species occupying adjacent but distinct fitness peaks. Add to these the twelve technologically innovative species and we can see that, just as biological evolution leads to the wonderful complexity of life, economic evolution is leading to a wonderful complexity of life science business models. Even though we haven't completed our exploration, Darwin's imagery of a tangled bank already seems appropriate. Figure 18.4 and Figure 18.5 summarise our exploration of this complexity so far. In the next part of the book, I will move on to explore the terra incognita of customer intimate business models.

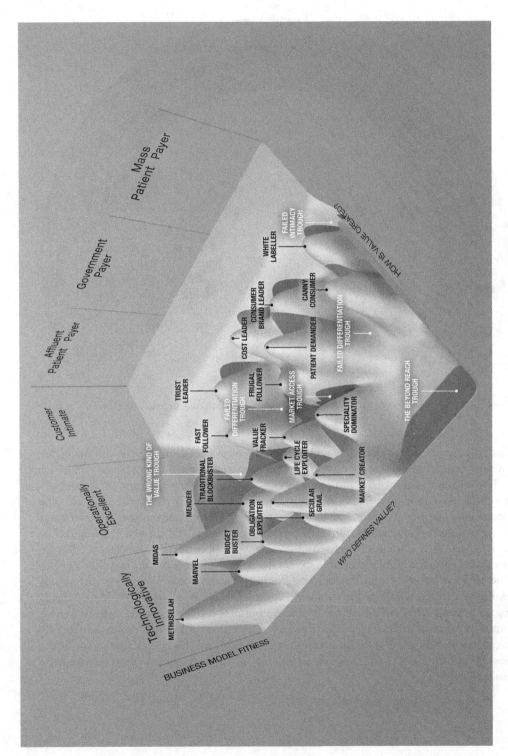

Figure 18.5 The emerging fitness landscape in technologically innovative and operationally excellent habitats

19 Customer intimate species emerging in the government payer habitat

So far in this third part of the book, I have discussed the emergence of models that create value by technological innovation or by operational excellence. In this section, I examine the emergence of models that create value through customer intimacy. Whereas technological innovators are the obvious descendants of research-based companies and operationally excellent companies the descendants of imitative, generic companies, customer intimate companies have fewer and less obvious ancestors in the life science sector. The genes (that is, the organisational routines) for customer intimacy are much less evolved in a sector traditionally focused on products. Customer intimacy as a concept is therefore less understood in the industry, and my exploration of its evolution is likely to be misunderstood unless I begin with some definition and clarification.

Like technological innovation and operational excellence, the idea of customer intimacy has its origins in the work of Michael Porter, although the term was actually coined by his followers, Michael Treacy and Fred Wiersema, as I mentioned in Chapter 7. Porter's work has been enormously influential and, like much great work, is very simple in essence.

Porter's contribution can be explained in four connected ideas. First, value is created by meeting needs. So technological innovation meets the need for product excellence (for example, in clinical efficacy) and operational excellence meets the need for low costs (for example, in low prices).

Second, within any market, customer needs are usually heterogeneous along multiple dimensions, not just a single 'good vs. cheap' axis. Within any mature product category, they vary along tangible, practical dimensions, such as ease of use and compatibility with other products. They also vary along less obvious dimensions, such as whether the customer seeks long or short term value or has a high or low need to feel innovative or confident in the product. This is an idea that Porter absorbed from marketing theorists like Theodore Levitt, and it led him to identify a third way of creating value: customer intimacy. This concept holds that a firm can create value with merely adequate products and operations by tailoring its offer more closely to the customer's specific set of needs. This was exactly how, in the 1920s, General Motors overcame Ford's incumbent advantages of scale and it is how smaller, independent retailers, restaurants and service businesses compete against giant, global competitors.

Porter's third idea was that being excellent (that is, clearly and demonstrably superior to the competition) is very expensive. Except in unusual conditions, such as embryonic markets or those where political factors make the market very imperfect (in the economists' sense of that word), most companies already make a pretty good offer to the market and have picked all the low hanging fruit. There are rarely any easy, quick, cheap wins. Being truly excellent is therefore difficult and expensive.

Porter's final and arguably most important idea was that, to a large degree, the three ways of creating value – product excellence, operational excellence and customer intimacy – are mutually exclusive. That is, the activity pattern required to achieve any one of these things often contradicts the other two or, at best, has little synergy with them. So, for example, the money invested in understanding an innovative new mode of action or in being the lowest cost producer or in understanding the intricacies of customers' non-clinical needs have little influence on one another.

Combining these ideas, Porter recognised that there were three fundamental ways to compete and that it is almost always necessary to choose one of these to the exclusion of the others. Customer intimacy, the tailoring of the product and the offer around it to meet the specific, contextual and extended needs of the customer, is the third of those three approaches and the one least familiar to the life sciences industry, which is typically strongly product-oriented (in research-based companies) or cost-oriented (in generic, follower companies).

Yet customer intimacy is a viable, possible route to creating value, optimising risk-adjusted return on investment, ensuring survival of the interactor (the firm) and thus amplification of the replicators (the organisational routines). Orgel's Second Law suggests, and biological analogues imply, that evolution will find and use any possible route to survival. The life sciences industry is familiar with the product excellence route and, especially in recent years, has become familiar with the operational excellence route. The customer intimacy route is one that the industry has not yet explored to the same extent. But, given the pressure for survival, we should expect and look for the emergence of customer intimate models.

To look for the emergence of such models, I followed the same method as in other habitats; I collected, organised and re-organised the activities of companies in the industry according to similarities and differences between their decisions. Again, I was imitating Linnaeus's method. As with technological innovation and operational excellence, I began my search in the habitat most familiar to life science companies, that where the government is the payer. Later, I will describe the habitats where affluent and less affluent patients are the payers.

Two evolutionary choices

As before, my search for customer intimate adaptations in the government payer habitat did not start with preconceived categories. Instead, I looked for emerging patterns in the observed activity of companies. I was also guided by examples of customer intimate activity in other sectors and I looked for analogous activity that could not be described as either technologically innovative or operationally excellent. The exploration involved trying to see past marketing and investor relations hype, which describes almost every business activity as being simultaneously innovative, efficient and customer focused. Whilst accepting that all business models involve at least a modicum of technological innovation and operational efficiency, I was looking for examples in which value was being created primarily by identifying and addressing varied, often non-obvious, customer needs. Examples from other business to business markets point to two broad ways that this typically happens. First, uncovering value that lies in the interstices between parts of the customers' value chain, such as when logistics companies work with manufacturing companies in the automotive sector. Second, the creation of value outside the traditional focus of activity, such as the merchandising activity of sports clubs and car companies. Despite the very obvious and important differences between these examples and life science companies, these analogues helped me to identify patterns of customer intimacy emerging in life science markets. As in the other habitats, these patterns revealed evolutionary choices about the best way to optimise risk–adjusted return on investment. In particular, two evolutionary choices emerged.

Management vs. prevention

> *I think that you will see much more of an emphasis on problem solving models, the things that address population health issues not simply particular point-in-time interventions. So devices that enable earlier intervention and prevention, I think will be more prominent. There's going to be an emphasis on early detection and management as well as prevention. I do see that happening.*
>
> **David Nexon, AdvaMed**

For customer intimate companies, a key determinant of risk-adjusted rate of return is the choice of which customers to address. That choice influences the size of the return because different markets vary in size and profitability. It also influences the level of risk because the nature of the customer influences the probability that customer intimacy activities will deliver the intended benefits and profits. In healthcare, the most fundamental 'which customers?' choice is whether to address the ill or the well. In other words, it is a choice between patients who have some illness or injury or those who have not yet become ill or injured. It is a choice between management and prevention.

Already ill patients are easier to target, more motivated to engage with the company and are generally a much better understood, and therefore less risky, population. Traditionally, ill patients have been the default choice for most life science companies, indeed for most healthcare systems. On the other hand, patients who are well, who are not yet ill or injured, are a much larger population and offer a potentially larger volume market. Perhaps more importantly, the value that can be created from successful prevention (that is, the improvement in healthcare outcomes that can be achieved per unit spend) is much greater than that possible via the management of the already ill or injured. Although it varies greatly between disease areas and patient categories, the old English idiom that 'an ounce of prevention is worth a pound of cure' is generally applicable in healthcare contexts. This is especially true for those long-lasting chronic conditions, such as diabetes, cardiovascular and respiratory diseases, that threaten to engulf government healthcare budgets.

For life science companies looking to create value through customer intimacy, the evolutionary choice to focus on the ill and injured or the well emerges from the data. Either choice is a trade off between risk and return. Depending on the context, either choice may optimise risk-adjusted rate of return. It may also be possible for a business model to choose somewhere along the illness–wellness spectrum although, in practice, this seems not to occur. In any case, as a guide to understanding how customer intimate business models are emerging, the management vs. prevention choice is a useful taxonomic division.

Low or high integration

> *A big portion of my business focuses on hospital operations management. It's driving much more of an operational factory approach where you can simulate care pathways and you can really work on optimising the flow of patients. In some hospitals, I can go to the emergency room and I wait for four hours for an initial diagnosis, then I wait for two hours for a CT scan, then I wait for four hours for the results of that CT scan, then I wait for a bed. So we are interested in how do you streamline the hospital process in the same way*

that you would streamline a production schedule within a factory. It's an analogy that we are applying in terms of different technology such as hospital simulation.

Michael Swinford, GE Healthcare

When a business model seeks to optimise risk-adjusted rate of return, there is typically a natural limit created by the total market for the product. The returns associated with a market are usually limited to that theoretical maximum; a company can extract no more than 100 percent of the market's profit pool and usually far less. However, customer intimacy approaches often appear to bend that rule. In the logistics and sports merchandise examples cited earlier, companies extract value far greater than the limits of the transport or sports market by releasing value beyond the limits of the product-defined market.

An important evolutionary choice therefore involves whether to stay within the boundaries of the product-defined market or to expand activity beyond those boundaries. In the government payer healthcare context, this equates to a decision about how much to integrate with the healthcare system's value chain. At one extreme, life science companies can choose to supply only products or only products and closely associated services – a low integration choice. At the other extreme, they can choose to provide products and/ or extensive services that go far beyond their traditional product categories. This involves doing some of the activity formerly carried out by the customer and is a high integration choice. Low integration is easier, more familiar and less risky. High levels of integration are harder; they require new capabilities and, being less familiar, they are more risky. However, because it goes beyond the traditional boundaries of the market, the potential returns from high integration greatly exceed those from low integration. This is especially true in disease areas and treatment pathways that involve multiple stages and span internal boundaries within healthcare systems, such as those involving both diagnosis and treatment and primary and secondary care. Every connection between healthcare processes and every boundary between functions provides an opportunity for value to be created by more effective and efficient integration.

Hence, for life science companies looking to create value through customer intimacy, the evolutionary choice between low and high integration emerges from the data. Either choice is a trade off between risk and return. Depending on the context, either choice may optimise risk-adjusted rate of return. It may also be possible for a business model to choose somewhere along the integration spectrum although, in practice, the choice seems to polarise. In any case, as a guide to understanding how customer intimate business models are emerging, the low vs. high integration choice is a useful taxonomic division.

There are other choices that determine the risk-adjusted rate of return of a customer intimate business model and which could serve as differentiating traits to help us understand and categorise emerging business models. A number of other factors, such as relatedness to products and impact on service efficacy, did indeed emerge from my work but these two stood out as the most useful differentiating traits. Like spines and cell nuclei, they are criteria against which the innumerable choices made in practice by life science companies can be usefully assessed and categorised.

To a large degree, these two evolutionary choices are independent of each other; the first choice doesn't seem to have much influence on the second. So, as with the other habitats, this means that they can be combined to form a taxonomy of theoretically possible business models, as shown in Figure 19.1.

As with its equivalent taxonomies in other habitats, it is important to remember three caveats with regard to Figure 19.1. It applies only to customer intimate models in the

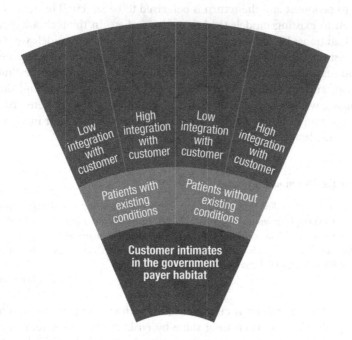

Figure 19.1 A taxonomy of customer intimate companies in the government payer habitat

government payer space; the four models are theoretical predictions, and we should not be surprised to find some business models that don't fit easily into any one category; and, like all taxonomies, Figure 19.1 is an approximation.

Notwithstanding those caveats, this model guides our understanding of industry evolution. It allows us to make sense of the business models we observe in practice and suggests a species flock of customer intimate models in the government payer space. As with the other habitats, this taxonomy is not a preconceived framework that I imposed on the data. Rather, it is a taxonomy that emerged from the data and that we can use to systematise and clarify our understanding of reality. In the remainder of this section, I will discuss some of the evidence for this framework and how it leads to an observed taxonomy of customer intimate models in the government payer habitat. I will begin with those models concerned with managing illness or injury before addressing the models concerned with prevention.

Manager models

> *We implemented a large deployment in Cape Verde, connecting nine islands in the whole population via Telemedicine. So before they evacuate any one, before they transport anybody from island to island they have to use Telemedicine unless it's a serious emergency. That makes a significant difference to the costs of their healthcare system.*

> **Manoel Coelho, GlobalMed**

The evolutionary choices embodied in new business models are aimed at optimising the risk/return balance, since it is this which will ensure the replication of the organisational routines. Unsurprisingly in other habitats, we saw models emerge earliest where the risk is perceived to be lowest and the return is perceived to be largest. This means that models that are closest to existing models tend to evolve earliest. In the technological innovator habitat, the Traditional Blockbuster and Life Cycle Exploitation models were examples of this. In the customer intimate context, we should expect new models to emerge that are closest to and share the most organisational routines with existing business models. Since the majority of current business models are based on treating the ill and injured, rather than maintaining wellness, we should expect new models to emerge here first. Indeed this 'gradualist' evolution of business models that manage the already ill or injured is what first emerges from the data.

The Treatment Enabler model

> We have a company called Vree Healthcare, a mobile based company that manages interaction between patients, hospitals, physicians and care givers. The first product that they brought to market was called Transition Advantage and is designed to prevent hospital readmissions, unnecessary hospital readmissions. And then we have a company called Telerx which is again a consumer, patient, care giver interaction company using mobile technology to better manage patient care.
>
> **Jay Galeota, Merck**

This Treatment Enabler model is characterised by a focus on patients who already have some health problems and on creating value by enabling treatment regimes. Characteristically, this model leaves ownership of the patient in the hands of the healthcare system and does not integrate deeply into that systems value chain. It therefore avoids the investment needed to build deep insight into the treatment pathways or to build the capabilities needed to combine closely with its customers' processes. In doing so, it foregoes some potential returns but, if it is successful, this model offers high fitness since it creates substantial returns at relatively low risk. The fact that this model primarily uses customer intimacy to enable treatment led me to label it the Treatment Enabler model.

The Treatment Enabler model is an example of gradualist evolution, since almost all previous life science industry models have been based on this low integration approach, helping the healthcare system to manage the already ill or injured. What is relatively novel about the Treatment Enabler model is that it is not based on technological innovation or operational excellence but on understanding and addressing the non-clinical needs of patients and healthcare systems.

Unsurprisingly, evidence of this is emerging in areas where addressing only clinical needs has proven insufficient. The most obvious examples are chronic diseases such as diabetes; respiratory diseases, principally COPD and asthma; and cardiovascular disease. In these cases, treatments already exist that, used correctly, allow most patients to live reasonable lives. But poor adherence to treatment leads to complications and exacerbations and concomitant cost implications for governments. The business models that are emerging to address this are based on customer intimacy and seek to address the non-clinical needs that might improve adherence to treatment, such as ease of use. The simplest examples of this are in respiratory, with the push by GSK, AstraZeneca, Chiesi and others to develop 'triple' combination therapies and smart drug delivery devices. AstraZeneca's investment in Adherium, developers of 'smart' inhalers, is just one example in a pattern of such investments that point to firms developing a customer intimate Treatment Enabling business model.

In diabetes management there is a wave of activity aimed at improving monitoring and compliance that is quite distinct from the development of new medicines in this therapy area. This includes Mayo Clinic's joint venture with Gentag to develop smartphone-based diabetes management, and Medtronic's work on closed loop insulin pumps, the so-called artificial pancreas. In cardiovascular disease, St Jude's Merlin patient monitoring system is aimed at improving outcomes and reducing costs via individual monitoring of patients at home. A broader approach to patient monitoring is the aim of Cerner and Qualcomm's recent collaboration; it is aimed at creating value not simply through more effective products or lower costs but by tailoring patient management more closely to the individual. In a hospital setting, costs and patient outcomes are often made worse by the development of pressure ulcers, and their avoidance has long been important to in-patient care. GE Healthcare's multi-sensing hand-held probe aims to enable this part of the treatment process. What unites these and other examples are that they create value not primarily through technological innovation (although all have elements of that) or through operational excellence (although all are aimed at optimising health economic outcomes). Rather, all of these approaches aim to create value by customer intimacy, by understanding and addressing customer needs at a more granular level than simply clinical indication. In addition, each of these approaches is aimed at managing patients who are already ill or injured. Finally, each model involves supplying the healthcare system in a relatively low involvement manner. Taken together, these three evolutionary choices of customer intimacy, existing conditions and low involvement, are the characteristics of the Treatment Enabler model.

The fact that the Treatment Enabler model is a small, gradual step from existing approaches does not imply that this model is inferior to other, more radically innovative models. The costs of drugs and devices typically make up around 10 percent of the overall costs of managing a disease or injury. This places a tight limit on the value that can be created by reducing the costs of those products or by replacing them with improved versions. It also means that much of the remaining 90 percent of the total value opportunity is available to customer intimate business models, of which the Treatment Enabler is one. Its low integration approach may limit how much value it can create, but the evidence in areas like respiratory disease, diabetes compliance and pressure ulcer avoidance suggests that there is still a large, deep pool of value to be tapped here.

Like all other business models, the Treatment Enabler is emerging as a result of the selection pressures created by the six great shifts. The value shift creates a positive selection pressure when the Treatment Enabler model creates real health economic value, as it seems to do in some of the example contexts mentioned earlier. The global shift fragments large, homogeneous clinically-defined markets into many smaller sub-markets, an environment in which any kind of customer intimacy is a competitive advantage. As the Mayo Clinic example demonstrates, the Treatment Enabler often requires the collaborative, networked business models favoured by the holobiont shift. Since it is not technologically innovative, the systeomic shift has less direct impact on the Treatment Enabler than it does on some other models, but its indirect effects are still significant, for example, when it enables our holistic understanding of a condition such as diabetes and its consequences. The information shift is an important positive selection pressure, as smart inhalers exemplify. The trimorphic shift, which favours polarising value chains, can be seen acting when, for example, telemedicine companies focus on their technology only because they can rely on other organisations to focus on medicines and patient care. Considering all the selection pressures as a whole, the Treatment Enabler model's emergence in the government payer habitat seems strongly favoured by the environment's selection pressures.

The Risk Manager model

The model shifts from selling products to invoicing for services per capita, based on the patient we're respon-
sible for. But more importantly, we commit to sharing risks. We have major programmes of this kind in
Europe where we commit to realising significant annual savings from process efficiencies.

Angelo de Rosa, Medtronic

Like its cousin the Treatment Enabler, the Risk Manager model is characterised by a focus on patients who already have some underlying condition. Where it differs is that, to a greater or lesser extent, it integrates into the healthcare system and takes ownership of the patient. The significance, cost and difficulty of doing so should not be understated. The new organisational routines and capabilities involved are extensive and are often different from those required by existing, low integration models. This model therefore involves significant investment with the aim of releasing otherwise inaccessible returns. If it is successful, this model offers high fitness by creating substantial returns that outweigh the additional risk. The fact that this model uses customer intimacy to manage risk that formerly belonged to healthcare providers led me to label it the Risk Manager model.

The Risk Manager model is an example of a more significant evolutionary change than the gradualist Treatment Enabler. It is genetically (that is, its routineome is) more differentiated from a company that simply makes and sells products. However, the ancestors of such models have existed for some time. In areas such as dialysis, medical nutrition and managing thrombosis, some life science companies have made significant steps towards integrating with healthcare systems. The same can be seen in some medical device and in-vitro diagnostic categories, where supply and servicing arrangements have sometimes blurred into running the service on behalf of the healthcare providers.

The Risk Manager model is different from the Treatment Enabler model and more evolved than these ancestor models, in that it takes an evolutionary step along a continuum of integration with the healthcare system. Unsurprisingly, evidence for its emergence is less developed than for the Treatment Enabler, but it is still significant. The most prominent example of this is Medtronic, which is developing Risk Manager models from its existing product franchises, principally by a series of acquisitions and alliances that are meant both to expand its product portfolio and to gain capabilities in managing services. It began with cardiac catheter labs and, with the acquisition of Dutch company Diabeter, is signalling a parallel model in diabetes care. Similarly, its large acquisition of Covidien seems designed to allow it to build a Risk Manager model in the huge operating room market. In the market to monitor post-acute care patients, Medtronic's Cardiocom business has partnered with LHC to provide services to home healthcare companies. As the earlier quote from Michael Swinford illustrates, GE Healthcare is prominent in the development of this model too. In these and other cases, the model involves moving from selling the products to delivering the service in which the product is used. A similar model can be seen emerging in Cardinal Health's acquisition of AssuraMed. Again, a company that primarily supplied medicines and devices is acquiring the capabilities to take on the risk, and realise the returns, further down the healthcare value chain. The development of the Risk Manager model is also observed in diagnostics and imaging. Here, Quest and Bracco both appear to be evolving towards forms of Risk Manager. Other medical technology groups are beginning to acquire the risk of designing the healthcare infrastructure, as Philips Healthcare is doing in India.

As different as they are, the Treatment Enabler and Risk Manager models have in common the evolutionary choice of focusing on patients who are already ill or injured. Whilst this choice is closest to existing industry models and implies less need for new organisational routines, the trade off is to turn away from the massive returns available from preventing illness. It is those models that I will discuss next.

Preventer models

I often compare human healthcare with that of a cow. On a modern farm, the cow has an RFID tag. Every health event is catalogued. If it gets sick, the vet is notified. The cow gets great, longitudinal, continuous healthcare. GM do a similar thing with my car, so that if there's a problem it is addressed before a break down. Human healthcare will have to move in that direction.

Elias Zerhouni, Sanofi

As I explored models that focus on prevention rather than management of illness and injury, my exploration took me into parts of the life science fitness landscape where few traditional healthcare companies have dared to venture. To prevent illness and injury is much easier in principle than it is in practice because causes are often multifactorial and lifestyle related. If this were not so, prevention would already be more important than management. Consequently, preventative models are likely to demand a lot of new organisational routines and capabilities not currently possessed by traditional life science companies, which evolved in the management of illness habitat.

Importantly, this need for new 'DNA' has three implications for the course of industry evolution. First, if the needs to be addressed are often behavioural and complex, it suggests that customer intimate companies may have the edge over technologically innovative companies in creating value here. Second, it suggests that the incumbent life science companies, with their legacy of organisational routines suited to illness management, may be relatively slow at evolving towards fitness peaks that require routines for illness prevention. Finally, in a previously unoccupied habitat where legacy DNA may be a disadvantage, we might expect new, non-life science companies without that legacy to evolve into this space first and faster. Indeed those three considerations do seem to be influencing the industry's evolution in this part of the fitness landscape.

The Extrinsic Nudge model

Obesity is by and large a disease of the poor, that's clear. Often, you will read in the press about people eating fried food and junk food, and processed food in the supermarket [being] way cheaper than the healthy food. And that's a big problem. I think that the people who govern our countries are realising that something has to be done to make the patient more responsible for their own health. And I think we're seeing more and more of that.

Bruno Strigini, Merck

The Extrinsic Nudge model is characterised by a focus on patients who are generally well, and on creating value by enabling the continuation of wellness. Characteristically, this model enables and influences behaviour that maintains wellness rather than attempting to directly control the factors or behaviours that might lead to illness. This limited influence on behaviour mitigates the difficulty and risk associated with trying to change human behaviour but, in doing so, it foregoes the potential returns of being more involved in, and directive of, patients' lives. If it is successful, this model offers high fitness, since it opts for relatively low risk whilst still creating substantial returns. Inspired by Cass Sunstein and Richard Thaler's book (171), I labelled this model the Extrinsic Nudge model.

As an evolutionary step, the Extrinsic Nudge model is somewhere between the Treatment Enabler and the Risk Manager. It is gradualist in one sense, taking a low integration approach, but novel in focusing on prevention. This implies a degree of emergence somewhere between its two cousins. Extrinsic Nudge models have some antecedents, for example in medicines that discourage smoking and in substitutes for addictive drugs, but the models we see emerging now go well beyond those in scope and potential. What is relatively novel about the Extrinsic Nudge model is that although it often uses a degree of technological innovation, it is mostly about nudging patients to either maintain wellness or prevent the progression of minor conditions to more serious ones. As I will discuss in Chapter 20, maintaining wellness is an area where there is some parallel evolution between the government payer and patient payer habitats. There is and will be overlap and exchange between these two habitats, which will partly depend on local regulatory and economic conditions. For the moment at least, however, we can see the distinct emergence of an Extrinsic Nudge model in the government payer habitat.

When looking for examples of prevention models, the most striking feature of the data is how much it is restricted to one area: weight management and obesity. On reflection, this seems quite rational; of all the illness prevention measures that governments could wish for, obesity stands out as the single most important. Its implications for epidemiology, from cardiovascular disease to cancers to diabetes, are huge and undisputed. Unsurprisingly, therefore, examples of Extrinsic Nudge models are mostly found in the area of weight control. Roche's Xenical is perhaps the most obvious example here, and over-the-counter Alli is also an example of the overlap with patient payer markets. Further evidence of the emergence of this model is the development of other medicines for obesity, such as Novo Nordisk's Saxenda for chronic weight management and Shire's Vyvanse for binge eating. These examples point to the emergence of the Extrinsic Nudge model, but the history of obesity drug development also points to the complex nature of the problem (172). Surgical intervention, such as gastric bands, and new devices, such as the Obalon weight-loss balloon or Gelesis's oral capsules, are more examples of the Extrinsic Nudge model in the government payer habitat. Beyond obesity, smoking cessation products, such as GSK's Zyban and Pfizer's Chantix, are the other principle evidence of the Extrinsic Nudge model.

Despite the small extent to which this model has emerged, the examples of it are varied. At first sight, it is hard to see the similarity between, for example, Chantix and Obalon. However, they share the key characteristics of the Extrinsic Nudge model. They create value primarily through customer intimacy, understanding and addressing customer needs at a granular level. Each of these approaches is aimed at preventing the development of illness. Finally, like the Treatment Enabler model, the Extrinsic Nudge model involves supplying the healthcare system in a relatively low involvement manner. These three evolutionary choices – customer intimacy, illness prevention and low involvement – define the Extrinsic Nudge model in the customer intimacy/government payer habitat.

The currently limited emergence of the Extrinsic Nudge model belies its potential importance to the life sciences market. Government payers generally recognise that trends, especially in lifestyle related diseases, threaten to overwhelm healthcare systems and government budgets, and that the reactive treatment paradigm has its limits. This implies a large pool of value available to effective Extrinsic Nudge business models. As with the Treatment Enabler, its low integration approach will limit how much value it can create but there is surely a large market opportunity, especially in obesity and other lifestyle conditions.

Like all other business models, the Extrinsic Nudge model is emerging from variations of organisational routines that are favoured by selection pressures created by the six great shifts. The value shift favours Extrinsic Nudge models that create real health economic value. The global shift spreads the market opportunity related to lifestyle diseases and also creates 'leapfrogging' opportunities for health systems that wish to avoid mimicking the west's problems. The complex nature of lifestyle related diseases often requires the new routines and collaborative, networked business models made possible by the holobiont shift. The systeomic and information shifts favour a holistic understanding of the links between disease and lifestyle. The polarising value chains of the trimorphic shift simultaneously allow innovation in specialised areas, greater customer understanding and global distribution, without the need to build a large organisation. Looked at overall, the emergence of the Extrinsic Nudge model seems assured. It is only the need to develop new organisational routines, and the weight of legacy routines, evolved to enable illness management, that is slowing that emergence.

The Social Demander model and the Big Brother trough

I think taxpayers and then governments will get very tired of paying for people who have no interest in looking after themselves. Whereas in the past we've said 'OK, if you're morbidly obese as a result of your lifestyle choices then that's very sad and we will help you.' But now it's such a well-documented problem that if you don't look after yourself, it has health consequences, that I'm not so sure that society will tolerate that.

Julian Bradwell, Proteus

The evolutionary choices and theoretical framework that emerged from my research data predict a business model in which, rather than simply nudged or enabled, the behaviour of currently healthy patients is controlled with the aim of avoiding illness or injury. One might imagine, for example, implanted diagnostics that detect smoking or excessive drinking by pregnant women, or perhaps even sugar intake by the morbidly obese or diabetic. This model would have high potential evolutionary fitness because, if successful, it would improve health outcomes, and so generate returns, for acceptable levels of risk. Since this model is characterised by societal demands on the patient, I labelled it the Social Demander model.

If examples of the Social Demander had been uncovered in my research, it would have supported the taxonomy in Figure 19.1, but none did. There are, however, extensive indications of moves in this direction. Some government healthcare providers are incentivising pregnant mothers towards healthier lifestyles with cash rewards. Some insurance companies are rewarding active lifestyles with reduced premiums. The highest level of control is seen by government payers restricting access to some treatments, such as in-vitro fertilisation or addiction therapy, on condition of behavioural changes. Similarly, in some countries, social security benefits are dependent on adherence to vaccination programmes. But, at time of writing, no evidence has emerged on life science companies in the government payer habitat developing a model that attempted to preserve wellness via high levels of control or involvement in patient lifestyle choices.

That said, to use a favourite adage of researchers, absence of evidence in not evidence of absence. It may simply mean that such models have not emerged yet but will in the future. There is a plausible, evolutionary explanation for this hypothesis. Whilst a Social Demander model would be favoured by the six shifts and their selection pressures, they would be disfavoured by other selection pressures from the social environment that have not so far been considered. For example, the values of many societies disfavour business models that impinge on personal freedom or the right to privacy. Similarly, many societal values disfavour the deliberate social or racial discrimination implied by lifestyle control. This is evidenced in public health programmes nominally targeted on the basis of income but focused, de facto, on certain ethnic or social groups. Those negative selection pressures would explain the non-emergence of the Social Demander model, but would also predict the conditions under which such models could emerge. For example, in societies where individual freedoms were valued less than communal benefits, such as in Singapore, we already see high levels of behavioural control by the government. In many countries, there is already a perception that treatments for 'self-inflicted' lifestyle conditions are less worthwhile than those for, say, childhood cancers. Finally, public and therefore political opinion in some societies is beginning to turn against those who deliberately choose unhealthy lifestyles (173). It is not difficult to imagine circumstances in which those circumstances combine to change societal values and begin to favour, in some contexts, a Social Demander model.

For these reasons, I have concluded that this part of the landscape currently includes both a Social Demander peak and an adjacent fitness trough. The peak represents conditions where the six great shifts overcome social resistance and the trough the reverse situation. A business model in this trough could have low fitness because of negative selection pressures created by some societal values in favour of freedom, privacy and equality. I labelled this part of the fitness landscape the Big Brother trough, in reference to Orwell's dystopian vision; but current trends mean that those societal values and selection pressures may well shift. If so, the selection pressures from the six shifts, which favour the Social Demander model, may well see the emergence of business models resembling my aforementioned imagined approaches.

A species flock of customer intimate models in the government payer habitat

In exploring the habitat described in this section, where the government pays and value is created by customer intimacy, we have moved some distance from the habitat that is most familiar to most of today's life science companies. Accordingly, the business models that we have predicted and observed are emerging only gradually and, even then, only in proportion to their closeness to existing models. The Treatment Enabler is most developed,

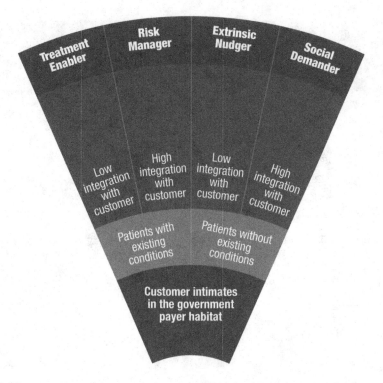

Figure 19.2 The emergence of customer intimate models in the government payer habitat

followed by the Extrinsic Nudge and the Risk Manager with the Social Demander still only a possibility, predicted in theory to emerge when, as seems likely, social values change and reduce the risks of the Big Brother trough.

The fact that these models have not yet strongly emerged does not mean that they are unimportant. On the contrary, the huge financial pressures and healthcare demands faced by governments, together with the limited ability of technological innovation and operational excellence models to meet that challenge, strongly suggests that the customer intimate models will become very important.

In *The Future of Pharma*, I predicted the emergence of three customer intimate models – the Value Picker, the Disease Manager and the Lifestyle Manager – that would occupy the government payer habitat. My subsequent work has developed those ideas and the three, or possibly four, business models described in this section are similar to those in the earlier book, but more clearly understood. As described for the other habitats in preceding sections of this book, this represents a species flock of business models that, in providing a range of risk and return options, widens investors' options, draws in capital and therefore constructs its own habitat. This species flock is shown in Figure 19.2 and Figure 19.3.

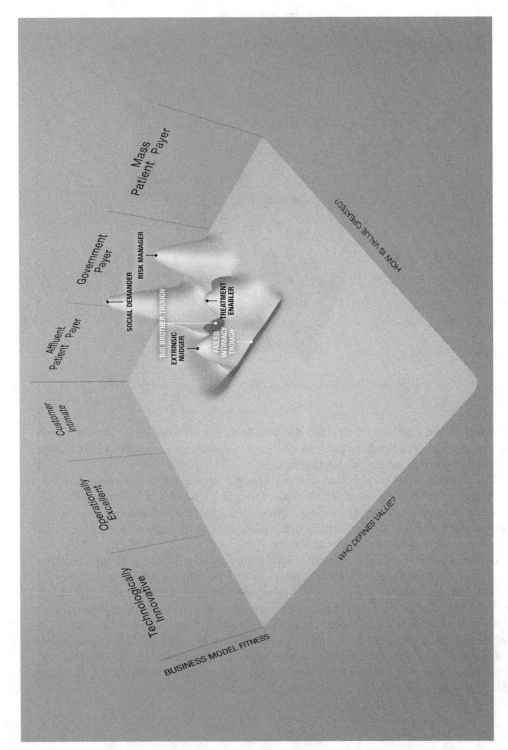

Figure 19.3 The emerging fitness landscape of customer intimate business models in the government payer habitat

20 Customer intimate species emerging in patient payer habitats

Whether they choose to compete via technological innovation, operational excellence or customer intimacy, the most familiar habitat for most life science companies remains the one in which governments pay. For most firms, this is the habitat in which they evolved and which has shaped, by the Darwinian evolution process of variation, selection and replication, the industry's 'gene pool' of organisational routines. Other habitats, in which the payer is the patient, have historically played only a secondary role in shaping the industry's business models.

However, as I have already discussed, changes in both the social and technological environments are leading to a relative diminution of the government role as payer and the growth of the patient payer gap, this latent market for healthcare that patients want but that governments will not or cannot pay for (see Figure 16.1 in Chapter 16). Of course, this habitat is neither new nor currently unpopulated. It has previously been addressed by over-the-counter medicine companies, some medical devices companies (for example in mobility aids and sports injury devices) and, especially in emerging markets, by low cost generic medicines. The patient payer habitats also increasingly overlap with the government payer habitats through co-payments and other contributory mechanisms.

For the last few decades at least, the habitats where the patient payer is dominant have generally come second to government payer habitats as a focus for life science companies. Only now are environmental changes causing these parts of the landscape to grow, fragment and gain in relative importance. And, just as biological species such as pigeons and foxes have adapted to occupy newly expanding, food rich urban habitats, so business models are evolving to fill the expanding patient payer habitats where there is opportunity to make a good risk-adjusted return on investment. I have already discussed the technological innovator and operational excellence models that are emerging to occupy patient payer habitats. In this section, I will discuss customer intimate models that are emerging to occupy that habitat where the patient, not the government, is the payer.

In my search for emerging customer intimate models in the patient payer habitat, I followed the same Linnaean method as I did other habitats. I collected masses of examples of real world decisions by companies and then repeatedly organised and re-organised them according to underlying similarities and differences between those decisions. The first observation that emerged from this process reinforced my findings in the technologically innovative and operationally excellent habitats: because of the polarisation of wealth distribution, the patient payer habitat is very heterogeneous.

The patterns of customer intimate activity in the life science sector point to three broad categories of patient payer. At the lowest levels of discretionary income, the Beyond Reach trough stretches across the landscape. It is wide in the technologically innovative habitat, narrows in the operationally excellent habitat and widens again in the customer intimate habitat. Although shrinking as economic growth raises millions out of poverty, there remain many millions, especially in emerging markets, that cannot be reached by any customer intimate model. To the extent that they can access any medical technology, they will rely on operationally excellent lowest cost models.

At the other extreme, there are the very wealthy, often characterised as the top few percent of the world's population. Because of their relatively small numbers, I will discuss the models in this wealthy habitat as an addendum towards the end of this section. Between these two extremes lies a broad habitat where patient payers have some discretionary income to allocate to healthcare. They purchase healthcare, medicines and medical technology that their governments cannot or will not pay for. Clearly, this is a broad category that includes a very wide range of purchasing power. Its boundaries are blurred and vary geographically, depending on how much state provision of healthcare there is and what form that provision takes.

What we see emerging in this latter, middle income area suggests it is naïve to try to be precise about those fuzzy, shifting boundaries. In this area, discretionary healthcare purchasing power is only loosely correlated to income or wealth and is heavily influenced by disease type, government provision and personal motivations. So, although I focused on looking for models emerging in this middle class area, it became clear that traditional demographic or economic categories revealed little here. One can observe relatively poor patients in emerging markets devoting considerable resources to healthcare because their governments will not pay for life-saving treatments. At the same time, one can observe relatively rich patients in developed markets relying on their governments to pay for relatively minor treatments. Eschewing a traditional, demographic approach, I continued to search for patterns in the evolutionary choices made by firms in this habitat, some traditionally life science firms and others not.

Two evolutionary choices

As in my exploration of the government payer habitat, my search for customer intimate adaptations in the patient payer habitat was guided by examples of customer intimate activity in other sectors. This prepared me to look for examples of creating value in the gaps between treatment activities and beyond the core patient–treatment process. Seeking out customer intimate approaches meant I looked in particular for activity that was focused on the granularity of customer needs, but which was neither technologically innovative nor operationally excellent. As before, this involved discounting some of the marketing and investor relations hype and allowing that all business models involve some degree of technological innovation and operational efficiency. As in the government payer habitat, this search process revealed that firms are making a number of evolutionary choices about the best way to optimise risk-adjusted return on investment in this habitat. In particular, two salient evolutionary choices emerged.

Management vs. prevention

> *Health is a very long term issue. You may be a thirty year old guy who has been healthy all your life. Then you marry and gain ten pounds. Then you have kids and put on another ten pounds and do less exercise. By the time you're middle aged, you've got a twenty year history of factors that predispose you to ill health. It's obviously much better to avoid arriving at that point.*

> **Michael Simpson, Caradigm**

As always, a key determinant of risk-adjusted rate of return is the choice of which patient payers to address. Traditionally most companies adopt the generally easier and less commercially risky approach of finding and treating patients with existing conditions, rather than looking those who are currently well. That choice is a trade off against the much larger possibilities to create value by maintaining wellness. This remains true even when competing for patients with existing conditions may mean competing with government payer models. The choice between focusing on management or prevention therefore has a fundamental influence on evolutionary success in the patient payer habitat. Depending on context, either choice may optimise risk-adjusted rate of return. It may also be possible for a business model to choose somewhere along the illness-wellness spectrum although, in practice, this seems not to occur. In any case, as a guide to understanding how customer intimate business models are emerging, the management vs. prevention choice is a useful taxonomic division in both government payer and patient payer habitats.

Low vs. high perceived health risk

I think that the unpredictability of human beings and the inconsistency of their behaviours are influencing health outcomes now, perhaps more so than the medicines and the advances in healthcare. Factors such as smoking, weight gain, poor diet, alcohol consumption. All of these factors are now at a point where they're offsetting the incremental benefit that the advances in medicine can provide.

Jay Galeota, Merck

A patient payer's motivation to allocate discretionary income to healthcare is heavily influenced by their state of health; a minor, transient condition creates less motivation than a debilitating, persistent one. And for those without existing conditions, this same argument takes the form of health risk. Those who through some combination of attitude, lifestyle and genetic predisposition have a significant perceived risk of developing a serious condition will typically be more motivated to allocate their discretionary income to healthcare than the lucky, well patient payer with a healthy lifestyle and no genetic predispositions. Overlaying these motivational factors are individual attitudes, ranging from the inappropriately complacent to the obsessively hypochondriac; but the underlying point remains that patient payers, whether ill or well, vary in their real and perceived levels of health risk. The choice between focusing on patients with differing perceived health risks presents customer intimate firms with another evolutionary trade off: focus on fewer, easier-to-get and more profitable, high risk patients or a greater number of harder-to-get and lower margin, low risk patients. In any given context, the choice of one over the other will imply greater or lesser evolutionary fitness. This choice therefore provides another dimension for understanding the emergence of customer intimate business models in the patient payer habitat.

In addition to these two dimensions, other evolutionary choices emerged from the research. These included factors such as aesthetic implications, as with cosmetic surgery, and emotive implications, as with paediatric markets. Such choices can and do determine the risk-adjusted rate of return of a customer intimate business model in the patient payer habitat. They could also serve as differentiating traits to help us understand and categorise emerging business models. However, the two factors highlighted here were most salient in the data. Like mammary glands and the number of hooves are to biologists, they are criteria against which the innumerable choices made in practice by life science companies can be usefully assessed and categorised.

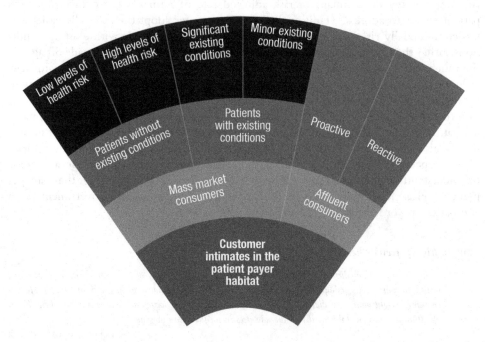

Figure 20.1 A taxonomy of customer intimate business models in the patient payer habitat

To a significant degree, management vs. prevention and level of perceived health risk are two evolutionary choices that are independent of each other; perceived health risk can vary within both ill and well populations. As with the other habitats, this independence means that they can be combined to form a taxonomy of theoretically possible business models, as shown in Figure 20.1.

Existing condition models

When customer intimate business models choose to focus on managing illness or injury, rather than maintaining wellness, they typically address markets that are smaller and have lower risk than markets of currently well customers. For most life science companies, it is also a choice to change less and rely more on existing, well developed organisational routines. As I discussed in Chapter 19 when I discussed models emerging in the government payer habitat, it is a more gradualist approach than focusing on the maintenance of wellness. Existing condition models are to the patient payer habitat what the Treatment Enabler or Risk Manager model are to the government payer habitat. Unsurprisingly, because it is more 'genetically similar' to current models, we see models that manage existing conditions evolving earlier and more quickly than models that focus on maintaining wellness. As predicted by the evolutionary choices shown in Figure 20.1, we see two existing condition models emerging.

The Self Carer model

The current drug market is very stiff. There are names used that no one can pronounce, leaflets you cannot understand and sometimes the side effects worse than the disease. That was for my partner and me the reason

to say it should be better. We make medical self-care tools for all kinds of home, garden and kitchen aches,
bladder infections to cold sores. Our motto is: be careful with your body! . . . People are getting smarter. We
first search the internet before we go to the doctor. There is more need to take care of ourselves.
Pieternella Bouter, Medical Brands

The Self Carer model focuses on patient payers with relatively minor, usually temporary, conditions that government payers do not address to the satisfaction of the patient. It therefore avoids the business risk involved in identifying and engaging with patient payers who are not currently ill and, in doing so, forgoes the returns available from those customers. When it is successful, the Self Carer model offers high fitness because it is relatively low risk, whilst still creating substantial returns. The fact that this model typically involves the patient payers caring for themselves, with little or no involvement from healthcare professionals, led me to label it the Self Carer model.

Quite obviously, the Self Carer model is a very gradualist evolutionary step, the near-descendant of current consumer healthcare models such as over-the-counter medicines and simple medical technology like first aid dressings, support bandages, incontinence products and so on. In markets with less extensive healthcare systems and in some more developed systems where co-payment is significant, the Self Carer model blurs into the government payer habitat and is closely related to the Treatment Enabler model.

The most obvious examples of the Self Carer model are the consumer health divisions of pharmaceutical companies that extend the lives of their technology into the patient payer habitat. GSK with antiviral products such as Zovirax, and AstraZeneca with its proton pump inhibitor Nexium, are both examples of treatments that extend the previously limited scope of prescription only medicines. In medical devices, we can observe the same trend from very simple consumer products to more sophisticated products that would, formerly, been obtained through healthcare professionals. Knee and other musculoskeletal supports, transcutaneous electrical nerve stimulation (TENS) and in-ear thermometers are all examples of this. In terms of both technology and therapy areas, what patient payers can buy is growing significantly. Overall, the picture is of a Self Carer model emerging that is much larger, more varied and more profitable than its less evolved ancestors in over-the-counter and First Aid.

The evolutionary forces that I described as the six great shifts are shaping this emergence of the Self Carer model. The global shift, by creating middle class patient payers across a much wider geography, is creating a larger market and is selecting against locally focused companies, which were historically dominant in this habitat. In developed markets, some aspects of the value shift, expressed through treatment rationing and mechanisms such as co-payments, are redrawing the boundary between treatments that are provided by governments and those that are not. This has the effect of growing the habitat for the Self Carer model. The information shift, via the internet and social media, is enabling patients to diagnose, prescribe and obtain treatments for minor ailments, substantially reducing the role of healthcare professionals. It also makes it possible for companies to identify and engage patient payers with minor ailments more easily. The trimorphic and holobiont shifts make it possible for companies to develop organisational capabilities needed by Self Carer models, without needing to build the entire value chain within one company. The growth of contract manufacturers in this area is an example of this. The systeomic shift, with its long term implications, seems to have the least direct influence on the Self Carer model but we can expect to see technologies trickle down over time into the patient payer space. Overall, the six great shifts are selecting for the Self Carer model, in which value is created for patient payers not through innovative technology or operational efficiency but through ever more granular understanding of their diverse motivations and via value propositions that are increasingly specific to their needs. This is the essence of customer intimacy.

The State Gap Filler model

> *In 2006, a $1,000 deductible was rare, except for people at small companies. Today, almost half of insured workers face a deductible of $1,000 or more, and for 36 percent of people at small employers the number is twice that high. Moreover, the burden of high deductibles isn't evenly distributed: Companies where more than one-third of workers earn $23,000 or less have deductibles that are 29 percent higher, on average, than companies where fewer workers are paid at that low level.*

> **Christopher Flavelle, Bloomberg**

The State Gap Filler model focuses on patient payers with existing, significant illness or injury, often chronic in nature, that government funded health systems (or state-subsidised health insurance, as in the US) does not address to the satisfaction of the patient. Like the Self Carer model, it avoids the risk involved in identifying and engaging with patient payers who are currently well and forgoes the returns available from those customers. However, it does require investment in identifying those patients whose needs take them out of the government payer habitat. It also involves the investment and risk of creating some form of value that is not provided by the government payer. When it is successful, the State Gap Filler model offers high fitness because it creates substantial returns for modest risk levels. The fact that this model typically involves the patient payers choosing to fill the gap between their needs and state (or insurance provider) provision, typically with some involvement of healthcare professionals, led me to label it the State Gap Filler model.

As a customer intimate approach focused on patient payers with existing conditions, the State Gap Filler is a close relation of the Self Carer model but with an important difference: it largely focuses on conditions that are significant and often chronic. In developed and, increasingly, some developing markets, these conditions are often addressed to some degree by government payers, so the State Gap Filler is also closely related to the Treatment Enabler model. However, it is distinguished from the Treatment Enabler by its focus on needs that government payers do not address. Such unmet needs can include the cosmetic, ease of use, efficacy and, in some cases, simple availability. The State Gap Filler model is therefore gradualist in a product sense; it typically involves products that are already sold to government payers in some context. But it shows more radical evolution in its customer focus. As a result, it has emerged rather less than the Self Carer model.

In diabetes care, products such as blood glucose meters, specialised footwear and various forms of sugar free medicine are available over-the-counter but not as reimbursable, prescribed products. In respiratory medicine, mild asthma can be medicated with over-the-counter formulations of epinephrine or ephedrine. In medical devices, some State Gap Filler business models are emerging partly because it is easier to get registration as an over-the-counter product; Mentholatum, with its light therapy products in the EU, is an example of this. In diagnostics, pregnancy testing devices are an obvious example of a State Gap Filler model, meeting needs for immediacy and convenience that health systems often do not. More recently, home tests for sexually transmitted diseases have emerged as another, similar example of the State Gap Filler model.

This variety of examples, varied as they are in product type, share the characteristic features of the State Gap Filler. All of them target patient payers with significant medical conditions, who are willing to allocate some of their discretionary income to address healthcare needs that are not met by state or insurer provision, such as confidentiality, ease of use or availability.

In the emergence of State Gap Filler models, we can see the influence of the selection pressures arising from the six great shifts. Many of these pressures act upon the model in the same way as they do on the related patient payer models. The value shift shrinks the government payer habitat and so allows the patient payer habitat to grow. The global shift leads to growth of this habitat beyond developed economies. The information shift, via the internet and social media, enables patient payers to obviate healthcare professionals, to a greater or lesser extent. The range of new capabilities required by the State Gap Filler model, such as managing consumer distribution channels and regulatory and product development expertise, are made easier by the trimorphic and holobiont shifts. The systeomic shift is, perhaps, a less significant pressure on this model; but it can be expected to influence the model over the long term by extending its technological reach. Yet again we can understand the evolution of a new model in terms of the six great shifts, and, like the other customer intimacy models, the basis of competition by this model is not technological innovation or operational excellence but the ability to address customer needs at an ever more refined level.

Wellness models

When customer intimate business models choose to focus on maintaining the health of currently well patients rather than managing patients with existing conditions, they are choosing much larger potential markets. But typically this carries higher commercial risk because well patients are less likely to engage than those driven by current illness. For most life science companies, wellness maintenance is also a choice to change significantly from their current model and so it usually involves the development of new organisational routines and capabilities, for example those that enable the influencing of lifestyle and behaviour choices related to wellness. As in the government payer habitat, this need for new routines has significant implications. The more the organisational routineome needs to change, the longer the new species will take to emerge and the more hindered incumbent companies may be by legacy routines and capabilities. As we will see, these considerations are indeed influencing the industry's evolution in this part of the fitness landscape. For most companies, therefore, wellness maintenance models are a more radical, less gradual evolutionary step than the two existing condition models that I discussed earlier. They are the patient payer cousins of the Extrinsic Nudge or Social Demander models. Unsurprisingly, because they are less genetically similar to most current models, we see models that maintain wellness evolving later and more slowly than models that focus on managing illness or injury. As predicted by the evolutionary choices shown in Figure 20.1, the data reveal the emergence of two wellness enabler models in this habitat.

The Self Manager model

We're seeing the rise of the so-called 'quantified self' movement, a movement towards using technology to monitor and manage our own health. The early signs of this are in, for example, the number of 'Kickstarter' projects in this area, or what's on show at consumer electronics exhibitions. Even more interesting is the combination of new sensors and monitors with mobile technology. I think we're heading towards a future where health tracking wearables and implants are commonplace.

Kai Gait, GSK

The Self Manager model focuses on consumers who are generally well and on creating value by enabling the continuation of wellness. Like its close cousin the Extrinsic Nudge model, this model enables and nudges behaviour that maintains wellness. Where it differs from its cousin in the government payer habitat is that it focuses on consumers who are willing to pay for help in maintaining their health. A further difference from its government payer cousin is that, whilst governments tend to focus on those with underlying genetic or lifestyle predispositions, such as the overweight or smokers, the consumer version of this model does not. The Self Manager model therefore involves another risk/return trade off; it puts at risk the significant investment needed to engage with healthy consumers in the hope of accessing this large potential market. If it is successful, this model offers evolutionary fitness when it takes moderate risks and achieves substantial returns. The fact that this model typically involves the patient managing their lifestyle – from food intake to exercise to various physiological parameters – led me to call it the Self Manager model.

The Self Manager model involves many organisational routines and capabilities that are new to the traditional life sciences industry. In as much as they currently exist, they can be seen in two other industries. The first and closest of these is the part of the foodstuffs business that makes health benefit claims, including dietary supplements. The second and more distant is the health and fitness industry of gyms, sports clubs and, to an extent, personal physicians, all of whom offer assistance in maintaining wellness. As the Self Manager model emerges, two main streams of evolution are visible. The first are the descendants of health foods and supplements sector. Current models in this area have not diverged very far from these origins and they are characterised by questionable value that is poorly supported by science. However, it seems clear that a more effective model is emerging, as implied by its new labels, such as nutritional health, functional food and nutraceuticals. The most prominent example of this is Nestlé Health Science, which is investing heavily in areas such as infant metabolism, stem cell development and dermatology. A recent review of research activity in this area also points to the development of this model in the prevention of conditions as varied as Parkinson's disease, obesity and allergies (174), whilst a KPMG report identified endocrine conditions and diabetes, cardiac, gastrointestinal and brain health as nutraceutical hot spots (175).

The second stream of evolution flows from the convergence of traditional fitness management with information technology. This area has seen an enormous but fragmented spurt of technological development, mostly based on mobile and wearable devices such as activity and metabolism trackers and associated apps. Business models in this area focus on measuring activity and behaviour, and using this information to influence behaviour change, rather than the supply of products such as foods or additives. As often happens during the early emergence of business models, value creation in this area is limited by technology fragmentation. Aircraft technology, for example, blossomed only when engine technology and materials technology converged with aircraft design. In the same way, we are beginning to see the convergence of technologies necessary to transform the Self Manager model in examples such as Samsung, Apple and Philips. The future trajectory for this model seems likely to include collecting more varied biological information, using big data and artificial intelligence to generate recommendations, appropriate foods and medicines and, as we see already with some US insurers and employers, financial incentives that reward healthy behaviour.

The behaviour of innovative consumers, summarised as the Quantified Self movement, is an early signal of where the market is headed. It is not hard to anticipate the development of medical technology that combines implantable biosensors (already a US Department of Defense project) wearable technology, big data and artificial intelligence to enable easy, constant measurement of activity, diet and biomarkers and that uses that information to advise individual behaviour. These two evolutionary paths to the Self Manager model – nutritional health and behaviour monitoring – seem likely to converge on a model that monitors wellness, tells you how maintain it and provides the foodstuffs to do so.

The emergence of the Self Manager model, early, uneven and as fragmented as it currently is, demonstrates both how apparently different businesses are in fact closely related and how their model is favoured by selection pressures. Nestlé, Apple and many other disparate businesses are all targeting healthy patient payers with an offer of wellness maintenance. Further, they do so not with leading edge technology or operational excellence but by addressing unmet, granular, individual needs that are often emotional and behavioural as much as clinical. Like the other patient payer models, the value and global shift are growing this habitat whilst the trimorphic and holobiont shifts are making it easier for firms to adapt to it, creating a habitat-growing feedback loop. The information shift and, to a lesser extent, the systeomic shift are making the model technologically possible, particularly its behavioural monitoring strand. Together, these selection pressures point to an almost inevitable emergence of the Self Manager model.

The Future Shaper model

> Very soon patients will have a virtual cloud: data points of very heterogeneous. multiscalable data. Everything from molecular and cellular all the way up to social networks. It will have the analytical tools to aggregate, to mine, to integrate and to model the data on each individual so that you can both optimise wellness and avoid disease.
>
> **Leroy Hood, Institute for Systems Biology**

Today, prognostic tests and profiling, combining genomics, biomarkers and lifestyle analysis, can already come quite close to predicting our lifespan and what stands between us and a long and healthy life. But the social and technological environmental shifts that I have described point to a rapidly emerging future, in which we are able to predict with a high degree of confidence, not only the degree to which our health is at risk, but also the detailed nature of that risk. Combined with the emergence of the patient payer gap, this points to the emergence of a business model with three distinct characteristics. First, a focus on consumers who are not currently ill or injured. Second, a focus on those with a high perceived health risk. Finally, a focus on those who are willing and able to allocate discretionary income to changing their predicted future. These first and last characteristics are shared with the Self Manager model, but the second is distinctive to this new model.

This model is a departure from that of current, typical life science firms and so involves significant evolution of their organisational routines. Such change makes it a relatively high risk model and predicts slower emergence than gradualist models. If successful, it will be so because it creates sufficient value for sufficient consumers to offset that greater risk. Because of its distinct focus on changing previously unalterable health destiny, I labelled it the Future Shaper model.

Little of the routineome needed for the Future Shaper model can be found in existing life science business models. Some can be seen in diagnostic and imaging companies, in particular those associated with screening programmes. Some can be seen in the vaccines industry, which is based on anticipating and pre-empting health risk. But for the most part, the Future Shaper model is quite far removed from its ancestors. The test for BRCA gene that informs the decision by some women to undergo preventative mastectomy is a primitive example of the Future Shaper model, and there are similar ones in bowel, prostate and ovarian cancer. Whilst most life science business models remain focused on treating illnesses once they have developed, we can see the emergence of business models that have the characteristics of the Future Shaper.

The interesting thing is that they are emerging often not from incumbent life science companies but from information technology companies. The high profile example is Calico, the sister company of Google under the Alphabet umbrella. Working in partnerships with companies such as AbbVie, Calico is bringing capabilities in big data to the market, with the aim of predicting and preventing illness. An interesting and strongly consumer-oriented example is 23andMe, offering individuals the opportunity to predict genetic predisposition and hence inform steps to pre-empt illness. J. Craig Venter's Human Longevity Inc., with its mission to prolong healthy lives, is also part Future Shaper although, from this early stage, it could develop into closely related models in the technological innovator/wealthy consumer habitat. In more traditional life science companies, vaccination offered to consumers, beyond the scope of government payer national immunisation programmes, is an antecedent of Future Shaper models. Businesses that encourage grandparents to purchase immunisations as christening gifts are an interesting example of this. More models of this type will surely emerge, and it is not hard to predict a business model that offers an immunisation or medication programme based on an individual's genetic predispositions. Such a model, aimed at patient payers, preventative and tailored around individual predispositions and emotional drivers, has all three characteristics of the Future Shaper model.

The Future Shaper model, which is emergent rather than emerged, reveals again the actions of selection pressures. The value and global shifts grow the habitat and the trimorphic and holobiont shifts enable the model in another habitat-growing feedback loop. More immediately than for the Self Manager model, the information shift and the systeomic shift in particular are making the Future Shaper model possible, especially big data and personalised medicine. Like the Self Manager model, the only thing postponing its emergence is the time needed for the variation, selection and replication of new organisational routines and their incorporation into new organisational structures.

Customer intimate models in the affluent patient payer habitat

Our model has evolved from an emergency service for those living in isolated locations, such as small islands or yachts, to a broader family practice that includes critically important executives and their families.

Daniel Carlin, WorldClinic

We provide access to the best medical care for individuals who travel a lot. It involves a proactive approach to managing the patient, access to his health records, to the appropriate healthcare systems, whether that's a physiotherapist or a cardiologist.

Gary Bell, Invictus

My research suggests that the four models discussed earlier – the Self Carer, the State Gap Filler, the Self Manager and the Future Shaper are emerging at varying speeds in the habitat where patients are the payer and value is created by customer intimacy. However, as I described earlier in this section, polarisation of wealth distribution means that patient payers are a very heterogeneous group. These four models all focus on mass market patient payers with significant discretionary income but who are not necessarily very wealthy. I have already described how the Beyond Reach trough will extend to the customer intimacy part of the fitness landscape, leaving those patients with no discretionary income a very limited choice of models such as the White Labeller. However, I have not yet discussed those wealthy enough to be able to afford a level of customer intimacy beyond that available to the mass consumer.

In business volume terms, this is a small habitat and evidence for business models in this part of the landscape is thin. In *The Future of Pharma*, I predicted a Health Concierge model and indeed this is emerging but, again, evolution has been smarter than I am and a number of model variants can be seen developing in this space. The most important choice differentiating them is the degree to which they manage or prevent illness. WorldClinic is a salient example of a model that is evolving from a reactive, illness management model to one that involves wellness maintenance. Its value proposition is based around telemedicine technology and exceptional customer intimacy for affluent patient payers. Whilst it began with patients who require treatment of some kind, their model also involves elements of wellness maintenance to provide a 'total care platform'. For this type of model, the label Health Concierge remains appropriate. Less customer intimate approaches use a holobiont model to achieve a less comprehensive, treatment-oriented model in conjunction with an array of healthcare providers. Invictus is an example of this. In effect, these are brokerage models, intermediaries that bring together value from multiple suppliers. Hence my choice to label this the Healthcare Broker model.

The Health Concierge and the Healthcare Broker models combine elements of all four of the patient payer, customer intimate models described earlier in exotic and relatively rare forms. They are barely recognisable as life science companies, even though they depend on a great deal of life science technology. However, it is not hard to imagine existing life science companies combining their knowledge assets, organisational routines and capabilities into holobionts with health providers and others to create these two models. These are favoured by selection pressures in the same way as the four mass market models and, much as mass market financial service companies, automotive companies and airlines all find it worthwhile to service small numbers of very wealthy customers, it seems likely that life science companies will do the same.

A species flock of customer intimate models in the patient payer habitat

In exploring the habitat described in this section, where the patient pays and value is created by customer intimacy, we have moved even further from the habitats familiar to most life science companies, where governments pay and competition is based on technological innovation or operational excellence. This implies a great change in organisational routines and we should expect the degree and speed of emergence to vary. Exactly as we would expect among the four mass market models, the Self Carer model is most developed, the Future Shaper the least and the Self Manager and State Gap Filler Models somewhere between the two. The few sightings of the Health Concierge and Healthcare Broker models barely yield enough data to comment, and the examples challenge our definition of a life science company. But examples in other industries, from wealth management to executive jets, imply that Orgel's Second Law will apply and models will develop in all customer intimate habitats.

Customer intimate business models in the patient payer habitat should be expected to look rather different from their cousins in the government payer habitat and more different still from their further-removed relations in the technologically innovative and operationally excellent habitats. We might expect to see very different strategies and capabilities, organisational and capital structures emerge. But these differences, equivalent to the phenotypic differences between humans and other mammals, don't mean that they are not life science companies. They still offer health and ultimately their revenue streams come from the same sources that pharmaceutical and medical technology companies seek to tap. As with the customer intimate, government payer models, huge financial pressures and healthcare demands faced by governments, together with the limited ability of technological innovation and operational excellence models to meet that challenge, strongly suggest that these models will become very important.

In *The Future of Pharma*, I predicted the emergence of a single customer intimate model for each of two consumer habitats: the trust manager and the health concierge. My subsequent work has developed those ideas and suggests that they were in fact two species flocks, with four and two species respectively. As in the other habitats, these species flocks are favoured by the selection pressures that create their habitat and enable their evolution. Further, the flocks provide a range of risk and return options, widening investors' options, drawing in capital and driving their own habitat construction. These species flocks are shown in Figure 20.2 and Figure 20.3.

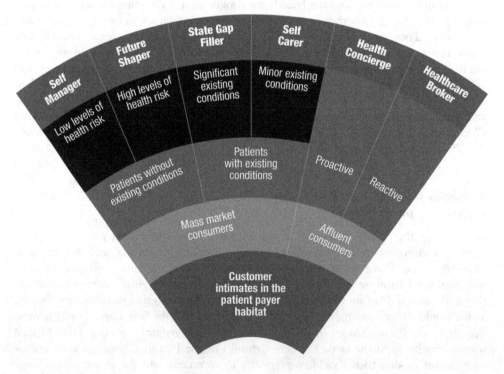

Figure 20.2 The emergence of customer intimate models in the patient payer habitat

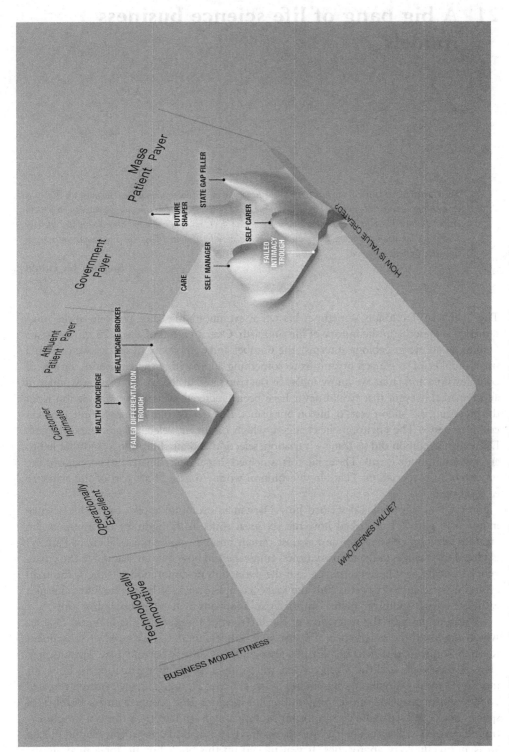

Figure 20.3 The emerging fitness landscape of customer intimate business models in the patient payer habitat

21 A big bang of life science business models

The Cambrian explosion is the key event in the history of multicellular animal life. The more we study the episode, the more we are impressed by its uniqueness and of its determining effect on the subsequent pattern of life's history. These basic anatomies that arose during the Cambrian explosion have dominated life ever since, with no major additions. The pattern of life's history has followed from the origins and successes of this great initiating episode.

Stephen Jay Gould

The Cambrian Explosion, sometimes known as evolution's big bang, was one of the most remarkable episodes in the history of life on Earth. Over a period of about 25 million years (a blink of an eye in geological terms), the number and complexity of species went from a small number of single cell organisms to something approaching the enormous variety of complex flora and fauna we know today. In the true sense of the words, it was a wonderful and remarkable event that would never have been predicted by simple extrapolation from the preceding 3.3 billion years of life on our planet. But, to an evolutionary scientist, it makes complete sense. The environment changed, which meant the selection pressures changed. Darwinian evolution did its thing – variation, selection and amplification – and that led to an expansion in life forms. Those life forms helped shape their habitats and accelerated the process of mass speciation. That's how evolution works. You and I are part of the evidence of that event.

In Part 1 of this book I described how Darwinian evolution applies to the life science industry. In Part 2, I described how the six great shifts in the industry environment are creating selection pressures for and against certain business model traits. Then, in Part 3, I explored the changes in the industry fitness landscape and how they are leading to the emergence of many new business models and the extinction or diminution of others. From an evolutionary science perspective, this also makes complete sense. What we are living through is the life science industry's own Cambrian explosion, our own evolutionary big bang.

I began to describe the speciation of the life science industry in *The Future of Pharma*, which suggested the emergence of seven new business models. Five years of subsequent research confirms this general idea but also confirms Orgel's Second Law. Evolution is cleverer than I am, and the seven models were only a rough approximation of how our industry is really evolving. As shown in Figure 21.1 and Figure 21.2, my research revealed twenty-six fitness peaks and corresponding business models, grouped into a number of species flocks and separated by significant fitness troughs. In fact, even this is a simplification. Each peak will certainly have sub-peaks and business model variations around disease areas and technology approaches. If you picked up this book hoping for a nice, simple

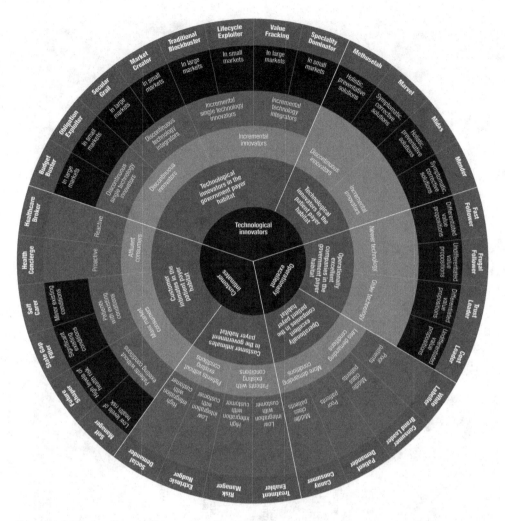

Figure 21.1 The speciation of life science business models

answer to the question How will the life sciences industry evolve? then I am afraid that any honest, well researched answer is going to disappoint you. I hope, however, that my answer has interested you.

The first three parts of *Darwin's Medicine* have been descriptive. I have described how evolutionary science applies to the life science industry, how the environment is changing and how those changes will shape the industry. I have deliberately avoided prescription. I have not made any attempt to suggest what companies should do. I have tried to explain rather than to stipulate and to elucidate rather than recommend.

However, to paraphrase Karl Marx, the point is not just to explain the world but to change it. So in the final, fourth part of this book I move from professor to advisor, making recommendations for how firms might adapt to the changing, expanding, fragmenting and exploding life science market.

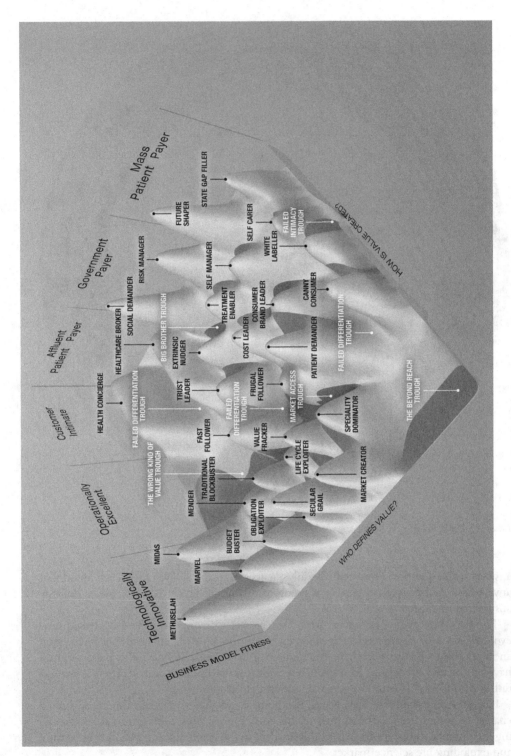

Figure 21.2 The emerging fitness landscape of life science business models

Part 4

Guiding the blind watchmaker

All appearances to the contrary, the only watchmaker in nature is the blind forces of physics, albeit deployed in a very special way. A true watchmaker has foresight: he designs his cogs and springs, and plans their interconnections, with a future purpose in his mind's eye. Natural selection, the blind, unconscious, automatic process which Darwin discovered, and which we now know is the explanation for the existence and apparently purposeful form of all life, has no purpose in mind. It has no mind and no mind's eye. It does not plan for the future. It has no vision, no foresight, no sight at all. If it can be said to play the role of watchmaker in nature, it is the blind watchmaker.

Richard Dawkins

22 Introduction

From description to prescription

The first three parts of this book contain a lot of information and ideas. Even if you are already familiar with my earlier research for *The Future of Pharma* and therefore chose to skip Part 1, I have ranged over concepts and information from economics, strategic management theory and a various scientific and technical disciplines. Such is the knowledge base needed to understand the evolution of the life science industry. But I am very aware that busy people read books like this differently from academics or compared with how they might read a novel. I know that many of you will have skipped or skimmed some of the preceding pages; others will have had enforced gaps between reading sessions whilst you have attended to work or family life. For a few readers, these words are the first you have read in this whole book. For all those reasons, I think it is worth beginning this fourth and final section of *Darwin's Medicine* with the briefest of restatements of what I have described so far. If you don't feel you need that, please feel free to skip to the end of this introduction and continue reading at Chapter 23.

I began *Darwin's Medicine* with a reprise of my ideas from *The Future of Pharma*, extended to cover the wider life sciences sector including medical technology. The starting premise for my work is that, to paraphrase J. Stanley Metcalfe, evolutionary theory doesn't belong to the biologists alone. It is a fabulously powerful idea that explains the behaviour of any complex adaptive system. The life sciences sector, with its multitude of organisational entities, each connected to others in numerous ways and each adapting to their environment, merits that label as much as a rain forest, the microbes in your intestines or the tangled English hedgerow that Darwin mused over at the end of *The Origin of Species*. The key semantic point I stressed in Part 1 was that when scientists, whether they are biological or management scientists, use the term evolution they don't simply mean gradual change, as a layman might. We mean the process of variation, selection and replication and amplification. The way that this process of Darwinian evolution explains and shapes the development of complex adaptive systems such as the life science industry is the guiding principle of both this book and its predecessor.

Among the key concepts in evolution are replicators, interactors, species and the environment. This is true for both biologists and management scientists. In biology, the replicators are genes, the interactors are organisms and species are groups of organisms sharing mostly the same genes. In a management science context, the replicators are organisational routines, the interactors are organisations and a group of organisations that share mostly the same routines is a business model. Just as shared genes mean that members of a species share phenotypic traits such as physiology, morphology and behaviour, organisations sharing the same routines also share phenotypic traits such as structures, processes and strategies. When biologists refer to the environment, they are referring to both the physical environment, such as the weather and the geography, and the biological environment, such as predators, prey and symbionts. When management scientists talk about the environment they tend to follow Nelson and Winter's categories and refer to the technological and sociological environments. Hence, for life science companies, information technology, biological discoveries and material science are aspects of the technological environment; demographics, social attitudes and macroeconomics are aspects of the sociological environment.

As I gratefully acknowledge, I picked up the idea of Darwinian evolution as a management, rather than biological, theory from Nelson and Winter and the many others who have followed them. In *The Future of Pharma*, I applied these ideas to an industry I began to work in almost forty years ago. In that earlier book, I predicted that changes in the industry's two environments would shape and fragment its fitness landscape, which is another idea I had adopted from the biologists. I predicted that, as firms adapted to the fragmentation of the fitness landscape into multiple habitats, new species of pharmaceutical company (that is, new business models) would emerge and there would be the concomitant extinction of other, older models. Taking Stephen Jay Gould's idea, I suggested this speciation would be another burst of evolutionary change to punctuate the equilibrium of the system. I compared it to an earlier burst of evolution in the late nineteenth and early twentieth centuries that led to the emergence of the modern industry and the demise of apothecaries.

The Future of Pharma and its ideas were very well received by the industry executives who were its intended audience. Many of its predictions have proved remarkably accurate in the few years since it was written. But, even as I submitted the book to the publisher, my research had done what all good research is supposed to do; it had raised more questions. In *The Future of Pharma*, I had observed and recorded environmental changes shaping the industry but I had not fully understood the selection pressure mechanism that explained that process. I had also restricted my research and analysis to pharmaceutical companies but I could see, even then, that the intra-industry distinctions (pharma, medtech, diagnostics, biotech etc.) that I and the rest of the industry commonly use were artificial. A better understanding would explore the life sciences industry more widely. Finally, although I was confident in my predictions of seven emerging business models, I knew that they were likely to be approximations and that a more detailed picture lay beneath. I could already see examples of companies within the same category that were quite different, suggesting that neither my research nor the emergence of new models was yet complete. These shortcomings of *The Future of Pharma* led to the research for and writing of *Darwin's Medicine*.

In this book, I've reprised its predecessor (Part 1), investigated the mechanism of selection pressures (Part 2) and uncovered the emergence of new business models (Part 3). In the next few paragraphs, I'll summarise Part 2 and Part 3 before setting out what I will cover in this final, fourth part of the book.

In Part 2: An Immeasurably Superior Power, I sought, in Winston Churchill's words, to find the great simplicities that arise from the great complexity of our industry's changing environment. As anyone familiar with the life science industry knows, the changes currently taking place in the sector's environment are innumerable, significant and complex. Starting with Nelson and Winter's physical and social environmental categories, I developed a framework to capture and collate the innumerable bits of information uncovered from company announcements, industry press reports, interviews with executives and various other sources. To this mass of data I applied an inductive approach, meaning that I examined and re-examined the evidence until consistent, coherent patterns emerged. In this kind of 'trying to understand' research, the laborious inductive approach is much more effective than the more commonly used deductive approach, which is aimed at proving some preconceived hypothesis.

The aim of my research was to understand how the environmental changes combined to either favour or disfavour certain business models. From this work emerged the six great shifts described in detail in Part 2. There are three key points to draw from these findings. First, each of the shifts is the aggregate of many different changes in the environment. Although it is tempting to assign singular importance to a particular factor, such as bioinformatics or demographics, it is both more accurate and more insightful to understand the way such specific factors combine to create fundamental shifts. Second, each of the six shifts creates selection pressures. They don't cause business models to change in a simple cause–effect way. Changes to organisational routines occur either because executives choose to make them or through the entropy of organisational life. These changes are then either selected for or selected against by the six shifts. It is the cumulative effect of this variation–selection process, followed by replication and amplification, that leads to the emergence of new business models. Finally, the relationship between selection pressures and business models is not simple or unidirectional. At any given time, all six sets of pressures are acting on every organisation in the industry and, as they adapt, industry business models influence the environment. For example, the value shift influences industry pricing practices. In turn, these influence payer budgets which then contribute to the value shift in a complex feedback loop. Overall, Part 2 achieved its aims. It elucidated the mechanisms by which changes in the industry's environment shape the emergence of business models and so helped to inform Part 3.

The analysis in Part 2 did not contradict what I had uncovered during the research for *The Future of Pharma*, but it did answer some of the questions raised by the earlier work. In particular, the selection pressures that I elucidated pointed to the same basic fitness landscape of nine primary habitats. These lay at the intersection of three ways of creating value (technological innovation, operational excellence and customer intimacy) and three types of value definer (government payers, affluent patients and mass market or poor patients). However, the interaction of the six great shifts and their resultant selection pressures also pointed to a degree of fragmentation *within* the habitats, a fragmentation that I had only begun to uncover in *The Future of Pharma*. It was towards the understanding of this habitat fragmentation, and the speciation of business models implied by it, that I then directed my research.

In Part 3: Evolution Is Cleverer Than You Are, my goal was to uncover and describe the emergence of business models under the selection pressures of the six great shifts. Again, I used an inductive approach to identify patterns in the mass of data. This revealed a fundamental feature of the industry's evolution. In biology the evolutionary fitness of a genome is represented by the reproductive success of its interactor (the organism). In the same way, in business the evolutionary fitness of its 'genome' of organisational routines – its routineome – is represented by the success of its interactor (the organisation). But in business, longevity and the replication and amplification of organisational routines is determined by risk-adjusted rate of return on investment. Thus, just as we can see biological adaptations as evolutionary 'choices' to optimise reproductive success in the face of environmental selection pressures, we can see organisational adaptations of the business model as evolutionary 'choices' to optimise the risk/return ratio in the face of selection pressures from the technological and sociological environments.

This line of thought, that business models emerge as the result of risk/return trade off choices, illuminated my examination of what life science companies and new entrants are actually doing in the real world. It revealed the emergence of species flocks in most of the nine habitats, groups of business models that are closely related but different, characterised and differentiated by their specific set of evolutionary choices. In total, twenty-six different business models, at differing stages of emergence, emerged from my research. In the industry's fitness landscape, they are separated by fitness troughs where compromise business models that, to use an English idiom, are neither fish nor fowl, have relatively low evolutionary fitness. This advance on *The Future of Pharma* model, with its much greater complexity and much higher resolution of different models, has three salient implications. First, it implies great expansion in the numbers and variety of business models in the life science industry, compared to the present. Many will look very different from current industry models, and they will look more different from each other than do the current, closely related set of models. Second, in another example of complex adaptive system behaviour, the models will feedback into the sociological and technological environments. They will do this by offering a variety of models providing a multitude of risk/return options attractive to many investors and, to some extent, these will create their own habitats. Finally, the emergence of these many and varied business models will be accompanied by the extinction of those life science business models with which we have become familiar and which currently characterise the sector. In that sense, we will see the survival of the fittest.

So to capture 'the story so far': the convergence of evolutionary forces is leading to our industry's equivalent of the Cambrian explosion, that period in life's history when the number of species expanded dramatically and life as we know it, in all its beauty and complexity, took over the surface of the planet.

Part 3 builds on this, to paint a detailed, closely argued description of a future for the life sciences industry. However, it is a description and not a prescription. It contains no recommendations for how life science firms (and those firms wishing to enter the sector) should adapt to the future. This is an important omission because, whilst biological evolution is driven by random mutation of genes, industry evolution is driven, at least in part, by the thoughtful, deliberate decisions of the intelligent people who lead its organisations. They need and value guidance as to how they should adapt to the future of their industry, which is, socially and economically, among the most important on Earth.

In this fourth and final part of the book, I move from description to prescription. In my many discussions with industry executives, they posed many questions about how to adapt to the future. They ranged from the detailed and operational to the high level and strategic. They concerned issues that were specific to their own company and were general to the industry. But, for all their variety, their questions resolved down to four key questions:

- Which fitness peak(s) should we climb?
- What capabilities does our new business model need?
- How should we design a capable holobiont?
- How do we build our core capabilities?

These form the structure for the rest of Part 4. In the following sections, I will synthesise what I learned from my research to provide answers to those questions.

23 Which fitness peak(s) should we climb?

This question is the most fundamental of all those that any organisation can ask itself. None of the other questions can be answered until this one has been resolved. The question itself rests on two premises that flow from the research described in Part 3. First, the landscape occupied by the life sciences industry is fragmenting into many different fitness peaks, each of which demands a business model with different routines, capabilities and traits. Second, it is either impossible or unwise for a single organisation to maintain every business model, so that choosing between them is a necessary prerequisite to answering all of the other questions, which concern how to build the chosen model or models.

The alternative to asking this question is to ignore the future and to adapt to the six great shifts on an ad hoc basis, making individual choices and hoping that they add up to a steady ascent of a fitness peak. To choose an ad hoc approach over a planned route is a brave decision, to speak euphemistically. At best, it might lead to the optimal habitat via a slower, circuitous and wasteful route. Or it might lead to adaptation to a habitat that is less attractive or harder to occupy than some viable alternative. More likely, given the attrition rate of natural selection, an ill-informed, ad hoc adaptation might lead a firm to stumble into one of the many fitness troughs, whose steep, slippery walls prevent escape. The question of 'which peaks?' becomes more, not less, important in larger firms that can simultaneously climb several different fitness peaks with different business models. In such cases, it becomes important to allocate neither too much resource nor too little to them and to manage the portfolio of business models so as to achieve synergy and balance risk. Multi-model organisations that fail to do this are worth less than the sum of their parts and effectively destroy value. This is visible to investors and other stakeholders who punish firms as a result. So, for any organisation, the question of which fitness peak or peaks to climb is both important and a necessary first step in deliberately managing the organisation's evolution.

The short answer to the question Which fitness peak(s) should we climb? is simply 'it depends'. Any fitness peak may be optimal, but no choice is optimal for all organisations. The best choice for any firm is contingent on many different factors. It is when we address the follow up question, What does it depend on? that the discussion becomes more interesting and the answer more useful. In my research and work with industry leaders, I observe firms grappling unconsciously with this question when they perceive themselves to be simply making choices about, for example, market entry or product development. From these observations of practice, it is clear that the question is answered in four, sequential stages of reification, criteria choice, assessment and resource allocation, as shown in Figure 23.1 and described in the remainder of this section of the book.

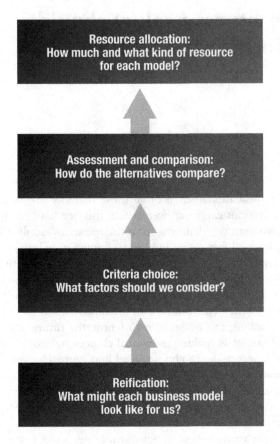

Figure 23.1 The four-stage process of fitness peak selection

Stage 1: reifying the available options

As illustrated in Figure 21.2 in Chapter 21, the emerging fitness landscape of the life sciences industry is a serried range of twenty-six fitness peaks separated by troughs of varying size and shape. There is no shortage of options for a firm to choose from, and the challenge is to compare them rationally and choose wisely. In Part 3, I characterised the business models that would occupy each peak in terms of their evolutionary choices – the degree of innovation, the size of market and so on. These characterisations are a useful taxonomy and enable leaders to make sense of their options. In practice, however, they are insufficiently detailed to allow an organisation to compare options. For example, it is impossible to meaningfully compare a Secular Grail with a Self Manager in the abstract. To make meaningful comparisons, what is needed is a clear picture, if not necessarily detailed, of the business model your organisation would need, if it were to occupy any given fitness peak.

For almost all organisations, this picture of a future business model is path dependent. By that I mean simply that it is strongly influenced by the organisation's history and the set of current assets, culture and resources that have arisen from that history. For example, when Pascal Soriot became CEO of AstraZeneca in 2012, he surveyed the landscape and could, in theory, have considered diversifying into entirely new therapy areas or even away from pharmaceuticals into medical technology or diagnostics. Self-evidently, this would have not used many of AstraZeneca's existing assets and resources. His choice to develop a set of technologically innovative business models in the government payer habitat, based around therapy areas in which AstraZeneca was already established, was largely dictated by his firm's history and resultant existing capabilities. GSK's exit from and re-entry into oncology, and development of its vaccines and consumer businesses, show similar path dependency. In medical technology, Stryker have visualised their Secular Grail model as involving the integration of orthopaedic implant technology with robotics. Medtronic have reified their Risk Manager model in their Hospital Solutions Business unit. So, in most cases, firms begin to reify their options by asking the question, What might that business model look like for us? and recognise the strong influence of path dependent existing assets and resources.

The problem with this approach is that, for most companies, path dependency is amplified by the limitations of managerial imagination. Executive teams, typically immersed in the culture of their organisations and comfortable discussing the customers and products with which they are familiar, struggle to identify and reify business model options that are not very similar to their current model. This can be seen in the tendency of historically research-based firms to stick to the government payer and the technological innovation habitat; they are relatively reluctant to look at patient payer habitats or other modes of value creation. Organisations that overcome this tendency demonstrate either a lack of path dependency, such as J. Craig Venter's Human Longevity Inc., or a yielding to force majeure, as seen in Roche's development of patient payer oncology models in China.

In practice, pragmatic approaches to reifying business models balance two opposing forces. On the one hand, they quickly, almost instinctively, discard business models that would ignore path dependent effects completely. To use the phrase coined by *In Search of Excellence*, firms still tend to 'stick to their knitting'. On the other hand, they also challenge themselves to widen their imagination and consider fitness peaks that are quite dissimilar from their current models. To do so rigorously, they need a framework that identifies their range of options and defines the risk/return trade offs that characterise each option. Used with care and contextualised to the specific context of any particular organisation, the twenty-six model fitness landscape, as seen in Figure 21.2, provides that framework.

So, Stage 1 involves using the fitness landscape to identify all possible options and then, balancing path dependency and originality, narrowing those down to small number of options. This is followed by sketching out what each of those possible models would mean for the firm, given its current and likely focus. For example, a Risk Manager for a pharmaceutical company in the diabetes therapy area would involve integrating into that particular part of the healthcare system in order to optimise outcomes. Then the firm would identify the key traits needed to operate in this area, such as patient management and health economic outcome management. This would naturally conclude with a broad outline of markets, products and other key choices for this model. By the end of Stage 1, the firm has moved from a multitude of abstract options to a manageable number of reified, concrete options described in sufficient detail that they may be assessed and compared.

Stage 2: deciding the assessment criteria

Stage 1 results in a list of reified business model options, each a set of evolutionary choices about where and how to compete that, if executed well, would allow a firm to successfully occupy a particular fitness peak. Expressing the options as specific choices about products and markets makes them sufficiently concrete that they may be compared and evaluated, with the aim of allocating resources or discarding the option. The simplistic and common approach to performing this comparison between business model options uses traditional financial assessments, for example, prioritising the option that generates the optimal discounted cash flow analysis. Such simplistic approaches are inadequate for two reasons. First, because the assessments for each model are looking into the medium and long term, any quantitative assessment must be based on imprecise estimates and so carries significant uncertainty. Second, by assessing only the potential returns of each model, this approach pays insufficient attention to risk, that is to say the probability of successfully developing the business model. A more sophisticated decision about which fitness peak or peaks to aim for must counter these two weaknesses. In practice, it must consider two, largely independent sets of factors: those relating to the relative attractiveness each fitness peak and those related to probability that the firm might successfully occupy that peak.

The first set of relative attractiveness factors stems from the simple fact that, in any given reified case, each fitness peak will differ in volume, profit pool, growth rate and other factors that determine its attractiveness. These characteristics are particular to the reified fitness peak; as such, they will vary between therapy areas or product categories. For example, a firm operating in the market for mobile patient monitoring systems may look at the government payer market for improving compliance by chronically ill patients (an example of a Treatment Enabler model). It may also consider the market in which healthy consumers use such equipment to maintain their health (a Self Manager model). In the case of patient monitoring systems, the latter may be larger, more profitable, faster growing and more attractive than the former. In another market, say for lipid lowering drugs, the two equivalent models may have their relative attractiveness reversed. This case specificity of fitness peak attractiveness reinforces the need to reify the options before beginning their assessment and comparison.

The second set of success probability factors stems from another simple reality that not all fitness peaks are equally easy to occupy. They will differ in how easy it is to access the market, to develop the value proposition and to build the necessary core organisation and holobiont. Note that success probability is a function of the gap between the organisation's current assets, resources and capabilities and what the fitness peak demands. For example, two different firms may both assess the same Secular Grail model to develop a cure for intractable epilepsy, a model that might involve a combination of deep brain stimulation, patient monitoring, therapeutic drugs and novel drug delivery technology. For a firm whose capabilities lie in incremental development of single technologies via its own resources, this model would be difficult and the probability of success would be relatively low. By contrast, a firm with strong capabilities in integrating technology and accomplished at building holobiont structures with complementary firms would have a higher probability of success in building exactly the same model. However, if the same two firms assessed the opportunity to extend and augment traditional epilepsy drugs (a Life Cycle Exploitation model) then the success probabilities would be reversed.

Critically, these two sets of factors (the attractiveness of a fitness peak and the probability of success in building it) are multifactorial. That is, they are each made of several

Table 23.1 Criteria for assessing fitness peak options

Typical component factors for assessing the attractiveness of a business model	Typical component factors for assessing the organisation's ability to occupy a fitness peak
Volume size of market	Closeness of current new product development capabilities to those needed by new model
Profit pool available	Closeness of current operational capabilities to those needed by new model
Growth trends in volume	Closeness of current customer relationship management capabilities to those needed by new model
Growth trends in profit pool	Closeness of current organisation structure to that needed by the new model
Level of direct competitive intensity faced by this model	Closeness of current organisational culture to that needed by the new model
Internal synergy of this model with others (i.e. synergistic effects arising from interaction of resources within the firm)	Closeness of current network of alliances and relationships to that needed by the new model
External synergy of this model with others (i.e. synergistic effects arising from interaction between customers)	Closeness of asset and resource scale to that needed by the new model

sub-component factors. In Table 23.1, I list factors that are commonly used by firms when performing this stage of the process in practice. However, it is important to note that these lists are illustrative and are neither exhaustive nor compulsory. Firms may add other factors into either column if it reflects their particular context. Equally, firms may select a subset of these factors rather than use them all. In practice, three to six factors are commonly chosen from each of the two sets of component factors.

In practice, it is often helpful to think of these two lists of factors in terms of the biological analogue, as if the organisation were choosing from a number of possible physical habitats. The attractiveness factors are then analogous to whatever makes a habitat attractive: how big is the habitat? How much food is there in this habitat? Are either of those two things shrinking or growing? How many other creatures will be hunting for the same food? Will the skills I use to hunt in this habitat be useful in others? Are there any adjoining habitats? In the same way, the organisation's probability of success in occupying the peak is analogous to how much a creature would need to adapt in order to thrive in that habitat: how much do I need to change my ability to innovate, be efficient and manage customers? How much do I need to change my organisation and its network? Am I the right size to thrive in this habitat?

In practice, organisations tend to begin by creating lists of assessment criteria that are quite long and include all of the aforementioned factors plus one or two that are very case specific. For example, publicly traded firms often add likely shareholder reaction to attractiveness factors, whereas firms that are protected from the equity market, such as by family shareholding, do not. By contrast, family firms may add closeness to the owners' vision to the factors that affect the probability of success. Conservative organisations may add volatility or stability as attractiveness considerations whilst those driven by venture capital may do the opposite. For example, we can see that GSK has considered counter-cyclicity as a factor when choosing to have both government payer and patient payer models. Overall, this process of clarifying the assessment criteria is the essential second stage in the process of choosing fitness peaks and business models. The outcomes of Stage 2 are therefore two lists, one of attractiveness factors and one of risk factors, that are specific to the firm. These values enable the next stage of assessing the alternatives in a rational manner.

Stage 3: assessing and comparing alternative fitness peaks

By completing Stages 1 and 2 thoughtfully and rigorously, a leadership team creates a set of alternative, reified business models and a set of criteria for assessing and comparing them. These criteria run along two dimensions: how attractive is this fitness peak to us and what is the probability that we can occupy it successfully? The first question allows for variation in attractiveness between models and in what is important to different firms. The second question recognises that the degree of adaptation needed is inversely proportional to the organisation's ability to build the model well enough and quickly enough to compete strongly. This assumption is a reflection of the axiom 'Natura non facit saltum' (Nature does not make a leap); it is a phrase from Linnaeus but also a recognition of business reality – organisational change is costly in time and resources and inherently risky.

The work done in Stages 1 and 2 has therefore enabled the third stage, which involves using those two sets of criteria, as exemplified in Table 23.1, to assess the alternative, reified business models. In turn this third stage enables the fourth, the final stage of allocating resources between alternatives.

In practice, it is the assessment of alternative business models that requires most work and the highest level of strategic judgement. Simplistically, firms often approach this task by trying to quantify each factor for each model and then aggregating those numbers to develop a ranking. In practice this approach is inadequate for two reasons. First, quantitative assessment remains bedevilled by uncertainty of the future, made worse when assessing intangible factors such as closeness to current organisational culture. Second, ranking of this sort gives little guidance about how resource allocation might vary over time and in type of resource. Simplistic ranking therefore reduces the ability to allocate resources differentially between models over time.

Both of these weaknesses have important practical ramifications for both multi-model organisations and for single model organisations trying to transition from one business model to another. It is important to address these weaknesses and to ensure that the assessment and comparison process intelligently incorporates all of the firm's explicit and tacit knowledge, rather than becoming a 'dumb' spreadsheet exercise. In practice, effective assessment of business model alternatives is a craft rather than a science. In particular, I observe three embedded habits that are necessary to compare business models effectively.

Organisationally-appropriate weighting of attractiveness factors

Just as with an individual's choice of marriage partner, what makes a business model attractive varies greatly between organisations. Large, mature organisations, for example, heavily discount business models that are small scale, because they do not meet the organisation's growth needs. Capital-intensive firms place more weight on profit pool and growth because they need high returns to justify their investment. Firms transitioning from one model to another, or adding another model to their portfolio, place a higher weight on the value of synergy between models, and so on. Typically, effective organisations often award significant weight to a small number of factors, perhaps three or four, and choose to regard others as not strategically significant. When this is not done and a larger number of factors are awarded small weighting, the assessment of attractiveness yields unclear results that fail to distinguish between options. Hence the craft involved in this assessment is to allocate weighting to attractiveness factors decisively and in a way that accurately reflects the organisation's situation. The aim here is to avoid blurred, compromise weightings that could apply to any organisation in the sector.

Model-appropriate weighting of probability factors

The organisational change needed to build a business model obviously depends on the model and the organisation's starting position. But the relative importance of each change is also dependent on the model. So, for example, the development of new product development capabilities is more important when trying to build one of the technologically innovative business models than it is when trying to build one of the operationally excellent models. Organisational scale and networks are more important when the reified model involves a large, global organisation than for a small, niche business model. As with attractiveness factors, effective organisations award significant weight to a small number of factors and choose to regard others as not strategically significant. Again, when a larger number of factors are awarded small weights (as often happens in politicised decision processes) the assessment of the organisation's ability to build the model yields an indistinct outcome. As with the attractiveness assessment, the craft involved in this assessment is to allocate weighting to the factors decisively and in a way that accurately reflects the demands of the fitness landscape and the potential business model. The aim here is to avoid a long list of similarly weighted factors that is very similar for all models.

Relative, not absolute, ranking of alternatives

When comparing alternatives, it is not the absolute values of each criterion that is important but the value relative to the comparator set. For example, comparing a group of reified models may result in the finding that all are large but differ significantly in their size. Or that all are difficult to build but that there is a wide span of difficulty. In this case, using absolute values would cluster all the models as attractive but difficult, which does little to inform the decision about resource allocation. Effective organisations award rank models in relative terms, so that the best is always given a high assessment, the lowest a low assessment and intermediate models are spread proportionately across the range. This avoids the uninformative clustering outcome that often occurs if absolute values are used. Again, there is a craft involved in ranking the alternatives in a way that accurately reflects the relative characteristics. The aim here is to avoid tight, indistinguishable clusters and to distinguish clearly between alternative models in both attractiveness and the organisation's ability to develop the model.

In practice, the assessment and comparison process is necessarily a matter of knowledge-based judgement rather than objective, quantitative but simplistic calculation. The assessment process itself is usually iterative, with each iteration raising questions and discussion, and that debate leading to another, more informed iteration. This also raises interesting questions of organisational behaviour and culture. Organisations with a strongly scientific culture often exhibit a preference for hard data and more objective certainty; but this is naïve in conditions where much of the data is uncertain and many of the criteria cannot be objectively measured. Other organisations seem to have a cultural preference to follow management intuition, even when some useful data are available. In practice, this stage of the process needs to combine careful judgement with as much rigour as possible. In this, it is no different from any other strategic management process, but the importance of balancing judgement and number-crunching is particularly important in this case because it is susceptible to culture and cognitive biases. Awareness and management of such biases is a key task of the leaders who direct this process.

Stage 4: allocating resources between alternative business models

The outcome of Stage 3 is an assessment of each model along the two dimensions (attractiveness of the fitness peak and organisational ability to occupy that peak). As shown in the example in Table 23.2 and Table 23.3, the assessment can be a single figure that is a weighted aggregate of the component factors.

Clearly, the calculations shown in these tables are illustrative examples. In practice, the models would be assessed and compared and the process reiterated to improve the judgements on which the scores are based. The depth of thought and internal discussion that is needed to develop such tables belies their superficial simplicity. However, it is in that discussion where leadership teams genuinely contribute to the evolution of their firms.

Whether the assessments and their aggregation are carried out using this arithmetical process or some other method, the aim is to produce a business model portfolio chart in

Table 23.2 Calculation of business model attractiveness

Attractiveness factor	Factor weighting %	Relative score of reified model A	Relative score of reified model B	Relative score of reified model C	Relative score of reified model D
Profit pool available	30	9 – largest profit pool	2 – smallest profit pool	8 – large profit pool	3 – small profit pool
Level of direct competitive intensity faced by this model	30	5 – median competitive intensity	3 – high competitive intensity	9 – lowest competitive intensity	2 – highest competitive intensity
Internal synergy of this model with others (i.e. synergistic effects arising from interaction of resources within the firm)	20	8 – highest internal synergy	6 – median internal synergy	7 – high internal synergy	2 – internal conflict
Growth trends	20	8 – fast growing	3 – low growth	9 – fastest growing	2 – declining
Weighted aggregate attractiveness score for this model	100	$(9 \times 30) + (5 \times 30) + (8 \times 20) + (8 \times 20) = 740$ (High attractiveness)	$(2 \times 30) + (3 \times 30)+(6 \times 20) + (3 \times 20)=$ 330 (Low attractiveness)	$(8 \times 30) + (9 \times 30) + (7 \times 20) + (9 \times 20) =$ 830 (Highest attractiveness)	$(3 \times 30) + (2 \times 30) + (2 \times 20) + (2 \times 20) =$ 230 (Lowest attractiveness)

Table 23.3 Calculation of business model risk

Risk factor	Factor weighting %	Relative score of reified model A	Relative score of reified model B	Relative score of reified model C	Relative score of reified model D
Adaptation of NPD capabilities	35	2 – low risk	2 – low risk	8 – highest risk	7 – high risk
Adaptation of SCM capabilities	15	2 – low risk	1 – lowest risk	5 – median risk	6 – median risk
Adaptation of CRM capabilities	15	3 – low risk	3 – low risk	5 – median risk	6 – median risk
Adaptation of culture	35	1 – lowest risk	2 – low risk	9 – highest risk	8 – highest risk
Weighted aggregate attractiveness score for this model	100	$(2 \times 35)+(2 \times 15) + (3 \times 15) + (1 \times 35) = 180$ (Lowest risk)	$(2 \times 35) + (1 \times 15) + (3 \times 15) + (2 \times 35) = 200$ (Low risk)	$(8 \times 35) + (5 \times 15) + (5 \times 15) + (9 \times 35) = 745$ (Highest risk)	$(7 \times 35) + (6 \times 15) + (6 \times 15) + (8 \times 35) = 705$ (High risk)

Table 23.4 A portfolio comparison of business models

	Low relative attractiveness	*High relative attractiveness*
High relative risk	Avoid or Withdraw (e.g. Model D)	Build (e.g. Model C)
Low relative risk	Manage (e.g. Model B)	Focus (e.g. Model A)

which all of the models to be compared are shown in a chart similar to Table 23.4, which is populated with the examples from Table 23.2 and Table 23.3.

A chart like the simplified example of Table 23.4 provides strong guidance for a leadership team trying to decide which peaks to climb and how to allocate resources between business models. At its simplest interpretation, it makes one of four recommendations for each business model under consideration.

Focus

Models in this part of the chart are those that are relatively easy to develop, meaning they are likely to be a close fit with current resources, assets and capabilities. They are also relatively attractive, typically with large, growing markets with significant internal synergy. In this case, organisations should focus on this fitness peak with the aim of building a strongly competitive model in the short to medium term. Usually, this involves the reallocation of significant existing resources but does not require much reconfiguration of the firm assets and capabilities.

Build

Models in this part of the chart are those that are relatively difficult to develop, probably requiring extensive development of resources, assets and capabilities. They are however relatively attractive, typically with fast growing markets with less competition. In this case, organisations should aim to build this model in the medium to long term. Usually, this involves the allocation of lesser resources in the short term but growing to significant allocations later. In addition, it typically involves significant reconfiguration of the firm assets and capabilities.

Manage

Like Focus models, models in this part of the chart are relatively easy to develop, meaning they are likely to be a close fit with current resources, assets and capabilities. However, they are relatively unattractive, typically with static or shrinking markets with intense competition. Often models in this area are existing models that happen to find themselves sitting on top of a new but not especially attractive fitness peak. In this case, organisations should aim to manage this fitness peak, maintaining a competitive model but with minimal resource allocation. Usually, this involves the reallocation of significant currently existing resources away from this model, towards Build and Focus models, in such a way as to minimise impact on competitiveness.

Avoid or withdraw

Models in this part of the chart are those that typically would be difficult and risky to build, being far from current resources, assets and capabilities. They are also relatively unattractive, being either small, unprofitable or both. In this case, organisations should avoid this fitness peak by withholding or divesting resources from this business model and diverting them to Build or Focus models.

Some readers will see the roots of this approach in other techniques such as the Boston Matrix or Directional Policy Matrix, which also address the issue of resource allocation between entities that vary in their risk and returns. Like all strategic management tools of this type, the approach provides guidance but should not be interpreted as an inviolable instruction. It works best as a guide to management thinking and works worst as a blind, number-crunching exercise. In practice, leadership teams adopt three sets of habits to make the use of this technique pragmatically applicable:

1   They challenge and reiterate. If the recommendation for any model runs strongly counter to intuition, effective organisations reiterate the entire process. This results either in clearer justification of the original recommendation or a revised recommendation.
2   When the comparison of models places them near the borders of the quadrants, they graduate their response. For example, a model on the build/focus border might be chosen for medium term focus once some minor changes in organisational capabilities are in place. Similarly, a model on the focus/manage border might be chosen for management only if it seems that the trend is for rapid decline in attractiveness.
3   They use the resource flows implied by the chart to help them choose how many models to support. Typically, resources can be withdrawn from models at the left half of the chart and redirected to models in the right half of the chart. So a chart with

several currently large models in the withdraw or manage quadrants implies significant resource availability and a strategy that can sustain several build and focus models. Conversely, lack of left-half models implies that new resources will need to be found and that fewer right-half models can be supported.

The end result of Stage 4, and this process overall, is a rational choice about how to allocate resources between fitness peaks and, therefore, business models. Sometimes, the result is very simple – a clear recommendation to focus all resources on the development and deployment of one model. More often, the result is a decision to focus on one or more models, build others, manage others and avoid others. Most importantly, this choice is specific to the firm and its context, which means that it avoids the dangers of the 'herd mentality', seen when firms follow industry fashion. Having made this rational, firm specific choice about what to evolve into, the firm is now in a position to answer the subsequent questions regarding how to evolve.

Climb few, climb wisely

In this discussion, I have described the practice I observe when firms try to answer the most fundamental question about their future: which fitness peak shall we attempt to climb? The importance of this question for future decisions means that it must be answered with great care and careful process. Often, care is mistakenly conflated with volume of data and size of spreadsheets. Effective firms take a more thoughtful approach. Hence the four-stage process I have described as emerging from practice. For all its stage-by-stage simplicity, this process is as much judgement as analysis and as much craft as science. The answers that result of this process are sometimes clear but are often nuanced. Most of all, the value of this approach to choosing which peak to climb and which model to build lies as much in the discussion it enables as in the answer it provides. That answer is the basis and reference point for all of the other questions about adapting to the future. I will discuss those questions next.

24 What capabilities does our new business model need?

In the preceding section, I described the process of choosing which fitness peak(s) to climb and thus which business model(s) to develop. This choice is the first and most fundamental that organisations have to make as they adapt to the changing, fragmenting fitness landscape of the life science industry. The rationale of the choice process described is that, for each fitness peak, there is a business model of optimal fitness. Each of these models is characterised by a particular approach to creating value, a particular target group of value definers and a particular set of choices about how to optimise the balance between risk and return.

The process I described, based on observation of current, advanced practice, leads to a pattern of resource allocation between the peaks and their optimal fitness models. This allocation pattern is sophisticated and nuanced, based not simply on chasing the biggest market but on a multifactorial assessment of how attractive the model is and on the firm's ability to develop the required model, which implies the risk associated with that choice. In single model firms, this leads to the focusing of resources onto the model that combines maximum relative attractiveness of the fitness peak with the highest relative probability of the firm being able to develop that model successfully. In multiple model firms, the process leads to a portfolio strategy, guiding the allocation and withdrawal of resource between different models over time.

Diligent execution of the fitness peak selection process puts an executive team in the position where it has chosen which models to develop and, of equal importance, the ones from which to withhold or withdraw resource. When compared to the present, those choices may imply wholly new business models, only incremental adaptation from current models or something between those two extremes. This choice of model or models is the essential first step in deliberately managing an organisation's evolution. But it raises an obvious next question: how do I design and build that model? In my research and in my advisory work with life science companies, I note that leadership teams don't begin the design of a new business model without first envisioning what it will look like. They rarely phrase the question in terms of traits, as I have, but they do try to form a clear vision of what capabilities the new model needs, which of those will be developed inside the organisation and which we be accessed via a holobiont. In this chapter, I describe my findings about how firms address the question of which capabilities are needed and, in subsequent sections, I address the acquisition and accessing of those capabilities.

What is a capability?

A capability is simply the ability to perform a necessary task. Capabilities depend on having the appropriate resources, but they mustn't be confused with those necessary antecedents. Employing a group of clever scientists, for instance, isn't the same as being able to develop new products. Resources are transformed into capabilities when they are utilised during a set of organisational routines, by which I mean, following Nelson and Winter's concepts, a stable pattern of organisational activities. To make an analogy with a biological system, routines express themselves through capabilities in the same way that genes express themselves via proteins. Like proteins in a living system, capabilities do most of the work but they have their origins in organisational routines which, like genes, store and use what the organisation knows.

It has long been recognised that not all capabilities play the same role in allowing an organisation to thrive. Prahalad and Hamel famously developed the concept of *core capabilities*, by which they meant those that distinguished a firm in the market place. In my work, I found that the core capability concept has some value. There are clearly some capabilities that seem to be prominent in enabling a firm's competitive advantage. However, as I probed more deeply into the capabilities necessary for firms to evolve and occupy a fitness peak, I found that Prahalad and Hamel's concept was too limited. In particular, it was not sufficiently detailed to allow firms to specify the full set of capabilities needed in a new business model. Instead, I observed firms thinking in terms of three classes of capabilities. Again, executives rarely discriminated very clearly or gave these different types of capabilities specific labels but it became clear that in specifying the capabilities needed by their business model there were three distinct types, which I labelled as follows:

Hygiene capabilities

These are capabilities that are necessary to allow an organisation to operate in the market but do not provide any sort of competitive advantage. Rather, their absence would prevent a firm from operating. A trivial example would be the capability to process orders and issue invoices in a timely, accurate manner. For such essential but not differentiating capabilities, I adopted the name hygiene capability, derived from Frederick Herzberg's seminal two-factor theory.

Differentiating capabilities

These are capabilities that allow an organisation to perform value-creating tasks in a manner superior to the competition. They are similar in concept to Prahalad and Hamel's core capabilities but they are rather more narrowly defined as capabilities that contribute strongly to the evolutionary fitness of a business model. So, for example, the Secular Grail model demands a set of differentiating capabilities to integrate multiple innovative technologies in a way that creates more value than its alternatives.

Dynamic capabilities

These are capabilities that allow an organisation to acquire, shift or reshape its resources, so enabling the development of other capabilities, either hygiene or differentiating. An example would be the ability of a customer intimate firm to develop insight into the heterogeneity of its customers' needs. This dynamic capability, the ability to create new knowledge resources, enables the differentiating capability to develop tailored value propositions. The concept of dynamic capabilities, as discussed in Chapter 8, is taken from Teece and Pisano's seminal work.

These three categories of capability encompass the entire set of a business model's capabilities, which I have labelled the 'capabileome'. Just as the proteome (the entire set of proteins expressed by an organism) is characteristic of a species, the capabileome is characteristic of a given business model. Just as some proteins, such as collagen, are ubiquitous across many species, so the most basic and fundamental capabilities, usually hygiene capabilities, are found to be identical or very similar in all business models. Order processing, procurement and recruitment are all examples of such ubiquitous hygiene capabilities.

By contrast, differentiating capabilities are more specific to and characteristic of a species flock of business models. For example, capabilities for absorbing, managing and using new scientific knowledge are characteristic of technological innovator business models, just as testosterone is characteristic of vertebrates. Dynamic capabilities are more analogous to regulatory proteins, disabling or enabling the expression of hygiene and differentiating capabilities. As I will discuss, dynamic capabilities seem to be similar in every type of business model, but they differ in the specifics of their mechanisms. Hence in trying to understand and specify the capability set – the capabileome – of a chosen business model, it is important to remember that it is unique to that model but shares many differentiating capabilities with its cousins and shares some of its of hygiene capabilities with its very distant relatives. Its dynamic capabilities, meanwhile, are shared with other models but their mechanism seems to be model specific.

This clarification of what organisational capabilities are and how they are analogous to proteins in organisms is helpful. It forms the basis for understanding how firms design and develop the capabileome of their chosen business model. In the following sections, based on my research observations, I will suggest a staged process by which organisations might deliberately develop a specification for the capabileome of their chosen business model. Later, in Chapter 26, I will describe another process for how they might then build their capabileome.

Stage 1: further reification of the chosen model

Initial, outline reification of business model options is a necessary precursor to choosing between them. However, it is impossible to specify the capabileome of a business model without further, more detailed, reification of the model. At a superficial level, it is self-evident that a business model implies certain capabilities. Operationally excellent customers must have excellent capabilities in managing costs, for example. Similarly, it is almost tautological to say that customer intimate companies must have strong capabilities in value proposition design. But such obvious superficialities are not sufficiently detailed or specific to guide executive action. Again, it is necessary to create a clearer, more detailed picture of what the chosen model looks like for the organisation in question before beginning to design its capabileome in any way that is practically useful. Consequently, a reification stage, as described in Chapter 23 is a necessary first step in defining the model's capabileome. The examples given in that section illustrate typical examples of reification. Importantly, this envisioning of what the new business model might be, which balances the constraints of path dependence against the possibilities of the new landscape, informs not only choice of model but also the subsequent design of the model. In my experience, reification is often an iterative process. Firms envision the specifics of their business model to a degree sufficient to compare and choose from options and then undertake a second, more detailed reification loop to allow specification of the capabileome.

Stage 2: specifying hygiene capabilities

Like most basic biological proteins, many hygiene capabilities are typically common across all models but the details of their functioning are model specific. For example, all business models will have a set of organisational routines for creating, approving and authorising legal contracts, which will express themselves in contract management capabilities. But the details of contract management may differ both between and within species flocks. Another parallel with basic biological processes is that hygiene capabilities are both ubiquitous and, by virtue of their ubiquity, almost invisible. Like respiration and perspiration, many hygiene capabilities are practically autonomic capabilities. This is a virtue for existing business models because organisations need little time spent thinking about these capabilities. On the other hand, it presents a challenge for the designers of new models because it means that their leaders must find a way to consciously elucidate what hygiene capabilities are needed. If not, they risk building a model without a critically important hygiene capability.

From my observations of how firms specify hygiene capabilities, it emerges that leaders begin with a mental framework of four classes of hygiene capabilities, as summarised in Figure 24.1. Each class of factor reflects something that could easily prevent the model from doing business, whilst not contributing significantly to competitive advantage. These factors are as follows:

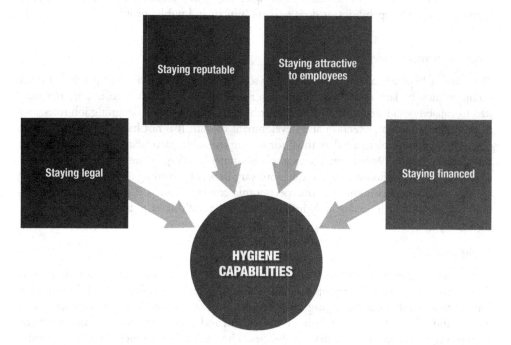

Figure 24.1 The four classes of hygiene capabilities

Staying legal

This class of hygiene capabilities is necessary so that the organisation is not prevented from doing business by force of law. Examples include, but are not limited to, capabilities in gaining and maintaining regulatory approval; obeying local, national and international trading laws; avoiding violations of antitrust or monopoly legislation; conforming to local employment law; and complying with environmental protection standards; This list of examples illustrates how, at a general level, such staying legal capabilities are ubiquitous across all or most models; but, at a detailed level, they are highly specific both to the model and to its particular variant in a given market and product category. Geographical spread of the model, for example, strongly influences the specifics of the hygiene capabilities needed to stay legal, as does product class or regulatory category.

Staying reputable

This class of hygiene capabilities is necessary so that the organisation is not prevented from doing business by force of public opinion and, since public opinion often acts via legislation, the capabilities for staying reputable connect strongly to those for staying legal. Examples include, but are not limited to, capabilities for ensuring transparency in business dealings; managing product access for very poor patients; managing gender, race and other diversity issues; managing crises that arise unexpectedly; and managing external critics and the media. As with the staying legal hygiene capabilities, this list of examples illustrates that the capabilities for staying reputable are ubiquitous across models but that, at a detailed level, they are highly specific both to the model and its particular context. The emotive nature of certain diseases, for example, shapes the detail of the necessary staying reputable hygiene capabilities, as does a firm's history and public profile.

Staying attractive to employees

This class of hygiene capabilities is necessary so that the organisation is not prevented from doing business by lack of appropriate human resources. Examples include, but are not limited to, capabilities in managing the employer brand; identifying and designing job roles; and managing recruitment, retention and development of staff. It is not hard to see that this set of capabilities is complemented by those for staying reputable, particularly those for employer brand management. Once again, the example illustrates how capabilities for staying attractive to employees are ubiquitous across models but vary in detail according to its particular variant and context. Macroeconomic and microeconomic conditions and the model's specific technology and market context strongly influence the design of this set of hygiene capabilities.

Staying financed

This class of hygiene capabilities is necessary so that the organisation is not prevented from doing business by lack of appropriate financial resources. Examples include, but are not limited to, capabilities in managing investor relations; sourcing investment capital; managing tax and related matters; managing cost controls and cash flow; and other management accounting and corporate treasury capabilities. The interactions of these hygiene capabilities with those for legality, reputation and employee attractiveness are obvious. Yet again, the example illustrates that capabilities for staying financed are ubiquitous across models but vary in detail according to the particular model, its variant and context. Geography, mode of value creation, scale and scope of the model all strongly influence the design of this set of hygiene capabilities.

This framework of four classes of hygiene capabilities provides a starting point for designing the hygiene part of the capabileome of the reified business model. The four categories include all or most of the necessary hygiene capabilities and, by considering these in the context of any given reified model, they allow the development of a comprehensive specification of this part of the capabileome. Table 24.1 shows an anonymised, simplified example.

Table 24.1 Hygiene capabileome specification for an anonymised medical device firm

Hygiene category	Generalised hygiene capability	Model-specific hygiene capabilities: The capability to . . .
Staying legal	Gaining and maintaining regulatory approval	• Build and maintain knowledge of the regulatory environment for this product category across target countries. • Design a regulatory approval strategy for this product class. • Design and execute a trials programme compliant with regulatory authority requirements. • Compile and submit necessary documentation to relevant authorities. • Manage relationships with relevant regulatory authorities across the product life cycle.
	Obeying local, national and international trading laws	• Build and maintain knowledge of the legal environment across target countries. • Design appropriate legal due diligence process to encompass all functions. • Operate appropriate legal due diligence process across all functions. • Develop and operate a legal challenge response process.
	Avoiding violations of antitrust or monopoly legislation	• Build and maintain knowledge of market abuse environment across target countries. • Design appropriate antitrust process into relevant business processes. • Operate appropriate antitrust process across all relevant business processes. • Develop and operate an antitrust challenge response process.
	Conforming to local employment law	• Build and maintain knowledge of employment law across target countries. • Design an appropriate legal due diligence process for human resource processes. • Operate an appropriate legal due diligence process across all human resource processes. • Develop and operate an employment law challenge response process.
	Complying with environmental protection standards	• Build and maintain knowledge of environmental protection law across target countries. • Design an appropriate environmental compliance process across all business processes. • Operate an appropriate environmental compliance process across all business processes. • Develop and operate an environmental law challenge response process.

(Continued)

Table 24.1 (Continued)

Hygiene category	Generalised hygiene capability	Model-specific hygiene capabilities: The capability to . . .
Staying reputable	Ensuring transparency in business dealings	• Design and maintain a transparency strategy for the business. • Execute and maintain the transparency strategy across all business functions. • Develop and operate a transparency challenge response process.
	Managing product access for very poor patients	• Design a patient access strategy. • Execute and maintain the patient access strategy across all relevant business functions. • Develop and operate a patient access challenge response process.
	Managing gender, race and other diversity issues	• Design a legally compliant diversity strategy for the business. • Execute and maintain a legally compliant diversity strategy for the business. • Develop and operate a diversity challenge response process.
	Managing crises that arise unexpectedly	• Design and maintain a crisis anticipation, early warning and response process. • Execute a crisis response process as necessary.
	Managing external critics and the media	• Design and maintain an external relations process. • Execute an external relations process.
Staying attractive to employees	Managing the employer brand	• Develop an employer brand strategy. • Manage the employer brand across all key constituencies. • Integrate the employer brand strategy with product and other brands.
	Identifying and designing job roles	• Identify and anticipate human resource needs across the business. • Develop human resource strategy consistent with business needs and market environment. • Translate human resource strategy into specific recruitment, retention and development plans.
	Managing recruitment, retention and development of staff	• Execute recruitment plans. • Execute retention plans. • Execute development plans.
Staying financed	Managing investor relations	• Build and maintain knowledge of the investor environment. • Develop and execute an investor relations strategy.
	Sourcing investment capital	
	Managing tax and related matters	• Build and maintain knowledge of the tax environment across our trading context. • Develop and execute a tax management policy.
	Managing cost controls and cash flow	
	Managing accounting and corporate treasury functions	• Develop management accounting and corporate treasury goals consistent with financial objectives and business strategy. • Develop financial control infrastructure and process. • Operation of financial control processes.

Even in this example, which I have simplified from a real case for both clarity and anonymity, it is obvious that the hygiene part of the organisation's capabileome alone can be very complicated. In the real world example of this process, the list of required hygiene capabilities typically stretches to 150–200 distinct items, the absence of any one of which would make it either impossible for the organisation to operate or put it at great risk of being unable to operate in the future.

This process of specifying a list of hygiene capabilities is therefore an important first step in specifying the complete capabileome of the chosen business model. For most firms, many of these hygiene capabilities will already exist in the organisation and will need little or only minor adaptation, as in the example of order processing, or else they are relatively easily sourced externally, as is often true of some regulatory approval capabilities. Others, such as those for patient access, might be wholly new to a firm if it moves from one business model to another. The important point to grasp is that the relative ordinariness of hygiene capabilities belies their fundamental importance. Without them, the firm cannot operate at even a basic level and so differentiating and dynamic capabilities are of merely academic interest.

Stage 3: specifying differentiating capabilities

Whilst, at a detailed level, the hygiene part of an organisation's capabileome may be specific to its business model, it will usually show broad similarity to that of other life science companies, even those operating very different business models. For example, the regulatory approval capabilities of two life science business models may differ significantly if one has chosen to be very technologically innovative in in-vitro diagnostics whilst the other has chosen to be a follower in generic pharmaceuticals. But, despite those differences, the two will both have regulatory approval capabilities that are recognisably those of a life science company and are quite different from, say, those of a defence company or utility company, which operate in very different regulatory environments.

This broad similarity between the capabileomes of different life science business models diminishes when we move from hygiene capabilities to consider differentiating capabilities. This is the part of the capabileome that allows firms not merely to operate but to create value more effectively than their competitors. As such, it differs substantially between business models that represent different evolutionary choices. That is not to say there is no similarity or overlap at all; the business models in each species flock (for example, those models in the government payer/technologically innovative habitat) will share many of their differentiating capabilities. Those differentiating capabilities shared by any one species flock will also overlap, to a degree, with those of adjacent species flocks (for example, those in other government payer habitats and those in other technologically innovative habitats). But the differentiating capabilities of species flocks in distant habitats (where, for example, there is no government involvement and no technological innovation) will be quite different. Importantly, business models within a species flock will, whilst sharing many differentiating capabilities, have at least some distinct and characteristic differentiating capabilities. These are the capabilities that reflect those evolutionary choices that define the business model.

Once a business model is chosen, reified and its hygiene capabilities specified, the next stage is to specify the differentiating part of its capabileome. Again, the goal is to ensure that all the essential differentiating capabilities are identified, none are neglected and no unnecessary differentiating capabilities are specified, as this implies wasted effort. This design of the differentiating capability part of a business model's capabileome falls into two parts:

1   Identifying the generalised differentiating capabilities that are specific to the chosen mode of value creation.

2   Expanding the generalised differentiating capabilities to those specific to the chosen, reified business model.

In the following sub-sections, I will describe an approach for specifying this part of the capabileome, based on my research observations and working with life science companies.

Stage 3.1: identifying the generalised differentiating capabilities
that are specific to the chosen mode of value creation

The idea that companies choose one of three ways to create value and de-prioritise the other two comes from Michael Porter (see Box 12.4 in Chapter 12) but is supported in my research observations of the life sciences sector. And, as in all industries, the chosen mode of value creation is the single most important factor in determining the differentiating capabilities required by any chosen business model. The choice of value-creation mode is also closely related to Porter's concept of the value chain. Hence, the differentiating capabilities of technological innovators lie mostly (although not exclusively) in the new product development part of their value chain, those of operationally excellent firms mainly in operations and supply chain, and those of customer intimate firms mostly in the sales and marketing part of their value chain. To be clear, that doesn't mean that firms ignore the other parts of the chain completely. It simply means that capabilities in the less critical parts of the value chain may become hygiene capabilities or may be different in nature. So, for example, a customer intimate or technological innovator company will still need reasonably efficient operations, but they will not differentiate on that basis. Likewise, an operationally excellent company will still need to innovate but instead of inventing new products it may prioritise circumventing patents and following quickly.

The differentiating capabilities demanded by each of the three modes of value creation are therefore distributed differently across the value chain and are different in nature for each model. Table 24.2 shows the broad, high-level differentiating capabilities that seem to be important to each value-creating mode in each part of the value chain. Note that I'm using the terms of value chain stage in the broad sense here, so that they correspond roughly to research and development, manufacturing and operations and sales and marketing.

Table 24.2 is not all-inclusive; different firms may identify other general differentiating capabilities. However, by using Table 24.2 as a guide, organisations can develop a first iteration of the general differentiating capabilities implied by their choice of value-creation mode. When reiterated and made as specific as possible to the organisation's context, this list of general differentiating capabilities becomes the input to the next, expansion stage of the process.

Stage 3.2: expanding the generalised differentiating capabilities
to those specific to the chosen, reified business model

In Stage 3.1, I recommended the development of a list of nine or so general differentiating capabilities, implied by choice of value-creating mode, using Table 24.2 as a guide. Self-evidently, for example, the ability of a technological innovator to differentiate itself depends on, among other capabilities, the ability to apply scientific knowledge to create innovative new products. Similarly, an operationally excellent company can compete only if it is able to maintain supply of imitative products at the lowest cost in its competitive set.

Table 24.2 Generalised differentiating capabilities important to each mode of value creation

Value-creating mode / Value chain stage	Technological innovation	Operational excellence	Customer intimacy
New product development	Maintain understanding of advancing scientific knowledge in all relevant disciplines. Apply scientific knowledge to create innovative new products. Develop new products to marketable status.	Acquire technological understanding necessary to develop imitative products. Apply technological knowledge to create imitative products. Develop imitative products to marketable status.	Acquire technological understanding necessary to create and deliver the customer intimate value proposition. Apply technological knowledge to create and deliver the customer intimate value proposition. Develop the customer intimate value proposition to marketable status.
Supply chain management	Identify operational requirements associated with innovative new products. Develop or source operational resources to manufacture and supply innovative new products. Maintain supply of innovative new products at acceptable costs.	Maintain understanding of technological knowledge associated with optimal efficiency. Develop or source operational resources needed to achieve industry leading cost base. Maintain supply of imitative products at lowest cost in competitive set.	Identify operational requirements associated with customer intimate value propositions. Develop or source operational resources needed to deliver customer intimate value propositions. Maintain delivery of customer intimate value propositions at acceptable costs.
Customer relationship management	Identify alignment between unmet clinical needs and new scientific advances. Select from new product possibilities on the basis of commercial viability. Develop and execute competitive strategies around selected new products.	Identify opportunities for profitable imitation. Select from imitative possibilities on the basis of commercial viability. Develop and execute competitive strategies around selected imitative products.	Develop deep understanding of heterogeneity of market needs. Develop innovative market segmentation and commercially viable targeting. Develop and execute competitive strategies around targeted segments.

This short list, as it stands, provides a useful but insufficiently detailed guide to senior executives responsible for building the firm's capabileome. The next step is to expand the list with enough detail to identify the component capabilities that constitute each of the general differentiating capabilities. Importantly, these component capabilities are specific to the chosen business model. For example, capabilities needed to maintain understanding of the scientific environment will vary between technologically innovative models that focus on one technology and those that integrate multiple technologies. Similarly, capabilities for maintaining supply of innovative products at the lowest cost in the competitive set will vary between operationally excellent models that focus on cost and those that attempt some degree of differentiation. The expansion of each of the general differentiating capabilities is therefore very case specific and must consider the details of the chosen, reified model.

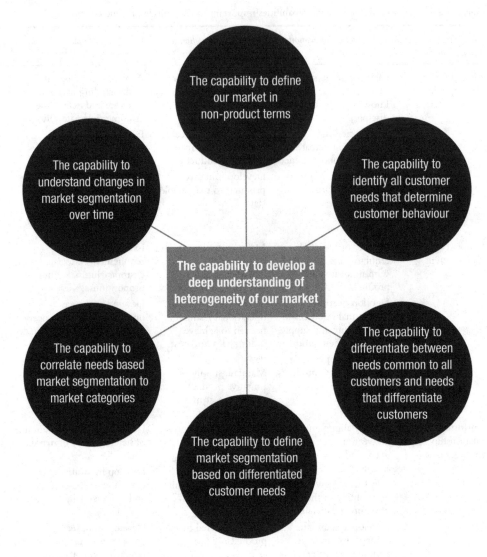

Figure 24.2 Model-specific expansion of capabilities to understand market heterogeneity

The example in Figure 24.2 shows the expansion of the general differentiating capability to develop a deep understanding of heterogeneity of market needs. Even in this simplified and anonymised form, it identifies six differentiating capabilities that are specific to this model. In practice, the expansion often produces more than this.

So the process for specifying the differentiating capabilities of a chosen model begins with identifying those generalised capabilities implied by choice of value-creation mode. This is not sufficient, however, and a full specification comes only from expanding those generalised capabilities in the context of reified model. As with the hygiene part of the capabileome, any chosen model has a large number of necessary capabilities. For example,

Table 24.2 suggests that each mode of value creation has around nine generalised differentiating capabilities although, in practice, the number is often higher. If each of these expands, as in Figure 24.2, to six differentiating capabilities that are specific to the model, then this part of the capabileome has at least fifty-four differentiating capabilities and quite conceivably more. Importantly, the interconnected nature of these capabilities means it is necessary to identify and acquire all of these differentiating capabilities. Together with the hygiene capabilities discussed earlier, even our simplified example now has over 100 necessary capabilities before we consider dynamic capabilities, as I do in Stage 4.

Stage 4: specifying dynamic capabilities

As I defined earlier, dynamic capabilities are those that reshape existing resources and so *enable* differentiating or hygiene capabilities. In this respect, they are analogous to regulatory proteins that switch other genes on or off. Like their biological analogue, dynamic capabilities are a more recent conception than hygiene and differentiating capabilities. As a result, they are less well defined and understood. Also like their biological analogue, they seem to play a role that is out of proportion to their numbers. This combination of importance and lack of definition led me to pay special attention to dynamic capabilities during my research, and I sought to understand which dynamic capabilities enabled resources to be changed and differentiating capabilities to be enabled. From my work, four broad types of dynamic capability emerged, as shown in Figure 24.3.

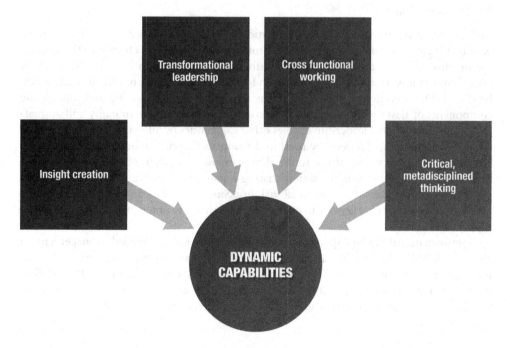

Figure 24.3 The four types of dynamic capabilities

Insight creation

This is a knowledge management capability that allows the organisation to create insight, meaning knowledge that is valuable, rare, hard to copy and that the organisation can act upon. Note that here I am using the term insight in the specific sense that I developed in my earlier work in this area (176). Importantly, whilst insight creation is sometimes conflated with market or customer insight, it can involve knowledge relating to any part of the value chain. Insight creation enables other capabilities by reshaping and improving knowledge assets and so providing knowledge that is necessary for those differentiating capabilities to function. For example, insight into how payers vary according to their risk attitudes enables a firm's differentiating capability to understand market heterogeneity and to develop and target extended value propositions. Similarly, insight into causes of cost variation in the supply chain enables firms to develop an industry leading cost base whilst insight into disease mechanisms can inform product design. In all cases, the ability to create some new piece of knowledge that the firm uses to create value is a dynamic capability.

The capability to create insight is often confused with the capability to gather, process and analyse data. In fact, whilst such data processing is often a necessary prerequisite to creating insight, it is rarely sufficient. On its own, data processing may lead to new knowledge but generally of the generic type is that is easily available to all firms in the sector and which does not enable differentiating capabilities. The creation of true market insight almost always requires inductive or deductive learning process (or a combination of both) in addition to data processing (177).

Transformational leadership

This is the capability that allows an organisation to envision a desired, future situation, the broad path towards that situation and to communicate that vision effectively throughout the organisation. My use of the term transformational leadership here is influenced by Bass's important work on the topic, although I am using it in a slightly narrower sense than he did (178). In particular, my observations emphasise the envisioning and influencing components of Bass's work rather than his considerations of ethics, morality and authenticity. Transformational leadership enables other capabilities by allowing firms to prioritise the differentiating capabilities they need to develop, so allowing resources to be allocated. For example, a clear vision of the future development of a given technology can enable, in a technological innovator, the differentiating capability of selecting from new product possibilities on the basis of commercial viability. Similarly, the clear communication of a vision of operational excellence can enable the disciplined maintenance of a low cost base supply chain.

Transformational leadership is often confused with either detailed management or charismatic leadership. In fact, attention to detail and charisma may contribute to transformational leadership, but they do not appear to be sufficient on their own. Rather, clarity of vision and consistency in using that vision to guide action seems to be central to the way in which transformational leadership enables differentiating capabilities.

Cross functional working

This is the capability that allows organisations to perform tasks across functional boundaries. My use of the term here is based on another of my research streams that covers two aspects of cross functional working: alignment of individual behaviours and optimising of the ratio of negative to positive intraorganisational conflict (179, 180, 181). Cross functional working enables other capabilities by minimising negative behaviours, such as politicking, and maximising positive behaviours, such as information sharing. For example, pooling of information about patent loss, customer needs and technological possibilities enables, in operationally excellent companies, the differentiating capability to identify opportunities for profitable imitation. Similarly, the optimisation of positive intraorganisational conflict between headquarters and operating affiliates enables, in global companies, the effective localisation of global competitive strategies.

The capability to work cross functionally is often confused with collaborative teamwork and structural devices such as brand teams and other matrix structure working groups. In fact, whilst such commonplace management techniques often contribute to cross functional working, they may also hinder it by blurring task ownership and encouraging compromise instead of consensus. Effective cross functional working involves the alignment of goals and removal of sources of conflict, such as shared resources and asymmetries of status.

Critical, metadisciplined thinking

This is the capability that allows organisations to process complex information more effectively. This capability combines two elements: the ability to combine knowledge from multiple disciplines and the ability to use that information in a rational, considered manner. Critical, metadisciplined thinking enables other capabilities by enabling better choices between options and overriding irrational, habitual decision making behaviour. For example, critical, metadisciplined thinking may avoid the allocation of resources between geographies on traditional, population-based lines and instead lead to resource allocation based on the existence of targeted, global segments. Similarly, more critical decision making may significantly change the assessment and comparison of fitness peaks, so altering choices about which fitness peak to climb and so shaping resource allocations.

Critical, metadisciplined thinking is often confused with evidence-based decision making. Whilst the use of data to support decisions is often a component of critical thinking, science-based firms often mistakenly assume that the only kind of data is quantitative and so restrict their evidence base. Critical, metadisciplined thinking is characterised by using multiple types of data and combining methods from both natural and social sciences.

Like hygiene factors, dynamic capabilities are broadly similar in nature across all business model types, but their detailed mechanism differs between models. Hence, the specification of what dynamic capabilities are needed follows a similar process to that for specifying hygiene and differentiating capabilities, namely elaboration and expansion of the four dynamic capability types in the context of the reified chosen model. Table 24.3 shows a simplified, anonymised example of this process.

As Table 24.3 shows, even in a simplified situation, the four classes can easily lead to a significant number of necessary dynamic capabilities.

Consolidating the capabilities specification

Although I have necessarily simplified, generalised and anonymised the examples in this section, I hope its general point remains clear. Just as no biological species is viable without

Table 24.3 A generic example of a dynamic capability specification

Category of dynamic capability	Model-specific capabilities
Insight creation	• The ability to identify and characterise critical knowledge gaps • The ability to define and execute inductive organisational learning processes • The ability to define and execute deductive organisational learning processes • The ability to combine multiple information sources to create relevant knowledge • The ability to differentiate insight from ordinary, non-insightful knowledge
Transformational leadership	• The ability to understand the key implications of situational change for the organisation • The ability to create a clear vision of the desired future situation • The ability to communicate the vision clearly throughout the organisation
Cross functional working	• The ability to identify key cross functional linkages and assess their efficacy • The ability to diagnose the causes of failures in cross functional working • The ability to manage the factors that optimise cross functional working
Critical, metadisciplined thinking	• The ability to identify those issues that would benefit from critical thinking • The ability to identify and use multiple epistemological perspectives relevant to those issues • The ability to gather, process and use knowledge from multiple sources to support critical thinking

a complete proteome that is specific to that species, no business model can operate and compete without a complete capabileome that is specific to that model. And, just as the human proteome is complex, with about 20,000 proteins, an organisational capabileome is also complex. When applying this process in practice, around 100 or 200 capabilities are usually identified, although that tends to ignore many of the taken-for-granted hygiene capabilities. More importantly, the process described in this section tends to highlight capabilities – hygiene, differentiating or dynamic – that have not previously been considered by the firm because they were not needed in their former business model. The ability of the process to identify such important but unconsidered capabilities is essential because, unlike when humans fail to express a protein, the lack of a capability may not be immediately obvious. For example, failure to attract staff, to create insight or to choose rationally from multiple product options are all gaps in a capabileome whose effects are subtle, slow acting and ultimately fatal.

When applied with care and rigour, the process described in this section delivers a long list (100 or 200 is a good rule of thumb) of necessary capabilities that characterise and are essential to the chosen business model. This list is the necessary starting point for the next stage in the process, acquiring those capabilities.

25 How should we design a capable holobiont?

In the preceding chapter, I introduced the idea of the capabileome: an organisation's full complement of capabilities that allow it to function and compete in its habitat. Using the biological analogue of the proteome, I argued that the capabileome, a reified business model's particular set of hygiene, differentiating and dynamic capabilities, is specific to and characteristic of that business model. The capabileome of any business model can and does overlap greatly with other, closely related models and, to a lesser extent, with more distant life science models. But it is a business model's capabileome that makes it what it is.

As well as being a defining characteristic, the capabileome of a reified business model is also a guide to executive action. Again, a biological analogy helps. If you wanted to build a functional human being with all its traits of speech, intelligence and the ability to walk upright, you would need to understand how the human proteome leads to those traits. The same would be true if you wanted to give one species, a chimpanzee say, those human traits. You would need to understand (among other things) the differences between the chimp and the human proteome as a preliminary step to modifying the proteome and then the animal.

In the same way, if you wanted to transform an existing life science company into one of the many new business models described in Part 3, one that would thrive in its newly selected environment, you would need a comprehensive understanding of how the new model's capabileome differs from that of its ancestor model. Without that understanding, your attempts to transform the old business model into the new would be fumbling in the dark.

In the approaches I described in Chapter 24, my intent was to enable executive teams to develop a target capabileome for their chosen new business model or models. That is, to develop the comprehensive list of hygiene, differentiating and dynamic capabilities that the new business model will need to climb the selected fitness peak. I help pharmaceutical and life science companies to do this and, when I do, the feeling in the room is often one of very palpable trepidation. Leadership teams are typically awed by the intimidating list of hygiene, differentiating and dynamic capabilities that they need to develop for their reified new business model. Even when they consider their existing capabilities and reduce their list to those that they still need to evolve, that list is always challenging. Furthermore, as a rule of thumb, the more attractive the new model is, the more challenging and intimidating the 'to evolve' gap is between old and new models and capabileomes.

This daunting gap between a firm's existing and target capabileomes raises an obvious and important question: how do we build these capabilities in our organisation? More to the point, perspicacious executives ask, how can we build these capabilities faster and better than our rivals, who are racing to occupy and dominate the same peak in our industry's fitness landscape? This is an important qualification of the question because it identifies the urgency of the evolutionary contest. It is not only necessary to acquire those capabilities, it is necessary to do so with greater efficiency and efficacy than our rivals. In most parts of the life sciences market, those rivals are very good companies staffed with bright, hardworking people. This makes our perspicacious question even more important to answer.

In fact, there are two ways for firms to build their target capabileome. The first, and by far the most common, is incrementalism or, in plain English, trial and error. Firms can try ways of doing something – acquiring a new product, for example, or reengineering a manufacturing process – and, if that adaptation works, keep doing it. If it does not work, then they can try another way of doing it and repeat until they find a good adaptation. This, broadly, is how biological evolution works and it is an *effective* process. The eyes through which you are reading this book are evidence of that efficacy. But it is also hugely *inefficient* process, wasting time and resources in fruitless searches up evolutionary dead ends.

Faced with a race against strong rivals, the common, default approach of incrementalism may be effective, but it is unlikely to be efficient. And against strong competitors, it is most unlikely to succeed. Unsurprisingly, I have observed in the practice of some exemplary firms a more deliberate, rational way of developing the target capabileome. In this section, I will describe my observations of how leaders deliberately accelerate the evolution of their firm's capabileome. As in the preceding sections, I will articulate their unspoken methods and explicate their implicit thinking in the form of an explicit, purposeful process that executives can use as practical guide. Before I do that, and in order to structure that process, it is important to qualify what is meant by the 'we' in our rhetorical question about how should we build our capabilities.

In the context of this question, 'we' can mean 'those of us who work in our firm' or 'those of us who work together to climb the fitness peak'. Importantly, those do not have to be the same people. The organisation's leadership will have to direct the construction of the target capabileome, but this does not mean that the entire capabileome needs to reside within the firm, as defined by its legal boundaries. Rather, as favoured by the selection pressures of the holobiont shift described in Part 2, the entity that needs to express the target capabileome is not a single business unit or firm but that network of firms, suppliers, partners and alliances that I called the holobiont. Yet again, biological analogies help: a fit human being needs a microbiome within its gut; algae, fungi and cyanobacteria live symbiotically to make lichen such an effective organism. In the same way, life science business models can best express their necessary capabilities via a holobiont of multiple organisations. This means that we are really considering the holobiont's capabileome rather than just that of the firm. Consequently, the answer to our question is best answered in two parts.

What should our capable holobiont look like?

This is a question of what part of our capabileome should lie inside our firm's legal boundaries, which should lie inside our suppliers, partners and allies, and what sort of relationship we should have with our holobiont network.

How should we develop our own capabilities?

This is a question of how to acquire or develop those capabilities that we have decided should lie inside our firm's legal boundaries.

These difficult questions require thoughtful answers. For that reason, I will answer them separately, based on my research observations, the first in the following pages of this chapter, the second in Chapter 26 titled, 'How Do We Build Our Core Capabilities?'

What should our capable holobiont look like?

In the simplest terms, the ultimate answer to this question is: it should look like whatever is necessary to express the target capabileome. This pragmatic principle that holobiont design should be led by capability requirements guides the decisions of effective companies. In practice, it is used to help answer a set of component questions: Who should we work with? What should they do for us? What sort of relationship should we have with them? What should we do ourselves? Answering these effectively is clearly necessary to design a capable holobiont. The quality of the answers to these questions strongly influences the evolutionary fitness of the holobiont.

In the context of a large, complex target capabileome, this simple set of questions proliferates into a very complex set of choices, often made more difficult by lack of hard information and subjectivity of interpretation. This difficulty leads to the common, satisficing practice most often observed in the life sciences industry. Typically, life science firms eschew complex questions by reducing them to narrower, functional tasks based on hard, objective data. Thus the decisions are delegated to departments such as, for example, procurement for the purchase of goods or services, manufacturing to outsource production and business development for acquiring intellectual property. This simplification substitutes the development of capabilities with the acquisition of goods or services and reduces the decisions to ones that are much easier to define and make. However, it also means that capabilities become commoditised and cannot be the source of competitive advantage.

In contrast to this traditional, functional approach, my observation is that some firms that take a more considered, strategic approach to building their capabileome use a four-stage process, shown in Figure 25.1 and described in the following paragraphs.

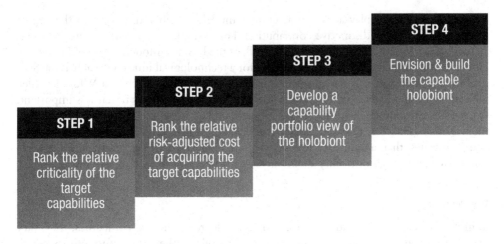

Figure 25.1 The holobiont design process

Stage 1: ranking the relative criticality of the target capabilities

The process of choosing a habitat, reifying the business model and identifying the target capabileome results in a long, often intimidating list of necessary capabilities. As daunting as this list is, in practice its most obvious feature is its variety and heterogeneity. It ranges from difficult and critically important capabilities, such as understanding the latest science in a given domain, for example nanotechnology, to the more mundane but still essential capabilities, such as being able to address the detailed requirements of local reimbursement approval systems. This heterogeneity is the first factor that influences firms in the design of their holobiont; effective firms rank the importance of capabilities and treat them differently when deciding whether to express them inside or outside of their firm's legal boundaries. All firms perform this capability ranking process, either deliberately or unconsciously, but firms vary in how they do it, and some firms are much more effective than others.

In less effective firms, informal or subconscious ranking simplistically estimates the relative importance of the capabilities, a concept that is often poorly defined and subjectively assessed. In addition to these weaknesses, this approach is fundamentally flawed because it ignores the interconnectivity of the different capabilities. In short, to force-rank the importance of very different capabilities is an overly simplistic and ineffective way to decide if they should stay in-house or be outsourced.

In contrast to this simplistic approach, more effective firms replace the ill-defined concept of capability importance with the more sophisticated concept of relative criticality, the extent to which the capability contributes to competitive strength of the reified business model in question. It is this dimension, which is better defined and easier to assess objectively than importance, that effective firms use to rank capabilities. Importantly, sophisticated firms recognise that relative criticality is multifactorial, the aggregate of several factors. These factors emerge repeatedly in practice although executives usually express them in varying ways and to varying degrees. Explicating what I see in practice, the following component factors of relative criticality emerge:

Capability salience

Whilst all capabilities play a role in a business model's viability, they vary in the degree to which they make a distinctive contribution. For example, a capability to protect intellectual property is necessary to many, if not all, of the business models described in Part 3. However, it is a much more salient capability for a technological innovator such as the Secular Grail model than it is for an operationally excellent model such as a White Labeller, who operates in a habitat where intellectual property protection is much less important. Conversely, capabilities in supply chain efficiency play a role in both those models, but their relative salience is reversed. Acquiring a salient capability makes more difference to competitiveness than acquiring a low salience capability, so high capability salience therefore correlates to high criticality of any given capability.

Capability rarity

Whilst most capabilities can be found to some degree in many companies, they vary greatly between market contexts in the extent to which they are found and to which they are developed. For example, the capability to prepare and submit local market access dossiers is typically well developed in the majority of life science companies. By contrast, the capability to map out the value chain of a healthcare system and identify areas where health economic value can be created is relatively rare and poorly developed. Acquiring a rare capability makes more difference to competitiveness than acquiring a common one, so high capability rarity correlates to high criticality of any given capability.

Capability complementarity

To some degree, all capabilities are interconnected, but they vary greatly in the extent to which they influence other capabilities. For example, the capability to develop integrated marketing communications programmes may influence some other capabilities, especially in the customer relationship management part of the value chain, but it has limited influence on product development and operations. By contrast, the capability to recruit and retain employees with key skill sets has significant influence on many other capabilities throughout the organisation. Acquiring a capability that complements many other capabilities makes more difference to competitiveness than acquiring one that has little influence on other capabilities, so high complementarity correlates to high criticality of any given capability.

Capability imitability

Ultimately, any capability can be imitated by rivals; however, they vary greatly in the extent to which they can be observed and then duplicated or substituted by competitors. Hence, the capability to tailor added value services to customers is necessarily visible to competitors as soon as it is expressed, making it relatively easy to mimic or substitute. By contrast, the capability to create insight into customer needs via organisational learning processes is much less visible to rivals and, being difficult and often implicit, it is much less imitable. Acquiring a capability that is hard to imitate makes more difference to competitiveness over time than acquiring an easy to copy capability; thus low imitability correlates to high criticality of any given capability. Note that the relationship is the inverse of the preceding three factors.

These four component factors allow the most effective firms to rank the relative criticality of each of their target capabilities in an objective, informed manner. In its simplest form, the ranking process is summarised in Table 25.1, in which Capability A has slightly

Table 25.1 An example of ranking relative criticality of targeted capabilities

Factor/Capability	Weighting	Capability A	Capability B	Capability C	Capability D
Capability salience	40	9 – high salience	2 – lowest salience	5 – median salience	10 – highest salience
Capability rarity	20	7 – high rarity	2 – lowest rarity	4 – low rarity	8 – highest rarity
Capability complementarity	25	7 – highest complementarity	4 – low complementarity	2 – lowest complementarity	6 – high complementarity
Capability imitability	15	8 – lowest imitability	3 – highest imitability	3 – highest imitability	4 – high imitability
Total	100	$(40 \times 9) + (20 \times 7) + (15 \times 8) + (25 \times 7) = 795$	$(40 \times 2) + (20 \times 2) + (15 \times 3) + (25 \times 4) = 265$	$(40 \times 5) + (20 \times 4) + (15 \times 3) + (25 \times 2) = 375$	$(40 \times 10) + (20 \times 8) + (15 \times 4) + (25 \times 6) = 745$

greater criticality than D (795 compared with 745), which has significantly greater criticality than C (375), which is somewhat more critical than B (265).

In addition to replacing the overly simplistic idea of capability importance with the
multifactorial construct of capability criticality, the example in Table 25.1 also illustrates
two other ways in which the most effective firms design their holobiont. They make *relative* assessments and weight each factor. As can be seen in this example, the salience, rarity,
complementarity and imitability of each capability are assessed not in absolute terms but
relative to all of the others. This reflects the reality that the capabilities are being judged
not in absolute terms but against each other in the 'competition' to be expressed inside
or outside the organisation's legal boundaries. Equally, the weighting of the capabilities
reflects the reality that each of the four component factors is more or less important in a
given context, as summarised in Table 25.2.

In essence, a capability is relatively critical to a business model if it is salient, rare, hard
to imitate and complements other capabilities. However, the relative contribution of these
four factors to overall relative criticality depends on the maturity of the market and the
breadth of capabilities that are important to competing in that habitat. Alert readers will
recognise that what effective firms are doing when they rank capabilities in this way is to
apply in practice the work of Jay Barney on Resource Dependency Theory (182). This
unconscious echoing of strategic management theory in the practice of executives demonstrates Lewin's oft-quoted assertion that there is nothing so practical as a good theory.

When diligently executed, this first stage of the process shown in Figure 25.1 has two
great practical outcomes. First, it transforms the target capabileome, as developed by the
process described in Chapter 24, from a long, intimidating list of very disparate capabilities into an ordered list, in which each target capability is accurately ranked according to
its relative criticality to the reified business model. Second, and arguably more importantly, the process gives the executive team a much deeper understanding of the capabilities needed to succeed in their chosen new habitat. The relative criticality ranking of
the target capabileome is, therefore, an important and necessary first step in designing

Table 25.2 Weighting guidelines for the component factors of relative criticality

Factor	Factor is weighted heavily when . . .	Factor is weighted lightly when . . .
Capability salience, which is related to how many capabilities make a significant contribution to success	Success in the chosen habitat is heavily dependent on a small number of capabilities.	Success in the chosen habitat is equally dependent on a large number of capabilities.
Capability rarity, which is related to how well capabilities are developed in this market context	The competitive environment is mature with many competent competitors having well developed capabilities.	The competitive environment is immature with most or all competitors having poorly developed capabilities.
Capability complementarity, which is related to the interconnectedness of capabilities	Success in the chosen habitat is equally dependent on a large number of capabilities.	Success in the chosen habitat is heavily dependent on a small number of capabilities.
Capability imitability, which is related to how difficult it is for competitors to copy or substitute a capability	The competitive environment is mature with many competent competitors able to imitate.	The competitive environment is embryonic with few competent competitors able to imitate.

the optimal holobiont for the new business model. It also it leads to the next stage in the process, that of assessing the relative risk-adjusted cost of acquiring each capability in the capabileome.

Stage 2: ranking the relative risk-adjusted cost of acquiring the target capabilities

Just as the many different capabilities of the target capabileome are very varied in their relative criticality to the business model (that is, the extent to which they contribute to competitive strength), they also vary in two other dimensions: the cost of acquisition and the probability that they can be successfully acquired and assimilated into the organisation. Capabilities may range from those that are relatively easy and cheap to acquire, such as the ability to financially quantify established markets, to those that are relatively difficult and expensive to acquire, such as the ability to demonstrate the value of novel integrated technologies to payers who are familiar only with assessing single and incremental technologies.

This variation in acquisition cost is only half the picture, however, because the true cost of acquiring a new capability is not simply how much has to be spent to either buy it in or develop it in-house. To make an accurate assessment, the financial cost of acquiring a new capability has to be adjusted for the probability of the acquisition being successfully assimilated into the company and implemented in practice. For example, many life science firms acquire the capability to quantify their markets by buying the services of IMS, the industry's dominant market information supplier. This may be expensive, but a firm can be relatively certain that that knowledge can be assimilated easily into its strategic planning and other processes. By contrast, the same firm might invest in training, for example in key account management skills, with much less certainty that the training investment will translate into new capabilities. When adjustment for this uncertainty is made, the acquisition cost of a capability that has a high probability of being assimilated successfully is, in effect, less costly that another capability with the same acquisition cost but a lower probability of assimilation success.

Heterogeneity in risk-adjusted cost of acquisition of capabilities is the second factor (after relative criticality) that influences firms in the design of their holobiont; firms rank the cost and assimilation risk of acquiring different capabilities and treat them differently when deciding whether to express them inside or outside their firm's legal boundaries. As with the criticality of capabilities, all firms perform this ranking process, deliberately or otherwise, but they vary greatly in how they do it, and the degree of rigour they apply is correlated to their effectiveness. Simplistic and ineffective ranking focuses only on the relative cost of acquiring different capabilities, a measure that often includes explicit but neglects implicit costs and so is often inaccurately estimated. In addition to its inaccuracy, this approach is fundamentally flawed because it ignores or understates the probability that the acquisition and assimilation process may partly or completely fail. In short, to simply rank the acquisition costs of very different capabilities is an overly simplistic and ineffective way to decide if they should stay in-house or be outsourced.

More sophisticated firms recognise that capabilities differ greatly in their relative risk-adjusted cost, that is, the total cost of acquisition adjusted for the probability that it will be assimilated and expressed successfully. As with the relative criticality of capabilities, sophisticated firms recognise that the risk-adjusted acquisition cost is multifactorial and the aggregate of several factors. These factors emerge consistently from my observation of practice, although they are usually expressed implicitly. What I see in practice is the following component factors of risk-adjusted cost of acquisition cost:

Capability acquisition cost

Obviously, the cost of acquiring new capabilities can vary hugely. In most cases, the acquisition of product development capabilities in some new technology or the cost of acquiring lowest cost operational capability in manufacturing is very large. The cost of acquiring regulatory capability in a new geography or legal compliance capability for a new product category is relatively small. This variation in acquisition cost is often even greater when the full acquisition cost, which includes embedding the capability into organisation in addition to acquisition, is considered. Since acquisition cost contributes the capital employed to acquire a particular capability, high acquisition cost correlates to a higher risk-adjusted acquisition cost.

Capability assimilation risk

It is sometimes assumed that capabilities can be acquired almost as if they were physical goods, for example, by purchasing an innovative, small company or by contracting a distribution arrangement. But this is not always the case. It is true that for simple capabilities, such as those to physically distribute a product or to perform certain basic manufacturing processes, realisation follows acquisition with almost 100 percent certainty. Buying in active pharmaceutical ingredients is an example of this. But more complex capabilities, for example those to work with key opinion leaders or to create a brand with particular values and salience, involve a much less certain linkage between investment and outcome. This capability assimilation risk has to be allowed for, so a high capability assimilation risk correlates to a higher risk-adjusted acquisition cost.

Capability permanence

It is often assumed that, once acquired, capabilities are permanent. However, it is naïve to assume this true in all cases. Some capabilities, especially dynamic capabilities such as cross functional working, seem to be culturally embedded and, once acquired, relatively permanent. Others, such as the ability to attract partners in a given research area or to procure materials at low cost, may be more transient and susceptible to changes in the market environment. Permanence or transience influences the effective cost of the capability and has to be allowed for, so low capability permanence correlates to a to a higher risk-adjusted acquisition cost. Note that, unlike the first two factors, capability permanence is inversely correlated to risk-adjusted acquisition cost.

Capability availability

Capabilities that are not currently possessed by the firm vary greatly in how available they are from outside the firm. Some capabilities are easily purchasable on the open market, with lots of choice and variety; a Google search for contract manufacturing services demonstrates this. Other capabilities are much harder to acquire. There is very limited choice in some areas of specialist distribution and technical support for many medical technologies in emerging markets, for example. The same is true of high reliability, regulatory compliant manufacturing capability in some specialised biotechnology areas. Capability availability, by increasing competition and choice, reduces the costs and risks of acquiring a capability, so high capability availability is correlated to lower risk-adjusted acquisition cost. Note that capability availability is inversely correlated to risk-adjusted acquisition cost.

As with criticality, these four component factors allow the most sophisticated firms to rank the risk-adjusted acquisition cost of each of their target capabilities in an objective, informed manner. In its simplest form, the process is summarised in Table 25.3, in which capability C (825) has a better risk-adjusted acquisition cost than D (770), which is somewhat better than A (235), which is better than B (215).

As with the similar method used for assessing relative criticality, the cost, risk, permanence and availability of each capability is assessed not in absolute terms but relative to all of the others and is weighted to reflect the particularities of market context, as shown in Table 25.4.

Table 25.3 An example of ranking relative risk-adjusted acquisition cost of targeted capabilities

Factor/Capability	Weighting	Capability A	Capability B	Capability C	Capability D
Capability acquisition cost	40	1 – highest cost	2 – high cost	10 – lowest cost	8 – low cost
Capability assimilation risk	20	3 – high risk	2 – highest risk	8 – lowest risk	6 – low risk
Capability permanence	15	4 – low permanence	3 – least permanent	4 – low permanence	8 – most permanent
Capability availability	25	3 – low availability	2 – lowest availability	6 – high availability	9 – highest availability
Total	100	$(40 \times 1) + (20 \times 3) + (15 \times 4) + (25 \times 3) = 235$	$(40 \times 2) + (20 \times 2) + (15 \times 3) + (25 \times 2) = 215$	$(40 \times 10) + (20 \times 8) + (15 \times 4) + (25 \times 6) = 770$	$(40 \times 9) + (20 \times 6) + (15 \times 8) + (25 \times 9) = 825$

Table 25.4 Weighting guidelines for the component factors of relative risk-adjusted acquisition cost of targeted capabilities

Factor	Factor is weighted heavily when . . .	Factor is weighted lightly when . . .
Capability acquisition cost	The resources available to fund capability acquisition are very limited.	The resources available to fund capability acquisition are ample.
Capability assimilation risk	The organisation is complex and has a poor record of assimilating new capabilities.	The organisation is simple and has a good record of assimilating new capabilities.
Capability permanence	The capabilities demanded by the market environment are stable.	The capabilities demanded by the market environment are changing quickly.
Capability availability	The potential to acquire capabilities is not hindered by intellectual property, legal, informational or other market imperfections.	The potential to acquire capabilities is hindered by intellectual property, legal, informational or other market imperfections.

To summarise, a capability has a high risk-adjusted cost of acquisition if it is costly to acquire, there is significant risk of not assimilating the acquired capability, the capability is transient and there is limited possibility of buying the capability on the open market. However, the relative influence of these factors on the risk-adjusted acquisition cost of acquiring capabilities depends on the organisation's resources and complexity and the market's stability and freedom from constraints.

When diligently executed, this second stage of the process shown in Figure 25.1 complements the first stage (the ranking of relative criticality) in two ways. First, it creates another ranked version of the capabileome, this time ordered according to relative risk-adjusted cost of acquiring each capability. Second, the leadership has a much deeper understanding not only of the criticality of the capabilities needed but also of the costs and risks of acquiring them. This understanding allows the leadership to begin the third stage of considering the holobiont's structure.

Stage 3: developing a capability portfolio view of the holobiont

If diligently executed, the processes suggested in the previous two steps will translate the intimidating list of capabilities to evolve into two lists, each containing those same capabilities but ordered in two different ways: by their criticality to the business model and by their risk-adjusted cost of acquisition. A very simplified example, based on Table 25.1 and Table 25.3, is shown in Table 25.5.

In this table it is the relative order of capabilities that is important rather than absolute value. High numbers equate to high criticality but low cost. When applying this process in practice, this means that it is less important to be very accurate in assessing the absolute measures of criticality and risk-adjusted cost, so long as the relative assessments are correct. In turn, this makes it less important to measure the sub-components of each with absolute accuracy and more important to assess relative values.

Equipped with these two rankings of the capabileome, the third stage in the process combines these two assessments to guide our choice of which capabilities we choose to keep within the firm, which we choose to express via our holobiont and, as I'll discuss, our choice of holobiont relationships.

In principle, the logic that underlies holobiont construction is similar to that involved in designing a multi-business corporate strategy or a multi-segment marketing strategy. That is because, in the same way as firms have limited resources to allocate between businesses and market segments, they have limited resources to allocate to the development and maintenance of capabilities. The important added complication in the case of holobiont design is capability ownership, the reality that a valuable capability which is not held inside

Table 25.5 An example of a combined ranking grid for capabilities

	Relative criticality (ranking)	Relative risk-adjusted cost (ranking)
Capability A	795 (1)	235 (3)
Capability B	265 (4)	215 (4)
Capability C	375 (3)	770 (2)
Capability D	745 (2)	825 (1)

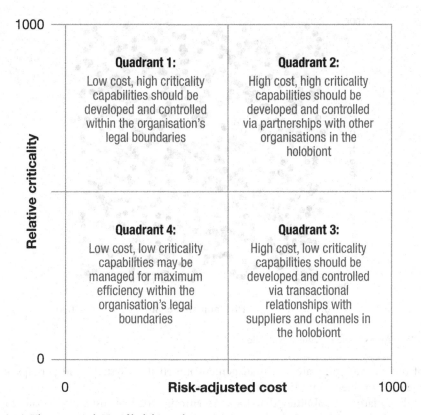

Figure 25.2 The strategic logic of holobiont design

the firm's legal boundaries is more likely to be appropriated by other firms. This logic of holobiont design is summarised in Figure 25.2.

This strategic logic is quite straightforward in application, although it is as practically difficult as it is valuable. The 200 or so ordered capabilities from a firm's version of Table 25.5 each have two values (relative criticality and relative risk-adjusted cost of assimilation) and they are used as coordinates to populate the firm's equivalent of Figure 25.2. Because the capabilities are assessed relative to each other, this results in a spread of capabilities across the figure and there are some capabilities in each of the four quadrants, as shown in Figure 25.3, in which each dot represents a target capability.

This populated figure is then used to guide the design of the capable holobiont. The quadrant in which each capability sits gives broad guidance as to how the firm should express each capability.

Quadrant 1: focus resources on the development and expression of low cost, high criticality capabilities within the firm's legal boundaries

In the terms of the transaction cost economists, this is a decision to 'make' rather than to 'buy' these capabilities. In practice, low cost, high criticality capabilities are likely to be:

- Hygiene capabilities that are not especially difficult or costly but have a disproportionate importance because of confidentiality, security or control issues. Examples

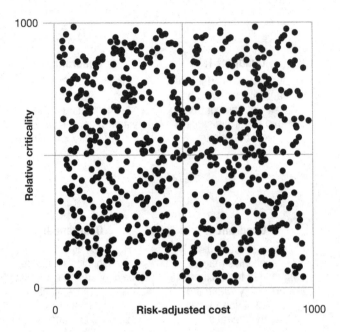

Figure 25.3 An example capability portfolio

of this include some areas of management information systems and perhaps adverse event or problem reporting for new products.

• Differentiating capabilities that have a criticality that is disproportionate to their relatively low costs or that are based on intangible assets. Examples of this include capabilities to manage brands or relationships with key government stakeholders.

• Dynamic capabilities involving issues of organisational behaviour and culture. This typically includes the four broad types of dynamic capability described in Chapter 24 (insight creation, transformational leadership, cross functional working and critical, metadisciplined thinking).

Quadrant 2: share resources to develop and express high cost, high criticality capabilities via partners in the firm's holobiont

In transaction cost economics terms, this can be seen as a form of 'buying' the capability; however, it is more accurate to describe it as co-creation of value, since it involves shared assets and resources and, typically, some complementarity between partners. Characteristically, this way of developing and expressing capabilities involves an interfirm relationship. It is a form of partnership rather than a purely transactional arrangement, in which the exchange is typically medium or longer term and involves higher degrees of mutual interests and trust. The value exchanged in partnerships is often not fully monetised as it includes tacit knowledge, know-how and relationship capital. In practice, high cost, high criticality capabilities are likely to be:

• Hygiene capabilities that are particularly difficult or costly but have relatively easily managed issues of confidentiality, security or control. An example of this would be partnering to share sales forces in order to address certain geographies.

- Differentiating capabilities that have not only high criticality and risk-adjusted costs, but whose risk-adjusted cost structure lends itself to mitigation by sharing. Examples of this include the development of technologically innovative value propositions that involve integration of multiple technologies. In these cases, not only is the cost and risk shared, the risk is also reduced by the combination of complementary knowledge bases.
- Dynamic capabilities where issues of organisational behaviour and culture are not significant but where synergies may be obtained. Examples of this include organisational learning by sharing fundamental research between firms working in the same disease area. At its most extreme, open source innovation is an example of this form of relationship, although joint technological development or shared manufacturing are more common examples.

Quadrant 3: divert resources from high cost, low criticality capabilities
by allowing them to be developed and expressed via transactional
relationships with suppliers and channels in the holobiont

This is the purest expression of 'buying' or outsourcing necessary capabilities in preference to 'making' them in-house. In practice, high cost, low criticality capabilities are likely to be:

- Hygiene capabilities that are difficult or costly, have no confidentiality, security or control issues, are freely available and lend themselves to economies of scale. Examples of this include undifferentiated manufacturing and operational capabilities, some sales force capabilities and some clinical development capabilities. All of these are evidenced by the growth of contract manufacturing, sales force and research organisations in the life science industry.
- Differentiating capabilities that are difficult, costly, have no confidentiality, security or control issues and whose criticality requires complementary capabilities that are held within the firm's legal boundaries. Examples of this include manufacturing capabilities to manufacture undifferentiated components or materials for highly differentiated products, routine clinical development capabilities that are necessary to complement more advanced studies and simple logistical support for distribution that complements highly skilled, value adding sales teams.
- Dynamic capabilities that are difficult, costly, have no confidentiality, security or control issues, lend themselves to economies of scale or scope and whose criticality requires complementary capabilities that are held within the firm's legal boundaries. Examples of this include the capability to gather market research information, such as when firms purchase information from IMS or enter into omnibus studies with the trade association. In these cases, the information purchased is a component of an organisational learning capability that is expressed in-house.

Quadrant 4: manage resources allocated to low cost, low criticality capabilities that must be
expressed within the organisation's legal boundaries

This is a form of 'making' the necessary capabilities that occurs typically when economic optimality is overridden by market imperfections. In other words, it involves capabilities that would be better to be outsourced but which, for some reason, cannot be. In practice, low cost, low criticality capabilities are likely to be hygiene capabilities that are not especially difficult or costly and have no confidentiality, security or control issues but for which there is no suitable supplier. The selection pressures of the holobiont shift make such capabilities increasingly rare. Examples include basic procurement capabilities or administrative capabilities whose relatively low cost, and the inertia against outsourcing, keeps them in-house but managed tightly to minimise costs. Differentiating and dynamic capabilities, which are typically relatively critical activities, rarely fall into this quadrant.

The application of the strategic logic of holobiont design is mostly straightforward but, in my experience of the practice of exemplary firms, there are two application issues that always occur: borderline capabilities and partnership design.

The first of these, borderline capabilities, occurs when capabilities seem to straddle quadrants. This is the case when the assessment of relative criticality and/or risk-adjusted acquisition cost leads to some capabilities being judged to be exactly in the middle, compared to the other necessary capabilities. This leads to the obvious question of which quadrant guidance should be followed. In many cases, a reiteration of the assessment, with more thought and closer comparison to other, similarly assessed, capabilities, resolves the issue and the capability is found to sit clearly in one quadrant or another. But, when this not the case, it is most often due to the capability being poorly defined. By that, I mean that the defined capability is in fact two or three capabilities that have been inadvertently conflated, considered as one and, since the component capabilities vary in criticality or risk-adjusted cost, the inadvertently combined capability is assessed as an average of its parts. For example, the capability to craft strong, segment specific extended value propositions may be better considered as three separate, component capabilities: to create insight into contextual market segments, to identify hidden value in the customer's value chain and to develop added value services. Dismantling the capability and assessing its component capabilities will almost always resolve this issue, with each component clearly in one quadrant or another.

The second of these practical issues, partnership design, occurs when it is clear that the capability is high cost and high criticality and should therefore be developed and expressed via a partnership. Commonly, the choice of partnership type is self-evident or enforced by circumstance, but occasionally this is not the case. Partnerships range from simple licensing to complete acquisition and from a simple one-way transfer of capabilities to a truly mutual arrangement, with pooling of capabilities. And along these two continua lie what seem to be an infinite number of combinations and legal arrangements. The exact choice of partnership arrangement is highly context dependent, but some additional guidance can be gained by considering the granularity of the space within the partnership quadrant. In that space, capabilities range from highly critical to little more than averagely critical and from very high risk-adjusted cost to only just above average risk-adjusted cost. The partnership quadrant can therefore be sub-divided into four further quadrants, see Figure 25.4.

In a simplified manner, Figure 25.4 shows that considering the granularity within the partnership quadrant forces trade offs between how much the firm needs the capability (how critical it is) and how much capital it has to put at risk to acquire that capability. These trade off choices are infinitely nuanced. Arguably the easiest decision of partnership model occurs when capabilities are of the highest criticality but only moderate risk-adjusted cost. These conditions typically imply the purchase of exclusive rights, real options purchases or perhaps a gradual acquisition. The next clearest choice occurs

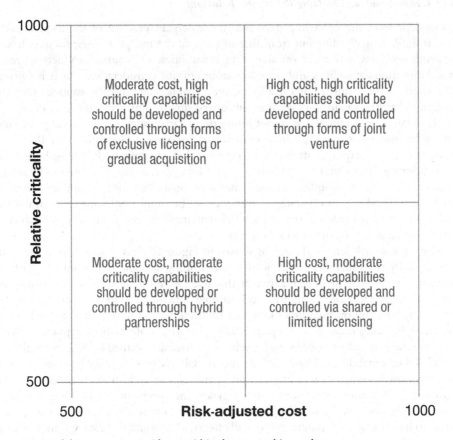

Figure 25.4 Holobiont structure guidance within the partnership quadrant

when the capability is only moderately critical but has a high risk-adjusted cost. These conditions typically imply a much more limited commitment of capital and the acceptance of the risk that the capability may be lost to or shared with a rival. Some context-limited licensing agreement, such as one restricted by geography or clinical application, is common in this case. The most challenging choices occur when the capability is of very high criticality but also of high risk-adjusted cost. In this situation, some form of joint venture is often employed. As well as sharing risk and knowledge, joint ventures often allow some of the capital at risk to be substituted for equity or other, non-cash, forms of capital. The fourth context, of moderate criticality and moderate risk-adjusted cost, seems to offer the most options for hybrid partnership arrangements. In this case, arrangements like shared ownership, combined licensing, part funding and option purchase seem to be common.

In this way, the ranking of capabilities in terms of criticality and risk-adjusted cost, followed by the use of those rankings to create a capability portfolio grid along the lines of Figure 25.3, provides guidance for whether the capability should be held inside or outside the organisation's legal boundaries, whether externally sourced capabilities should be transactional or partnership based and what the optimal form of partnership might be.

Stage 4: envisioning and building the capable holobiont

It is evident from the preceding steps that the emergent practice of the most effective firms is fundamentally different from that of most of the industry. Their focus is less on acquiring products and more on acquiring capabilities. Of course, products represent some innovation capabilities and these are an important consideration, but it is through the acquisition of a full set of capabilities, the capabileome (and the routines that create them) that firms gain long term evolutionary fitness. This capability-driven view is why companies are so interested in not losing those capabilities during the acquisition or partnership process. Genzyme's independence of Sanofi and Genentech's of Roche are both examples of acquirers attempting to ensure that capabilities they have bought are not lost during the acquisition. The shedding of jobs post-acquisition can also be seen as the de-duplication of capabilities or the removal of capabilities thought not needed in the new business model. This capability-driven view of building a holobiont, in contrast to a product-oriented approach, is the crucial differentiator between firms who are successful at building capable holobionts and those that are not.

Clearly, the fourth and final stage, as shown in Figure 25.1, is to move from the guidance given by the capability portfolio to a functioning, capable holobiont. As with the previous stages of the process, practice at this stage varies greatly from the ad hoc and opportunistic to the more thoughtful and planned. The most deliberate practice involves first envisioning the optimal holobiont and then taking the necessary steps to build it. The latter, building phase is a completely idiosyncratic, context-specific practice that is driven by the particular resources and needs of the firm and shaped by exigencies that are not related to capabilities. These include the availability of suitability partners, national protectionism (as with Pfizer's attempt on AstraZeneca) and, in the case of some US acquirers, tax inversion. That idiosyncrasy makes the mechanics of building the holobiont another book, and I won't address it here. By contrast, the envisioning stage does appear to have many common features in all effective firms and these *are* within the scope of this book.

The envisioning stage involves reifying a holobiont structure that would be capable of expressing the target capabileome. In practice, this reification is an interactive, fluid process, but it can be simplified into three steps:

Defining the organisational core

The reified vision of the capable holobiont begins with designing the organisation that can express the capabilities in Quadrants 1 and 4 of Figure 25.3. As with any organisational design, this process begins by defining the scale and type of resources – human, knowledge, capital and other – needed to express those capabilities. It then defines the way those resources will be structured into organisational entities such as departments and subsidiaries and the reporting and control relationships between them. The most important part of designing the organisational core is that it begins with 'What capabilities do we need to express?' and does not necessarily follow traditional structuring, by product category or geography, for example. We can see examples of this occurring in the way that both Johnson & Johnson and Medtronic have structured those parts of their businesses that are focused on customer intimate models. We can also see it in the structuring of market access functions aligned according to health systems type (e.g. when Canada is grouped with the EU rather than the US). Conversely, we see the limitations of more traditional organisational design with unwieldy and inefficient groupings such as EMEA (Europe, Middle East and Africa), which forces a multitude of disparate capabilities into an irrational structure.

Defining the holobiont's nodal structure

Following the definition of the organisational core, the next step of holobiont design is to define nodal structure, that is, the organisations that will express Quadrant 2 (high cost, high criticality) activities and the relationships between them. In practice, these activities are clustered around parts of the value chain – for example in early research, in late-stage development or extended value delivery. As with design of the core, the type and scale of capabilities to be expressed dictate the type and scale of holobiont partners, whilst concepts summarised in Figure 25.4 guide the choice of relationship. This definition of what capability is needed, at what scale and in what sort of relationship typically provides very clear guidance to the design of the nodal structure of the holobiont. This part of the reification process also involves identifying relationships between strategic partners, which may be via the core organisation or directly between those partners. This part of the holobiont can, therefore be very complex, especially if the target capabileome is particularly large one or very different from the firms current capabileome, as will be the case if the fitness peak to be climbed is either high, distant or both compared to the current business.

Defining the holobiont's transactional component

The definition of first the organisational core and then the nodal structure addresses capabilities in Quadrants 1, 4 and 2 respectively. It therefore makes it clear which Quadrant 3 capabilities are to be 'bought' from by suppliers or from channels to market. As with the two earlier steps, this involves defining the type and scale of resources needed to express those capabilities and therefore the number, scale and types of suppliers required, along with the relationships between suppliers. It also helps to differentiate between those (usually very few) transactional relationships to be managed on a long term (but still transactional) basis – sometimes called strategic suppliers – and those less critical suppliers that merit only low involvement or indirect procurement arrangements.

Working methodically through these three steps typically leads to an envisioned holobiont of the form shown in Figure 25.5. The example here, simplified for clarity, is for a Value Fracking model in respiratory medicine. It serves to illustrate the point that a functioning holobiont must express all the capabilities needed by the reified business model in order to climb the chosen fitness peak. Obviously, the precise content of this holobiont design is context specific but this figure serves to illustrate the concept.

It is the firm's own version of this figure – designed for its own reified model and target capabileome – that subsequently guides its activities for developing its own capabilities, finding and working with partners and finding and working with transactional suppliers and channels. The first of those activity sets, developing the firm's own capabilities, is the subject of Chapter 26.

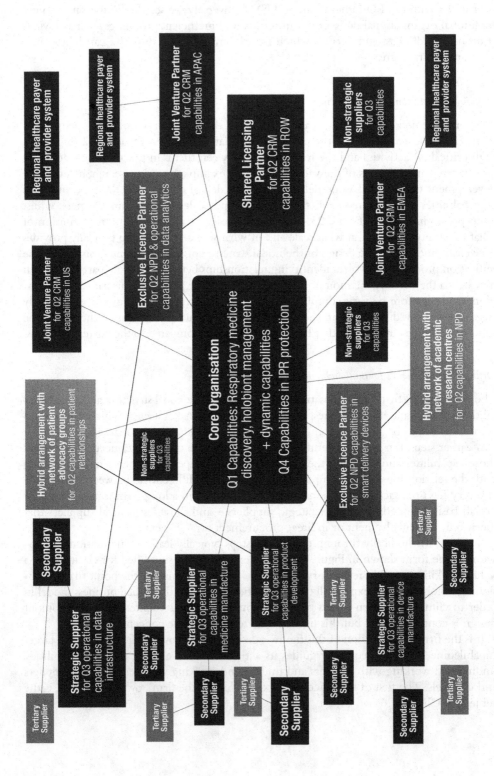

Figure 25.5 An example of holobiont design

26 How do we build our core capabilities?

As I begin this final section of Part 4 of this book, I want to review briefly what I've said so far about how life science firms might manage and accelerate their own evolution.

I take as self-evident that it is a necessary first step to understand the industry's environmental shifts and selection pressures (as described in Part 2) and the consequently emerging fitness landscape and business models (as described in Part 3). That understanding is a necessary but insufficient requirement for the leadership team of any life science company.

A firm could explore this new landscape by forever taking incremental steps, each of which individually seem eminently sensible but which collectively do not add up to clear direction of travel. Such a corporate 'random walk', to steal a term from physics, is as likely to lead to a fitness trough as a fitness peak. Even if that incremental perambulation did lead upwards it is likely to do so much more slowly than an informed and planned assault on the same fitness peak. In essence, I argue that firms that manage their own evolution have an advantage over those that adopt the trial and error methods of nature.

To deliberately manage a firm's evolution means to choose one or more of the industry's fitness peaks and then to build a business or businesses that can climb and then dominate that peak or peaks. I have already described how to do so in three sequential and connected steps:

First, choose the fitness peak or peaks to be occupied. I described a process for doing this by reifying the available business model options, deciding on the criteria by which to select from those options, making that assessment and then allocating resources between those models. (Chapter 23)

Second, identify the target capabileome of the chosen model. I described how effective firms begin by further reifying their model then specifying the full set of hygiene, differentiating and dynamic capabilities that are required for that model to function and compete. (Chapter 24)

Third, design a capable holobiont. I described the practice of building a portfolio view of capabilities, based on their criticality to the business model and their risk-adjusted cost of acquisition, then using that capability to direct the choice of partners, suppliers and channels that make up a capable holobiont. (Chapter 25)

The rigorous execution of these three steps will lead a company from its existing business model, which is well adapted to its old and disappearing habitat, most of the way towards a new business model that is well adapted to occupy its chosen fitness peak within its new, emerging habitat. I say most of the way towards because a final critical step is necessary. That step is to build those capabilities that are expressed not in the holobiont of partners, suppliers and channels but within the legal boundaries of the organisation itself. These capabilities, some Quadrant 1 and some Quadrant 4 as I styled them in Figure 25.2, are the firm's contribution to the holobiont. As such, they not only allow the firm to compete but they also make the firm attractive to holobiont partners.

The term core capabilities (otherwise rendered as core competencies) has been sorely abused and its meaning greatly blurred since Hamel and Prahalad's influential book (183). Perhaps because of its alliterative expression, many executives and consultants allow themselves the comfort of throwing the term around without the discomfort of trying to understand what it means (to steal and adapt a quote from President John F. Kennedy).

Let me be clear about which capabilities I mean when I talk about those that must be developed and expressed within the organisation itself. Principally, I mean those capabilities that sit in Quadrant 1 of our portfolio view of capabilities, as shown in Figure 25.3. That is, those capabilities that are relatively critical to the success of the business model and are relatively low in risk-adjusted cost. To a much lesser degree, I also mean the Quadrant 4 activities but, since these are less critical and typically much closer to existing capabilities, it is Quadrant 1 activities that do and should draw most attention from a firm's leadership. Exactly what these Quadrant 1 activities are is specific to the reified model but, in general, they will reflect the choice of how value is to be created (technological innovation, customer intimacy or operational excellence) and the choice of who defines value (affluent or mass market patient payer or government payer). To restate the obvious, core capabilities generally reflect the habitat chosen and specifically characterise the reified business model. It is the building of these model-specific Quadrant 1 capabilities that is the subject of this section.

Gene therapy for firms

To understand how evolutionary science guides the development of these capabilities, consider the analogy I used earlier, the idea of giving a chimpanzee human traits. Even though my simian cousin and I share most of our DNA, if I wanted him to do what I do – stand upright and give a conference speech, for example – then I'd somehow need to equip him with many traits that he doesn't currently possess. These would range from his skeletal structure, to his capacity for speech, to his instincts regarding social interaction. I could, if I wished, try to train the chimp to read academic papers, constructively criticise them, write a paper and present to an audience, but I suspect that my progress might be slow or limited. Whatever your opinion of academics, I hope we can agree that I am better adapted to the conference hall than my chimpanzee cousin, who is better adapted than I am to the rain forest of central Africa. To a large degree, a chimp's traits and evolutionary fitness stem from its DNA and, as a result, training can shape it only to a very limited extent.

This tongue-in-cheek analogy helps us to understand how life science companies can develop and express the core capabilities required of their new business model. In essence, evolutionary fitness means acquiring the relevant traits. Just as the chimp in the conference room needs the capacity to talk, so firms need, for example, the capacity to create technologically innovative value propositions that are accepted by payers. In biology, such traits are created by the actions of proteins, which do the work of biological systems. For example, the trait of speech requires, among others, the forkhead box protein P2 (FOXP2); in the same way, the capacity to create an acceptable value proposition requires, among others, a capability to understand what constitutes health economic value in the particular context in question. Biological traits require many complementary proteins, just as business traits require many complementary capabilities. And, just as proteins are expressed by

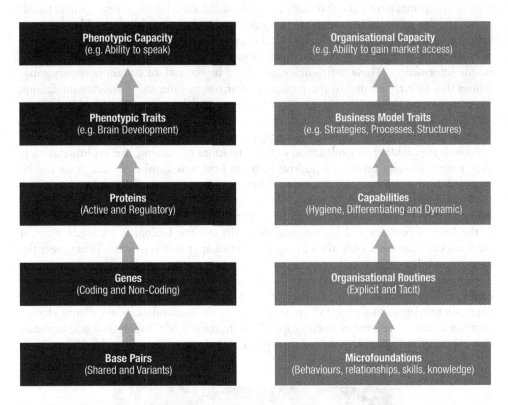

Figure 26.1 The parallels between biological and business model traits

genes such as the FOXP2 gene on chromosome 7, capabilities are expressed by organisational routines. For example, some of the routines for understanding value are routines for mapping a value chain in a healthcare system, a set of activities that lies in what we might think of as the customer relationship management chromosome. Finally, just as biological genes are made up of collections of nucleotides, routines are constituted by microfoundations, the nature of which I will discuss next. This extended analogy, summarised in Figure 26.1, is not merely an author's creative device; it illustrates why superficial attempts to build capabilities, such as training, often fail and why alternative, more fundamental approaches are necessary.

Training significant new capabilities into an organisation is analogous to training a chimp to do a professor's job (or indeed training a professor to survive in the jungle)! Such training might have limited success if the capability is simple and close to the chimp's existing skills. For example, a common chimpanzee called Washoe was taught some 350 words of sign language at the University of Nevada, Reno. But more complex tasks like writing that are unrelated to the animal's existing skills would have been beyond Washoe's capacity because she did not have the necessary neurological structures. That lack of neurological structure was due to the nature of her proteome which was, in turn, due to her genome's nucleotide sequence.

In exactly the same way, training a capability into an organisation can and does work well if that capability is simple and close to extant capabilities. For example, many life science companies have learned to use their skills in clinical trials to generate simple health economic data. But those same firms struggle to articulate compelling health economic value propositions because they lack critical organisational traits (typically at the interface of marketing and market access functions) in gathering and using real world health economic information. These deficiencies are caused by the lack of certain necessary capabilities that in turn are due to the nature of their routineome and its microfoundations, for example the dynamic capabilities for organisational learning. Just like Washoe, no amount of superficial training will help if the routineome and its microfoundations place fundamental limits on the organisation's capacity.

As well as providing an explanation of the limitations of training, this evolutionary science perspective also provides a positive view on how new capabilities and traits can be acquired. In my observations, significant adaptations occur successfully only when training is complemented or substituted by fundamental changes in activity, behaviour, personnel and process. In other words, adaptation is much more likely to be effective if addressed at the level of routines and microfoundations. To use our biological analogue again, if we want chimpanzees to talk then the only effective approach is genetically engineer the creature and then train it or its descendants.

Of course, the executives and firms I observe in my research don't usually think in terms of evolutionary science. But their practice does reveal a thoughtful, if often implicit, approach to adaptation through the management of microfoundations in order to change routines and so express the necessary capabilities. In the rest of Chapter 26, I will explicate that approach as a systematic, deliberate process of three steps, summarised in Figure 26.2.

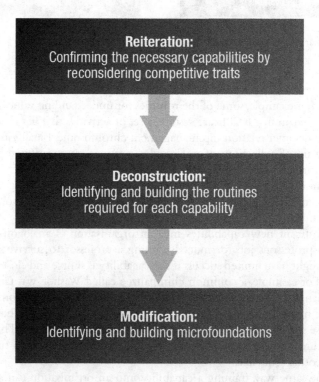

Figure 26.2 Three stages of capability building

Stage 1: reiteration – confirming the necessary capabilities by reconsidering competitive traits

Although the new business model's necessary capabilities have already been identified in Chapter 25, it is clear that the process of building a new business model is not strictly as linear as my prescriptions in this part of the book imply. When observing leadership teams in action, they frequently perform iterative loops at many points in the process with the aim of reviewing and improving their thinking. An example of this occurs at this stage, when they begin to build the capabilities of the core organisation. At this point, executives in effect ask themselves: are the Quadrant 1 capabilities we have identified so far sufficient to create the competitive traits that our business model needs to occupy its fitness peak?

This question represents a small (in terms of time invested) but valuable (in terms of benefit) enhancement of the capability building process. By this stage, following the selection of the fitness peak, the identification of the target capabileome and the design of the holobiont, the leadership team typically has a much clearer, fine-grained conception of their reified business model. They can therefore be clearer about the traits and capabilities that model needs. Figure 26.3 illustrates a simplified and anonymised example of reiteration process for a Secular Grail business model.

Even in this simplified example, there are ten capabilities identified as core. Some of these, such as those for bringing the technologies to market, are differentiating capabilities. Others, such as those for organisational design and creating actionable knowledge,

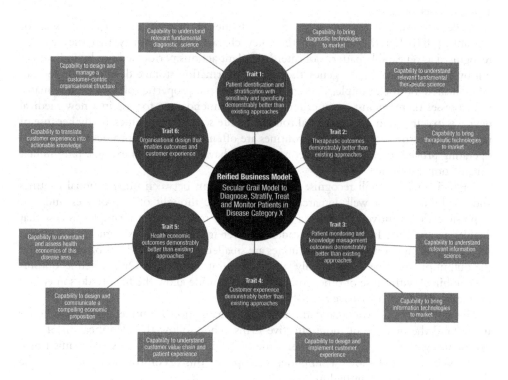

Figure 26.3 An example of the capabilities reiteration of a Secular Grail business model

are dynamic capabilities. For each reified business model, the equivalent of Figure 26.3 will look different, but this example serves to demonstrate how, by re-asking what capabilities are needed and by linking them to the competitive traits of that model, firms may clarify their core capabilities before moving on to how to create them. In practice, this reiterative step both refines previously identified core capabilities and often identifies some additional ones that were previously overlooked. This is the first of three ways that more effective firms differ from their less effective rivals in their approach to developing core capabilities.

One valuable practical lesson that emerges when firms carry out this process is that firms often see capabilities as a translational process. That is, an activity that translates inputs of some kind into outputs of another kind. For example, in Figure 26.2 some capabilities translate fundamental scientific knowledge into actionable technological solutions and others translate actionable technological solutions into marketable products. This view of capabilities as acts of translation is useful because it helps frame the next stage of identifying the required routines.

Stage 2: deconstruction – identifying and building the routines required for each capability

The Quadrant 1 capabilities identified by the process described in Chapter 25, and clarified by the reiterative process described above, differ greatly from each other. Each takes different inputs and translates them into different outputs, allowing the firm to do a particular activity that is essential to its model. But for all their dissimilarity, every capability arises from one or usually many organisational routines, just as proteins arise from the action of a set of genes.

Academics quibble over exactly how to define an organisational routine (see, for example, [184]) but they agree on their key characteristics, namely, that they can be recognised as repeatable patterns of interdependent actions performed not by individuals but by groups. As such, like genes, they act as information storage devices, and they can be replicated. So for example, a lab group that tests the properties of a set of new materials, assesses them against some criteria and recommends one for use in a new medical device is executing an organisational routine. In life science companies, partly because of regulatory pressures, organisational routines are often codified into protocols or standard operating procedures and a typical company will have thousands of explicit and implicit organisational routines.

Perceptive readers will recognise that the distinction between organisational routines and capabilities is not well demarcated. Both can be thought of as processes, and it is impossible to definitively separate a large, complex routine from a simple process that enables a capability. Indeed, some academics refer to capabilities as high-level routines. As a generalisation, organisational routines are smaller, self-contained sets of activities and the output of a routine is not usually very useful in its own right. Only when its outputs are combined with those of other routines does a routine allow the firm to do something distinctly useful – that is, have a capability.

This imperfect but workable definition of an organisational routine allows us to better understand the practice of more effective firms. They follow the identification of core capabilities with the deconstruction of those capabilities into the necessary organisational routines. Figure 26.4 shows a simplified example of this deconstruction for one of the dynamic capabilities identified in Figure 26.3.

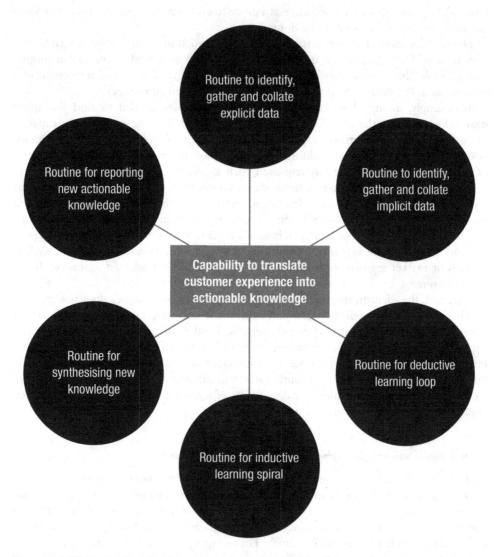

Figure 26.4 The organisational routines of creating actionable knowledge

Even this simplified example serves to illustrate that each capability arises from a number of distinct but complementary routines. In this case, the capability translates data from varied sources into actionable knowledge. It therefore involves routines for gathering two very different kinds of data (implicit and explicit), processing them via two very different but complementary methods (inductive and deductive), synthesising that learning and then communicating the results in a form that can be used. This deconstruction of capabilities into constituent routines is the second of three ways that more effective firms differ from their less effective rivals in their approach to developing capabilities in the core organisation. In contrast to this deconstruction into routines, those less effective firms merely define tautologically a single process such as a 'customer experience improvement process'. In practice, this is less effective as a guide to creating the capability because it does not make explicit what needs to be done.

The identification of the organisational routines needed for each capability enables the firm to build them. In practice, many routines may need to be built. Even in our simplified example, the ten core capabilities in Figure 26.3 might, if each had six component routines as in Figure 26.4, lead to sixty necessary organisational routines.

Interestingly, in my observations, life science companies seemed to find this quite straightforward once the need for a routine was identified. This suggests that the capability to build routines (a dynamic capability) is common in the industry. A complementary observation was that routine building and codification is much more common in parts of the value chain that are heavily regulated, such as clinical development, manufacturing and some aspects of marketing communications, than in less regulated activities, such as leadership, strategic planning and sales. Together, these two observations suggest that, once identified, the dynamic capability to build routines is itself an evolutionary adaptation to regulated environments. For example, business models that codify clinical trial processes are selected for by the regulatory environment whilst those that don't codify a SWOT analysis or market segmentation process (for example) are not selected against with the same pressure.

That said, the identification and building of organisational routines does not guarantee that those routines will function and express the necessary capabilities. Partly this is because the absence of even one or two organisational routines can prevent or limit the expression of a capability. For example, a consideration of Figure 26.4 will reveal how building five out of six of the routines is not sufficient to create actionable knowledge. But building and even documenting a routine is also insufficient if the organisational routines are no more than mere statements or documents of activities. To function, they need they appropriate microfoundations, as I will discuss next.

Stage 3: modification – identifying and building microfoundations

Organisational routines, those sequences of repeatable, interdependent activities performed by a group and which contribute to a capability, perform the same role in organisations that genes do in organisms; they store information about how to do things. As information carriers, they vary in their effectiveness and their efficacy, especially when their output is not binary and is hard to assess objectively. For example, a routine for assessing alternative materials is relatively easy to standardise, a routine for critically assessing strategic options much less so. And just as the functioning of a gene is dictated by its nucleotide sequence, the functioning of a routine is determined by its microfoundations.

After reiterating the trait-capability linkage and deconstructing capabilities into component organisational routines, the third way in which effective companies differ from the less effective lies in the way they deliberately manage the microfoundations of their core capabilities. My observations of practice in this area are based on the work of Teppo Felin, Nicolai Foss and their colleagues (185). My work identifies four classes of microfoundation, the management of which lies at the basis of developing core capabilities:

Attributes of individuals

As a group activity, an organisational routine's 'raw material' is the people in that group. In particular, it is the congruence between the knowledge, abilities and behaviours of the group members and the characteristics of the task that determine the efficacy of the routine. For example, the attributes of a group that assures the compliance of marketing communications messages must include legal knowledge, judicial abilities and attention to detail. By contrast, a team responsible for designing that creative marketing communications message probably needs less of those, but instead requires knowledge of communications psychology, writing ability and a high degree of originality. As thought experiment, imagine swapping the attributes of these two complementary groups; it would result in low creativity and legally non-compliant routines. This illustrates the importance of congruence between attributes and the routine. Figure 26.5 similarly explicates the attributes required for executing the routine for inductive learning, one of the six routines from Figure 26.4.

Even this simplified example demonstrates that each routine requires a characteristic set of knowledge, abilities and behaviours. Amplified across multiple routines, this demonstrates the challenge of building even a single new Quadrant 1 capability. Importantly, this set of knowledge, abilities and behaviours does not need to be exhibited by every member of the routine-enacting group. If the group functions well, different individual characteristics combine and complement to create an effective group. This attribute-pooling mechanism highlights the importance of the three other classes of microfoundations, all of which contribute to the functioning of the group.

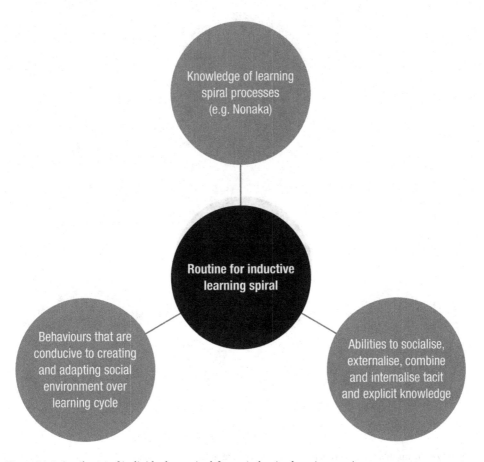

Figure 26.5 Attributes of individuals required for an inductive learning routine

Team structure

The group responsible for executing a particular routine is typically small but it is often multidisciplinary and its membership often overlaps with groups responsible for executing other organisational routines. Along with the need to combine attributes constructively, this means that the structure of the group is important. Key dimensions of structure are flatness vs. hierarchy, scope of activity and connectivity to other groups. For example, a group that has to integrate technologies to create a new product would typically need a flattish structure (to pool knowledge effectively) and a broad scope of activity (to identify value across boundaries). Further, they must be connected at one end to the group whose routines understand basic technology and at the other to the group whose routine commercialises the product. Again, a thought experiment that considers that same group with a rigid hierarchical structure, narrow scope and weak connections serves to illustrate the need for congruence between team structure and routine; the result would be unlikely to be an effective product. Figure 26.6 shows the team structure required for executing the routine for inductive learning, complementing the attributes shown in Figure 26.5.

Again, even a simplified example demonstrates that each routine requires a congruent team structure. Of course, overlapping membership and connectivity means that team

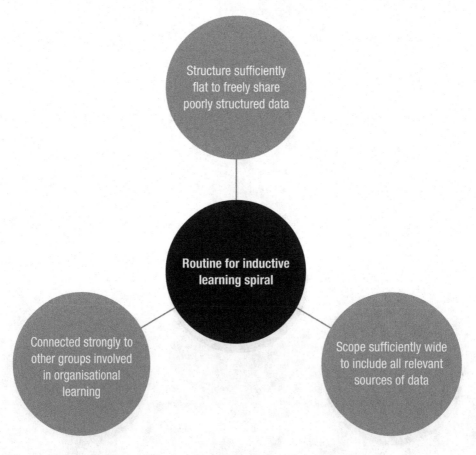

Figure 26.6 Team structure considerations for an inductive learning routine

structure cannot be designed on a routine-by-routine basis. In practice, it is designed at the level of capabilities or sometimes capability groups but with consideration of the individual routines. If the team is structured well it typically functions well, but this can be undermined by conflict either within or between routine groups. This leads to the third microfoundation of organisational routines.

Conflict management methods

All human groups conflict both within themselves and with other groups. This conflict often results in a range of behaviour from petty politicking to majorly destructive behaviour and so is generally considered universally negative. However, intraorganisational conflict can be either positive or negative (177), and the goal of conflict management methods is to optimise the former over the latter. Optimising positive conflict over negative involves management of three factors: antecedents of conflict (such as physical separation, status hierarchies and shared resources); commitment to the firm rather than the group; and congruent goal setting. The challenge is that optimising these factors is very context specific and often a trade off. Putting colleagues in the same physical location

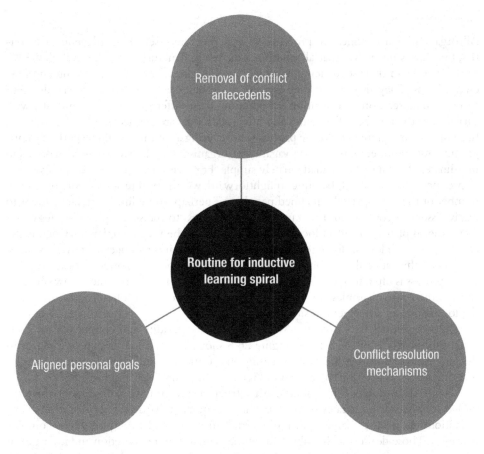

Figure 26.7 Conflict management considerations for an inductive learning routine

may have costs; lessening commitment to the group may reduce motivation; and setting congruent goals may be limited by management information systems. The challenge is to invest in conflict management where it is most likely and most harmful, and to do so in a context specific, not generic manner.

Figure 26.7 shows a simplified version of the conflict management considerations required for executing the routine for inductive learning, complementing the attributes shown in Figure 26.5 and team structure shown in Figure 26.6.

As before, even this simplified example demonstrates that each routine-executing group requires a particular consideration of its intraorganisational conflict issues. In practice, the more varied, the more physically separated and the more managed-by-quantified objectives, the more potential for intraorganisational conflict exists and the more need for conflict management there is. Equally, the more interconnected a group is with other groups and the more critical its routines, the greater the importance of managing conflict. Given the trends in life science companies for tightly managed, international cross functional teams, the importance of this microfoundation is self-evident.

An appropriately structured team with the congruent attributes and optimised, positive conflict should execute its routine well and so contribute to the necessary core capability. However, one class of microfoundation remains to be considered.

Group process

All organisational routines are processes in that they are a set of interdependent activities, but that is not to say that all routines are equally structured or identically designed. Routines vary in their sequencing, with varying degrees of linearity, branching and reiterative loops. They also vary in their rigidity, with their executors being allowed different amounts of discretion in execution. In addition, they differ greatly in complexity, with variation in the number of activities and how much they are connected to other routines. In a completely rational world, the process for executing a routine would be perfectly congruent to its requirements, but the vagaries of organisational behaviour may make them inordinately bureaucratic or inadequately simple. For example, a process to approve a set of product claims ought to be quite straightforward, with a fixed process involving a small number of the appropriately qualified people and perhaps some limited iterative loops to resolve issues of contention. In comparison, the process to translate a global strategy into a set of local plans that reflect local conditions ought to be very complex, varying greatly case by case, with lots of discretion, reiteration and several interconnected activity streams. In practice, this rational correlation between routine and process is often not this way and group process is often too simple or too complex in relation to the routine. In my observations of these two examples, for instance, the approval of claims is often too complex and the localisation of strategies too simple.

Effective routines have processes whose sequencing, rigidity and complexity are congruent to the needs of the routine. Figure 26.8 shows a simplified version of the process design considerations required for executing the routine for inductive learning, complementing the considerations described in Figure 26.5, Figure 26.6 and Figure 26.7.

As with the examples for attributes, team structure and conflict management, this simplified example demonstrates that each routine requires a particular set of process considerations. In practice, larger and more varied routines tend to require more complex processes. Those dealing with ambiguous inputs demand more discretion and less rigidity. Those dealing with difficult problems tend to require more complex sequencing. Given

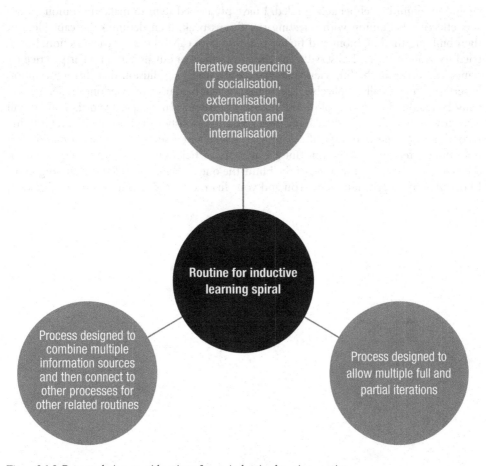

Figure 26.8 Process design considerations for an inductive learning routine

the enormous variation between routines within a life science company, it is not difficult to see the importance of designing a congruent process for each routine.

Astute readers will have noticed a little author's wordplay in my description of the microfoundations. Using the words I chose, they can be remembered as ATCG, which biologists will remember as the four nucleotides of DNA. This is deliberate; I intend it to remind the reader that these four things lie at the very base (pun intended) of all capabilities. What is more, the analogy with protein expression, genes and base-pairs reminds us that how these microfoundations combine and interact is very complex indeed. It takes only small weaknesses – the organisational equivalent of a single-nucleotide polymorphism – to make one firm highly effective and another ineffective.

A one eyed watchmaker

In this part of the book, I have borrowed Richard Dawkins's wonderful metaphor in an attempt to communicate that, in a manner analogous to genetic engineering, organisational evolution might be deliberately guided. I have prescribed steps to make this guiding process effective, beginning with selecting the fitness peak, then defining the capabileome, then building the holobiont and finally building core capabilities. In each section, I have tried to explicate what I observe to be the most effective but usually implicit practice by senior executives in the life science industry. I am under no illusion that this prescription is perfect or universally applicable. I recognise that, at best, my prescriptions render a company half-sighted as they explore the industry's evolving landscape. Even then, they will only be effective if they both take my prescriptions seriously and also apply them with due recognition of their firm's specific context. That may not sound much and I could wish for a more effective prescription. But it is perhaps sufficient because, to take a quote from the Genesis Rabbah, 'In the street of the blind, the one eyed man is called the guiding light.' I hope that my suggestions allow you and your firm to be the industry's guiding light.

Conclusion
The grandeur of the life sciences industry

There is grandeur in this view of life, with its several powers, having been originally breathed into a few forms or into one; and that, whilst this planet has gone cycling on according to the fixed law of gravity, from so simple a beginning endless forms most beautiful and most wonderful have been, and are being, evolved.
Charles Darwin, *The Origin of Species*

I will end this book with a confession; with respect to the life sciences industry, I am what we English call a snob, an elitist, one who holds that not everyone and everything is of equal value to society. Now, to be clear, those are not my views with respect to human beings. Quite the opposite. However, they are my views about industry sectors. I must confess to a prejudice in favour of the life sciences sector and against other industries. When I work with a company that is curing a life-destroying disease or one which is restoring the life quality of someone who is seriously injured, I feel respect, admiration and some degree of pride that I have worked in this area, in various capacities, for almost my entire adult life. By contrast, when I survey my local shopping mall and observe endless fashion stores, fast food outlets and shops selling 'chindogu', I sometimes despair for the human race. Similarly, when I read in my newspaper of the enormous amounts of human ingenuity and effort that are allocated to financial services or the video games industry, I ponder what the world would look like if those same people devoted their energies to activities that were more useful to society. For all its many limitations and imperfections, the life sciences sector is, in my view, the world's most important industry.

If you share that view with me, then what I say next may appear self-evident. It is important – very important indeed – that we understand the future of the life sciences industry. Moreover, it is important that we deliberately direct the evolution of our industry and its companies towards a future in which it continues to contribute to society. Such a positive future is by no means assured. Left to itself, Darwinian evolution is a random and incredibly wasteful process without direction. There is therefore no guarantee that our industry, which has contributed so much to human wellbeing, will continue to do so. It could reach an evolutionary dead end, where innovation stalls or where its benefits remain restricted to a wealthy few. Equally, as recent pricing trends suggest, it could so abuse its social environment that it stimulates a response that sets the industry back for decades. Even if its evolution continues on a positive trajectory, our industry's progress might be much slower and more wasteful than is necessary. To assume an ever better future for the life sciences industry is naïve.

What our industry needs is the equivalent of transhumanism, the intellectual movement that aims to transform the human condition by deliberate use of technology. I am sceptical of transhumanism, not least because of its ethical implications. When explored in fiction, from Huxley's *Brave New World* to the movie *Blade Runner*, transhumanism is frightening, but its life science industry analogue is not. Transforming the life science industry, by understanding and directing its evolution, is something we can and should do for the benefit of society as a whole. It is even more appealing when considered next to the alternative, which is to preside over a random walk across the industry's fitness landscape that, at best, will be slow and wasteful and, at worst, will lead into one or more fitness troughs.

So my challenge to those who lead the industry is to seize this opportunity. Use evolutionary science to direct the evolution of your organisation, and hence our industry, just as you use your knowledge of natural sciences to direct the development of your products. Taking up that challenge means first answering two fundamental questions. I wrote *Darwin's Medicine* to answer those questions.

What does the future of the life sciences industry look like?

The life science industry of the future will differ from that of the present in many ways; but three dissimilarities with the present are most salient.

It will be much bigger

When I began my career in 1978, the industry's focus was on curing the ill or injured in the western world, whose care was paid for by governments. Today, that focus is a little broader, but not unrecognisably so. Although the industry addresses more countries, curing sickness rather than maintaining wellness is still the dominant approach and governments (or their proxies) remain the most important purchaser. The future will be very different. The life sciences industry will be as much concerned with maintaining wellness as with curing sickness, if not more so. Only a small proportion of the earth's then population of 10 billion will be outside of the industry's remit, and their governments' roles will have receded in relative terms, as patient payers grow in importance. Today, about 10 percent of the world's gross domestic product is spent on healthcare. As a result of this broadening focus, that number will rise inexorably. Long term projections suggest that, over a generation or two, the figure will rise to 30 percent.

This much larger healthcare market has both positive and negative implications. Obviously, it presents a growth opportunity for life science companies. Conversely, but not so obviously, it demands focus. No company can be a dominant player in 30 percent of the world's economy. Even if it were possible, it would not be politically acceptable. This demand for focus leads to the second major dissimilarity between now and the future.

It will be more fragmented

The life science industry as we know it evolved in a relatively limited habitat of sick westerners and their governments or proxy payers. Despite globalisation, today's environment is still dominated by that habitat. Although emerging markets and out of pocket payments are no longer irrelevant, current business models are still best explained by the selection pressures of the historical environment, in the same way that human behaviour is often best explained by our hunter–gatherer past.

The future will look very different. At the highest level, the industry landscape will be divided according to who defines value and how value is created. Those nine major habitats will play a much more balanced role in shaping the industry. Across this fragmented landscape, there will exist perhaps twenty-six different peaks, each representing a set of evolutionary choices aimed at optimal evolutionary fitness. Alongside those peaks, and dividing them, will be number of deep fitness troughs, representing an extinction threat to maladapted business models. Each peak will be occupied by a business model, equivalent to a biological species, and each model will have innumerable disease area variants and technology variants, equivalent to sub-species. Today, we can categorise life science companies with a handful of terms and a few more disease area labels. In the future, the speciation of business models will make such simple categorisations meaningless. We will live in a cacophonous jungle, not a monotonous lawn.

This heavily fragmented market has both positive and negative implications. Obviously, each peak represents an opportunity for life science companies to adapt their model and so achieve optimal evolutionary fitness, which will be characterised by optimal risk-adjusted rate of return. The obverse of this is that fragmentation threatens extinction. The environment will be more complex and competition both more varied and more intense. Companies that make the wrong choice of fitness peak, or worse don't make a choice at all, are unlikely to survive. Even those that do will survive only if they climb their chosen peaks faster and better than their rivals. This requirement to evolve quickly and effectively leads to the third major dissimilarity between now and the future.

It will be more networked

Historically, the dominant organisational form in the life science industry has been the integrated company, which has created most of its value through its own employees, working within its distinct organisational boundaries. Recent years have seen a marked trend towards outsourcing and cooperation, but the industry remains dominated by self-contained firms, often large and incorporating multiple business units that represent diverse evolutionary choices.

The future will look very different. Even when operating under an umbrella legal entity, core organisations will be smaller and each one will be focused on a particular business model. These smaller entities will be focused on one part of their value chain but will form part of a holobiont of symbiotic organisations that together express the capabilities needed to occupy their chosen fitness peak. Today, many life science companies count their employees in four or five digits. In the future, a couple of hundred is likely to be the typical size of an operating unit, but it will be linked to many other similarly sized holobiont partners.

This networked market has both positive and negative implications. Obviously, networks represent an opportunity for life science companies to adapt relatively easily, mitigate risk and remain flexible in comparison to their integrated predecessors. By contrast, holobionts threaten failure if not built and managed well. They demand capabilities that are not needed in traditional, integrated organisations. Companies that fail to identify what capabilities their fitness peak demands or fail to attract and manage holobiont partners will not be able to compete.

Of the many ways that our future industry will differ from the present, these three will be the most important. These changes, along with the constraints of path dependence and culture that hinder organisational adaptation, mean that it is almost inevitable that the roll call of tomorrow's industry leading companies will look very different from today's. This sobering thought leads to the obvious question for both existing companies and new entrants – how to adapt so as to be on that future list rather than to be a footnote in the industry's history.

How can we adapt to the future?

Surviving and thriving in the future I have described earlier will demand innumerable small and large decisions, but two choices will have most influence on a firm's survival.

Which fitness peak shall we occupy?

The large, fragmented and competitive environment described earlier demands that firms choose which fitness peak they will occupy. Whilst large firms may host multiple, relatively autonomous business models, every business model will need to aim for a peak and avoid troughs. Traditionally, such corporate strategy decisions have begun with choices of technology, clinical indication, product or geography. But these categories are poor guides to the risk and return involved; a choice on any of these four dimensions might include a range of possible returns and risks. When guided by evolutionary science, strategic choices should begin with what fitness peak to aim for. Surely, this will then be reified in terms of technology, clinical indication, product and geography; but the strategic choice should begin with those evolutionary trade offs, such as which habitat and which peak within each habitat.

The choice of which peak to occupy is idiosyncratic, by which I mean it relates specifically to the individual case and that there is no single best choice for all organisations. Because this choice is necessarily case specific, industry fashions and 'best practice' often lead firms in the wrong direction. The choice of peak will depend upon its attractiveness and how easy it is to occupy, both of which are multifactorial and strongly influenced by the firm's assets, culture and history. Firms that make idiosyncratic choices, using processes that allow for those issues, are likely to make the right choice. Firms that follow fashion or begin with the product, technology, geography or clinical indication are likely to head in the wrong direction.

How will we build our holobiont?

The need to adapt well and quickly to the chosen fitness peak dictates the design, construction and management of an appropriate holobiont. Evolutionary science dictates that this is guided by the organisational routines and capabilities required by the chosen fitness peak. Traditionally, the choice of interfirm arrangements have been led by operational issues such as product licensing, distribution presence or economies of scale or scope, but these factors are poor indications of the underlying capabilities and make insufficient allowance for the importance of the capabilities or the risks in assimilating them. When guided by evolutionary science, holobiont design should begin with the requirements of the fitness peak and will then allow for differences in the relative importance and relative risks in acquiring and expressing the necessary capabilities.

Holobiont construction and management is again idiosyncratic and case specific. Thoughtlessly copying the practice of others ignores the peculiarities of the firm's situation. The choice of partners and the relationships between them will depend on the capabilities needed and what capabilities the firm brings to the holobiont, all of which vary in criticality and risk. Firms that construct their holobiont deliberately, using processes that allow for those issues, are likely to make the right choice. Firms that do not apply deliberate thought and planning to the growth of their holobiont, and instead are led by opportunistic or tactical issues, are unlikely to be successful.

Of the many choices upon which evolutionary success depends, these two are the most important. Every firm in the life sciences industry will make these choices. The only question is whether those choices will be made deliberately, using thoughtful processes based on an understanding of how evolutionary science applies to our important industry, or made accidentally, as the result of a myriad of smaller choices and in ignorance of Darwin's powerful idea.

That choice, between using evolutionary science to guide your firm's future or hoping that your many smaller choices will add up to a successful evolutionary strategy, is the first decision you have to make.

Whenever you see a successful business, someone once made a courageous decision.
Peter Drucker

References

1. Smith BD. *The Future of Pharma: Evolutionary Threats and Opportunities*. London: Gower; 2011.
2. Klepper S. Industry Life Cycles. *Industrial & Corporate Change*. 1997;6(1):119–43.
3. Jinsoo Y. A Theory of Industry Life Cycle. *Journal of Economic Development*. 2000;25(1):155.
4. McGahan AM. How Industries Change. *Harvard Business Review*. 2004;82(10):86–94.
5. Nelson RR, Winter SG. *An Evolutionary Theory of Economic Change*. Cambridge, MA: Harvard University Press; 1982.
6. Edwards JR. Reconsidering Theoretical Progress in Organizational and Management Research. *Organizational Research Methods*. 2010;13(4):615–19.
7. Flannery MA. *Alfred Russel Wallace: A Rediscovered Life*. London: Discovery Institute; 2011.
8. Bowler PJ. *Evolution: The History of an Idea*. Berkeley, University of California Press; 2003.
9. Popper KR. Natural Selection and the Emergence of the Mind. *Dialectica*. 1978;32:339–55.
10. Dennett DC. *Darwin's Dangerous Idea*. London: Allen Lane; 1995.
11. Dawkins R. *The Selfish Gene*. Oxford: Oxford University Press; 1976.
12. Velben T. Why Is Economics Not an Evolutionary Science? *Quarterly Journal of Economics*. 1898;12(3):373–97.
13. Beinhocker ED. *The Origin of Wealth: Evolution, Complexity and the Radical Remaking of Economics*. London: Random House; 2006.
14. Hodgson GM, Knudson T. *Darwin's Conjecture: The Search for General Principles of Social and Economic Evolution*. Chicago: Chicago University Press; 2010.
15. Murmann JP. The Coevolution of Industries and Important Features of Their Environments. *Organization Science*. 2013;24(1):58–78.
16. Wright S. Evolution in Mendelian Populations. *Genetics*. 1931;16:97–159.
17. Hull J. The Second Industrial Revolution: The History of a Concept. *Storia Della Storiagrafia*. 1999;36:81–90.
18. Vogel MJ, Rosenberg CE. *The Therapeutic Revolution*. Philadelphia, University of Pennsylvania Press; 1979.
19. Metcalfe JS. *Evolutionary Economics and Creative Destruction*. London: Routledge; 1998.
20. Treacy M, Wiersema M. *The Discipline of the Market Leaders*. London: Harper Collins; 1995.
21. Smith BD. Emerging Models. Pharmaceutical Market Europe. April 2013.
22. Buchanan M. *Forecast: What Physics, Meteorology and the Natural Sciences Can Teach Us about Economics*. 1st ed. London: Bloomsbury; 2013.
23. A Billion Shades of Grey. *The Economist*. 2014 4/26/2014.
24. Fund UNP. Ageing in the Twenty-First Century: A Celebration and a Challenge 2012 [updated 2012. Available from: http://www.unfpa.org/sites/default/files/pub-pdf/UNFPA-Exec-Summary.pdf].
25. Why Population Ageing Matters: A Global Perspective: National Institute on Ageing 2007 [Available from: https://www.nia.nih.gov/research/publication/why-population-aging-matters-global-perspective].

26. Larry Summers at the IMF Economic Forum. 2013 [Available from: https://www.youtube.com/watch?v=KYpVzBbQIX0].

27. King S. *When the Money Runs Out: The End of Western Affluence.* New Haven, Yale University Press; 2014.

28. Age Invaders. *The Economist.* 2014 4/26/2014.

29. Morath E, Radnofsky L. Medical Price Inflation Is at Slowest Pace in 50 Years. *Wall Street Journey.* 2013 9/18/2013.

30. Newhouse J. Medical Care Costs: How Much Welfare Loss. *Journal of Economic Perspectives.* 1992;6(3):3–21.

31. Okunade AA, Murthy VNR. Technology as a "Major Driver" of Healthcare Costs: A Cointegration Analysis of the Newhouse Conjecture. *Journal of Health Economics.* 2002;21(1):147–59.

32. Martin JJ, Gonzalez MP, Garcia MD. Review of the Literature on the Determinants of Healthcare Expenditure. *Applied Economics.* 2011;43(1):19–46.

33. Baumol WJ. Social Wants and Dismal Science: The Curious Case of the Climbing Costs of Health and Teaching. *Proceedings of the American Philosophical Society.* 2006;37(4):612–37.

34. Erixson F, van der Marel E. *What Is Driving the Rise in Healthcare Expenditures? An Inquiry into the Nature and Causes of the Cost Disease.* ECIPE Working Paper 05/2011. 2011.

35. Eggleston K. *Healthcare for 1.3 Billion: An Overview of China's Health System.* Asia Health Policy Programme Working Paper 28. 2012.

36. Indonesia: The Humongous Healthcare Plan. BBC World Service Assignment 2013 [Available from: http://www.bbc.co.uk/programmes/p02rs56m].

37. Page B. How Well Is the NHS Meeting Public Expectations? *Think Differently Blog.* 2012 11/22/2012.

38. The World Health Report 2008: The World Health Organisation 2008 [updated 2008. Available from: http://www.who.int/whr/2008/en/].

39. Weindling P. From Infectious to Chronic Diseases: Changing Patterns of Sickness in the Nineteenth and Twentieth Centuries. In: Wear A. editor. *Medicine in Society: Historical Essays.* Cambridge: Cambridge University Press; 1992. pp. 303–17.

40. Olesen J, Leonardi M. The Burden of Brain Diseases in Europe. *European Journal of Neurology.* 2003;10(5):471–7.

41. Tulchinsky TH, Varavikova EA. What Is the "New Public Health"? *Public Health Reviews.* 2010;32:25–53.

42. Carrera-Bastos P, Fontes-Villalba M, O'Keeke JH. Western Diet and Lifestyle and the Diseases of Civilisation. *Research Reports in Clinical Cardiology.* 2011;2:15–35.

43. Nugent R. Chronic Diseases in Developing Countries: Health and Economic Burdens. *Annals of the New York Academy of Sciences.* 2008;1136:70–9.

44. Johansson A. Looking to 2060: Long Term Global Growth Prospects. 2012 November. Report No.: OECD Economic Policy Papers No. 03.

45. Quah D. The Global Economy's Shifting Centre of Gravity. *Global Policy.* 2011;2(1):3–9.

46. Bank W. Remarkable Declines in Global Poverty but Major Challenges Remain 2013 [updated 4/17/2013. Available from: http://www.worldbank.org/en/news/press-release/2013/04/17/remarkable-declines-in-global-poverty-but-major-challenges-remain].

47. Burrows MJ. Global Trends 2030: Alternative Worlds: Office of the Director of National Intelligence 2012 [updated 2012 December. Available from: http://www.dni.gov/index.php/about/organization/national-intelligence-council-global-trends].

48. Steenkamp JB, Hofstede GT. International Market Segmentation: Issues and Perspectives. *International Journal of Research in Marketing.* 2002;19:185–213.

49. Smith BD, Awopetu B. Mind Set and Market Segmentation in Pharmaceutical Industry: An Assessment of Practice in the UK. *Journal of Pharmaceutical Marketing and Management.* 2006;17(3/4): 101–16.

50. Schoonveld E. *The Price of Global Health.* 1st ed. Farnham: Gower; 2011.

51. Unlocking Pharma Growth: Navigating the Intricacies of Emerging Markets: McKinsey and Co 2012 [Available from: http://www.mckinsey.com/~/media/mckinsey/dotcom/client_service/pharma%20and%20medical%20products/pmp%20new/pdfs/emerging_markets_compendium_2012.ashx].

52. Porter ME. *The Competitive Advantage of Nations*. London: Palgrave McMillan; 1998.

53. Chase-Dunn C, Lara-Millan A, Niemeyer R. Biotechnology in the Global Political Economy. 2004 [Available from: http://irows.ucr.edu/research/biotech/isa04biotech.htm].

54. Congressional Hearing on India's Industrial Policy Centers on Pharmaceutical Patents. 2013 [Available from: http://infojustice.org/archives/30038].

55. Williams Z. Trade Agreement Trends. 2014 [Available from: http://www.globalpolicyjournal.com/blog/25/08/2014/trade-agreement-trends].

56. Globalisation and the Shifting Balance in the World Economy 2012 [Available from: http://dgff.unctad.org/chapter1/1.html].

57. How Globalised are Specific Industries 2012 [updated 2012. Available from: https://www.dpdhl.com/content/dam/presse/specials/gci/2012/dhl-gci-2012-chapter3.pdf].

58. Topal C. The Globalisation of China's Life Science Industry: Flashpoints in Sino–US Trade Relations 2014 [updated 4/4/2014. Available from: http://www.nbr.org/research/activity.aspx?id=413].

59. Margullis L. Symbiogenesis and Symbionticism. In: Margullis L, Fester R, editors. *Symbiosis as a Source of Evolutionary Innovation: Speciation and Morphogenesis*. Boston: Massachusetts Institute of Technology; 1991. pp. 1–14.

60. Roxburgh C, Lund S, Atkins C, Belot S, Hu WW, Pierce MS. Global Capital Markets: Entering a New Era 2009 [updated 2009. Available from: file:///C:/Users/BrianSmith/Downloads/MGI_Global_capital_markets_Entering_a_new_era_gcm_sixth_annual_full_report.pdf].

61. World Investment Report 2014 Geneva 2014 [updated 2014. Available from: http://unctad.org/en/PublicationsLibrary/wir2014_en.pdf].

62. Coase R. The Nature of the Firm. *Economica*. 1937;4(16):386–405.

63. Williamson OE. Transaction Cost Economics: The Origins. *Journal of Retailing*. 2010;86(3):227–31.

64. Teece D, Pisano G. The Dynamic Capabilities of Firms: An Introduction. *Industrial & Corporate Change*. 1994;3(3):537–56.

65. Burton TM. Medical Device Recalls Nearly Doubled in a Decade. *The Wall Street Journal*. 2014 3/21/2014.

66. Gaffeny A. Number of Drug Recalls Surges at FDA, Led by Mid Level Concerns. 2014 [Available from;http://www.raps.org/Regulatory-Focus/News/2014/08/11/20005/Number-of-Drug-Recalls-Surges-at-FDA-Led-by-Mid-Level-Concerns/].

67. Weston AD, Hood L. Systems Biology, Proteomics and the Future of Health Care: Toward Predictive, Preventative and Personalized Medicine. *Journal of Proteome Research*. 2004;3(2):179–96.

68. Kuhn T. *The Structure of Scientific Revolutions*. 50th Anniversary ed. Chicago: University of Chicago Press; 1962.

69. Trask RL. *Mind the Gaffe: The Penguin Guide to Common Errors in English*. London: David R Godine; 2005.

70. Lauerman J. Faroes' 50,000 Residents Leap into DNA Testing Quagmire. *Bloomberg*. 2013 2/25/2013.

71. Dewey FE, Pan S, Wheeler MT, Quake SR, Ashley EA. DNA Sequencing: Clinical Implications of New DNA Sequencing Technologies. *Circulation*. 2012;125:931–44.

72. Breker M, Schuldiner M. The Emergence of Proteome Wide Technologies: Systematic Analysis of Proteins Comes of Age. *Nature Reviews: Molecular Cell Biology*. 2014;15:453–64.

73. Ezzatollah F, Mesbah-Namin SA, Farahzadi R. Biomarkers in Medicine: An Overview. *British Journal of Medicine and Medical Research*. 2014;4(8):1701–18.

74. Babuin L, Jaffe A. Tropinin: The Biomarker of Choice for Detection of Cardiac Injury. *Canadian Medical Association Journal*. 2005;173(10):1191–202.

75. Hahm G, Glaser JJ, Elester EA. Biomarkers to Predict Wound Healing. *Plastic and Reconstructive Surgery*. 2011;127:21S–26S.

76. Cuellar JM, Scuderi GJ, Cuellar VG, Golish SR, Yeomans DC. Diagnostic Utility of Cytokine Biomarkers in the Evaluation of Acut Knee Pain. *Journal of Bone and Joint Surgery*. 2009;91:2313–20.

77. Sander JDY, Keith J. CRISPR-Cas Systems for Editing, Regulating and Targeting Genomes. *Nature Biotechnology*. 2014;32:9.

78. Khalil AS, Collins JS. Synthetic Biology: Applications Come of Age. *Nature Reviews: Genetics.* 2010;11:367–79.

79. Sawyer E. Bio 2.0: Dissecting the Next Revolution in Biology. Synthetic Biology is on Its Way to Treating Human Disease 2012 [updated 2012. Available from: http://www.nature.com/scitable/blog/bio2.0/synthetic_biology_is_on_its].

80. Kämpf MM, Christen EH, Ehrbar M, Daoud-El Baba M, Charpin-El Hamri G, Fussenegger M, Weber W. A Gene Therapy Technology Based Biomaterial for the Trigger Inducible Release of Biopharmaceuticals in Mice. *Advanced Functional Materials.* 2010;20(15):2534–8.

81. Thornton J. *Janet Thornton – The Importance of Genomics and Bioinformatics for the future of Medicine and Agriculture.* 2014 Bernal Lecture. Birkbeck, University of London; 2014.

82. Ideker T, Galitiski T, Hood L. A New Approach to Decoding Life: Systems Biology. *Annual Review of Genomics and Human Genetics.* 2001;2:343–73.

83. Bruggeman FJ, Westerhoff HV. Trends in Systems Biology. *Trends in Microbiology.* 2007;15(1):45–50.

84. Villoslada P, Steinman L, Baranzini SE. Systems Biology and Its Application to the Understanding of Neurological Diseases. *Neurological Progress.* 2009;65:124–39.

85. Moor JB, Weeks ME. Proteomics and Systems Biology: Current and Future Applications in Nutritional Sciences. *Advances in Nutrition.* 2011;2:355–64.

86. Park JH, Lee SY, Kim TY, Hyun UK. Application of Systems Biology for Bioprocess Development. *Trends in Biotechnology.* 2015;28(8):404–12.

87. Nichlolson JK. Global Systems Biology, Personalized Medicine and Molecular Epidemiology. *Molecular Systems Biology.* 2006;2:1–6.

88. Feala JD, Abdulhameed MD, Yu C, Dutta B, Yu X, Schmid K, Dave J, Tortella F, Reifman J. Systems Biology Approaches for Discovering Biomarkers for Traumatic Brain Injury. *Journal of Neurotrauma.* 2013;30(13):1101–16.

89. Martins-Green M, Vodovotz Y, Liu P. Systems Biology Applied to Wound Healing. *Wound Repair and Regeneration.* 2010;18(1):1–2.

90. Bradbury MS, Hedvig H, Heath JR. *Systems Biology and Nanotechnology.* 1st ed. London: Springer; 2007. p. 1411–30.

91. Farokhzad OC, Langer R. Impact of Nanotechnology in Drug Delivery. *ACS Nano.* 2009;3(1):16–20.

92. Bliss M. *William Osler: A Life in Medicine.* Oxford, Oxford University Press; 2007.

93. Bryan CS. What Is the Oslerian Tradition. *Annals of Internal Medicine.* 2015;120(8):682–7.

94. Loscalzo J, Barabasi AL. Systems Biology and the Future of Medicine. *Interdisciplinary Review of Systems Biology in Medicine.* 2011;3(6):619–27.

95. Mardinoglue A, Nielsen J. Systems Biology and Metabolic Modelling. *Journal of Internal Medicine.* 2012;271(2):142–54.

96. Andreozzi P, Viscogliosi G, Servello A, Marigliano B, Ettorre E, Marigliano V. Predictive Medicine in Cardiovascular Diseases: What Next? *Prevention and Research.* 2015;1(1):53–9.

97. Sautin M, Suchkov S. Opportunities of Predictive Medicine at the Treatment of Diabetes Mellitus Complications. *EPMA Journal.* 2014;5(Suppl 1): A73.

98. Levey DF. Genetic Risk Prediction and Neurobiological Understanding of Alcoholism. *Translational Psychiatry.* 2014;4(e391).

99. Carlson B. P4 Medicine Could Transform Healthcare, but Payers and Physicians Are Not Yet Convinced. *Biotechnology Healthcare.* 2010;7(3):7–8.

100. Machlup F. *The Production and Distribution of Knowledge in the United States.* New York: Literary Licensing LLC; 1962.

101. Hilbert M, López, Priscilla. The World's Technological Capacity to Store, Communicate, and Compute Information. *Science.* 2011;332(6025):60–5.

102. Moore GE. Cramming More Components onto Integrated Circuits. *Electronics.* 1965;38(8): 114ff.

103. Moore's Law Is Dead: The Future of Computing. *The Connectivist.* 2013 10/13/2013.

104. Aron J. First Nanotube Computer Could Spark Carbon Revolution. *New Scientist.* 2013 9/25/2013.

105. Van Loock P. Shaping the Future of Quantum Computing. *Physics.* 2014;7(56).

106. Brown M, Krauss D. In-Memory Revolution: Tech Trends 2014. 2014 2/21/2014. [Available from: http://dupress.com/articles/2014-tech-trends-in-memory-revolution/].

107. Van Noorden R. The Rechargeable Revolution: A Better Battery. *Nature*. 2014;507(7490):26–8.

108. Rani S. The Promise of Nanotechnology for the Next Generation of Lithium-Ion Batteries. *Nanotech Insights*. 2014 April.

109. West DM. Improving Health Care through Mobile Medical Devices and Sensors 2013 [Available from: http://www.brookings.edu/research/papers/2013/10/22-improving-health-care-mobile-medical-devices-apps-sensors-west].

110. Armstrong-Smith I. You Wear It So Well. *The Analytical Scientist*. 2014 3/31/2014.

111. Bell L. Michael J Fox Teams with Intel to Use Big Data and Wearables in Parkinson's Research. *The Inquirer*. 2014 8/14/2014.

112. Bank W. Mobile Phone Access Reaches Three Quarters of Planet's Population: World Bank; 2012 [updated 7/17/2012. Available from: http://www.worldbank.org/en/news/press-release/2012/07/17/mobile-phone-access-reaches-three-quarters-planets-population].

113. World Fixed Broadband Forecast. 2014. [Available from: http://quantum-web.com/world-fixed-broadband-forecast/].

114. Emerging Trends in Mobile and What They Mean for Your Business 2014 [updated 5/8/2014. Available from: http://www.nielsen.com/us/en/insights/news/2014/emerging-trends-in-mobile-and-what-they-mean-for-your-business.html].

115. Adler E. The 'Internet of Things' Will Be Bigger Than the Smartphone, Tablet, And PC Markets Combined. *Business Insider*. 2014 4/21/2014.

116. Niewolny D. How the Internet of Things Is Revolutionizing Healthcare. 2015. [Available from: https://cache.freescale.com/files/corporate/doc/white_paper/IOTREVHEALCARWP.pdf]

117. Henry Mayo Memorial Hospital. http://www.microsoft.com/windowsembedded/en-us/customer-stories-details.aspx?id=44 [Internet]. 2015 [Available from: http://www.microsoft.com/windowsembedded/en-us/customer-stories-details.aspx?id=44].

118. Morse A. Novartis and Google to Work on Smart Contact Lenses. *Wall Street Journal*. 2014 7/15/2014.

119. Marks P. Fabric Circuits Pave the Way for Wearable Tech. *New Scientist*. 2014 9/4/2014.

120. de Lange C. Clothes with Hidden Sensors Act as an Always-On Doctor. *New Scientist*. 2014 4/3/2014.

121. Horowicz-Mehler N, Tao C, Faulkner EC, Doyle JJ. An Analysis of Real World Data Trends in Global HTA Markets. *Value in Health*. 2014;17(3):A28–A29.

122. Timm J, Renly S, Farkash A. Large Scale Healthcare Data Integration and Analysis Using the Semantic Web. *Studies in Health Technology Informatics*. 2011;169:729–33.

123. Garrett B. A World Run on Algorithms 2013 [updated 7/24/2013. Available from: http://www.atlanticcouncil.org/images/publications/a_world_run_on_algorithms.pdf].

124. Cattell J, Chilukuri S, Levy M. How Big Data Can Revolutionize Pharmaceutical R&D. *McKinsey Quarterly*. 2013 [Available from: http://www.mckinsey.com/industries/pharmaceuticals-and-medical-products/our-insights/how-big-data-can-revolutionize-pharmaceutical-r-and-d].

125. Henschen D. Merck Optimizes Manufacturing with Big Data Analytics. *Information Week*. 2014 4/2/2014.

126. Proof Social Media Matters to Patients (and to Pharma Marketers) 2014 [updated 2014 January. Available from: http://www.precise.co.uk/media/152729/Pharma%20Market%20Research.pdf].

127. Fink JLW. Compliance Made Easy: High-Tech Systems Remind Patients to Take Their Meds. *Entrepreneurship Theory and Practice*. 2010 11/1/2010.

128. Pharma CRM Helps in Salesforce Effectiveness. *Global Vision Technology Blog*. 2014 11/19/2014 [Available from: http://blog.global-visiontech.com/pharma-salesforce-effectiveness/].

129. Lazer D, Kennedy R, King G, Vespignani A. The Parable of Google Flu: Traps in Big Data Analysis. *Science*. 2014;343:1203–5.

130. Musen MA, Middleton B, Greenes RA. Clinical Decision-Support Systems. In: Shortliffe EH, Cimino JJ, editors. *Biomedical Informatics*. 1st ed. London: Springer; 2015. p. 643–74.

131. Terry K. IBM Watson Helps Doctors Fight Cancer. *Information Week*. 2015 2/8/2015.

132. Dilsizian SE, Siegel EL. Artificial Intelligence in Medicine and Cardiac Imaging: Harnessing Big Data and Advanced Computing to Provide Personalized Medical Diagnosis and Treatment. *Current Cardiology Reports*. 2014;16(1):441.

133. Krol B. Berg and the Pursuit of the Body's Hidden Drugs. *Bio IT World*. 2014 8/28/2014.

134. Somrak M, Luštrek M, Šušterič J, Krivc T, Mlinar A, Travnik T, Stepan L, Mavsar M, Gams M. Tricorder: Consumer Medical Device for Discovering Common Medical Conditions. *Informatica*. 2014;38:81–8.

135. Hernadez D. Artificial Intelligence Is Now Telling Doctors How to Treat You. *Wired*. 2014 6/2/2014.

136. Doerfer Companies and Universal Robotics Partner for Flexible Medical Device Assembly Automation. *Med Device Online*. 2014 2/5/2014.

137. Gams M, Horvat M, Ozek M, Lustrek M, Gradisek A. Integrating Artificial and Human Intelligence into Tablet Production Process. *AAPS PharmSCiTech*. 2014;15(6):1447–53.

138. Curcio D, Longo F, Mirabelli G, Papoff E, editors. *Pharmaceutical Routes Optimization Using Artificial Intelligence Techniques*. IDAACS; 2007 [Available from: http://ieeexplore.ieee.org/xpl/articleDetails.jsp?reload=true&arnumber=4488412].

139. Candan G, Taskin MF, Yazgan HR. Demand Forecasting in Pharmaceutical Industry Using Artificial Intelligence: Neuro-Fuzzy Approach. *Journal of Military and Information Science*. 2014;2(2):41–9.

140. Porter ME. *Competitive Advantage*. New York: Free Press;1985.

141. Sheth J, Sisodia RS. Revisiting Marketing's Lawlike Generalisations. *Journal of the Academy of Marketing Science*. 1999;27:71–87.

142. Noor W, Kleinrock M. Pharma 50. Pharmaceutical Executive. 2013 [Available from: http://www.pharmexec.com/2013-pharm-exec-top-50].

143. Thompson H. The Future of Devices Is Generic. *Medical Device and Diagnostic Industry*. 2013 9/23/2013.

144. Saxena V. New Paradigms in Diagnostics: Graphene and a Single Drop of Blood. *Fierce Medical Devices*. 2014 11/20/2014.

145. Brenan C, LaMarr B. Recent Technology Advances Transforming Pharmaceutical Drug Discovery and Development. *Drug Discovery World*. 2015 [Available from: http://www.ddw-online.com/drug-discovery/p146756-recent-technology-advances-transforming-pharmaceutical-drug-discovery-and-development-summer-09.html].

146. Varelis, JS. Here's How to Revamp R&D and Enhance Productivity. *Medical Device and Diagnostic Industry*. 2014 5/19/2014.

147. Snyder GH, Cotteleer MJ, Kotek B. 3D Opportunity in Medical Technology. 2014 4/28/2014. [Available from: http://dupress.com/articles/additive-manufacturing-3d-opportunity-in-medtech/].

148. Janvilisri T, Bhunia AK, Scaria J. Advances in Molecular Diagnostics. *BioMed Research International*. 2013 [Available from: http://dx.doi.org/10.1155/2013/172521].

149. Handfield R. Major Trends Impacting the Pharmaceutical Supply Chain Ecosystem. *NC State University Supply Chain Resource Cooperative*. 2014 3/29/2014.

150. *Med Tech Supply Chain Management Trends and Leading Practices*. PriceWaterHouseCooopers; 2013.

151. Key Logistics Trends in the Life Sciences 2013 [updated 2013. Available from: http://www.dpdhl.com/en/media_relations/press_releases/2013/dhl_study_predicts_distribution_channels_for_pharmaceutical_manufacturers.html].

152. Jack A. McKeeson Takeover of Celesio to Trigger Sector Consolidation. *Financial Times*. 2013 10/27/2013.

153. Trends in Biopharmaceutical Manufacturing. 2015 [Available from: http://www.pharmtech.com/top-trends-biopharmaceutical-manufacturing-2015].

154. Conroy S. Frugal Innovation, Frugal Manufacturing Will Drive Medtech Trends in the Next Decade. *Medical Design*. 2012 7/24/2012.

155. Law D. On the Cutting Edge: Innovation Trends in Medical Manufacturing. *Medical Manufacturing*. 2013 5/31/2013.

156. Green W. Apple and Google 'Will Have Big Impact on Pharma Supply Chains. *Supply Management*. 2014 9/15/2014.

157. Challener C. Pharma Outsourcing Driving Need for Cloud-Based Services. *PharmTech.* 2014 9/29/2014.

158. Festel G, De Nardo M, Simmen T. Outsourcing of Pharmaceutical Manufacturing. *Business Chemistry.* 2014 [Available from: http://www.businesschemistry.org/article/?article=197].

159. Trends in 3D Printing of Customised Medical Devices. *Medical Plastics News.* 2013 6/25/2013 [Available from: http://www.medicalplasticsnews.com/news/technology/trends-in-3d-printing-of-customised-medical-devices/].

160. Raghupathi W, Raghupathi V. Big Data Analytics in Healthcare: Promise and Potential. *Health and Information Science Systems.* 2014;2(3) [Available from: https://hissjournal.biomedcentral.com/articles/10.1186/2047-2501-2-3].

161. Greene JA, Kesselheim AS. Pharmaceutical Marketing and the New Social Medical. *New England Journal of Medicine.* 2010;363:2087–9.

162. Toumi M, Flostrand S, Millier A. Segmentation of Regional Payers. *Journal of Medical Marketing.* 2013;11(3):244–53.

163. Smith BD. Superior Segmentation. *Pharmaceutical Market Europe.* 2012 4/19/2012.

164. Adamaski J. Correspondence Risk Sharing Arrangements for Pharmaceuticals: Potential Considerations and Recommendations for European Payers. *Health Services Research.* 2010;10:153.

165. Alvesson M, Sandberg J. *Constructing Research Questions.* 1st ed. London: Sage; 2013.

166. Gould SJ. *Wonderful Life: Burgess Shale and the Nature of History.* London: Vintage; 2000.

167. Zimmer C. The New Science of Evolutionary Forecasting. 2014 [Available from: https://www.quantamagazine.org/20140717-the-new-science-of-evolutionary-forecasting/].

168. Belanov S; Bychkov, Dmitri; Benner, Christian; Ripatti, Samuli; Ojala, Teija; Kankainen, Matti; Lee, Hong Kai; Tang, Julian Wei-Tze; Kainov, Denis E. Genome-Wide Analysis of Evolutionary Markers of Human Influenza A(H1N1)pdm09 and A(H3N2) Viruses May Guide Selection of Vaccine Strain Candidates. *Genome Biology and Evolution.* 2015 [Available from: http://gbe.oxfordjournals.org/content/early/2015/11/27/gbe.evv240.abstract].

169. Agarwal A, Ressler D, Snyder G. The Current and Future State of Companion Diagnostics. *Pharmgenomics and Personalised Medicine.* 2015;8:99–110.

170. Haruya M, Kano S. A New Look at the Corporate Capability of Personalized Medicine Development in the Pharmaceutical Industry. *R&D Management.* 2015;45(1):94–103.

171. Sunstein C, Thaler, Richard. *Nudge: Improving Decisions about Health, Wealth and Happiness.* London: Penguin; 2009.

172. Rodgers RJ; Tschöp, Matthias H; Wilding, John PH. Anti-Obesity Drugs: Past, Present and Future. *Disease Models and Mechanisms.* 2012;5(5):621–6.

173. Brown RCH. Moral Responsibility for (Un)healthy Behaviour. *Journal of Medical Ethics.* 2013 [Available from: http://jme.bmj.com/content/early/2013/01/10/medethics-2012-100774.abstract].

174. Nasri H; Baradaran, Azar; Shirzad, Hedayatollah; Rafieian-Kopaei, Mahmoud. New Concepts in Nutraceuticals as Alternatives for Pharmaceuticals. *International Journal of Preventative Medicine.* 2014;5(12):1487–99.

175. Nutraceuticals: The Future of Intelligent Food. 2014 [Available from: https://www.kpmg.com/ID/en/industry/CM/Documents/neutraceuticals-the-future-of-intelligent-food.pdf].

176. Smith BD, Raspin PJ. *Creating Market Insight.* 1st ed. London: Wiley; 2008.

177. Smith BD, Wilson HN, Clark M. Creating and Using Customer Insight: 12 Rules of Best Practice. *Journal of Medical Marketing.* 2006;6(2):135–9.

178. Bass BM. From Transactional to Transformational Leadership: Learning to Share the Vision. *Organisational Dynamics.* 1991;18(3):19–31.

179. Smith BD. Turf Wars: What the Intraorganisational Conflict Literature May Contribute to Our Understanding of Marketing Strategy Literature Implementation. *Journal of Strategic Marketing.* 2011;19(1):25–42.

180. Smith BD. Maybe I Will, Maybe I Won't: What the Connected Perspectives of Motivation Theory and Organisational Commitment May Contribute to Our Understanding of Strategy Implementation. *Journal of Strategic Marketing*. 2009;17(6):469–81.

181. Smith BD. Capturing an Elusive Phenomenon: Developing and Testing a Multiple Perspective Model of Marketing Strategy Implementation. *Journal of Strategic Marketing*. 2013;21(5): 16–40.

182. Barney JB. Firm Resources and Sustained Competitive Advantage. *Journal of Management*. 1991;17(1):99–120.

183. Prahalad CK, Hamel G. The Core Competence of the Corporation. *Harvard Business Review*. 1990; 68(3):79–91.

184. Feldman MS, Pentland Brian T. Reconceptualising Organisational Routines as a Source of Flexibility and Change. *Administrative Science Quarterly*. 2003;48:94–118.

185. Felin T, Foss NJ, Heimeriks KH, Madsen TL. Microfoundations of Routines and Capabilities: Individuals, Processes, and Structure. *Journal of Management Studies*. 2012;49(8):1351–74.

Index

Note: Italicized page numbers indicate tables and figures.